Microsoft Support Network

In the event you cannot install Microsoft® Office for Windows® or an Office application, please refer to the telephone support offerings below. Microsoft's support offerings range from no-cost and low-cost electronic information services (available 24 hours a day, 7 days a week) to annual support plans and CD-ROM subscription programs. Please check the Technical Support section in online Help for detailed information.

Microsoft support services are subject to Microsoft's then-current prices, terms, and conditions, which are subject to change without notice.

Standard Support

No-charge support from Microsoft support engineers is available via a toll call between 6:00 A.M. and 6:00 P.M. Pacific time, Monday through Friday, excluding holidays. In Canada, call between 8:00 A.M. and 8:00 P.M. Eastern time, Monday through Friday, excluding holidays.

- In the United States for:

  - Microsoft Office for Windows, call (206) 635-7056
  - Microsoft Access for Windows, call (206) 635-7050
  - Microsoft Excel for Windows, call (206) 635-7070
  - Microsoft PowerPoint® for Windows, call (206) 635-7145
  - Microsoft Word for Windows, call (206) 462-9673
  - Microsoft Schedule+, call (206) 635-7049

- In Canada, for technical support for Microsoft Office applications, call (905) 568-2294.

When you call, you should be at your computer and have the appropriate product documentation at hand. Be prepared to give the following information:

- The version number of the Microsoft product that you are using
- The type of hardware that you are using, including network hardware, if applicable
- The exact wording of any messages that appeared on your screen
- A description of what happened and what you were doing at the time
- A description of how you tried to solve the problem

D1305666

Priority Support

The Microsoft Support Network offers priority telephone access to Microsoft support engineers 24 hours a day, 7 days a week, excluding holidays, in the U.S. In Canada, the hours are from 6:00 A.M. to midnight, 7 days a week, excluding holidays.

- In the United States, call (900) 555-2000; $1.95 (U.S.) per minute, $25 maximum. Charges appear on your telephone bill. Not available in Canada.

- In the United States, call (800) 936-5700, at $25 (U.S.) per incident; in Canada, call (800) 668-7975, at $30 (CDN) per incident. These services are billed to your VISA, MasterCard, or American Express card.

Text Telephone

Microsoft text telephone (TT/TDD) services are available for the deaf or hard-of-hearing. In the United States, using a TT/TDD modem, dial (206) 635-4948. In Canada, using a TT/TDD modem, dial (905) 568-9641.

Product Support Worldwide

The following list contains Microsoft subsidiary offices and the countries they serve. If there is no Microsoft office in your country, please contact the establishment from which you purchased your Microsoft product. This list provides only basic technical support phone and fax numbers; other services such as BBS and sales numbers may be available. For additional subsidiary information, check the Product Support Worldwide section in online Help.

When you call, you should be at your computer and have the appropriate product documentation at hand. Please follow the guidelines listed above under "Standard Support."

Area	Telephone Numbers	Fax Numbers	Area	Telephone Numbers	Fax Numbers
Argentina	(54) (1) 815-1521	(54) (1) 814-0372	Liechtenstein	See Switzerland	
Australia	(61) (02) 870-2131	(61) (02)805-0519	Luxembourg	(32) 2-5133274 (Dutch-speaking) (32) 2-5023432 (English-speaking) (32) 2-5132268 (French-speaking)	
Austria	Microsoft Excel: 0660-6511 PowerPoint: 0660-6511 Word: 0660-6513	022-68 16 2710			
Belgium	02-5133274 (Dutch-speaking) 02-5023432 (English-speaking) 02-5132268 (French-speaking)		Mexico	(52) (5) 325-0912	
			Netherlands	02503-77877 (Dutch-speaking) 02503-77853 (English-speaking)	
Bolivia	See Argentina		New Zealand	64 (9) 357-5575	64 (9) 358-0092
Brazil	(55) (11) 871-0090	(55) (11) 241-1157	Northern Ireland	See United Kingdom	
Caribbean	(214) 714-9100	(809) 273-3636	Norway	(47) (22) 02 25 50	(47) (22) 02 25 70
Chile	56 2 232 4467	56 2 233 5917	Papua New Guinea	See Australia	
Colombia	(571) 618 2255	(571) 618 2269	Paraguay	See Argentina	
Czech Republic	(+42) (2) 245 10554	(+42) (2) 266020	Poland	(+48) (2) 6216793 or (+48) (71) 441357	(+48) (2) 6615434
Denmark	(45) (44) 89 01 11	(45) (44) 89 01 44	Portugal	(351) 1 4412205	(351) 1 4412101
Dubai	(971) 4 513 888	(971) 4 527 444	Republic of China	(886) (2) 508-9501	(886) (2) 504-3121
Ecuador	(593) (2) 463-094		Republic of Ireland	See United Kingdom	
England	See United Kingdom		Russia	(+7) (095) 267-8844 or (+7) (095)158-6963	(+7) (502) 224 50 45
Finland	(0358) (90) 525-502-500	(46) (0)8 752 29 00			
France	(33) (1) 69-86-10-20	(33) (1) 69-28-00-28	Scotland	See United Kingdom	
French Polynesia	See France		Singapore	(65) 220-7202	(65) 227-6811
Germany	Microsoft Access: 089/3176-1180 Microsoft Excel: 089/3176-1120 PowerPoint: 089/3176-1120 Word: 089/3176-1131	089-3176-1000	Slovenia	(+386) (61) 1232354	
			Slovak Republic	(+42) (7) 312083	(+42) (2) 266020
			South Africa	(Toll free): 0 802 11 11 04 (27) 11 445 0046	(27) 11 445 0045 or
			Spain	(34) (1) 803-9960	(34) (1) 803-8310
Greece	(30) (1) 6893 63 1 through (30) 1 6893 635	(30) (1) 6893 636	Sweden	(46) (8) 752 09 29	(46) (0)8 752 29 00
Hong Kong	(852) 804-4222	(852) 560-2217	Switzerland	Microsoft Access: 01/342-4121 Microsoft Excel: 01/342-4082 PowerPoint: 01/342-4082 Word: 01/342-4087 Technical Support (French-speaking): (41) (22) 738 96 88	01-831 09 69
Hungary	(36)(1) 2MSINFO (267-4636)	(+36) (1) 268-1558			
India	(91) (11) 646-0694				
Ireland	See United Kingdom				
Israel	972-3-613-0833	972-3-613-0834			
Italy	(39) (2) 7039-8351	(39) (2) 7039-2020	Turkey	(90) 212 2585998	(90) 212 2585954
Japan	Microsoft Access: (81) (3) 5454-2378 Microsoft Excel: (81) (3) 5454-2320 Word: (81) (3) 5454-2321	(81) (3) 5454-7955	United Kingdom	(44) (734) 271000	(01734) 270080
			Uruguay	See Argentina	
			Venezuela	58.2.910046; 58.2.910510	58.2.923835
Korea	(82) (2) 531-4800	(82) (2) 563-5194	Wales	See United Kingdom	

Getting Results
with Microsoft® Office
for Windows® 95

Version 7.0

Microsoft Corporation

Microsoft, MS, MS-DOS, Bookshelf, FoxBASE+, FoxPro, Microsoft Press, Multiplan, PivotTable, PowerPoint, TipWizard, Visual Basic, Windows, Wingdings, and XL design (the Microsoft Excel logo) are registered trademarks, and AutoSum, IntelliSense, Microsoft At Work, Where do you want to go today?, and Windows NT are trademarks of Microsoft Corporation in the USA and other countries.

The Microsoft Excel Solver program was developed by Frontline Systems, Inc., P.O. Box 4288, Incline Village, NV 89450-4288. Portions of the Microsoft Excel Solver program code are copyright 1990, 1991, and 1992 by Frontline Systems, Inc. Portions are copyright 1989 by Optimal Methods, Inc.

The Microsoft Excel Solver program uses GRG2 nonlinear optimization code developed by Leon Lasdon, University of Texas at Austin, and Allan Waren, Cleveland State University. Linear and integer problems use the simplex method with bounds on the variables and the branch and bound method, implemented by John Watson and Dan Fylstra, Frontline Systems, Inc.

The Microsoft Excel Analysis ToolPak was developed by GreyMatter International, Inc., 173 Otis Street, P.O. Box 388, Cambridge, MA 02141.

The Microsoft Data Map was developed by MapInfo Corporation, One Global View, Troy, NY 12180-8399.

The Microsoft Excel Spreadsheet Solution Templates were developed by Village Software, 186 Lincoln Street, Boston, MA 02111.

The Seven Habits of Highly Effective People, copyright 1995, Covey Leadership Center.

Clip Art copyright 1993 by 3G Graphics Inc., from their IMAGES WITH IMPACT® for Windows collection. All rights reserved.

Graphic filters licensed from Access Softek, Inc. Copyright 1995 Access Softek, Inc.

PhotoCD portions copyright 1992 by Eastman Kodak. All rights reserved.

International Hyphenator licensed from Houghton Mifflin Company. Copyright 1991–1993 by Houghton Mifflin Company. All rights reserved. Reproduction or disassembly of embodied computer programs or algorithms prohibited.

Graphics Filters portions copyright 1991-1994 by ImageMark Software Labs. All rights reserved.

ImageStream Graphics Filters® copyright 1995 ImageMark Software Labs, Inc.

CorrecText® Grammar Correction System copyright 1993 by INSO Corporation. All rights reserved. Underlying technology by Language Systems, Inc. Reproduction or disassembly of embodied programs or databases prohibited.

No investigation has been made of common-law trademark rights in any word. Words that are known to have current registrations are shown with an initial capital. The inclusion or exclusion of any word, or its capitalizations, in the CorrecText® Grammar Correction System databases is not, however, an expression of the developer's opinion as to whether or not it is subject to proprietary rights, nor is it to be regarded as affecting the validity of any trademark.

International CorrectSpell™ copyright 1993 by INSO Corporation. All rights reserved. Reproduction or disassembly of embodied programs and databases prohibited.

Soft-Art Dictionary and Soft-Art dictionary program: copyright 1984–1994, Trade Secret, Soft-Art, Inc. All rights reserved.

Adobe, Adobe Type Manager, Aldus, Persuasion, PostScript, and TIFF are trademarks of Adobe Systems, Inc.

America Online is a registered trademark of America Online, Inc.

Paradox is a registered trademark of Ansa Software, a Borland Company.

Classic is a registered trademark licensed to Apple Computer, Inc., and Apple, AppleTalk, Macintosh, and TrueType are registered trademarks, and AppleMail, AppleScript, Geneva, Power Macintosh, PowerBook, PowerShare, PowerTalk, and QuickDraw are trademarks of Apple Computer, Inc.

Artisoft and LANtastic are registered trademarks of Artisoft, Inc.

Avery is a registered trademark of Avery Dennison Corporation.

Banyan and VINES are registered trademarks of Banyan Systems, Inc.

Borland, dBASE, dBASE II, dBASE III, dBASE III PLUS, and dBASE IV are registered trademarks, and Quattro Pro is a trademark of Borland International, Inc.

Document No. 66085-0795
OEM Document No. 000-11315
Printed in the United States of America

Contents

Introduction

What Have We Done to Your Manual?

By Pete Higgins, Group Vice President,
Microsoft Applications and Content Group

We thought you might ask! The best way to answer this question is to tell you about the goals we've set for ourselves in producing this book: make it relevant to the work you do; make it more graphical; make it easier to scan and digest; and make it fun to browse through, and more friendly overall.

We spent a lot of time thinking about these goals. We learned a great deal about the tasks you use software to help you accomplish, and we learned about the jobs you perform in your organizations. We then worked to determine how we could most effectively use the book format to show you what Microsoft® Office applications can do for you.

So You Don't Have Time to Learn?

Historically, we've focused on *documenting* our products—that is, explaining how they work, often in intricate detail. However, you've told us that your primary focus is on getting your work done, not learning our products! This motivated us to rethink our approach. We not only assessed what we've done in the past, but we also thought about makers of other types of products and how they provide assistance to their users.

For example, when you buy a car, you need enough information about how the car works to enable you to drive it safely; you don't necessarily need to understand all the workings of the internal combustion engine. If you later find that you need more information, you can always consult an expert or refer to the owner's manual or a repair manual. And when you're planning to drive your car from point A to point B, you probably just want to know the most direct route, not every possible route.

We realize that you have a job to do; you need to get from point A to point B. Our job is to provide you with a "map" and steer you in the right direction so that you can get there as quickly and efficiently as possible. If you need more information along the way, it's right there at your fingertips in our new online user assistance system—all you have to do is ask the Answer Wizard!

Tell Us What You Think!

We want your feedback! Tell us what you like or don't like about this book and the new user assistance that we've built into the Microsoft Office applications. Tell us what you think about the Answer Wizard. Tell us if you notice mistakes. We can handle it!

You can send your comments in electronic mail to:

offc95ua@microsoft.com

Or you can send a letter to:

Office UA Feedback
Microsoft Corporation
One Microsoft Way
Redmond WA 98052
USA

(The addresses above are for comments pertaining to the *Getting Results* book, built-in user assistance, and the Answer Wizard only.)

Although we can't promise that we'll be able to answer all of your responses, we'll certainly try our best. You can be sure, however, that we'll read them all; your feedback is very valuable to us!

Sources for Additional Information

Depending on the tasks you need to do, you may need additional information about using Microsoft Office applications. Chances are that you'll find the information you need in one or more of the resources described below and on the following pages.

The Microsoft Network: Gain Easy Access to Information

From product discussion forums to technical documents, you'll find a wealth of information about Microsoft Office applications on The Microsoft Network, Microsoft's online information service. To learn how to sign up for and connect to The Microsoft Network, look up **Microsoft Network** in Windows® 95 online Help. To connect directly to specific Office application information sources, click The Microsoft Network on your Office application's Help menu.

Visit the Microsoft Home Page on the Internet

Microsoft maintains a wide array of news and information on the World Wide Web on the Internet. Your gateway to this information is the Microsoft Home Page.

The address? **http://www.microsoft.com**

Microsoft Press Publications Complete the Picture

Microsoft Press publications are an integral part of the Microsoft Office information spectrum. Designed to complement the material included in your Microsoft Office package, Microsoft Press® books for Office applications range from step-by-step tutorials and general how-to guides to technical references and programming guides. Look for the titles in the following list at your local bookstore.

To find the Microsoft Press retailer nearest you, or to order books directly, call 1-800-MSPRESS (1-800-677-7377) in the United States. In Canada, call 1-800-667-1115.

Outside the United States and Canada, fax 206-936-7329, or write to the following address:

International Coordinator
Microsoft Press
One Microsoft Way
Redmond, WA 98052-6399
USA

General Tutorials

Step by Step series (various authors); editions for Microsoft Office, Microsoft Excel, Microsoft Access, Word, and PowerPoint® for Windows 95	The quick and easy way to get started with Microsoft Office and the various Office applications.
The Way Word Works (Dorling Kindersley) *The Way Excel Works* (Dorling Kindersley)	These colorful, visually oriented how-to guides are perfect introductions to Microsoft Word and Microsoft Excel.

User's Guides

The Ultimate Microsoft Office Book, second edition (Eric Stroo)	Learn helpful techniques for using Microsoft Office applications in combination with one another.
Running series (various authors); editions for Microsoft Office, Microsoft Excel, Microsoft Access, Word, and PowerPoint for Windows 95	Provides all levels of computer users with a one-stop, example-filled user's guide and reference to working with Microsoft Office and the various Office applications.

Quick Reference Guides

Field Guide series (Stephen L. Nelson); editions for Microsoft Office, Microsoft Excel, Microsoft Access, Word, and PowerPoint for Windows 95	Concise, visual, and easy-to-follow quick reference guides for Microsoft Office for Windows 95 applications; of special appeal to beginning and intermediate users.

Programming Tutorials

Microsoft Excel/Visual Basic for Windows 95 Step by Step (Reed Jacobson)	Learn how to use the Visual Basic® programming language built into Microsoft Excel to automate spreadsheet tasks and create custom applications.
Microsoft Access/Visual Basic for Windows 95 Step by Step (Evan Callahan)	Learn how to use the Visual Basic programming language built into Microsoft Access to automate database tasks and create custom applications.

Installation and Administrative Guide

Microsoft Office for Windows 95 Resource Kit (Microsoft Corporation)	The essential technical and strategic resource for systems administrators and others whose job it is to implement Microsoft Office for Windows 95 throughout an organization.

Programming Guides and Technical References

Microsoft Excel/Visual Basic for Windows 95 Programmer's Guide (Microsoft Corporation)	Learn how to customize the operation of Microsoft Excel for personal use, create macros to streamline routine tasks, and build custom applications.
Developing Microsoft Excel 95 Solutions with Visual Basic for Applications (Eric Wells)	Use the Microsoft Excel object model and Visual Basic to create business applications that turn raw data into useful information.
Microsoft Excel Developer's Kit, third edition (Microsoft Corporation)	Technical information and sample code for software developers who want to use Microsoft Excel as an application development platform.
Microsoft Excel Worksheet Function Reference, second edition (Microsoft Corporation)	A printed version of the Microsoft Excel online reference for worksheet functions.
Microsoft Excel/Visual Basic Reference, second edition (Microsoft Corporation)	A printed version of the Microsoft Excel online reference for Visual Basic.
Microsoft Word Developer's Kit, third edition (Microsoft Corporation)	Learn how to customize Word for personal use, create macros to streamline routine tasks, and build custom applications.
Developing Client Server Applications with Microsoft Office and BackOffice (Eric Wells)	Use Microsoft Office and BackOffice to build information systems that will convert raw data into useful information.

Programming Guides and Technical References *(continued)*

Microsoft Guide to Object Programming with Visual Basic 4 and Microsoft Office 95 (Joel Dehlin and Matt Curland)	Create customized business applications using Microsoft Visual Basic 4 custom objects and Office 95.
Developing Applications with Microsoft Office for Windows 95 (Christine Solomon)	Provides corporate developers, consultants, and managers with the concepts and techniques they need to plan, develop, and implement customized business applications using Microsoft Office and related technologies such as OLE, ODBC, and Visual Basic for applications.
Microsoft Jet Database Engine Programmer's Guide (Microsoft Corporation)	A technical sourcebook for the database engine used in Microsoft applications, including Microsoft Access for Windows 95 and Visual Basic 4.

Credits

Lead   Kathryn Hamilton

Contributing Writers   Evan Callahan, Kathi Davidson, Mark Dodge, John Guarino, Jim Holtzman, Ann Laporte, Sharon Lawson, Charlotte Lowrie, Janet Wilson

Editors   Carmen Almodovar, Ann Becherer, Laura Brenner

Illustrator   Leslie Newman

Book Designer   Mary Tjarnberg

Designers   Aileen Burke, Jennifer Jacobson, Daniela Lammers

Copy Editor   Linda Moschell

Indexer   Julie Kawabata

Production   Margot Ayer, Kristin Lynn Bergsma, Chris Chisholm, Hubert Dolan, Lori Fields, Phyllis Grossman, Donna Johnston, Katrina Kennard, Luanne LaLonde, Erin Pearson

Additional Contributors   Michael Anderson, Shelley Greer, Shawn Klaisner, Valerie Klaisner, Nailah Shami, Bruce Vanderpool

---

This book is dedicated to Charlie Golder, without whom many of us wouldn't be writing user assistance materials for Microsoft today, and without whose continuing inspiration our lives would be far less rich.

PART 1

Your First Day at the Office

Contents

Introducing Microsoft Office

Get to Know Microsoft Office and Its Applications

Welcome to Microsoft® Office for Windows® 95. Office is a set of powerful applications designed to work together as one program. In partnership with Windows 95, Office helps you concentrate on what's really important: working with your information and sharing it with others, quickly and efficiently.

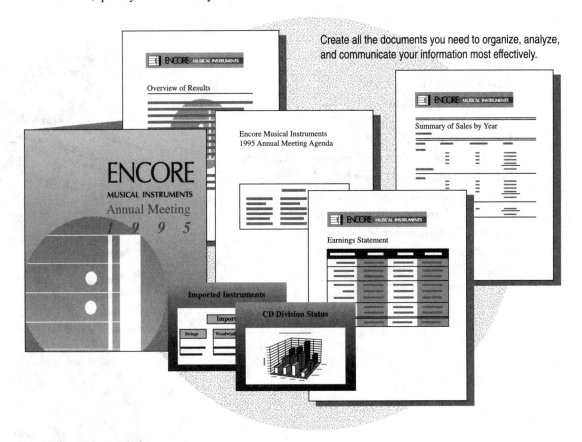

Create all the documents you need to organize, analyze, and communicate your information most effectively.

Which applications does your edition of Office include?   Microsoft Office Standard includes Microsoft Word, Microsoft Excel, Microsoft PowerPoint®, and Microsoft Schedule+. Microsoft Office Professional includes these applications and Microsoft Access. For details on new features included in Office and its applications, see "What's New in Microsoft Office," page 10.

Which Office Applications Should You Use?

The applications you use in a work session vary depending on what you want to do. While the possibilities are unlimited, this section suggests a few of the tasks you can accomplish quickly and efficiently using Office.

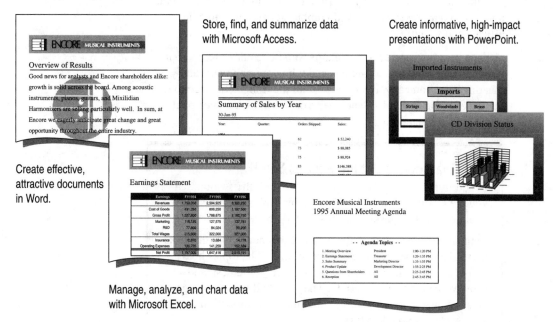

Store, find, and summarize data with Microsoft Access.

Create informative, high-impact presentations with PowerPoint.

Create effective, attractive documents in Word.

Manage, analyze, and chart data with Microsoft Excel.

Organize your time and coordinate with others using Schedule+.

Create great-looking documents with Word Develop business plans, letters, memos, reports, and all the documents your organization needs. Usually, you won't have to start from scratch; wizards and templates do a lot of the work for you.

Crunch numbers with Microsoft Excel Organize and analyze data in worksheets, charts, and maps. Consolidate your organization's budgets and create forecasts to use for future planning. For smart decision-making, compare alternative scenarios using what-if analysis.

Keep track of data with Microsoft Access   Manage customer contacts, orders, inventory, or any other kind of information you need to track. Find the data you need quickly and summarize it in professional-looking reports.

Present your plans and results with PowerPoint   Prepare high-impact presentations that will keep your audience attentive. To increase the appeal of your presentations, add graphics, charts, multimedia effects, and sound.

Manage your time and set up meetings with Schedule+   Keep your Appointment Book up to date by scheduling appointments and meetings electronically. Keep track of all the things you need to do in an electronic To Do List and keep your business and personal contacts in a Contact List.

Use This Book to Get the Results You Want

In addition to "Your First Day at the Office," the section that you are reading now, this book contains topics that illustrate common business tasks like those listed above.

In the table of contents or the index of this book, find the tasks most like the ones you need to accomplish. The topics help you determine which applications will serve you best, and show you what you need to do. They also tell you how to get detailed instructions, examples, and related information on your screen as you do a task.

For some tasks, you use one Office application. For others, the topics show you how you can use the applications together to get the most from Office.

 Sample documents show what you can do   The Office applications provide samples that may help you get started. For example, open a sample letter, presentation, workbook, or database to get ideas for your own work. To find samples, browse through the folders installed with the application you're using.

Get a jump start on your document   Use a template or an existing document, and modify it as needed. For details, see "About Creating and Opening Documents and Databases," page 46.

Put Information Together the Way You Need It

Office provides powerful ways to combine information from its applications. For example, you can place data and charts from Microsoft Excel into a sales letter you write in Word and then mail the letter to your customers using a Microsoft Access mailing list.

Sometimes you create whole documents that are closely related. In those cases, even when you have documents created in different Office applications, you can bind them together, save, and print them as a single document.

Data and chart added to a text document

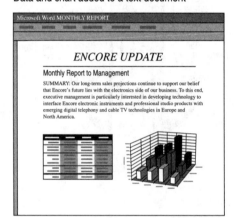

Different types of documents bound together with Office Binder and saved as one file

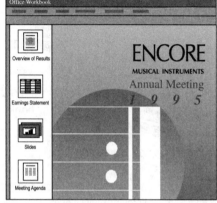

Use Office in Your Workgroup and Beyond

It's not enough to create your own documents and manage your own data; you also need to communicate and share information with coworkers and customers. Groups can review documents and view presentations online, and can work together in shared lists and databases. Send or route documents electronically, or post them in public folders on the network.

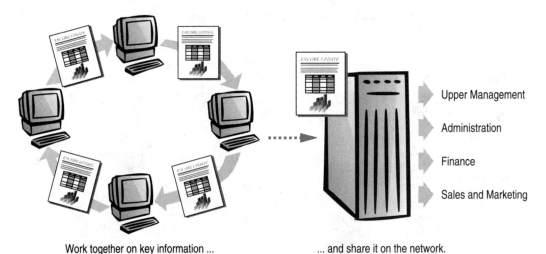

Work together on key information ...   ... and share it on the network.

Get your coworkers' comments on your document or workbook In Word documents and Microsoft Excel workbooks, give and receive feedback online without printing the document. For details, see "Have Your Team Review a Word Document," page 333, and "Share a Workbook with a Coworker," page 338.

Find out more about sending and publishing documents on a network For details, see "Share Documents Electronically," page 326.

Make your electronic mail messages look great Compose, edit, and format your electronic mail messages in Word for easy reading and a professional look. For details, see "Share Documents Electronically," page 326.

Get Going with Productivity Tools

The Office applications share a consistent design in many areas, making it easy to keep working as you switch among the applications and different documents. To get the most out of your work sessions, take advantage of the Office applications' productivity tools, including wizards, toolbar buttons, and shortcut menus.

Productivity tools include toolbars with buttons for common tasks ...

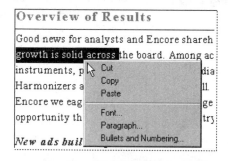

... shortcut menus with the commands you need alongside your work ...

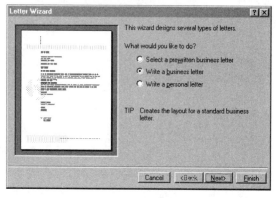

... and wizards that automate complex tasks in a few steps.

Manage your work with the Microsoft Office Shortcut Bar   The Microsoft Office Shortcut Bar provides quick access to many basic tasks and frequently used documents. For example, you can use the Shortcut Bar to quickly find and open documents. Customize the Shortcut Bar to display frequently used folders in toolbar form, with their contents represented as buttons. For details, see "Take a Shortcut to Work," page 36.

Use improved online assistance while you work   To go to Help topics that offer step-by-step instructions, visual examples, and other information you need to do your task, ask the Answer Wizard a question in your own words. For details, see "Get Assistance While You Work," page 30.

Microsoft Office Shortcut Bar

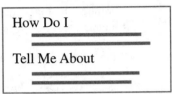

Online assistance provides quick information while you work.

Let IntelliSense Technology Handle Repetitive Tasks

To minimize repetitive, time-consuming tasks, Office applications provide IntelliSense™ technology. The IntelliSense features understand what you are trying to do and help you do it. For example, IntelliSense features can do the following:

- AutoCorrect catches and corrects common typing mistakes so you don't have to fix them.

- AutoComplete and AutoText finish entering some types of information so you do less repetitive typing.

- AutoFormat formats an entire document so you don't have to apply formatting yourself.

For details, look up **AutoCorrect**, **AutoComplete**, **AutoText**, and **AutoFormat** in the online index for the application you are using.

If You Are Switching to Office

A special welcome! Thank you for giving Office a try.

You can open existing files from many other applications, including WordPerfect®, Lotus® 1-2-3®, and Quattro Pro™. Click Open (File menu) and select the file type you want to open.

For former WordPerfect and 1-2-3 users, online Help is available to ease your transition. In Word, click WordPerfect Help (Help menu) to get information on switching. In Microsoft Excel, click Lotus 1-2-3 Help (Help menu) for information.

For details, look up **Lotus 1-2-3**, **WordPerfect**, **Quattro Pro**, or the name of the application you are switching from in the online index for the Office application you are using.

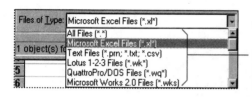

In the Open dialog box, click Files Of Type, and select the type for the file you want to open.

Next Steps

To	See
Create a new document, find an existing document, and customize the Office Shortcut Bar	"Take a Shortcut to Work," page 36
Learn how to get online Help	"Get Assistance While You Work," page 30
Get started using Word	"Create Your First Word Document," page 57
Get started using Microsoft Excel	"Create Your First Microsoft Excel Workbook," page 70
Get started using PowerPoint	"Create Your First PowerPoint Presentation," page 82
Get started using Schedule+	"Schedule an Appointment," page 314
Get started using Microsoft Access	"Use Your First Microsoft Access Database," page 91
Combine information from more than one Office application	"Use Office Applications Together," page 103

What's New in Microsoft Office

New features, improved design, revamped online Help, and extended IntelliSense technology make this the most productive Office ever. Use wizards and templates to get a fast start on creating high-quality documents, workbooks, and presentations. Share work with others across the network. Use Schedule+, a new addition to the Office family, to manage personal tasks and appointments. If you have Microsoft Office Professional, use the new and improved Microsoft Access wizards and other features to take the work out of creating and maintaining databases.

Finding more information   Each application in Office has extensive online Help that provides easy access to hundreds of subjects online. This topic often refers you to the application's online index for more details. To display an online index, double-click the Help button on the application's Standard toolbar, or click Help Topics (Help menu), and then click the Index tab.

Help button

"What's new" information is also available in online Help. For details, look up **what's new** in the online index.

The Most Productive Office Yet

To help you be your most productive, IntelliSense technology has been extended to speed your most common tasks and to provide you with the information you need when you need it. And Office works hand-in-hand with Windows 95 to help you streamline and organize your work environment.

Work Smarter, Not Harder

- Quickly create and open documents, view the contents of folders, schedule appointments, and send mail with the Office Shortcut Bar. For details, see "Take a Shortcut to Work," page 36.

- Copy files, worksheets, tables, and charts by "dragging and dropping" them on the desktop, into other applications, documents, or mail messages, or to different folders on your computer. For details, look up **drag-and-drop editing** in the application's online index.

- Collaborate with your coworkers by sending them files through electronic mail or by posting copies in a folder on the network where all interested parties can view them. For more information, see "Share Documents Electronically," page 326.

- Enjoy the convenience of having your application automatically correct typos as you make them. For details, look up **AutoCorrect** in the online index.

Find the Documents You Need

- Make it easier to identify your documents by using descriptive filenames with multiple words and spaces, such as National Sales Meeting Presentation. For more information about long filenames and other Windows 95 features, see your Windows 95 documentation and online Help.

- When you can't remember the name of a file, but do remember a word or phrase it contains, use the newly designed Open dialog box features to search for the file. For more information, see "About Creating and Opening Documents and Databases," page 46.

- Organize related files, such as all the documents, worksheets, and presentations you need for your next sales meeting, by storing them in a single Office Binder. For more information, see "Use Office Applications Together," page 103.

- Or, locate related files by recording summary information, such as Author's Name, Subject, Title, or Comments, or keywords and phrases of your own choosing when you save each file. When you want to find related files, simply search for one or more of the summary fields or for a keyword or phrase. For more information, see "About Creating and Opening Documents and Databases," page 46.

Get Help Where and When You Need It

- When you know what you want to do, but don't know what to call it to get the help you need, ask the Answer Wizard in your own words. The Answer Wizard quickly displays step-by-step instructions, examples, and other information to help you get the job done fast. For more information, see "Get Assistance While You Work," page 30.

- When you want to know more about a screen item, such as a command, a toolbar button, or a dialog box, find out quickly with a ScreenTip. To get a ScreenTip, click the Help button on the application's toolbar or the question mark button within a dialog box, and then click a screen item for a brief explanation. For more information, see "Get Assistance While You Work," page 30.

Help
button

Question mark
button

- Need help finding Help? Choose Help Topics from any Office application's Help menu. You'll find a list of all Help topics, an index of Help terms, and a tab that lets you access the Answer Wizard.

- If you have the CD-ROM version of Office, you have access to this book online. To display the online version, click the Getting Results Book button on the Office Shortcut Bar. Then, search for topics using keywords of your own choosing, or quickly display related Help topics.

Getting Results Book button

- If you have the CD-ROM version of Office, you have the Office CD Value Pack, a collection of application extras that include clip art, maps, sounds, presentation enhancements, and utilities such as Word Viewer. For details on what's included in the Office CD Value Pack and how to access its contents, see the online Help file Valupack.hlp, located in the ValuPack directory on the Office CD.

Preview Office-Compatible Applications

- If you have the CD-ROM version of Office, you can view short demonstrations of applications created by other vendors to work closely with Office. These applications have the familiar look and feel of Office and offer similar menus, toolbars, and accelerator keys, as well as easy ways to share information with Office applications. For information on viewing the demonstrations, see the online Help file Valupack.hlp in the ValuPack directory on the Office CD.

What's New in Microsoft Word

Everyday Tasks Made Fast and Easy

- Instead of checking the spelling in your entire document at once, let Word flag your spelling mistakes as you type with Spell It. You can make corrections at your leisure quickly by viewing a pop-up list of suggested changes. For details, look up **checking spelling automatically** in the Word online index.

- Speed text editing by having Word automatically fix capitalization errors and common misspellings using the improved AutoCorrect feature. AutoCorrect now learns your personal preferences for capitalization and spelling as you type. AutoCorrect also automatically inserts special characters such as arrows, copyright symbols, and other symbols when you type special shortcuts. For details, look up **AutoCorrect** in the Word online index.

- Let Word automatically create bulleted lists and borders as you type. For details, look up **AutoFormat** in the Word online index.

- Use a simple mouse movement to quickly toggle between selecting a single word and a single letter with improved AutoSelect. For details, look up **AutoSelect (automatic word selection)** in the Word online index.

- Add addresses to your faxes, memos, and letters with one click using the Address Book feature. For more information, look up **address book** in the Word online index.

Insert Address button

Work Smarter, Not Harder

- Create professional-looking resumes, newsletters, and reports quickly by using the new, professionally designed templates provided with Word. Templates provide a layout, heading styles, and other design elements for your documents, so all you need to do is type over the "placeholder" text. For more information, see "Create Your First Word Document," page 57.

- Let Word show you better ways to get the job done with the TipWizard®, which watches you as you work and offers suggestions for faster, easier ways to accomplish your task. For example, if you type a single line of text without a period and then start a new paragraph, the TipWizard automatically applies a heading-level style. For details, look up **TipWizard** in the Word online index.

- Replace words and all their variations with the improved Find and Replace commands. For example, in addition to finding the word "purchase" and replacing it with the word "buy," you can also replace "purchasing" with "buying" and "purchased" with "bought." For details, look up **finding words, all forms** in the Word online index.

- If you have the CD-ROM version of Office, you have access to Imager, a utility that enables you to easily insert scanned images into your Word documents and PowerPoint presentations. For details on accessing and using Imager, see the online Help file Valupack.hlp in the ValuPack directory on the Office CD.

Online Communication with Style

- Write, format, and edit electronic mail messages with Word. For details, see "Share Documents Electronically," page 326, or look up **email, mail editor** in the Word online index.

Highlight button

- Call attention to review comments you make in documents or replies you embed in electronic mail messages by using the Highlight button. For details, look up **highlighter pen** in the Word online index.

- If you have the CD-ROM version of Office, you have Word Viewer, an easy-to-use standalone utility that lets users who do not have Word view and print Word documents. For details on accessing and using Word Viewer, see the online Help file Valupack.hlp in the ValuPack directory on the Office CD.

Use Word with Other Office Applications

Insert Address button

- Easily insert names and addresses from your Schedule+ Contact List or Microsoft Exchange personal address book into your letters, memos, and faxes using the Address Book feature. You can also use the Word Mail Merge feature and Letter, Memo, and Fax Wizards to access address information quickly. For details, see "Create a Mailing," page 177, or look up **address book** in the Word online index.

What's New in Microsoft Excel

Everyday Tasks Made Fast and Easy

- Save typing when you enter data in lists or databases with AutoComplete. When you begin typing text in a cell, Microsoft Excel checks the surrounding cells for similar data and, if it finds it, automatically completes the entry for you. For more information, see "Create a Business Contact List in Microsoft Excel," page 300.

- Quickly format numbers by choosing from a list of examples in the improved Format Cells dialog box. For more information, see "Make Your Microsoft Excel Worksheet Look Great," page 206.

- No need to create temporary formulas to total the values of cells in a worksheet. Now, when you select a range of cells, Microsoft Excel automatically displays the sum of their values. For details, look up **AutoCalculate** in the Microsoft Excel online index.

Manage Data Effortlessly

- Quickly set up invoices and expense tracking, business planning, financial analysis, and personal budgeting worksheets with one of the new, professionally designed templates provided with Microsoft Excel. For more information, see "Figure the Monthly Payment on a Loan," page 515.

- Create electronic forms for your workbooks with the Template Wizard With Data Tracking, and then use the forms to gather data from your coworkers and send the data to a database without retyping. For more information, see "Create a Form for Online Customer Quotes," page 198.

- Share Microsoft Excel lists and databases with your coworkers. Now, more than one person can edit a list or database simultaneously over a network. For more information, see "Share a Workbook with a Coworker," page 338.

Work Smarter, Not Harder

- Use CellTips to document your worksheets or to provide comments on a coworker's worksheet. For details, look up **CellTips** in the Microsoft Excel online index.

- Show data, such as sales by region or population, geographically with Microsoft Data Map. For more information, see "Display Data on a Map," page 246.

Use Microsoft Excel with Microsoft Access

If you have Office Professional or Microsoft Access for Windows 95, Microsoft Excel makes it easy to share data and use Microsoft Access forms and reports right from your worksheet.

- Summarize Microsoft Excel data in a sophisticated report by using the Microsoft Access Report Wizard right from your worksheet. For more information, lookup **Access Report Wizard** in the Microsoft Excel online index.

- Simplify entering data into your Microsoft Excel list or database by using Microsoft Access forms. For more information, look up **Form Wizard (Microsoft Access)** in the Microsoft Excel online index.

- Move data from a Microsoft Excel worksheet into a Microsoft Access database without retyping by using the Convert To Access command. For details, look up "Move a Product List into Microsoft Access," page 379.

What's New in Microsoft PowerPoint

Create Stellar Presentations Effortlessly

- Set up your presentations in no time at all by using the new, professionally designed templates provided with PowerPoint. The templates provide structure, format, and content for a variety of sample presentation types. Pick the presentation type you want, and then type over the suggested content to personalize your presentation. For more information, see "Customize the Appearance of Your Presentation," page 264.

- Or, if you want to create a presentation from scratch, use the AutoContent Wizard. Not only does the wizard help you choose the organization and format for your presentation, it also helps you tailor your presentation to a specific audience and a given length of time. For more information, see "Create Your First PowerPoint Presentation," page 82.

- Simplify overhead presentations and printed output or jazz up electronic presentations with *design templates*. The design templates provide different presentation styles or looks. For more information, see "Create Your First PowerPoint Presentation," page 82.

Accent Your Message with Visual and Audio Effects

- Bring your presentations to life by using the Animation Effects toolbar to animate titles, text, and art with sound, motion, and other effects. For more information, see "Prepare for an Electronic Presentation," page 280.

- Let Auto Clip Art suggest clip art that will add impact and increase audience retention. You can also add visual appeal with textured effects, two-color gradient fills, and customizable color schemes. For more information, see "Get Your Point Across with Graphics," page 271.

- If you have the CD-ROM version of Office, you have an entire library of presentation images, design templates, video clips, and sounds at your disposal. For details on accessing and using this library, see the online Help file Valupack.hlp in the ValuPack directory on the Office CD.

Make Final Preparations Quickly

- Save yourself potential embarrassment by proofing your presentation for spelling, punctuation, and formatting errors with Style Checker. For details, look up **Style Checker** in the PowerPoint online index.

- Do you work in color but print in black and white? Quickly preview your color presentation using Black and White view. For more information, see "Quickly Prepare a Black & White Presentation," page 256.

- Take your complete presentation anywhere you go. Make sure all linked files and multimedia files are included, and compress and save them on multiple disks with the Pack and Go Wizard. For details, look up **Pack and Go** in the PowerPoint online index.

- Review a presentation with your workgroup across the network with Presentation Conferencing. For more information, see "Give an Electronic Presentation," page 288.

Impressive Presentation and Follow-up

- During your presentation, navigate between slides to review or preview important points with Slide Navigator. For details, look up **Slide Navigator** in the PowerPoint online index.

- Access your speaker's notes, capture audience comments, and keep track of time while controlling a presentation on a second computer with the Stage Manager tools available with Presentation Conferencing. For details, look up **Presentation Conferencing** in the PowerPoint online index.

- Hold more effective meetings by jotting down audience comments and notes and automatically creating an action item list with Meeting Minder. When you're back at your desk, quickly export your meeting notes to Word or Microsoft Exchange for easy publication. For details, look up **Meeting Minder** in the PowerPoint online index.

Use PowerPoint with Other Office Applications

- Incorporate text, tables, art, and charts from Word documents or Microsoft Excel worksheets into your slides by dragging and dropping them. For more information, see "Get Your Point Across with Graphics," page 271.

- Print training materials or handouts from your slides in Word with Write-Up. For more information, see "Transfer Information Between PowerPoint and Other Applications," page 268.

What's New in Microsoft Schedule+

Because Schedule+ is included with Office for the first time, all the features may be new to you. If you have used Schedule+ in the past, you'll find the new Schedule+ makes it easier than ever to manage your schedule, contacts, and to do list.

Meet, with No Hassle at All

- Quickly schedule meetings with your coworkers with the Meeting Wizard. For more information, see "Schedule a Meeting," page 320.

- Run better meetings by sending agendas or documents you want attendees to review along with your meeting requests. For more information, see "Schedule a Meeting," page 320.

- Don't worry about time zone differences when you set up meetings with people around the world. Schedule+ automatically adjusts meeting times no matter where the attendees are located. For details, look up **time zones** in the Schedule+ online index.

Organize Your Contacts

- Keep important information about your key business and personal contacts a click away by recording names, telephone numbers, and other important facts about your associates in the Schedule+ Contact List. For more information, see "Manage Contacts with Schedule+," page 296.

- Make it easier to find related contacts by grouping them. For more information, see "Manage Contacts with Schedule+," page 296.

Organize Your Tasks

- Keep yourself organized by creating an electronic To Do List, then schedule time for tasks by dragging them into your Appointment Book. For more information, see "Keep a To Do List," page 317.

- Make it easy to find related tasks by grouping them by project. For more information, see "Keep a To Do List," page 317.

Personalize Schedule+

- Organize your Appointment Book, To Do List, and Contact List to emphasize the scheduling, task, and contact information that's most important to you. For details, look up **views** in the Schedule+ online index.

- Customize how you view Schedule+: Add and remove tabs, and change the appearance of each tab to suit your needs. For details, look up **tabs** and **views** in the Schedule+ online index.

Use Schedule+ with Other Office Applications

- Stay in touch with your contacts by creating a mailing list from your Schedule+ Contact List with the Word Letter Wizard. For more information, see "Create a Mailing," page 176.

- Build a more elaborate project schedule by exporting your Schedule+ To Do List to Microsoft Project or Microsoft Excel. For details, look up **exporting** in the Schedule+ online index.

Take Your Schedule with You

- When you'll be away from your desk, print a copy of your schedule that fits into your paper day planner. For details, see "Schedule an Appointment," page 314.

- If you have a Sharp® Wizard or a Timex® Data Link wristwatch, download your schedule to your device. For details, see **exporting** in the Schedule+ online index.

What's New in Microsoft Access

If you have Office Professional, you have access to a rich set of new database features: new Microsoft Access wizards that help you create databases from scratch or from existing data, improved form and table design features, improved filters, enhanced analysis features, and all the power of Microsoft Visual Basic® for applications.

Create a Database Effortlessly

- Quickly create any of a number of common business or personal databases, such as an order entry database or a music collection database, with the Database Wizard. The wizard creates the tables, forms, and reports you need, so all you need to do is enter your data. For details, look up "Track Your Business Contacts in Microsoft Access," page 306.

- Move data from a Microsoft Excel worksheet into a Microsoft Access database without retyping by using the Convert To Access command. For details, look up "Move a Product List into Microsoft Access," page 379.

- Avoid retyping text you have in another application by importing it with the Text Import Wizard. For details, look up **importing with Text Import Wizard** in the Microsoft Access online index.

- After importing data from a Microsoft Excel worksheet or other "flat-file" database, let Microsoft Access reorganize it into tables for you with the Table Analyzer Wizard. For details, see "Move a Product List into Microsoft Access," page 379.

Find the Information You Need Fast

- Find information with just a few mouse clicks using Filter By Form and Filter By Selection. Just select the information you want, and Microsoft Access quickly finds all records that contain that information. For details, look up **Filter By Form** or **Filter By Selection** in the Microsoft Access online index.

- Improve the speed at which your database finds the information you need by using the Table Analyzer Wizard to maximize your database's performance. For details, see "Move a Product List into Microsoft Access," page 379.

Create Impressive Forms and Reports

- Quickly format your reports and forms in a distinctive, consistent style with AutoFormat. For more information, look up **AutoFormat** in the Microsoft Access online index.

- Quickly copy formatting characteristics from one item to another using the Format Painter. For details, look up **Format Painter** in the Microsoft Access online index.

- Spruce up your forms by using the new Formatting toolbar in Design and Datasheet views. For details, look up **Formatting toolbar** in the Microsoft Access online index.

- Jazz up your forms and reports with background pictures. Now more controls have a transparent background to let watermarks show through. For details, look up **background pictures** in the Microsoft Access online index.

Work Smarter, Not Harder

- If you use a shared database on a laptop, use Database Replication to synchronize the data on your laptop with data in the master copy of the database on your desktop computer. For details, look up **database replication** in the Microsoft Access online index.

- Automate repetitive tasks and create custom applications in Microsoft Access with Microsoft Visual Basic. For introductory information, see "Automate Repetitive Tasks in Microsoft Access," page 553.

Use Microsoft Access with Microsoft Excel

- Use the analyzing power of Microsoft Excel PivotTable® dynamic views to summarize Microsoft Access data right on your form or report. For details, see "Create a Sales Summary from a Microsoft Access Database," page 465, or look up **PivotTable** in the Microsoft Access online index.

- Simplify entering data into your Microsoft Excel list or database by using Microsoft Access forms. For more information, look up **Form Wizard (Microsoft Access)** in the Microsoft Excel online index.

- Create sophisticated, detailed reports from Microsoft Excel data by using the Microsoft Access Report Wizard. For more information, look up **reports, creating** in the Microsoft Access online index.

Next Steps

To	See
Find out more about Office	"Introducing Microsoft Office," page 2
Find out more about Windows 95	Microsoft Windows 95 documentation, or choose Help from the Windows 95 Start menu
Get answers to your questions about how you can best complete your tasks	"Get Assistance While You Work," page 30

Install and Start Microsoft Office

Get Up and Running in a Few Easy Steps

If Office is already installed on your computer You can skip ahead to the section on starting Office. If you need to modify your Office installation—for example, add Equation Editor or remove graphics converters to free up disk space—see "Add or Remove Office Components," later in this topic.

If Office isn't already installed You can install Office on your own computer or on a network location. Once Office is available on the network, other users can install it on their computers, or they can save disk space by running a shared version of Office over the network. When you install Office, you can include just the components you want—ranging from a minimal version suitable for computers with limited disk space to the entire set of Office components.

Key Features

Office Setup

Registration Wizard

Install Office from floppy disks or a CD-ROM on a computer or on a network location.

From its network location, install Office on individual computers ...

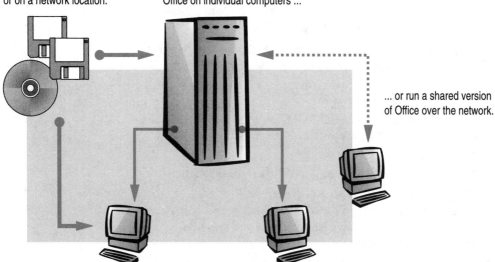

... or run a shared version of Office over the network.

Plan to use Word as your email editor? For best performance, we recommend that your computer have at least 12 MB of memory.

Install Office on Your Computer

Want to install Office directly on your hard disk—or install Office in a way that conserves disk space?   You can use the Office Setup program to install Office directly on your hard disk from a CD-ROM, floppy disks, or a network location. If you want to save disk space, you may be able to run a shared version of Office over the network (if your network administrator provides this option). Or, conserve disk space by installing Office so that it runs from your CD-ROM.

Which Office components should you install?   Office Setup is easier than ever since it recommends which components to install and where to install them. For example, you'll probably want to choose the Typical option, which installs commonly used Office components. If you're not sure which components to install, don't worry—you can always run Setup again to add or remove them.

Upgrading from a previous version of Office?   By default, the Setup program replaces your current version of Office with Office for Windows 95. If you do not want this, specify a different directory location for Office for Windows 95 when prompted by Setup. Even if you choose to replace your current version of Office, Setup preserves the documents, templates, and other files you created so you can continue using them in Office for Windows 95.

Important   If you're using a virus-detection utility, disable it before you run the Office Setup program. Also, close any open Windows applications.

▶ **To install Office on Windows 95**

1   If you're installing from a CD-ROM, insert the Office CD in the CD-ROM drive. Click the Install Microsoft Office button and skip to step 5.

   If you're installing from floppy disks, insert the first Setup disk (Disk 1) in drive A or B.

   If you're installing from a network location, connect to it. (Make sure to write down the drive letter because you may need to use it if you run Setup again.)

2   Click the Start button, click Settings, and then click Control Panel.

3   Double-click the Add/Remove Programs icon.

4   On the Install/Uninstall tab, click the Install button.

5   Follow the Setup instructions on the screen.   [?] For Help on dialog box options, click this button.

▶ **To install Office on Windows NT™**

1 If you're installing from a CD-ROM, insert the Office CD in the CD-ROM drive. Click the Install Microsoft Office button and skip to step 4.

   If you're installing from floppy disks, insert the first Setup disk (Disk 1) in drive A or B.

   If you're installing from a network location, connect to it. (Make sure to write down the drive letter because you may need to use it if you run Setup again.)

2 In Program Manager, click Run (File menu).

3 Type the location you're installing from plus the word **setup** (for example, type **a:\setup** or **x:\msoffice\setup**).

4 Click OK, and then follow the Setup instructions on the screen.

? For Help on dialog box options, click this button.

How Do You Register Office?

Registration ensures that you will be notified of future product updates, have access to Microsoft product support services, and qualify for the Microsoft product repair and replacement plan.

If you have a modem and you're installing on Windows 95 The Registration Wizard starts when you finish installing Office. This wizard helps you fill out the registration form and can automatically send it to Microsoft.

If you don't have a modem, or if you're installing on Windows NT Fill out your Office registration card and send it to Microsoft.

Install Office on a Network

For instructions on installing and administering Office on a network, see the Network Readme file (NETWORK.TXT) on the first Setup floppy disk (Disk 1) or on the CD-ROM. If you've already installed Office, you'll also find the Network Readme file in your Office folder, or you can look up Network Install Readme in the Getting Help section of the Office online Help table of contents.

For more details on installing Office on a network, you might want to purchase the *Microsoft Office for Windows 95 Resource Kit*, which is available wherever computer books are sold and directly from Microsoft Press®.

Add or Remove Office Components

Once you install Office, you can run Setup again at any time to add Office components—such as PowerPoint, Equation Editor, or add-in files—or remove them to free up disk space. You can also restore the previous installation (if files are accidentally corrupted or deleted), or uninstall Office.

For Help, double-click. In the Office online index look up: **installing Microsoft Office components**

If you originally installed an application using its own Setup program rather than Office Setup   By default, Office Setup will remove previous versions of applications and install newer versions. If you accept the defaults, you should use Office Setup to add or remove components, or to reinstall or uninstall an application. If you do not allow Office Setup to remove a previous version of an application, you must use the original Setup program (not Office Setup) to make changes to that application.

Important   If you're using a virus-detection utility, disable it before you run the Office Setup program. Also, close any open Windows applications.

▶ **To add or remove Office components on Windows 95**

1 If you originally installed Office from a CD-ROM, insert the Office CD in the CD-ROM drive.

   If you originally installed Office from floppy disks, insert the first Setup disk (Disk 1) in drive A or B.

   If you originally installed Office from a network, connect to the network location using the same drive letter.

2 Click the Start button, click Settings, and then click Control Panel.

3 Double-click the Add/Remove Programs icon.

4 Click the Install/Uninstall tab.

5 Select the Office application, and then click the Add/Remove button.

6 Follow the Setup instructions on the screen.

For Help on dialog box options, click this button.

▶ **To add or remove Office components on Windows NT**

1 Start Office Setup just as you did when you first installed Office.

2 Follow the Setup instructions on the screen.

 You've installed a Word or Microsoft Excel add-in file—now how do you activate or "load" it? For details, look up **add-in programs** in the Word or Microsoft Excel online index.

Start and Quit Office

To start an Office application on Windows 95 Click the Start button, click Programs, and then click the application you want.

To start an Office application on Windows NT Double-click the application's icon in the Microsoft Office program group.

To quit an Office application Click Exit on the application's File menu.

 To quickly start an Office application and create a new document at the same time Click the Start A New Document button on the Office Shortcut Bar. (For details, see "Take a Shortcut to Work," page 36.)

For Help, double-click.
In the Office online index look up:
starting applications

Start A New Document button

Next Steps

To	See
Get instructions on installing and administering Office on a network	The Network Readme file (NETWORK.TXT) in the Office folder, or look up Network Install Readme in the Getting Help section of the Office online Help table of contents
Get late-breaking information about Office	The following Readme files in the Office folder or in the folders for the individual applications: OFREADME.TXT (Office) BINDER.TXT (Office) WDREADME.TXT (Word) XLREADME.TXT (Microsoft Excel) ACREADME.TXT (Microsoft Access) PPREADME.TXT (PowerPoint) SCREADME.TXT (Schedule+)
	Or, look up the appropriate Readme file in the Getting Help section of the application's online table of contents
Get help on using and customizing the Office Shortcut Bar	"Take a Shortcut to Work," page 36

Get Assistance While You Work

Use Online Help to Get the Right Information Quickly

Maximize productivity by minimizing the time you spend learning how to use Office and its applications. Expanded and improved *online assistance* helps you get your work done faster. For example, to identify unfamiliar items on the screen, you can display ScreenTips.

For more in-depth assistance, ask the Answer Wizard questions in your own words, and then quickly go to step-by-step instructions, visual examples, and more. Or, look up index entries like those listed with the topics in this book to find out how to perform your task.

What if online Help is not available? Run Office Setup to install it. For details, see "Install and Start Microsoft Office," page 25.

Find Out What's on the Screen

When you're not sure what an item you see on the screen is or what it does, display a *ScreenTip*, which offers a brief explanation. ScreenTips are available for commands, parts of dialog boxes, screen areas such as scroll bars, and toolbar buttons.

Unless a dialog box is displayed, activate ScreenTips by clicking the Help button.

Help button

When you're working in a dialog box, activate ScreenTips by clicking the question mark button.

Question mark button

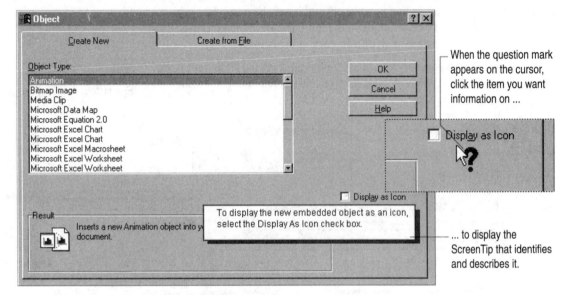

When the question mark appears on the cursor, click the item you want information on ...

... to display the ScreenTip that identifies and describes it.

 To close a ScreenTip or to remove the question mark from the mouse pointer Press ESC, or click the Help button or the question mark button again.

What's the difference between ScreenTips and ToolTips? ToolTips are one kind of ScreenTip. ToolTips identify toolbar buttons when you point to them; you don't need to click the question mark button first. To display ToolTips, click Toolbars (View menu), and select the Show ToolTips check box.

To get Help on dialog box options in Schedule+ Click the Help button in the dialog box. ScreenTips are not available in Schedule+.

Ask for Help in Your Own Words

Usually you know exactly what you want to do, but if you don't know what to call your task, getting helpful information can be a challenge. With the new Answer Wizard, you don't need to know exactly what something is called to get help. Just type a question in your own words, and the Answer Wizard lists online Help topics that can assist you with your task.

To go directly to information that helps you complete the task, choose a topic listed under "How Do I." To understand the task better, choose a topic listed under "Tell Me About." The resulting topic varies depending on your choice; it may be a step-by-step procedure, a visual example illustrating the task, a ScreenTip describing a screen item, or reference information.

Display the Answer Wizard by double-clicking the Help button, or by clicking Answer Wizard (Help menu). If necessary, click the Answer Wizard tab.

Help button

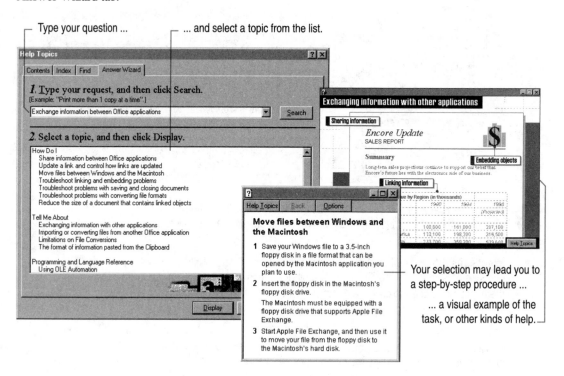

Type your question ...

... and select a topic from the list.

Your selection may lead you to a step-by-step procedure ...

... a visual example of the task, or other kinds of help.

If the topic you selected isn't exactly what you wanted Double-click the Help button again. Your last six questions and the resulting topic lists are still available, so you can select another topic. You might need to rephrase your question to find the topic you need.

To get help when you're using the Office Shortcut Bar Click the Answer Wizard button on the Shortcut Bar to work with the Answer Wizard or the online index.

Answer Wizard button

Look Up Information in the Online Index

There's another way you can find the online Help you need: Look up entries in the *online index*. The topics in this book include index entries (such as the entry you see to the right of this paragraph) related to the tasks being covered. To use the online index, double-click the Help button, and then click the Index tab.

For Help, double-click. In the online index look up:
Help

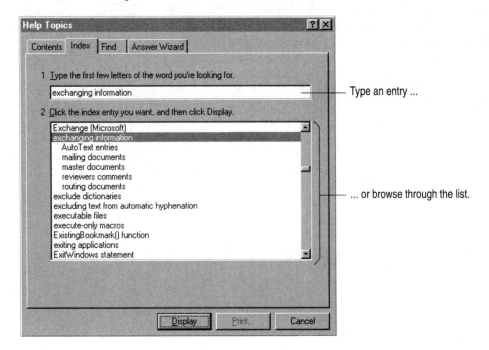

Type an entry ...

... or browse through the list.

To close a Help topic window   Click the Close button.

Special help on switching from another product   If you're switching from WordPerfect to Word, or from Lotus 1-2-3 to Microsoft Excel, check the Help menu for commands that provide information on switching.

How do you get Help when you're using an add-in?   When you're working with an add-in application, such as Microsoft Graph, WordArt, or Microsoft Data Map, get online Help by choosing commands from the add-in's Help menu.

Easy Office connections to The Microsoft Network   Getting access to online information and forums for Office applications is as easy as clicking a command on the Help menu. Click The Microsoft Network (Help menu), and then click the type of information that you want. For more information, look up **Microsoft Network** in Windows 95 online Help.

View this entire book online   If you have the CD-ROM version of Office, you have access to *Getting Results with Microsoft Office* online. To display the online version, click the Getting Results Book button on the Office Shortcut Bar. Then, search for topics using keywords of your own choosing, or quickly display related Help topics.

How do you see online Help in Schedule+?   Choose Help Topics from the Help menu, and then click the Index tab.

Close button

Getting Results Book button

Work Smarter with the TipWizard

When you are working in Word or Microsoft Excel, use the TipWizard to discover quicker, easier ways to work. When you display the TipWizard, it observes the way you work and displays tips that can simplify and speed your tasks.

For example, the TipWizard may suggest that you click a toolbar button instead of choosing a command and working in a dialog box.

For details, look up **TipWizard** in the Word or Microsoft Excel online index.

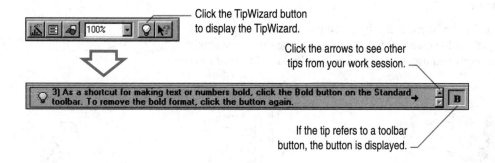

Click the TipWizard button to display the TipWizard.

Click the arrows to see other tips from your work session.

3] As a shortcut for making text or numbers bold, click the Bold button on the Standard toolbar. To remove the bold format, click the button again.

If the tip refers to a toolbar button, the button is displayed.

Take a Shortcut to Work

Using the Microsoft Office Shortcut Bar

The Microsoft Office Shortcut Bar provides convenient shortcuts
you can use to work with your documents and Office applications.
The Shortcut Bar complements the Windows Start menu; use it for
creating and opening documents quickly, setting up appointments,
and more.

Customize the Shortcut Bar by placing it where it's most useful,
changing its look, adding buttons to access the documents and
applications you use most often, and displaying additional toolbars.

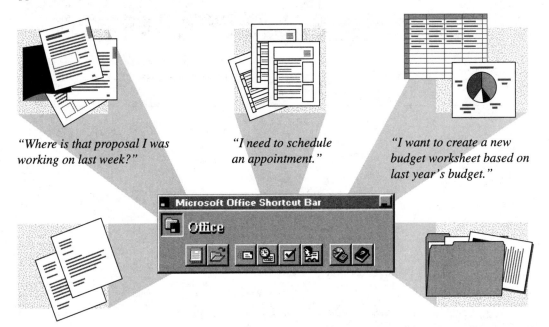

*"Where is that proposal I was
working on last week?"*

*"I need to schedule
an appointment."*

*"I want to create a new
budget worksheet based on
last year's budget."*

*"I need to write a great
sales letter, fast!"*

*"What documents did I save
in my book project folder?"*

Get a Quick Start on a New Document

Ordinarily, to create a new document, you would use the Windows Start menu to start the application you need. Then you would click New on the application's File menu to create the document.

With the Office Shortcut Bar, get a jump-start on creating a document. To display the Shortcut Bar, click the Start button on the Windows taskbar, click Programs, and then click Microsoft Office Shortcut Bar. Then click the Start A New Document button, select the tab containing the type of document you want, and double-click the document or template of your choice. The application you need starts automatically.

 For Help, click the Answer Wizard button.
In the Office online index look up:
Shortcut Bar
creating documents

Start A New Document button

Select the type of document you want to create.

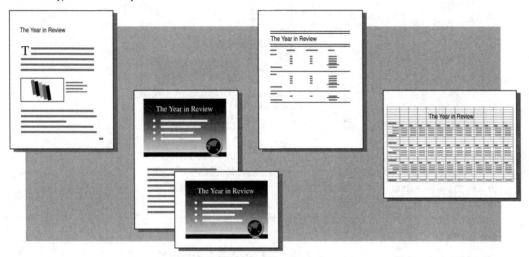

Often, you can use a template or existing document instead of starting from scratch.

 Save time and effort by using a template   Get going fast without starting from scratch: Use a template as the basis for your document. Office applications provide ready-to-use templates, or you can create your own; you can even use an existing document as a template. Templates are available by clicking New (File menu). For details, see "About Creating and Opening Documents and Databases," page 46.

Open Documents More Quickly

When you want to work with an existing document, open it easily from the Office Shortcut Bar. You don't have to start an application first; opening the document starts the appropriate application automatically.

Click the Open A Document button, display the folder containing the document, and double-click the document to open it.

For Help, click the Answer Wizard button.
In the Office online index look up:
opening documents

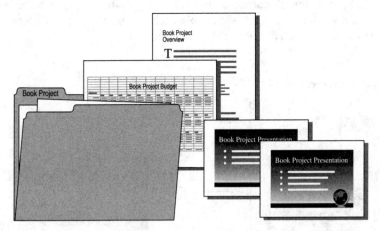

Open A Document button

 What if you don't know where the document is? You can search for it. At the bottom of the Open dialog box, specify the characteristics you want to search by, for example, all the documents with "Book Project" in the filename. There are other ways you can search and other criteria you can use for searching. For details, look up **finding documents** in the Office online index.

Take shortcuts to your favorite documents and folders Cut down on the time you spend getting to the documents and folders you use most often. In the Open dialog box, use the Add To Favorites button to create shortcuts to documents and folders in various locations and to add them to your Favorites folder. For example, you might want a shortcut to a network folder that you access frequently. For details, see "About Creating and Opening Documents and Databases," page 46.

Look In Favorites button

Add To Favorites button

Using the Windows Start Menu and Taskbar with Office Applications

To start an application When you want to begin work by starting the application instead of creating or opening a document as described earlier, use the Start menu. (However, you can add application buttons to the Shortcut Bar if you want. See "Add Buttons to Create Your Own Shortcuts," later in this topic.)

To switch among documents and applications that are open and running Use the taskbar for task switching; it shows you what documents and applications are currently open and running and provides the quickest way to switch among them.

For details, see your Windows documentation.

Position the Shortcut Bar and Change Its Look

Place the Shortcut Bar where it's most convenient while you work. The Shortcut Bar is docked along the right side of your screen by default, but you can dock it across the top instead, or float it in your workspace. Just drag it where you want it.

To change the look of the Shortcut Bar, click the right mouse button on the Shortcut Bar, and then click Customize. Then adjust the color and button settings on the View tab.

 For Help, click the Answer Wizard button.

In the Office online index look up:
Shortcut Bar, customizing
Shortcut Bar, moving

? For Help on dialog box options, click this button.

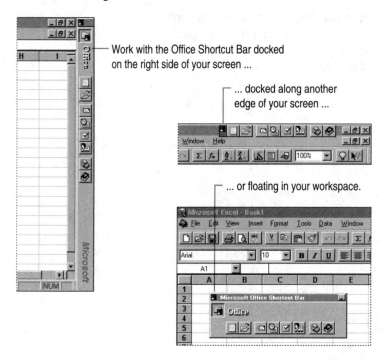

Work with the Office Shortcut Bar docked on the right side of your screen ...

... docked along another edge of your screen ...

... or floating in your workspace.

Hide the Shortcut Bar until you need it   Keep the Shortcut Bar out of the way but readily available by turning on the Auto Hide option. (Click the right mouse button on the Shortcut Bar.) For details, look up **hiding Shortcut Bar** in the Office online index. You can also minimize the Shortcut Bar so that it appears as a button on the taskbar.

Shortcut menus provide the commands you need   Quickly change the Shortcut Bar and individual buttons by using commands on a shortcut menu. Point to the item you want to change, and click the right mouse button. The shortcut menu displays commands available for the item.

If you are using a laptop computer or a low-resolution monitor   By default, the Shortcut Bar appears in the title bar area instead of at the right edge of the screen. This reduces the toolbar and button sizes so that they take the least amount of space on your screen. If you want to place the Shortcut Bar in the title bar area, click the right mouse button on the Shortcut Bar, click Customize, and then, on the View tab, select the Auto Fit Into Title Bar Area check box. For details, look up **shortcut bar, customizing** in the Office online index.

Add Buttons to Create Your Own Shortcuts

It's likely that you'll want to add buttons to the Shortcut Bar and use
it like a desktop to quickly access the documents and applications
you use most often. The Shortcut Bar and its buttons stay visible
when you work with applications maximized. Add buttons by
dragging icons from folders onto the Shortcut Bar.

 For Help, click the
Answer Wizard button.
In the Office online index look up:
buttons

Drag a document or application icon onto a toolbar.

 Display hidden buttons to create more shortcuts Additional built-in
buttons are available but not displayed on the Shortcut Bar. For example,
display the Screen Saver button to start your screen saver quickly. To
display hidden buttons, click the right mouse button on the Shortcut Bar,
click Customize, and then click the Buttons tab. Select the check boxes for
the buttons you want displayed.

Screen Saver button

Hide buttons you don't need To change the buttons displayed on the
Shortcut Bar, click the right mouse button on the Shortcut Bar, click
Customize, and then click the Buttons tab. To hide a button, clear its check
box.

Be careful with the Delete button! On the Buttons tab, if you click the
Delete button, the selected toolbar button is permanently deleted from the
toolbar. If you might want to add it again later, it's easier to hide the button
than to delete it.

Display More Toolbars

By default, the Office toolbar is displayed on the Shortcut Bar, but you can display more than one toolbar. For example, the Desktop toolbar contains shortcuts for connecting to a network and opening the My Computer window. To display a toolbar, click the right mouse button on the Shortcut Bar, click Customize, and then select the toolbar you want on the Toolbars tab.

When multiple toolbars are displayed, they are "layered" so you see the contents of one toolbar at a time. The titles of the other toolbars are still visible; to display a different toolbar, just click the one you want.

 For Help, click the Answer Wizard button.
In the Office online index look up:
toolbars

Create a toolbar to easily access documents such as those saved in a project folder.

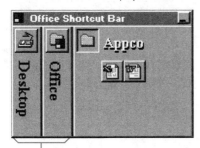

Click to display a different toolbar.

Change the look and button arrangement of a toolbar In the Customize dialog box, click the View tab to change the appearance of the Shortcut Bar, including the size of buttons and the color of the toolbar itself. Click the Buttons tab to add, remove, or change the positioning of individual buttons on a toolbar.

Add or remove a toolbar In the Customize dialog box, click the Toolbars tab to add, remove, or change the positioning of toolbars. Instead of removing a toolbar, you can hide it so that you can make it available again later.

Create a custom toolbar Click the Add Toolbar button on the Toolbars tab to create your own toolbar from scratch. You can create a toolbar for an existing folder, and a button will be created for each item the folder contains. For more information, see **toolbars, adding and removing** in the Office online index.

For Help on dialog box options, click this button.

What Else Can You Do with the Shortcut Bar?

Use the Shortcut Bar to quickly handle everyday tasks, such as scheduling your time, and to adjust settings with minimal interruption to your work flow.

Manage time and contacts   Access Schedule+ directly from the Shortcut Bar to take care of common time management tasks. To add a task to your To Do List, click the Add A Task button. To schedule an appointment, click the Make An Appointment button. To add an entry to your Contact List, click the Add A Contact button.

Send a message   To send an electronic mail message quickly with Microsoft Exchange, click the Send A Message button. For details, see your Microsoft Exchange documentation.

 For Help, click the Answer Wizard button.
In the Office online index look up:
Shortcut Bar
Schedule+

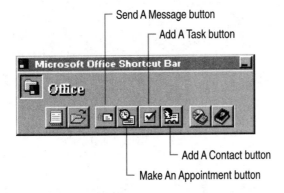

Send A Message button
Add A Task button
Add A Contact button
Make An Appointment button

 Combine several documents in a single file   Unhide the Microsoft Office Binder button on the Office toolbar. Then you can use this button to bind together related Word documents, Microsoft Excel workbooks, and PowerPoint presentations. Save and print bound documents as a single file. For details, see "Use Office Applications Together," page 103.

Microsoft Office Binder button

Get Help While You Work With the Shortcut Bar

Use the Answer Wizard and the online index to get detailed information about the Shortcut Bar and Office. Click the Help Topics button, and type a question in your own words, or look up index entries in the online index to view the online Help topics related to your task.

Click the Answer Wizard button
to find the online Help you need.

For details on using online Help, see "Get Assistance While You Work," page 30.

About Creating and Opening Documents and Databases

Microsoft Office makes creating new documents and databases easy by providing a special kind of document called a *template*. Templates are predesigned, ready-to-use documents into which you put your own information.

The Open command (File menu) offers more capabilities than ever to help you get to the documents and databases you've already created. The new Favorites folder and the improved Find File feature help you open the document you want quickly and easily.

You can use the templates provided, add your own templates to existing collections, and organize your own template collections. It's also simple to create documents from scratch by using a blank template.

Key Features

Templates

Open Command

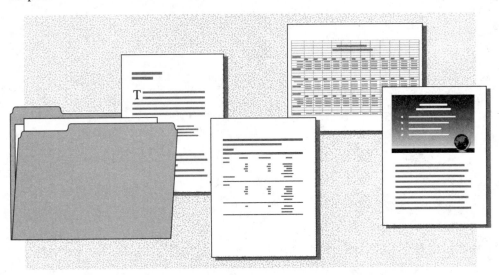

 Open any Word, Microsoft Excel, or PowerPoint document as a template Click the right mouse button on a document listed in the Windows Explorer, and click the New command on the shortcut menu that appears. This opens a copy of the document, leaving the original intact.

Create a New Document Based on a Template

To create a new document, click the Start A New Document button on the Office Shortcut Bar. The New dialog box appears, containing templates for all Office applications. When you use a template to create a document, the new document is a copy of the template and has no name. When you save it, the Save As dialog box appears so you can give the new document a unique name. The original template remains unchanged.

Important If you use the Open A Document button to open a template, the original template is opened for modification. Always use the Start A New Document button to create new documents based on templates.

For Help, click the Answer Wizard button.
In the Office online index look up:
Office Shortcut Bar
templates

Start A New
Document button

Open A
Document button

Browse through the tabs in the dialog box.

To create a document from scratch, select the General tab.

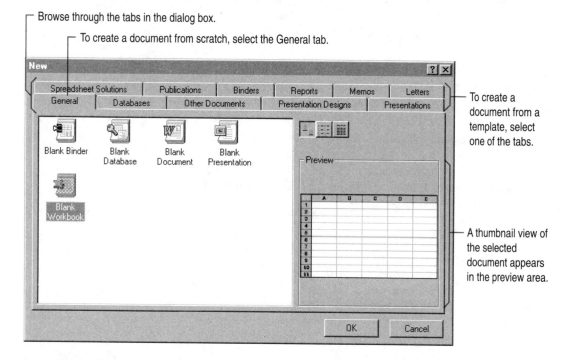

To create a document from a template, select one of the tabs.

A thumbnail view of the selected document appears in the preview area.

Note Templates behave slightly differently in each Office application. For more information about a particular type of template, look up **templates** in the application's online index.

Want to get a jump start on creating a Microsoft Access database? Use the Database Wizard. For details, look up **Database Wizard** in the Microsoft Access online index.

Create a document or database using a wizard   Wizards that you find in the New dialog box assist you one step at a time in the creation of a customized document, using information you supply. The Microsoft Access Database Wizard helps you quickly set up common business and personal databases, including ones for asset management, order entry, and music collection tracking. See **databases, creating** in the Microsoft Access online index.

Office Binder templates   The Office Binder provides a way to bring documents from different Office applications together in a single location. The Binder includes templates of its own, giving you a starting point for some typical tasks in which documents from multiple applications might be used together. For more information, see **Binder** in the Microsoft Office online index.

Drag documents into the New dialog box   With the New dialog box open, you can drag documents and templates into it from the Windows Explorer. When you create new documents based on existing documents you drag into the dialog box, they open as templates.

[?] For Help on dialog box options, click this button.

Create "custom applications" using templates   In Microsoft Excel and Word, templates can also provide custom toolbars, macros, menus, commands, and other special settings—essentially creating a customized application environment. For more information, see **templates** in the Microsoft Excel or Word online index.

Built-In Templates Covered in This Book

Some of the topics later in this book discuss how to use templates. See the following:

Microsoft Word

- "Write a Business Letter," page 120.
- "Create Letterhead and Matching Envelopes," page 133.
- "Create a Memo," page 125.
- "Create a Fax Cover Sheet," page 129.
- "Create a Simple Newsletter," page 141.
- "Create a Resume and Cover Letter," page 508.
- "Create an Online Manual," page 342.
- "Create a Thesis or Dissertation," page 523.

Microsoft Excel

- "Create a Form for Online Customer Quotes," page 198.
- "Figure the Monthly Payment on a Loan," page 515.

Microsoft PowerPoint

- "Customize the Appearance of Your Presentation," page 264.

Microsoft Access (Database Wizard)

- "Organize Your Music Collection," page 518.
- "Track Your Business Contacts," page 306.
- "Track Orders in a Shared Database," page 355.

Microsoft Office Binder

- "Use Office Applications Together," page 103.

Save Your Own Documents as Templates

You probably have documents you already use as unofficial "templates." Whenever you open, copy, and adapt the contents of an existing document, you use that document as a template. Protect your time investment by formally saving these documents as templates. Click Save As (File menu), and in the Save As Type drop-down list box, select the template format.

If you save a document in the Office Templates folder, it will appear on the General tab in the New dialog box. Subfolders within the Templates folder appear as tabs in the New dialog box displaying any documents they contain. You can create a tab by adding your own folder within the Template folder.

Important   Microsoft Access has no template format.

When you start a new document from the Microsoft Office Shortcut Bar, tabs containing templates for all Office applications appear in the New dialog box. When you click New (File menu) in one of the Office applications, only tabs containing templates for that application appear.

For Help, double-click.
In the application's online index look up:
saving documents

Create custom tabs for the New dialog box where you can store your own templates.

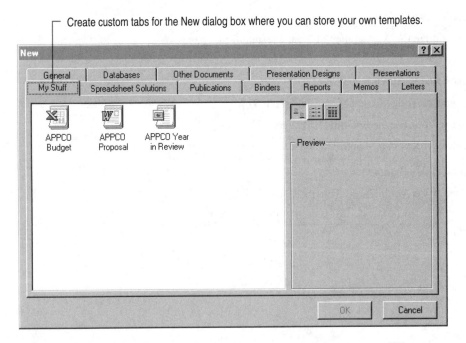

Too many tabs?   If you create more folders than can be displayed as tabs in the New dialog box, a "More" tab appears, listing additional folders.

? For Help on dialog box options, click this button.

Open Documents and Databases

Click the Open A Document button in the Microsoft Office Shortcut Bar, or click Open (File menu) in any Office application to get to the documents you need. Use the tools at the top of the Open dialog box to choose different views, create new folders, print documents, connect to network drives, and more. The boxes at the bottom of the Open dialog box help you find documents.

For Help, double-click.
In the application's online index look up:
opening documents
finding documents

- Use the Look In drop-down list to choose a drive and folder.

- The Files Of Type drop-down list displays the default file type for the active application, but you can select another type.

- You can enter any part of the name of the document you're looking for into the File Name box.

- You can find documents containing specific text or properties using the Text Or Property box.

- The Last Modified drop-down list is a quick way to narrow your search to time periods like "last week" or "last month."

Select a folder to look in.

Click to move up one folder level.

Click to display a thumbnail view of the selected document.

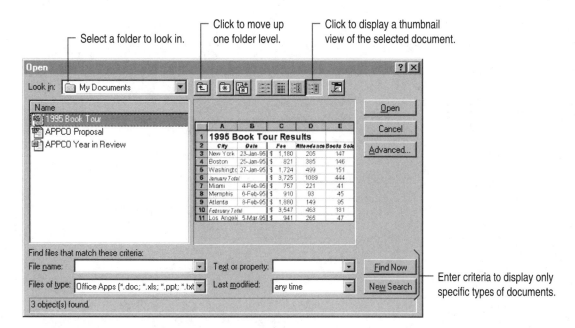

Enter criteria to display only specific types of documents.

 Open files as read-only Clicking the Commands And Settings button in the Open dialog box displays a drop-down menu with several helpful commands. The Open Read Only command opens the selected document so that you can view it without making inadvertent modifications to the original. For more information, see **read-only files** in the online index.

Commands And Settings button

Advanced Searches

When you want to specify precise search criteria to help pinpoint the file or group of files you want to find, click the Advanced button in the Open dialog box. Here you can select document or database properties, use And or Or as operators, and specify values to narrow a search. You can even search for variations on a word, such as "write," which will find occurrences of the words "write," "wrote," and "written."

You may want to search for documents more than once using the same advanced search criteria. You can save an advanced search by clicking the Save Search button. To repeat the search later, click the Commands And Settings button in the Open dialog box, click Saved Searches, and click the name of the search you want.

For Help on dialog box options, click this button.

Store and Retrieve Frequently Used Documents

If you are ever unsure where to put documents so you can find them quickly, here's an easy solution. The dialog boxes of both the Open and Save As commands (File menu) include buttons that activate a folder called Favorites. You can use Favorites any way you like.

When you select a document or folder and click the Add To Favorites button, a *shortcut* to that document is added to the Favorites folder. The original file or folder actually doesn't move. For more information about shortcuts, see your Windows documentation.

For Help, double-click.
In the application's online index look up:
Favorites folder

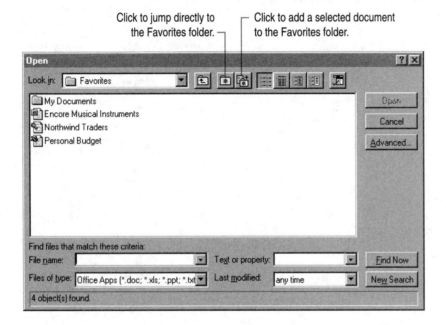

Click to jump directly to the Favorites folder.

Click to add a selected document to the Favorites folder.

Workgroup templates   Here is a handy way to make templates available to a workgroup without duplicating them on each person's computer. Click the right mouse button on the Microsoft Office Shortcut Bar title bar, and click Customize. Click the Settings tab, select User Templates Location, and then click the Modify button to specify a folder location anywhere on your computer or over a network. Any templates stored there are automatically made available in the New dialog box.

Favorites or My Documents?   The Favorites folder is a good place to store and look for folders and shortcuts to documents of interest, even ones not directly related to the work at hand, as well as those in remote network locations. The My Documents folder, on the other hand, is a good place to store documents on which you are currently working.

Make Your Documents Easier to Find

Not being able to locate a file can be as frustrating as losing your car keys. But, unlike your car keys, you can make Microsoft Office documents easy to find by specifying custom text or values, called properties.

Microsoft Office applications automatically define some properties for you, such as the author's name and the date the file was created. However, you also can set your own properties by clicking Properties (File menu). In Microsoft Access, click Database Properties (File menu). Click the Custom tab, and type the text or value you want.

You can use properties to "group" documents even when they are in different locations. For example, you can enter properties for project name or due date so that you or your coworkers can quickly find all documents with the same property. Say you are working on a project called Encore; enter that name in the Subject box in the Properties dialog box. When anyone wants to see all the files related to Encore, they can click Open (File menu) and type **Encore** in the Text Or Property box.

For more information, see **properties** in the online index.

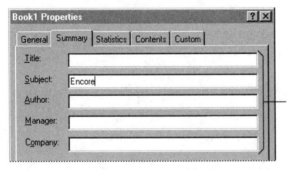

Type in properties you can use later to identify related documents.

Next Steps

To	See
Format Word documents	"Make Your Word Document Look Great," page 161
Use the Office Shortcut Bar	"Take a Shortcut to Work," page 36
Format worksheets	"Make Your Microsoft Excel Worksheet Look Great," page 206
Format charts	"Customize the Look of a Chart," page 236
Use PowerPoint presentation templates	"Customize the Appearance of Your Presentation," page 264
Use PowerPoint AutoContent Wizard	"Create Your First PowerPoint Presentation," page 82
Use the Office Binder and Binder templates	"Use Office Applications Together," page 103

Create Your First Word Document

You've come to the right place for a jump start to creating your first letter, memo, report, or whatever you want to write. You'll find easy-to-follow instructions on everyday tasks such as editing, formatting, saving, and printing. You'll get practical advice on how to do things the right way—and on what to do if something goes wrong. And, along the way, you'll find lots of timesaving tips, tricks, and shortcuts.

Word gives you a jump start on memos, resumes, reports, newsletters, and many other kinds of documents.

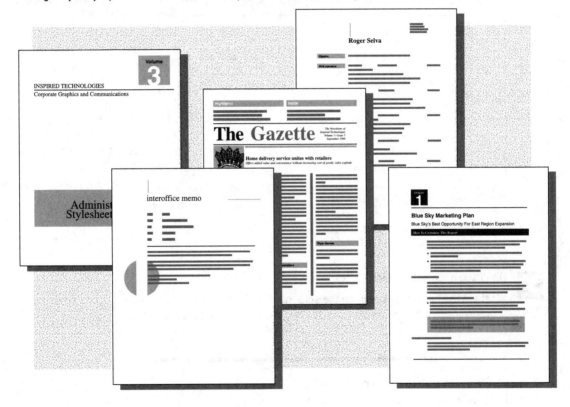

What's on the Word Screen?

When you start Word, the screen contains a fresh document surrounded by a "dashboard" of handy buttons, menus, and other tools that you can use to work on your document.

 For Help, double-click.
In the Word online index look up:
toolbars
viewing screen elements
nonprinting characters

— The blinking *insertion point* shows where the text you type will appear.

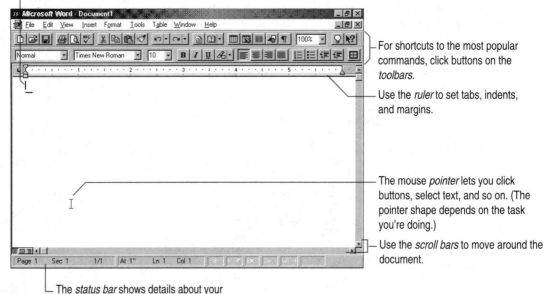

— For shortcuts to the most popular commands, click buttons on the *toolbars*.

— Use the *ruler* to set tabs, indents, and margins.

— The mouse *pointer* lets you click buttons, select text, and so on. (The pointer shape depends on the task you're doing.)

— Use the *scroll bars* to move around the document.

— The *status bar* shows details about your document, such as what page you're on.

 Don't see a toolbar or ruler?   Click Toolbars or Ruler (View menu).

What are the funny ¶ symbols on the screen?   Word uses such *nonprinting characters* to show the carriage returns, spaces, and tabs that you've entered. If you find them distracting, click the Show/Hide ¶ button.

¶
Show/Hide ¶ button

What Does the Scissors Button Do?

To find out about any toolbar button, just point to it.

— The button name appears, and the status bar also shows a brief description.

Create a New Document

You can easily create a new document from scratch. Or, save time by using a wizard or template that produces a ready-made document with an attractive layout and "fill-in-the-blanks" text.

For Help, double-click.
In the Word online index look up:
creating documents
templates, overview

To start a document from scratch, click the New button.

To start from a wizard or template, click New (File menu), click a tab, and then double-click the icon for the wizard or template you want.

The wizard or template produces a "skeleton" document that you can fill in.

So, What *Are* Wizards and Templates?

Wizards take you step-by-step through creating documents, while templates provide a preset layout. For details on templates, see "About Creating and Opening Documents and Databases," page 46.

What kinds of wizards and templates come with Word?

Letters, memos, resumes, reports, newsletters—just about any type of document you can imagine. To see the range of wizards and templates, click New (File menu). Or, preview each template by clicking Style Gallery (Format menu), clicking a template, and then clicking Example.

Type Text

Just start typing. When the text bumps up against the end of a line, don't press ENTER; Word automatically *wraps* the text to the next line. Press ENTER only when you want to start a new paragraph.

Speed typing   Even if you're a hunt-and-peck novice, you'd like to streamline text entry. We'll show you some shortcuts for inserting addresses, dates, and symbols and for fixing troublesome typos.

For Help, double-click.
In the Word online index look up:
address book
AutoCorrect
dates
symbols

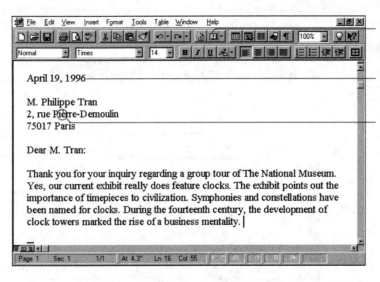

To insert an address from your personal address book, click the Insert Address button.

To insert today's date, click Date And Time (Insert menu).

To insert a character that's not on the keyboard—such as è, ®, or ✄—click Symbol (Insert menu).

Fix Typos and Insert Symbols on the Fly

To speed up text entry, Word works behind the scenes, automatically fixing typos and inserting symbols or hard-to-type words. For example, you might type: On wednesday, you'll recieve teh brochure i wrote called "wELCOME to Microsoft(r) WOrd." Word automatically fixes your sentence like this: On Wednesday, you'll receive the brochure I wrote called "Welcome to Microsoft® Word." Much better, isn't it?

What types of automatic corrections does Word make?   To see the list, click the AutoFormat tab (Options command, Tools menu), or click AutoCorrect (Tools menu). You can also add your own corrections to the list. If Word overzealously makes a correction, just click Undo (Edit menu) and Word "learns" not to make the same fix again.

Move Around in the Document

If you're a keyboard whiz, you may find it's easiest to zip around in the document by pressing direction keys such as RIGHT ARROW, HOME, or PAGE UP. If you're comfortable using the mouse, try the techniques shown in the following illustration.

 For Help, double-click. In the Word online index look up:
scrolling
pages, going to
going to, last editing location

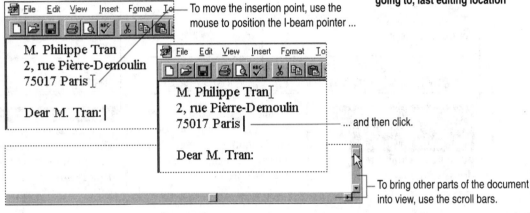

To move the insertion point, use the mouse to position the I-beam pointer ...

... and then click.

To bring other parts of the document into view, use the scroll bars.

You are here As you drag the scroll box on the vertical scroll bar, a page indicator shows where you'll land when you release the mouse button.

You scrolled the document and started typing, but the screen scrolled back to where you started As you scroll, the insertion point stays in the same place. To type in the location you scrolled to, just position the I-beam pointer and click.

Where Do You Want to Go Today?™

As you're navigating around in the document, you can easily go back to the previous location or jump to a specific page.

To go back to the last place you typed or edited Press SHIFT+F5. (You can press SHIFT+F5 up to three times to return to the previous three locations.)

To go to a specific page Click Go To (Edit menu). Type the page number, click Go To, and then click Close.

Select the Text You Want to Change

Now that you've typed some text, chances are you're ready for a change. Maybe you'd like to move a sentence or underline a word? First, you need to highlight, or *select*, the text so Word knows what you want to modify.

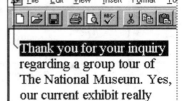 **For Help, double-click.**
In the Word online index look up:
selecting text and graphics
undoing actions

— To select any amount
of text, drag over it.

— To select a word,
double-click it.

— To select a line, click to the left of it.
To select multiple lines, click to the
left of a line and drag up or down.

File Edit View Insert Format To

Thank you for your inquiry
regarding a group tour of
The National Museum. Yes,
our current exhibit really
does feature clocks.

File Edit View Insert Format To

Thank you for your inquiry
regarding a group tour of
The National Museum. Yes,
our current exhibit really
does feature clocks.

File Edit View Insert Format To

Thank you for your inquiry
regarding a group tour of
The National Museum. Yes,
our current exhibit really
does feature clocks.

 You tried to select part of a word, but the entire word was highlighted
To turn off automatic word selection, click Options (Tools menu), click the Edit tab, and click Automatic Word Selection.

Bulk selections   To select a paragraph, double-click to the left of it. If you want to select a large area, click at the start of the selection, scroll to the end of the selection, and hold down SHIFT as you click. To select the entire document, hold down CTRL as you click to the left of a line.

Oops—How Do You Undo What You Just Did?

To undo a mistake—such as accidentally deleting a word—click the Undo button. If you decide to go through with the action after all, click the Redo button.

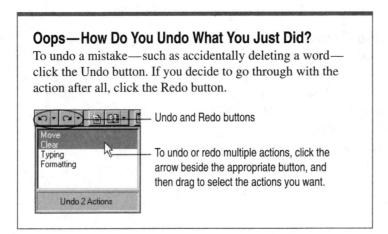

— Undo and Redo buttons

— To undo or redo multiple actions, click the
arrow beside the appropriate button, and
then drag to select the actions you want.

Insert and Delete Text

Insert text If you've already practiced moving the insertion point, you know how to insert text: Just click where you want to start inserting, and then type the new text.

Delete text To delete just a few characters, use the old reliable DELETE and BACKSPACE keys. Or, press INS and "overtype" the unwanted text, and then press INS again to continue inserting text. However, if you want to delete text in bulk, it's more convenient to use the techniques shown in the following illustration.

For Help, double-click. In the Word online index look up:
**moving insertion point
deleting text and graphics
overtype mode**

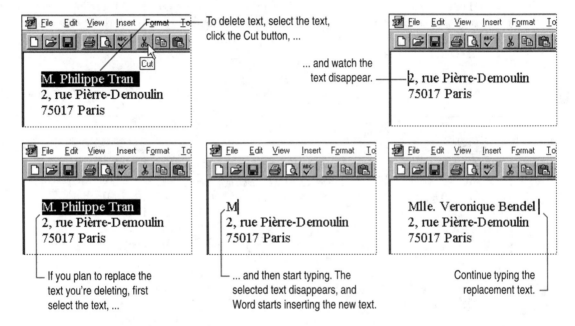

To delete text, select the text, click the Cut button, ...

... and watch the text disappear.

If you plan to replace the text you're deleting, first select the text, ...

... and then start typing. The selected text disappears, and Word starts inserting the new text.

Continue typing the replacement text.

You tried to insert text, but Word gobbled up the text as you typed You accidentally turned on Overtype mode. To fix this problem, just press INS. (The word "OVR" in the status bar should be dimmed.)

You selected text and started typing, but the selected text didn't disappear Click Options (Tools menu), click the Edit tab, and then click Typing Replaces Selection.

Want to delete one word at a time? Press CTRL+BACKSPACE to delete the word to the left of the insertion point, or press CTRL+DELETE to delete the word to the right.

Move and Copy Text

For the easiest way to move or copy text a short distance, use drag-and-drop editing. You can drag and drop text within a document, between different documents, or between many applications.

 For Help, double-click.
In the Word online index look up:
text, copying and moving

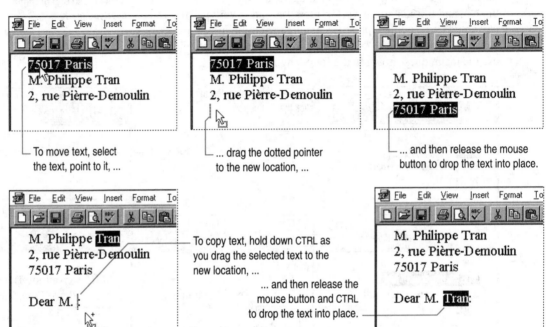

To move text, select the text, point to it, ...

... drag the dotted pointer to the new location, ...

... and then release the mouse button to drop the text into place.

To copy text, hold down CTRL as you drag the selected text to the new location, ...

... and then release the mouse button and CTRL to drop the text into place.

 **You tried to drag and drop, but nothing happened** Click Options (Tools menu), click the Edit tab, and then click Drag-And-Drop Text Editing.

Move or Copy Text a Long Distance

To move text, first select it, click the Cut button, click in the new location, and then click the Paste button. To copy text, select it, click the Copy button, click in the new location, and then click the Paste button. (You can paste the text as many times as you want; the text remains on the Clipboard—a temporary storage location—until you cut or copy more text.)

Cut, Copy, and Paste buttons

Change the Appearance of Text

You're probably not a desktop publisher or member of the art department, but you still want to make your documents look sharp and stylish. We'll introduce the most popular formats—so popular, in fact, that they're all packed onto a single toolbar.

For Help, double-click. In the Word online index look up:
formatting characters
formatting paragraphs

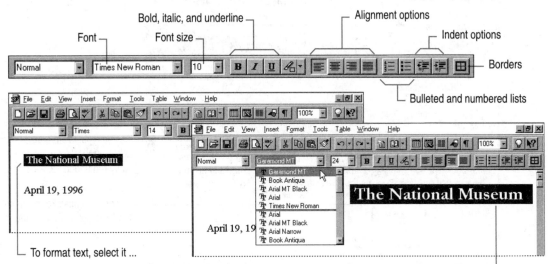

Font — Font size — Bold, italic, and underline — Alignment options — Indent options — Borders — Bulleted and numbered lists

To format text, select it ...

... and then click the formats you want, such as font, bold, and right alignment.

Want more formatting options? See "Make Your Word Document Look Great," page 161.

How do you get rid of a format? Once you start typing (say, in 16-point Arial® bold), the formats will stick around until you turn them off. For example, click the Bold button again to "unbold" text, or select a different font. You can also press CTRL+SPACEBAR to remove the character formats you've applied, or press CTRL+Q to remove the paragraph formats.

Character vs. Paragraph Formatting

You can apply *character formats* (such as fonts, *italic*, and SMALL CAPS) to any number of characters, ranging from a single comma to the entire document. *Paragraph formats* (such as alignment, indents, and line spacing) work for individual paragraphs only. (Remember that a paragraph includes everything you type until you press ENTER.)

Check the Spelling

Word can act as the reader over your shoulder—checking for spelling mistakes and typos "behind the scenes" as you type. This saves time since there's no more waiting for the spelling checker to review your document. And, there's no need to acknowledge every proper name, colloquialism, or abbreviation that Word questions.

 For Help, double-click.
In the Word online index look up:
spell checking
AutoCorrect

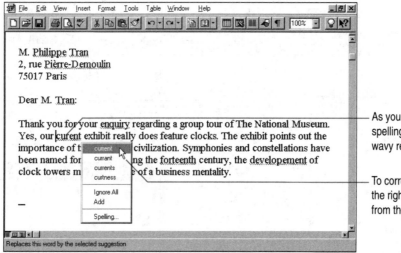

As you type, Word marks possible spelling mistakes or typos with a wavy red underline.

To correct a mistake, point to it, click the right mouse button, and select from the list.

 To jump to the next mistake   Double-click the spelling icon on the status bar. An "x" on the icon indicates that the document contains spelling mistakes; a check mark indicates that Word didn't find any mistakes.

Don't want to make the same mistake twice?   Point to the mistake, click the right mouse button, click Spelling, type or select a correction, and then click AutoCorrect. The next time you make the same mistake, Word will fix it for you.

Do you find the wavy red underlines distracting?   To temporarily hide the underlines, click Options (Tools menu), click the Spelling tab, and then click Hide Spelling Errors In Current Document.

Spelling icon

Spell Checking on Demand

If you want to free up memory, turn off automatic spell checking: Click Options (Tools menu), click the Spelling tab, and then click Automatic Spell Checking. Then, whenever you want to check the spelling, click the Spelling button.

Spelling button

Save, Preview, and Print a Document

To save the document, click the Save button. (If you're saving for the first time, Word asks you to name the document.) If you want to fine-tune the layout of the document before you print it, click the Print Preview button. Or, click the Print button to print right away.

 For Help, double-click.
In the Word online index look up:
printing, documents

Save, Print, and Print Preview buttons

— In print preview, click this button to switch between zooming in on the document or editing it.

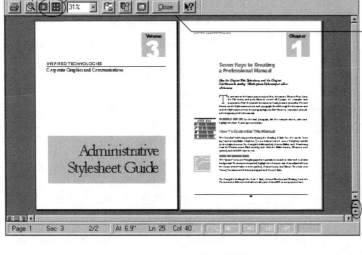

To switch between viewing one or multiple pages, click these buttons.

To return to the previous view, click this button.

To show the next or previous page, click these buttons.

 Help! How do you cancel a print job? Double-click the printer icon in the status bar.

How to Close a Document and Then Open It Again

When you finish working on a document, close it to free up memory. Just click Close (File menu).

To open an existing document, click the Open button or click its name at the bottom of the File menu. For details on easy ways to locate your documents, see "About Creating and Opening Documents and Databases," page 46.

Change Your View of the Document

Normal view: for everyday text editing   Chances are, you're working in normal view, which shows a simplified version of your document for speedier typing and editing. For example, dotted lines indicate page breaks, multiple columns appear as a single column, and you won't see top and bottom margins.

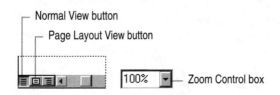

— Normal View button

— Page Layout View button

100% — Zoom Control box

Page layout view: what you see is what you get   If you want to see how your document will look when it's printed, switch to page layout view by clicking a view button or by clicking Page Layout (View menu).

What are all those other views?   The View menu includes a wide range of viewing options, such as full screen and outline. For details, look up **views** in the Word online index. Also, you can switch to print preview to adjust the layout before you print (see the previous section, "Save, Preview, and Print a Document").

Want to prevent eyestrain?   If you're a laptop user or just have difficulty reading text on the screen, you can *zoom*, or magnify, the screen. Just click the magnification you want in the Zoom Control box. You can also enlarge the toolbar buttons by clicking Toolbars (View menu), and then clicking Large Buttons.

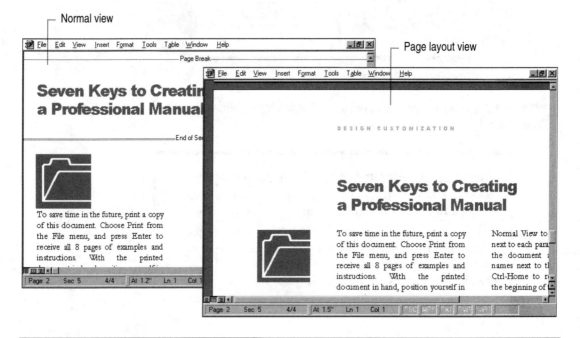

Normal view

Page layout view

Next Steps

To	See
Modify the formatting of your document, such as fonts, line spacing, and margins	"Make Your Word Document Look Great," page 161
Get information on how to complete tasks	"Get Assistance While You Work," page 30
Learn more about wizards, templates, and easy ways to create new documents	"About Creating and Opening Documents and Databases," page 46
Make the screen look the way you want and put your favorite tools on toolbars	"Customize Office," page 112
Find out how to include information created in other applications in your documents	"Use Office Applications Together," page 103

Create Your First Microsoft Excel Workbook

Make sense of your data by organizing, calculating, and analyzing it with Microsoft Excel. You work with your data on one or more *worksheets* in a *workbook*.

Begin by entering values and text. Save time by using formulas to automatically calculate values. Then make the data attractive and readable, and emphasize key information, by formatting it. Or display it graphically in a chart. Save the workbook file and print your work.

Printed sheets from a Microsoft Excel Workbook

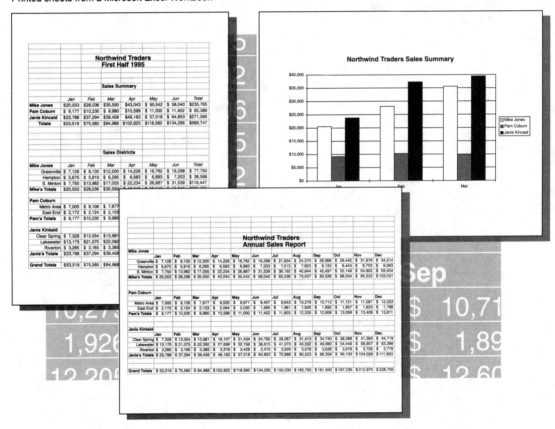

Create a Workbook File

To get started, create a workbook file. You can create a new, blank workbook; or, to save time, you can open an existing workbook, or *template*, and fill in your data.

For Help, double-click. In the Microsoft Excel online index look up: **workbooks, creating workbooks, opening**

To create a blank workbook, click the New Workbook button.

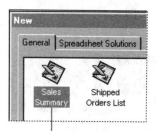

To work with a template, click New (File menu) and select the template you want.

 What's the difference between a workbook and a worksheet?
A workbook is a Microsoft Excel file containing one or more sheets; each worksheet is a "page" in the workbook where you enter and work with data. You can add worksheets and other kinds of sheets; for details, see "Add More Sheets to the Workbook," later in this topic.

Use workbooks you create as templates For details, see "About Creating and Opening Documents and Databases," page 46.

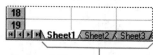

Each worksheet in a workbook has a named tab.

What's On the Screen?

When you create a new workbook, the Microsoft Excel window displays a worksheet with a grid of rows and columns. Each *cell* has a reference indicating its row and column location, for example, C3. The Standard and Formatting toolbars are displayed with buttons that provide easy access to common tasks.

For Help, double-click. In the Microsoft Excel online index look up: **display options**

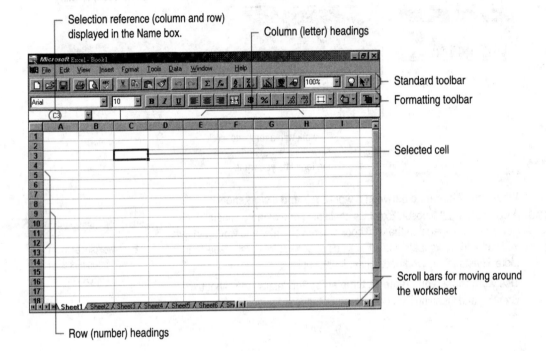

Selection reference (column and row) displayed in the Name box.

Column (letter) headings

Standard toolbar

Formatting toolbar

Selected cell

Scroll bars for moving around the worksheet

Row (number) headings

Work in Cells and Ranges

When you work with data in worksheet cells—for example, entering, copying, deleting, or formatting it—first you *select* the area to work in. The selection can be a single cell or a *range* (block) of cells.

After making your selection, perform the action you want. Data you enter and work with can be text, such as a list of names and addresses; values, such as revenues or units sold; or a formula that calculates a value.

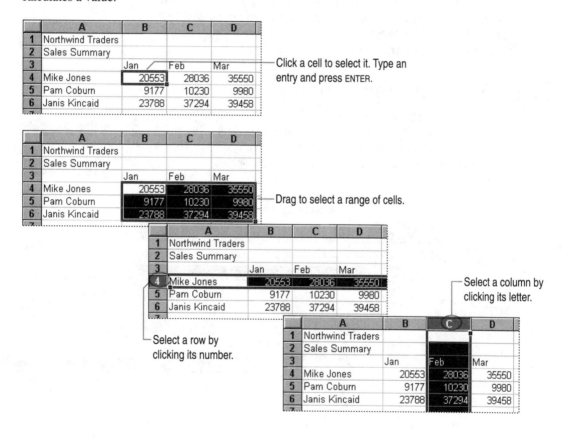

For Help, double-click. In the Microsoft Excel online index look up:
selecting cells
entering data

Click a cell to select it. Type an entry and press ENTER.

Drag to select a range of cells.

Select a column by clicking its letter.

Select a row by clicking its number.

To cancel an entry Press ESC. If you already pressed ENTER, click the Undo button.

If the entry is wider than the cell If the entry is text and the cell to the right is blank, the entry extends beyond the cell. If the cell to the right is filled, the text that fits in the cell is displayed and the rest is hidden. If the entry is a value, you see ##### (pound signs) displayed. Widen the column or change the number format to display the number correctly. For details, see "Change the Way Text and Data Look" later in this topic.

Work with commands right where you need them A *shortcut menu* contains the most useful commands for the cell or object you have selected. For example, when a cell or range is selected, the shortcut menu displays commands allowing you to cut, copy, paste, delete, insert, or format data. Click the right mouse button to display the shortcut menu.

Undo button

Enter Data Automatically

Avoid repetitive typing and save time by entering some kinds of data automatically. Enter the same information in several cells, or enter an incremental *series*. A series can be numerals, such as 10, 20, 30; ordinals, such as first, second, third; dates; or months.

For Help, double-click.
In the Microsoft Excel online index look up:
entering data, filling cells

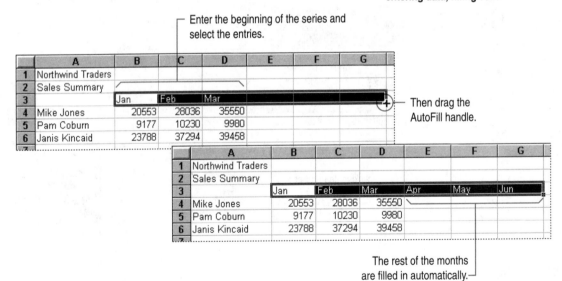

Enter the beginning of the series and select the entries.

Then drag the AutoFill handle.

The rest of the months are filled in automatically.

Modify the Data

When the information you are working with changes, or when you need to correct an error, edit data directly in the cell. Another way to modify data is by rearranging it; that is, moving and copying cell entries to different locations on the worksheet.

 For Help, double-click. In the Microsoft Excel online index look up: **cells, editing**

3		Jan	Feb
4	Mike Jones	20553	28036
5	Pam Coburn	91?7	10230
6	Janis Kincaid	23788	37294

To edit a cell's contents, double-click it ...

9189

... and make the change.

	A	B	C	D	E	F	G
1	Northwind Traders						
2	Sales Summary						
3		Jan	Feb	Mar	Apr	May	Jun
4	Mike Jones	20553	28036	35550	43043	50542	58040
5	Pam Coburn	9177	10230	9980	10599	11000	11402
6	Janis Kincaid	23788	37294	39458	49183	57018	64853

Select the cells you want to move and point to the border.

	A	B	C	D	E	F	G
1				Northwind Traders			
2				Sales Summary			
3		Jan	Feb	Mar	Apr	May	Jun
4	Mike Jones	20553	28036	35550	43043	50542	58040
5	Pam Coburn	9177	10230	9980	10599	11000	11402
6	Janis Kincaid	23788	37294	39458	49183	57018	64853

Then drag to the new location.

 If you want to copy cells instead of moving them Hold down CTRL while dragging.

To use the Cut, Copy, or Paste command Make your selection and click the right mouse button to display the shortcut menu.

If you make a mistake Click the Undo button.

To clear data from a cell Select the cell and press DELETE.

Check the spelling in your worksheet Select the area you want to check, or select a single cell to check the entire worksheet. Then click the Spelling button.

Undo button

Spelling button

Enter a Formula to Calculate a Value

Set aside your calculator! Instead, use *formulas* to calculate values on your worksheet. To create any formula, begin by typing = (equal sign). You can enter values directly in a formula, for example, by typing **=1+2+3**. Press ENTER to see the value resulting from the formula.

You can also calculate values in other cells by including their *cell references* in the formula. For example, the formula =A1+B2+C3 totals the values in these three cells.

Take advantage of Microsoft Excel *functions*, which are built-in formulas you can complete quickly. Use functions alone or within larger formulas. To create a formula that automatically totals values with the SUM function, click the AutoSum™ button. If the proposed range to be totaled is incorrect, drag to indicate the correct range and then press ENTER.

For Help, double-click. In the Microsoft Excel online index look up:
formulas, entering
calculating formulas
functions, entering in formulas

AutoSum button

─ Selected cell's formula displayed in formula bar

B4		fx	=SUM(B4:B6)			
	A	**B**	**C**	**D**	**E**	**F**	**G**
1				Northwind Traders			
2				Sales Summary			
3		Jan	Feb	Mar	Apr	May	Jun
4	Mike Jones	20553	28036	35550	43043	50542	58040
5	Pam Coburn	9177	10230	9980	10599	11000	11402
6	Janis Kincaid	23788	37294	39458	49183	57018	64853
7		=SUM(B4:B6)					

└ SUM function totals values for January

B7		=SUM(B4:B6)				
	A	**B**	**C**	**D**	**E**	**F**	**G**
1				Northwind Traders			
2				Sales Summary			
3		Jan	Feb	Mar	Apr	May	Jun
4	Mike Jones	20553	28036	35550	43043	50542	58040
5	Pam Coburn	9177	10230	9980	10599	11000	11402
6	Janis Kincaid	23788	37294	39458	49183	57018	64853
7		53518	75560	84988	102825	118560	134295

└ To total all months at once, select the range before clicking the AutoSum button.

Find the right function quickly and easily Click the Function Wizard button for help finding the function you need and building a formula. You can also use the Function Wizard to combine functions in a formula.

Display formulas instead of values on your worksheet Press CTRL+` (single left quotation mark) to switch between values and formulas.

See a running total of currently selected data The sum of the cells you currently have selected is displayed in the lower-right corner of the window. As the selection changes, the total is updated accordingly. For details, look up **AutoCalculate** in the Microsoft Excel online index.

Function Wizard button

Change the Way Text and Data Look

There are many ways you can modify the appearance of your worksheet. Before you make a change, remember to select the cell or range you want to apply the change to.

For Help, double-click. In the Microsoft Excel online index look up: **cells, formatting formatting cells, number format**

Make text bold or italic.

Change the font and size.

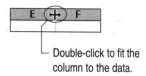

Use the Formatting toolbar to quickly change text and values.

	A	B	C	D	E	F	
1				Northwind Traders			
2				Sales Summary			
3							
4		Jan	Feb	Mar	Apr	May	
5	Mike Jones	$ 20,553	$ 28,036	$ 35,550	$ 43,043	$ 50,542	$
6	Pam Coburn	$ 9,177	$ 10,230	$ 9,980	$ 10,599	$ 11,000	$
7	Janis Kincaid	$ 23,788	$ 37,294	$ 39,458	$ 49,183	$ 57,018	$
8	Totals	$ 53,518	$ 75,560	$ 84,988	$102,825	$118,560	$

Underline values or text.

Align data left, right, or centered.

Format values as currency.

 For more formatting options Instead of using toolbar buttons, click the right mouse button to see the available formatting commands.

Save time by automatically applying formatting to a range Use an *autoformat*, which makes formatting changes for you all at once. Click AutoFormat (Format menu), and select the look you want.

If you see ###### in a cell Widen the column by double-clicking the right border of the column heading. When the cursor is placed over the column border, it changes as shown. Alternatively, you can change the number format for the cell or column.

For more ways you can change the look of a worksheet See "Make Your Microsoft Excel Worksheet Look Great," page 206.

E	↔	F

Double-click to fit the column to the data.

Add More Sheets to the Workbook

To organize your data, you can add more sheets to a workbook. These can be other worksheets; for example, one worksheet might contain a quarterly summary, and others could provide detailed data for each month of the quarter. Another kind of sheet you can add is a *chart sheet*, which displays data graphically.

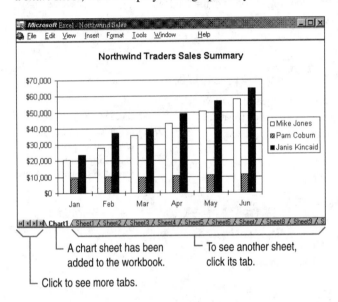

A chart sheet has been added to the workbook.

To see another sheet, click its tab.

Click to see more tabs.

 How many sheets can you add?   The number of sheets you can add to a workbook is limited only by available system memory. A new workbook contains 16 worksheets by default, but you can change this setting. Click Options (Tools menu), select the General tab, and specify your preference, between 1 and 255, in the Sheets In New Workbook box.

Add sheets that automate your work   Another sheet you can add to a workbook is a *module sheet*. A module sheet contains Visual Basic for applications code. For example, you might record or write macros that automatically open a workbook, select a cell or range, enter text, format data, or create a chart. For details, see "Automate Repetitive Tasks in Microsoft Excel," page 540.

Give workbook sheets meaningful names   Named tabs can help locate sheets in your workbook. Double-click the tab at the bottom of the window, and type the name you want.

For Help, double-click. In the Microsoft Excel online index look up:
worksheets inserting
chart sheets, inserting

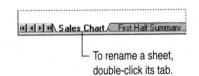

To rename a sheet, double-click its tab.

Save, Preview, and Print a Sheet

Be sure to frequently save the data you've entered and the changes you've made. To reduce trial and error and wasted paper, preview the currently displayed sheet before printing it.

Click the Save button to save the workbook. To view the current sheet as it will appear when printed, click the Print Preview button. You might need to adjust the page layout and view it again. To print without previewing, click the Print button on the Standard toolbar.

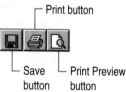

For Help, double-click.
In the Microsoft Excel online index look up:
saving
printing

Print button — Save button — Print Preview button

In the Preview window, click Zoom to get a close-up view. ⌐

If no changes are needed, click the Print button.

To return to work on your sheet, click the Close button.

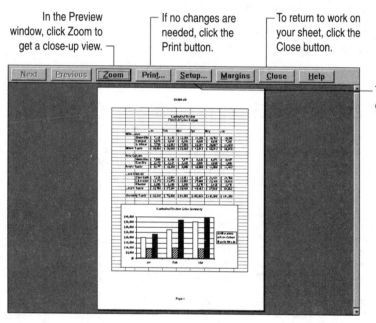

To adjust page layout, click the Setup button.

Print part of your worksheet   Select the area you want to print, click Print Area (File menu), and then click Set Print Area. Then click the Print button. To resume printing the entire worksheet, click Print Area (File menu), and then click Clear Print Area.

How can you change the page layout?   From the Print Preview window, click the Setup button. Otherwise, click Page Setup (File menu). Set the area of the worksheet that prints on the Sheet tab. Change the margins and alignment on the Margins tab. Orient the data horizontally or vertically on the page on the Page tab. Add or edit headers and footers on the Headers and Footers tab.

Use this workbook as a basis for others   If you want to create more workbooks based on this one, save it as a template. For more information, look up **templates, creating** in the Microsoft Excel online index.

If Your Data Is a List

Often a Microsoft Excel worksheet takes the form of a *list*, which is a labeled series of rows containing similar data.

Working with lists, you can:

- Show a subset of rows by filtering to see just the data you want.

- Sort the list alphabetically, numerically, or chronologically, or create a custom sort.

- Insert automatic subtotals without creating formulas.

- Compare and analyze data in a *PivotTable*, which is an interactive worksheet table that summarizes large amounts of data.

For information about working with lists, see "Create a Business Contact List in Microsoft Excel," page 300. For information about creating a PivotTable, see "Create a Sales Summary," page 446.

Original list with all sales for the first quarter

	A	B	C	D	E	F
1	Northwind Traders					
2	Employee Sales, 1st Quarter 1995					
3	Country	Last	First	Shipped Date	Order ID	Sale Amount
4	UK	Buchanan	B.L.	6-Jan-95	10869	$1,630.00
5	UK	Buchanan	B.L.	6-Jan-95	10872	$2,058.46
6	UK	Buchanan	B.L.	8-Jan-95	10874	$310.00
7	UK	Buchanan	B.L.	9-Jan-95	10866	$1,096.20
8	UK	Buchanan	B.L.	10-Jan-95	10870	$160.00
9	UK	Buchanan	B.L.	23-Jan-95	10899	$122.40
10	UK	Dodsworth	Annabella	6-Jan-95	10828	$932.00
11	UK	Dodsworth	Annabella	6-Jan-95	10871	$1,979.23
12	UK	Dodsworth	Annabella	9-Jan-95	10893	$5,502.11
13	UK	Dodsworth	Annabella	20-Jan-95	10889	$11,380.00

	A	B	C	D	E	F
1	Northwind Traders					
2	Employee Sales, 1st Quarter 1995					
3	Country	Last	First	Shipped Da	Order ID	Sale Amour
4	UK	Buchanan	B.L.	6-Jan-9	10869	$1,630.00
5	UK	Buchanan	B.L.	6-Jan-9	10872	$2,058.46
10	UK	Dodsworth	Annabella	6-Jan-9	10828	$932.00
11	UK	Dodsworth	Annabella	6-Jan-9	10871	$1,979.23

Click a column's arrow button to filter the list.

Filtered list showing one day's orders

Next Steps

To	See
Insert and delete cells, rows, and columns	**cells, inserting and deleting** in the Microsoft Excel online index
Find and replace data	**cells, finding and replacing** in the Microsoft Excel online index
Name cells and ranges, making them easier to identify and find	**cells, naming** in the Microsoft Excel online index
Link a formula to source data in another location	**formulas, linking** in the Microsoft Excel online index
Create charts that display your data graphically on the worksheet or on separate sheets.	"Create a Chart from Worksheet Data," page 216

Create Your First PowerPoint Presentation

Any time you communicate with a group of people, you are giving a presentation. The more important the message, the clearer you want your presentation to be. Also, the larger the audience, the easier the message must be to grasp. While information is not going to change itself to accommodate these realities, you can almost always communicate it better and more easily with PowerPoint.

Before you get started, you should know what you'll need. You may want to use one or more of the following items:

- Slides, displayed electronically using a computer, or printed on overhead transparencies, 35mm slides, or paper.
- Printed handouts for the audience.
- Notes the presenter can use for reference.

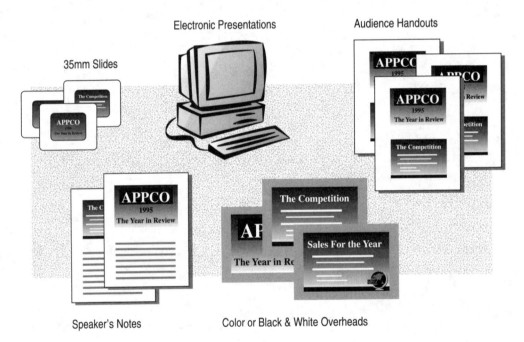

35mm Slides

Electronic Presentations

Audience Handouts

Speaker's Notes

Color or Black & White Overheads

Getting Around in PowerPoint

PowerPoint has five *views*, each giving you a different way of looking at your work. Activate each view with its corresponding button, located at the bottom of the main window.

Slide view Use this view when incorporating text and graphic elements, when creating "progressive disclosure" builds, and when modifying the appearance of a slide.

Outline view Work with slide titles and main text in this view. It's best for organizing and developing presentation content.

Slide sorter view This view is best for arranging and ordering slides, adding transitions, and setting timing.

Notes pages view Create notes for the presenter in this view. Draw and type anything you want onto a notes page.

Slide show This view is like a slide projector. Each slide fills the screen, and you can see the effects of transitions and timing.

For Help, double-click.
In the PowerPoint online index look up:
views

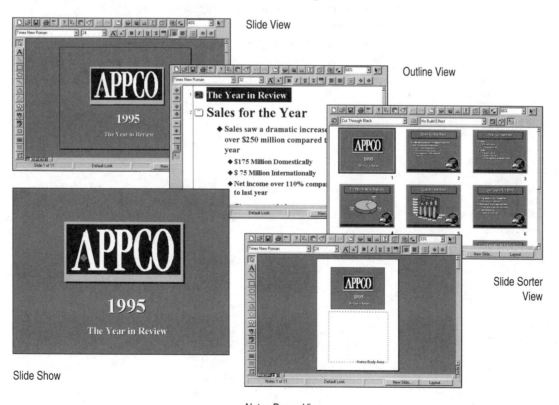

Slide View

Outline View

Slide Sorter View

Notes Pages View

Slide Show

Know your place   When you use the vertical scroll bar in slide view or notes pages view, a slide indicator pops up, telling you exactly where you'll land when you release the mouse button.

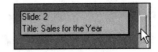

Get the Help You Need While You Work

Expanded and improved online assistance is just a click away. It's the fastest way to get information so you can keep working.

Ask the Answer Wizard   Type a question in your own words. The Answer Wizard lists online Help topics related to your question. Double-click the Help button and then click the Answer Wizard tab.

Look it up in the online index   Instead of typing a question, use index entries provided in this book to find online topics related to your task. Double-click the Help button and then click the Index tab.

For details, see "Get Assistance While You Work," page 30. Or look up **Help** in the online index.

Create a New Presentation

You can get a great deal of help creating and organizing your presentation by using the PowerPoint electronic assistant, the AutoContent Wizard. You choose a topic type from several general areas, and the wizard creates a skeletal presentation with suggestions about where to put different kinds of information and how to organize it into an effective presentation format.

You can certainly create a new presentation without the wizard, too! Just open a template or a blank presentation. The following shows the AutoContent Wizard's outline for a presentation designed to deliver a progress report.

 For Help, double-click.
In the PowerPoint online index look up:
presentations, creating

Each icon represents a slide.

The first slide is a title slide.

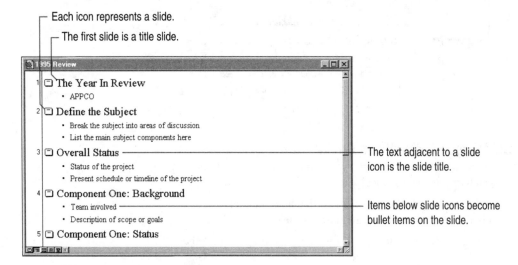

The text adjacent to a slide icon is the slide title.

Items below slide icons become bullet items on the slide.

Good news, bad news   The AutoContent Wizard's outlines, "Selling a Product, Service or Idea" and "Recommending a Strategy" are designed for typical presentation objectives. The "Communicating Bad News" outline provides a style to soften the blow as much as possible and helps you complete an unpleasant task.

Enter Your Own Text

By far the easiest and fastest way to edit the text in your presentation is using outline view, in which you can view and edit all the text in your presentation in one window, rather than one slide at a time, as in slide view. Just highlight the sample AutoContent text and type in your own text.

 For Help, double-click.
In the PowerPoint online index look up:
outline view
outlines

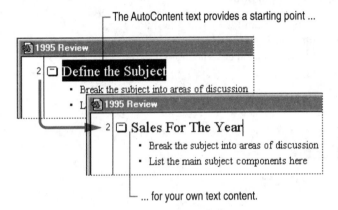

Guidelines for Working in Outline View

- To manipulate outline items, you can use the Outlining toolbar, which appears automatically in outline view.

- Each line of text you type in an outline automatically becomes either a slide title or bullet item on a slide.

- You can click to the left of a bullet item and drag it to another location.

- If you click the slide icon next to a slide title, you can drag the slide and all its subordinate text at once.

- To create a new bullet item, click at the end of an existing bullet item line and press ENTER.

- To create a new slide, first create a new bullet item, and then click the Promote button until the bullet becomes a slide icon.

Peeking at the slide   From outline view, you can quickly display a slide in slide view by double-clicking the icon next to the title of the slide you want to see.

Choose the Appearance You Want

After you add your information, it's time to decide how it should look. Use the Apply Design Template command (Format menu) to select one of the professionally created PowerPoint designs.

For Help, double-click.
In the PowerPoint online index look up:
Design Templates

Just three possible slide designs

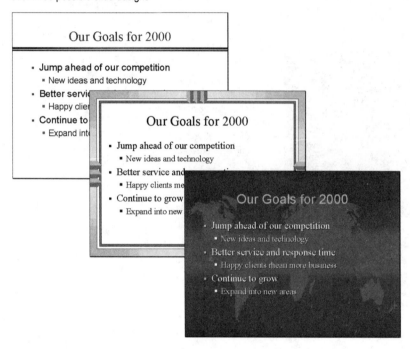

For more information about templates, see "Customize the Appearance of Your Presentation," page 264.

Add Graphics

The Insert Clip Art button starts the Microsoft ClipArt Gallery, a convenient way to browse and select clip art. Use the drawing tools on the Drawing and Drawing+ toolbars to focus attention on important information. Import graphics from other programs using the Object and Picture commands (Insert menu). For details about using graphics, see "Get Your Point Across with Graphics," page 271.

 For Help, double-click.
In the PowerPoint online index look up:
clip art
drawing
Insert Object

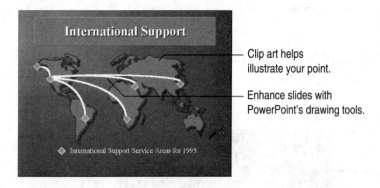

Clip art helps illustrate your point.

Enhance slides with PowerPoint's drawing tools.

Pictures at an exhibition   Click the Options button in the Microsoft ClipArt Gallery dialog box to organize the clip art into categories and add your own pictures to the gallery.

Check For Errors

How many times have you typed "adn" when you meant to type "and"? The AutoCorrect feature fixes this kind of common mistake for you automatically as you type.

Click AutoCorrect (Tools menu) to select options and add your own common typing and spelling errors to the list for automatic correction.

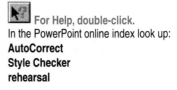 For Help, double-click.
In the PowerPoint online index look up:
AutoCorrect
Style Checker
rehearsal

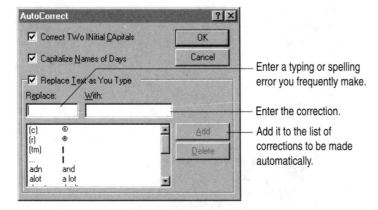

Enter a typing or spelling error you frequently make.

Enter the correction.

Add it to the list of corrections to be made automatically.

 Check spelling   Click Spelling (Tools menu) when it's time to proofread your presentation. For faster service, press F7.

Automatic style checking   The Style Checker performs a style audit of your presentation to detect everything from simple spelling errors to style and design errors specifically associated with presentations, like too many bullets on a slide, fonts too small for the audience to see, and many others. Click Style Checker (Tools menu).

Take a test drive   Try running your presentation on screen. You might find that you need to make some additional adjustments when you see it in sequence. To run the slide show, click the Slide Show button.

Slide Show

Rehearse and time your presentation   To help you rehearse and determine the length of your presentation, you can set the display time for each slide and have PowerPoint change slides for you using the PowerPoint rehearsal and transition features. For information, see "Prepare for an Electronic Presentation," page 280.

Getting Printed Materials

Getting it on paper or transparencies To print overheads, audience handouts, notes, or a presentation outline, click Print (File menu). You can use the Print toolbar button, but when you do, only slides are printed.

Custom handouts The Write-Up feature exports your presentation, including slide images and notes, to Microsoft Word, where you can create multipage handouts or notes pages. If you need handouts that include documents from several Office applications, use the Office Binder to collate them for easy printing. For more information, see "Create Presentation Handouts

and Speaker's Notes," page 259, and "Use Office Applications Together," page 103.

Getting 35mm slides or color overheads If you don't have access to a color printer or a 35mm film recorder, you can use a service bureau that specializes in such things. If you have a modem, you can send your order directly to Genigraphics® 24 hours a day. Finished slides can be delivered overnight. If you don't have a modem, use your favorite fast-delivery service. For more information, look up **service bureaus** in the PowerPoint online index.

Choose from a variety of output options.

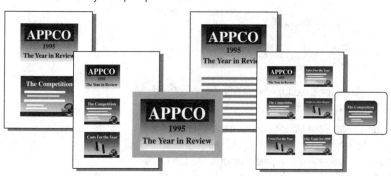

Next Steps

To	See
Produce handouts and other printed materials	"Create Presentation Handouts and Speaker's Notes," page 259
Create a presentation you can display on a computer	"Prepare for an Electronic Presentation," page 280
Add graphics	"Get Your Point Across with Graphics," page 271
Change the design	"Customize the Appearance of Your Presentation," page 264

Use Your First Microsoft Access Database

Most businesses maintain their vital information in databases. Customer lists, product inventories, and payroll schedules, for example, are often stored in database applications. Get control over your data by using Microsoft Access.

With Microsoft Access, you keep all your data in one place where it's easy to find just what you need when you need it. Updating data is a snap—change information only once, and Microsoft Access updates it everywhere else that it appears. And when you need to summarize information, you can create professional-looking reports that show just the information you need.

Key Features

Tables

Forms

Reports

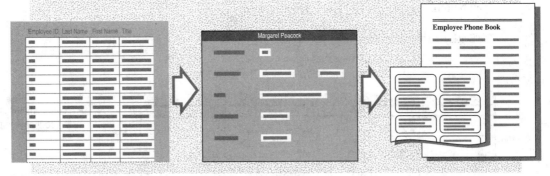

A table keeps all information about a single subject, for example employees, in one place.

A form makes it easier to enter and review information about employees.

A report makes it easy to summarize and print information.

Try It Out   To see how a database works, use the Northwind database and follow the discussion in this topic. To do so, you need to have Microsoft Office Professional or an individual copy of Microsoft Access installed. If this database isn't available on your computer, use the Microsoft Access Setup program to install it. For details, look up **installing Northwind Traders sample database** in the Microsoft Access online index.

View Information in a Database

Suppose that you are the new personnel manager of Northwind Traders, an import/export company. Your first task in your new position is to review and update employee data.

In a database, all facts about one subject, such as your company's employees, are stored in a single *table*. A table looks just like a Microsoft Excel worksheet, with columns, called *fields*, and rows, called *records*. A table can contain text, dates, and numerical values—anything you need to store.

To view employee data, open the Northwind database. Click the Open Database button, double-click the Access folder in the Look In box, double-click the Samples folder, and then double-click Northwind. Click Employees on the Tables tab, and then click the Open button.

 For Help, double-click. In the Microsoft Access online index look up: **tables, overview** **fields, described** **records, described**

Open Database button

The Employees table contains all employee records.

— A field contains a single fact about an employee. — The column selector

Employee ID	Last Name	First Name	Title	Birth Date	Hire Date	Ad
1	Davolio	Nancy	Sales Representative	08-Dec-48	01-May-92	507 - 20th A
2	Fuller	Andrew	Vice President, Sales	19-Feb-42	14-Aug-92	908 W. Cap
3	Leverling	Janet	Sales Representative	30-Aug-63	01-Apr-92	722 Moss B
4	Peacock	Margaret	Assistant Sales Manager	19-Sep-37	03-May-93	4110 Old Re
5	Buchanan	Steven	Sales Manager	04-Mar-55	17-Oct-93	14 Garrett H
6	Suyama	Michael	Sales Representative	02-Jul-63	17-Oct-93	Coventry Ho
7	King	Robert	Sales Representative	29-May-60	02-Jan-94	Edgeham He
8	Callahan	Laura	Inside Sales Coordinator	09-Jan-58	05-Mar-94	4726 - 11th.
9	Dodsworth	Anne	Sales Representative	27-Jan-66	15-Nov-94	7 Houndstoc
10	Hellstern	Albert	Business Manager	13-Mar-60	04-Apr-94	13920 S.E.
11	Smith	Tim	Mail Clerk	06-Jun-73	18-Feb-94	30301 - 166
12	Patterson	Caroline	Receptionist	11-Sep-72	18-Jun-94	16 Maple La
13	Brid	Justin	Marketing Director	08-Oct-62	04-Feb-95	2 impasse d
14	Martin	Xavier	Marketing Associate	30-Nov-60	18-Feb-95	9 place de l
15	Pereira	Laurent	Advertising Specialist	09-Dec-65	07-Mar-95	7 rue Nation
(AutoNumber)						

— A record contains all the facts about one employee.

— A new record goes here.

— Employee records are sorted by employee number.

 Can't see the contents of a column? Resize the column to fit the data it contains by double-clicking the right side of the column selector. For details, look up **resizing columns** in the Microsoft Access online index.

What Is a Relational Database?

A relational database like the Northwind database stores information in a collection of tables, each containing data about one subject. Because the tables are related, you can use information from more than one table at a time.

For example, you may want to combine information from an Employees table with an Orders table to create a report of total sales per employee for the past month. The two tables share one type of information (in this case, the employee ID number), but otherwise maintain unique data. Storing data in related tables is very efficient because you store a fact just once, which reduces disk storage requirements and makes updating and retrieving data much faster.

In a relational database, each table includes a field that is also included in another table so tables can share information.

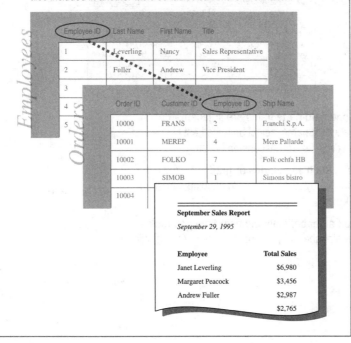

Sort Records Alphabetically

In the Employees table, records are listed by Employee ID number. But it's easier to review or find names when you see them alphabetically, so sort records alphabetically by last name.

 For Help, double-click. In the Microsoft Access online index look up: **sorting, records**

To sort employee records in alphabetical order, click the Last Name column heading ...

... and then click the Sort Ascending button.

Employee ID	Last Name	First Name	Title	Birth Date	Hire Date	Add
13	Eric	Justin	Marketing Director	08-Oct-62	01-Jan-94	2 impasse du
5	Buchanan	Steven	Sales Manager	04-Mar-55	13-Sep-92	14 Garrett Hil
8	Callahan	Laura	Inside Sales Coordinator	09-Jan-58	30-Jan-93	4726 - 11th A
1	Davolio	Nancy	Sales Representative	08-Dec-48	29-Mar-91	507 - 20th Av
9	Dodsworth	Anne	Sales Representative	27-Jan-66	12-Oct-93	7 Houndstool
2	Fuller	Andrew	Vice President, Sales	19-Feb-42	12-Jul-91	908 W. Capit
10	Hellstern	Albert	Business Manager	13-Mar-60	01-Mar-93	13920 S.E. 4
7	King	Robert	Sales Representative	29-May-60	29-Nov-92	Edgeham Ho
3	Leverling	Janet	Sales Representative	30-Aug-63	27-Feb-91	722 Moss Ba
14	Martin	Xavier	Marketing Associate	30-Nov-60	15-Jan-94	9 place de la
12	Patterson	Caroline	Receptionist	11-Sep-72	15-May-93	16 Maple Lar
4	Peacock	Margaret	Sales Representative	19-Sep-37	30-Mar-92	4110 Old Red
15	Pereira	Laurent	Advertising Specialist	09-Dec-65	01-Feb-94	7 rue Nationa
11	Smith	Tim	Mail Clerk	06-Jun-73	15-Jan-93	30301 - 166th
6	Suyama	Michael	Sales Representative	02-Jul-63	13-Sep-92	Coventry Hou
*	(AutoNumber)					

You can sort by more than one field if the fields are adjacent   For example, to sort by both last and first name, select both the Last Name and First Name columns, and then click the Sort Ascending button.

Does a field contain numbers, such as salaries or grades?   You can rank records from highest to lowest by clicking the field heading, and then clicking the Sort Descending button.

Sort Descending button

Want to see employees listed alphabetically the next time you look at the Employees table?   After alphabetically sorting employee records, click Save (File menu).

Find and Display Only the Information You Need

Northwind's sales manager has drafted a new set of sales guidelines, which he has asked you to distribute to all sales representatives. To find the names and addresses of just those employees, you *filter* the data.

 For Help, double-click. In the Microsoft Access online index look up:

filters
Filter By Selection

To find all Sales Representatives ...

... select Sales Representative ...

... and then click the Filter By Selection button.

Employee ID	Last Name	First Name	Title	Birth Date	Hire Date	Ad
13	Brid	Justin	Marketing Director	08-Oct-62	04-Feb-95	2 impasse du
5	Buchanan	Steven	Sales Manager	04-Mar-55	17-Oct-93	14 Garrett Hi
8	Callahan	Laura	Inside Sales Coordinator	09-Jan-58	05-Mar-94	4726 - 11th A
1	Davolio	Nancy	Sales Representative	08-Dec-48	01-May-92	507 - 20th A
9	Dodsworth	Anne	Sales Representative	27-Jan-66	15-Nov-94	7 Houndstoc
2	Fuller	Andrew	Vice President, Sales	19-Feb-42	14-Aug-92	908 W. Capi
10	Hellstern	Albert	Business Manager	13-Mar-60	04-Apr-94	13920 S.E.
7	King	Robert	Sales Representative	29-May-60	02-Jan-94	Edgeham Hc
3	Leverling	Janet	Sales Representative	30-Aug-63	01-Apr-92	722 Moss Ba
14	Martin	Xavier	Marketing Associate	30-Nov-60	18-Feb-95	9 place de la

Employee ID	Last Name	First Name	Title	Birth Date	Hire Date	Address	C
1	Davolio	Nancy	Sales Representative	08-Dec-48	01-May-92	507 - 20th Ave. E.	Seatt
9	Dodsworth	Anne	Sales Representative	27-Jan-66	15-Nov-94	7 Houndstooth Rd.	Lond
7	King	Robert	Sales Representative	29-May-60	02-Jan-94	Edgeham Hollow	Lond
3	Leverling	Janet	Sales Representative	30-Aug-63	01-Apr-92	722 Moss Bay Blvd.	Kirkla
4	Peacock	Margaret	Sales Representative	19-Sep-37	03-May-93	4110 Old Redmond Rd.	Redn
6	Suyama	Michael	Sales Representative	02-Jul-63	17-Oct-93	Coventry House	Lond
(AutoNumber)							

 Want to see just the sales representatives for a specific country? Click the country, and click the Filter By Selection button again.

Want to filter for just part of a field? For example, to find employees whose names begin with the letter P, select the P in Peacock, and then click the Filter By Selection button.

Want to show all employee records again? Click the Remove Filter button.

Remove Filter button

Need to find information that's contained in more than one table? Use a query to ask your database more sophisticated questions. For details, look up **queries, bringing together data from multiple tables, queries** in the Microsoft Access online index.

Make It Easier to Read Records

Now you're ready to review individual employee records, but you've found that the Employees table is difficult to read. The table is so wide that you need to scroll to see all fields, and it's difficult to distinguish one record from another.

The easiest way to review individual records is to use a form. To review records using the Employees form, click the Database Window button, click the Forms tab, click the Employees form, and then click the Open button.

 For Help, double-click. In the Microsoft Access online index look up: **forms, overview**

Database Window button

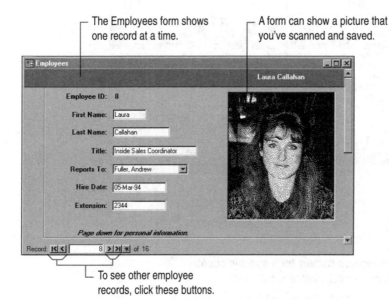

— The Employees form shows one record at a time.

— A form can show a picture that you've scanned and saved.

L— To see other employee records, click these buttons.

 If your table doesn't have a form   Create one by clicking the arrow next to the New Object button and then clicking AutoForm. Your new form will include all fields contained in the table.

New Object button

Want to create a form that contains only the fields you need?   Click the arrow next to the New Object button, click New Form, and then double-click Form Wizard and follow the instructions. For details, look up **forms, creating** in the Microsoft Access online index.

Add a Record to Your Database

When you need to add a new record, use the same form that you used to review records. Using a form makes it easy to see what to type in each field, and it can save typing if the form provides list boxes and other controls that help you enter the information you want.

If the Employees form isn't displayed, click the Database Window button, click the Forms tab, click the Employees form, and then click the Open button. To open a blank record, click the New Record button, the button with the asterisk (*) at the bottom of the form. Then enter information in the form.

When you move to another record or close the form, Microsoft Access saves the new record for you and adds it to the Employees table.

Microsoft Access automatically assigns the next available Employee ID number ...

... and provides a list of managers.

To add a new record, click here.

Did you make a mistake?   To undo a change to a field, click the Undo button. To undo changes to an entire record, click the Undo button again.

Undo button

Need to delete a record?   Select the record, and then click the Delete Record button. In some cases, Microsoft Access may not allow you to delete a record. For details, look up **referential integrity** in the Microsoft Access online index.

Delete Record button

Want to check your spelling?   Select a field and click the Spelling button.

Spelling button

Get the Help You Need While You Work

Expanded and improved online assistance is just a click away. It's the fastest way to get information so you can keep working.

Ask the Answer Wizard   Type a question in your own words. The Answer Wizard lists online Help topics related to your question. Double-click the Help button, and then click the Answer Wizard tab.

Look it up in the online index   Instead of typing a question, use index entries provided in this book to find online topics related to your task. Double-click the Help button, and then click the Index tab.

For details, see "Get Assistance While You Work," page 30. Or look up **Help** in the online index.

Update a Record

If you want to make a change to an employee record (for example, change the title of an employee who's been promoted), updating is simple. On the Employees form, just find the record you want to update, and then make the change. To find an employee name quickly, click the Last Name field, click the Find button, and then type the employee's last name.

 For Help, double-click.
In the Microsoft Access online index look up:
finding data

Find button

— Type the change ...

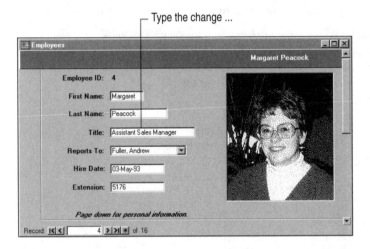

... and then move to another record or close the form to save the change.

 You don't have to know the complete name to find a record   Was the sales representative you met last week Dodsworth or Dodson? After clicking the Find button, type the part of the name you know, and then select the Any Part Of Field drop-down box in the Match field.

Print Just the Data You Need

Now that you've updated your employees data, you want to print a revised employee phone book for distribution to all employees.

When you want to summarize and print data, you create a report. You tell Microsoft Access exactly what you want to see, and it finds the data and lays it out in a professional, readable format. You can save your reports, too. That way, when the underlying data changes, you can print an updated report with just a few clicks of the mouse.

To create an employee phone book, click the arrow next to the New Object button, click New Report, and then double-click the Report Wizard. In the wizard, select the Employees table, and then double-click LastName, FirstName, and HomePhone. Then follow the instructions on the screen.

 For Help, double-click. In the Microsoft Access online index look up:
reports, overview
reports, creating
reports, printing

New Object button

Microsoft Access takes just the information you need from the Employees table to create a phone book.

Employee Phone Book

Last Name	First Name	Home Phone
Brid	Justin	88 83 83 11
Buchanan	Steven	(710) 555-4828
Callahan	Laura	88 83 83 16
Davolio	Nancy	(710) 555-4848
Dodsworth	Anne	88 83 83 17
Fuller	Andrew	(710) 555-5592
King	Robert	(71) 555-5586

 What else can you do with reports?   Group related data (such as all beverages, condiments, meats, or other categories of products in an inventory report), and then subtotal and total any numbers in the report. You can also create reports that combine data from more than one table, for example, how many sales orders each salesperson booked during the month. For details, see "Create and Enhance an Inventory Report," page 407, or look up **reports, defined** in the Microsoft Access online index.

Need Help Setting Up a Database?

Now that you've seen how a Microsoft Access database can help you manage your data efficiently, you're ready to set up your own database. But designing and creating a database may seem overwhelming. Where do you begin? How many tables do you need? Exactly what should you store in each table? How do you get your tables to work together, "to relate"? What about forms and reports?

With Microsoft Access, you don't need to be a database expert to set up a database.

The Microsoft Access Database Wizard helps you quickly set up common business and personal databases, including ones for asset management, order entry, and music collection tracking. The result is a complete database that contains all the tables, forms, and reports. All you need to do is add data.

For a list of the databases that you can create with the Database Wizard, click the Database Window button, and then click the New Database button.

If the Database Wizard doesn't create the type of database that you need Use the Table Wizard or create a table by entering data in a blank table, and then add the forms and reports you need by using the Form Wizard and the Report Wizard. For details on creating tables, see "Add Suppliers to Your Inventory Database," page 385, or **tables, creating** in the Microsoft Access online index. For details on creating forms, see "Create a Great Looking Product Form," page 400. For details on creating reports, see "Create and Enhance an Inventory Report," page 407.

Want to use an existing database? Microsoft Access has powerful, easy-to-use tools that manage information from other desktop databases, SQL databases, or applications such as spreadsheets or word processors. For details, look up **importing data from other programs and formats** in the Microsoft Access online index.

Next Steps

To	See
Set up a database that you share with your coworkers using the Database Wizard	"Track Orders in a Shared Database," page 355
Set up a specialized database without using the Database Wizard	"Design a Custom Inventory Database," page 378
Set up a database by importing a Microsoft Excel worksheet	"Move a Product List into Microsoft Access," page 379
Create a table	"Add Suppliers to Your Inventory Database," page 385
Create a form	"Create a Great Looking Product Form," page 400
Create a report	"Create and Enhance an Inventory Report," page 407
Find information in your database	**queries, overview** in the Microsoft Access online index

Use Office Applications Together

It's easy and convenient to use Office applications together. For example, you can:

Copy, move, and paste information When you want to insert information that won't need updating.

Link information When you want the most up-to-date information included in one or more documents.

Embed information When you want to include information that becomes part of your current document.

Store information in an electronic binder To organize and print files from Microsoft Excel, Word, and PowerPoint as a single unit.

Key Features

Linking
Embedding
Office Binder

If you're working on an annual report, create your financial information in Microsoft Excel.

Write the report in Word, and link information from Microsoft Excel so your report can be automatically updated.

Then create a professional-quality PowerPoint presentation from your Word report.

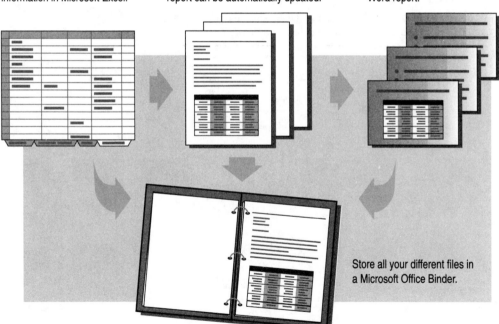

Store all your different files in a Microsoft Office Binder.

How Do I Know When to Copy and Paste, Link, or Embed Information?

The following table is a quick way to help you decide which method of sharing information to use.

If you want a copy of the information, and you	Then use
Don't care whether you have the most recent version of the original, or "source," information	Copy, move, and paste commands; or drag-and-drop editing
Want to edit the original information using the source application and have your changes reflected in both your document and the source document	Linking
Know you'll have ongoing access to the source document, and you want to minimize file size	
Want to share information among many documents, or among documents contained within an Office Binder	
Are not confident you'll have ongoing access to the source document, and you don't care about file size	Embedding
Want to edit the source information using the source application, and it's not important to have changes reflected in the source document	

Automatically Update Information Inserted from Another Application

You can link virtually any information among Office applications. For example, to make sure sales figures from Microsoft Excel are up to date in an annual report written with Word, copy and link the numbers. Then if the figures change, they can be automatically updated in the Word document.

Linking is a good method to use when you want to share the same information between many documents and when you want to share information among documents in an Office Binder.

For Help, double-click.
In the application's online index look up:
linked objects, overview

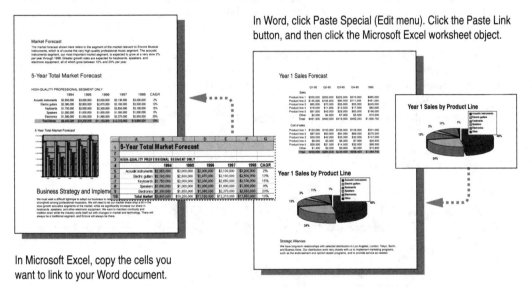

In Word, click Paste Special (Edit menu). Click the Paste Link button, and then click the Microsoft Excel worksheet object.

In Microsoft Excel, copy the cells you want to link to your Word document.

You can use the same method to link a Microsoft Excel chart to your Word document.

Want to control when links are updated? Click Links (Edit menu), and then click the name of the link you want. Click the Manual button to set the link to update only when you specifically request an update. For details on updating links, look up **linked objects, updating** in the application's online index.

Copy and Edit Information Using the Original Application

There are two types of information you can embed. You can copy and embed existing information. For example, you can embed numbers from an existing Microsoft Excel worksheet into your current Word document.

Or you can create and embed new information. For example, you can create a graphic object, record an audio clip, or create an equation using Equation Editor.

To embed existing information, copy the information, and then switch to your current document. Click Paste Special (Edit menu), and click the Paste button.

To create and embed new information, such as a WordArt or an Equation Editor object, click Object (Insert menu). On the Create New tab, choose the object you want. To embed an existing object, on the Create From File tab, type the name of the file you want to embed or click the Browse button and locate the file.

For Help, double-click.
In the application's online index look up:
embedded objects

? For Help on dialog box options, click this button.

A Microsoft Excel chart embedded in a Word document

To edit an embedded object, double-click it.

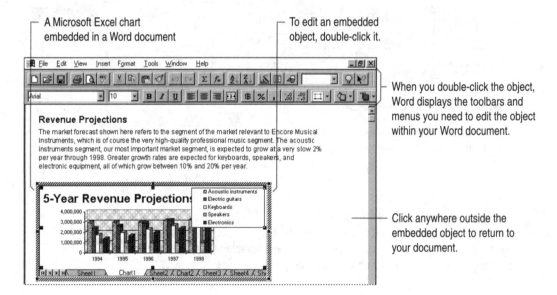

When you double-click the object, Word displays the toolbars and menus you need to edit the object within your Word document.

Click anywhere outside the embedded object to return to your document.

Need to keep file size to a minimum?   Link information instead of embedding it. Embedded objects increase file size because the object itself is stored in your document. A linked object, however, is stored in the source document. Only a representation of it is displayed within your current document.

Move or copy information among applications the easy way   In all Office applications you can select the information you want and then drag and drop it to move or copy it. For details, look up **drag and drop editing** in the application's online index.

Need Help editing an embedded object?   Double-click the object, and then click Help (Help menu), or press F1, and choose Help topics for the application in which the object was created.

Get the Help You Need While You Work

Expanded and improved online assistance is just a click away. It's the fastest way to get information so you can keep working.

Ask the Answer Wizard   Type a question in your own words. The Answer Wizard lists online Help topics related to your question. Double-click the Help button, and then click the Answer Wizard tab.

Look it up in the online index   Instead of typing a question, use index entries provided in this book to find online topics related to your task. Double-click the Help button, and then click the Index tab.

For details, see "Get Assistance While You Work," page 30. Or look up **Help** in the online index.

Other Quick and Easy Ways to Share Office Information

Each Office application includes convenient ways to transfer information quickly to other applications. For example, in Microsoft Access, click the OfficeLinks button to transfer database information to other Office applications.

You also can move a list created in Microsoft Excel to Microsoft Access and create a new database using the Convert To Access command (Data menu in Microsoft Excel). Or if you create a PowerPoint presentation and want to transfer it to Word to create speaker's notes, click the Report It button in PowerPoint.

 For Help, double-click.
In the application's online index look up:
importing
exporting

OfficeLinks button in Microsoft Access

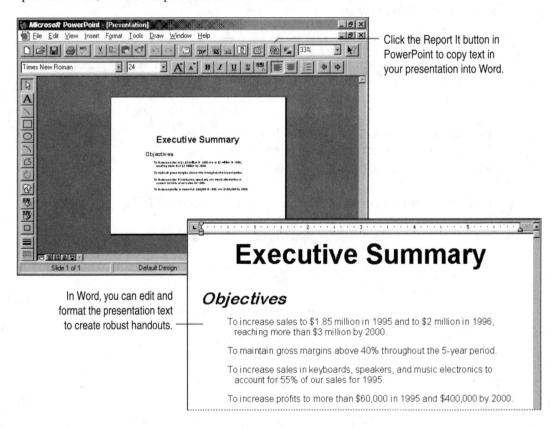

Click the Report It button in PowerPoint to copy text in your presentation into Word.

In Word, you can edit and format the presentation text to create robust handouts.

 Another easy way to transfer information between applications   First, make sure that the document into which you want to transfer information is open and its icon appears on the Windows taskbar. In the other application, select the information you want to transfer. Drag the selection onto the application's icon on the taskbar and continue holding down the mouse button until the application opens and you have dragged the selection where you want it.

Store and Organize Related Project Files in a Binder

Just as you put related papers on your desk in order, now you can organize related electronic documents in a single electronic binder. The documents always stay in the order you place them in, and they can be saved, moved, and printed as a single file.

For example, if you create an annual report, you can create, save, and arrange your Microsoft Excel financial worksheets, the Word report, and a PowerPoint presentation all in a single Microsoft Office Binder. When you're ready to print your annual report, you can print all the sections in the Binder as a single document.

To create a new, blank Binder, on the Office Shortcut Bar, click the Start A New Document button, and then click the General tab. Or to use a Binder template, click the Binders tab.

 For Help, click the Answer Wizard button.
In the Office online index look up: **Binder**

Start A New Document button

— Click to close the Binder pane.

— Drag here to move this section within the Binder pane.

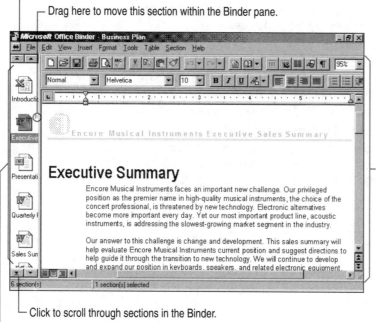

— This Word document is the active section in the Binder.

— Click to scroll through sections in the Binder.

— Binder sections

Important A Binder is most effectively used as a place to assemble related, finished documents. When editing documents in a Binder, you should be aware of some limitations. For details on these limitations, see BINDER.TXT in the Office folder in the folder in which you installed Microsoft Office.

Want to include Microsoft Access information?   Although you cannot add Microsoft Access database information as a separate Binder section, you can output Microsoft Access information to other documents, worksheets, and presentations, and then store those documents as sections in your Binder. For details, look up **OfficeLinks** in the Microsoft Access online index.

Save a section separately   When you want to save a Binder section as a separate document, drag it from the left pane to a new location, for instance, to the desktop.

Binder shortcut   To quickly add, delete, duplicate, or rename a Binder section, click the section's icon in the Binder pane using the right mouse button.

Use a Binder template   Office for Windows 95 comes with ready-to-use Binder templates, each designed around a task such as scheduling meetings and billing clients. Office Binder templates combine ready-to-use templates from Microsoft Excel, Word, and PowerPoint. To open a Binder template, on the Office Shortcut Bar, click the Office toolbar. Click the Start A New Document button, and then click the Binders tab.

Create your own Binder Template   When you create a Binder that you think would be a good starting point for other projects, save it as a template. To do this, add all the sections you want to your Binder, and then click Save Binder As (File menu). In the Save As Type box, click Binder Template. Then when you want to create a new Binder, choose this template.

Want to quickly share information between sections?   The easiest way to move information from one Binder section to another is to select the information you want to move, drag it over the section you want in the binder pane, and then press the ALT key to activate the section. Without releasing the mouse button, drag the information where you want it in the section.

Next Steps

To	See
Share the binder with coworkers	"Share Documents Electronically," page 326
Create a presentation quickly from a Word document	"Transfer Information Between PowerPoint and Other Applications," page 268
Analyze Microsoft Access information using a PivotTable	"Create a Sales Summary from a Microsoft Access Database," page 465
Use names and addresses in Microsoft Access to create a mailing	"Create a Mailing," page 176

Customize Office

Rearrange Your Work Environment to Suit Your Working Style

When you move into a new office, the first thing you do is adjust things the way you want them: You hang pictures, adjust your chair height, and rearrange the furniture.

You can adjust Office applications to match your working style as well. In each application, you can add, remove, or change commands on menus, buttons on toolbars, the way your screen looks, and the way your document looks each time you create one.

Key Features

 Toolbars

Toolbar Buttons

Menus

For quick access to commands you frequently use, add a toolbar button ...   ... or add a command to a menu.

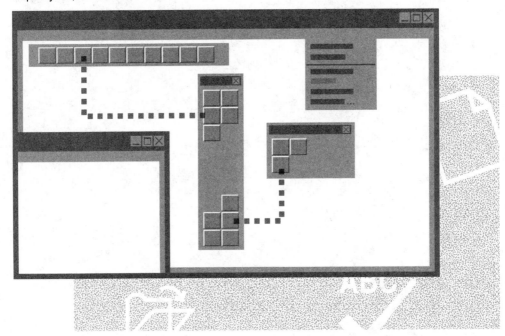

Adjust Your Screen Workspace

Perhaps the easiest way to customize Office applications is to adjust the amount of screen area available for your work. To have the maximum screen area available, click Full Screen (View menu) in Microsoft Excel and Word. Click Toolbars (View menu) to hide or display the toolbars you want.

In each Office application, you can specify which elements you see on the screen by clicking Options (Tools menu) and then clicking the View tab.

 For Help on dialog box options, click this button.

When you are editing or formatting a worksheet, you might want to turn off the Formula Bar to give you more space on the screen. Click Options (Tools menu), and then click the View tab.

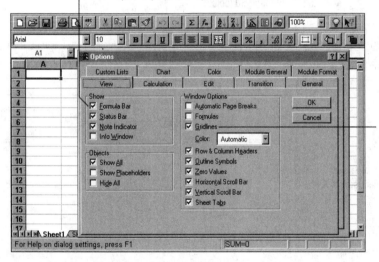

Checked items appear on the screen. Unchecked items do not.

Save and print different views The Microsoft Excel View Manager creates different views of a worksheet so you can see your data with different display options. Use it to display, print, and store different views without saving them as separate sheets. For details, look up **View Manager** in the Microsoft Excel online index.

Want to get rid of the dots, lines, and paragraph marks? You can determine which nonprinting elements, such as spaces, gridlines, page breaks, field codes, and formulas, you want displayed. Click Options (Tools menu), click the View tab, and then set the options you want.

Is the text on your screen too small? Use the Zoom Control box to magnify the display up to 200 or 400 percent for easy reading. In Microsoft Access, make sure you are in Print Preview or Layout Preview.

Zoom Control box

Customize a Toolbar with Your Favorite Tools

Just as you place items you often use close at hand, you can put your favorite buttons on application toolbars. You can also rearrange buttons and delete those you don't use.

Additionally, you can build your own custom toolbar. For example, you might create a toolbar with only the Microsoft Excel tools you use for doing your taxes.

For details on how to customize a toolbar or create a new one, look up **toolbars, customizing** in the online index of the application you want to customize.

For Help, double-click.
In the application's online index look up:
toolbars, customizing
toolbars, creating and deleting

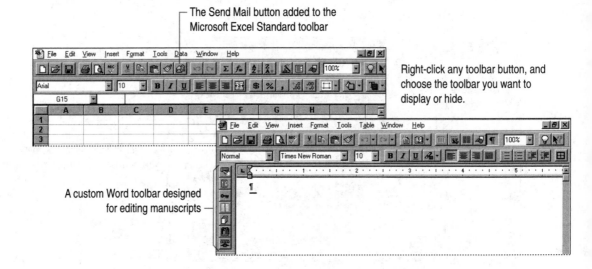

The Send Mail button added to the Microsoft Excel Standard toolbar

Right-click any toolbar button, and choose the toolbar you want to display or hide.

A custom Word toolbar designed for editing manuscripts

Want to move a toolbar to the side of the window? Click between any of the toolbar buttons, or on the title bar of a floating toolbar, and then drag the toolbar to where you want it.

Create a button for a macro You can create or record a macro and then assign a button to it and add it to a new or existing toolbar. For details on creating or recording a macro, see "Automate Repetitive Tasks in Microsoft Excel," page 540, "Automate Repetitive Tasks in Word," page 536, and "Automate Repetitive Tasks in Microsoft Access," page 553.

Choose your own button images or text When you add a command or macro to a toolbar, you can assign a button or text to it. Use one of the buttons provided, type the text you want, or create your own button image in a graphics application, and then copy it onto the button. Or, in Word or Microsoft Access, use the Button Editor to create a button image. For details, look up **toolbars, customizing** in the application's online index.

Create a new Microsoft Access toolbar button the easy way You can create a new toolbar button to open any object displayed within your Microsoft Access Database window by dragging it to the toolbar.

Menus and Other Things You Can Change

If the standard menus in Microsoft Access, Microsoft Excel, and Word do not contain the commands you use most often, you can add a new menu, delete an existing menu, or change menus so that they display the commands, formats, and macros you use most often.

For example, if you often have several document windows open simultaneously, you can add the Previous Window command and choose it to quickly return to your last document window. For details on customizing menus, look up **menus, customizing** in the application's online index.

And, in Schedule+ you can organize your Appointment Book, To Do List, and Contact List to emphasize the scheduling, task, and contact information that's most important to you. You can change how you view Schedule+, add and remove tabs, and change the appearance of each tab to suit your needs. For details, look up **views** in the Schedule+ online index.

There are many other elements you can change to make your working environment more comfortable and efficient. To discover which options you can change to suit your working style, click Options (Tools menu), or look up **customizing** in the application's online index.

For Help, double-click.
In the application's online index look up:
menus, customizing

Next Steps

To	See
Customize the Microsoft Office Shortcut Bar	"Take a Shortcut to Work," page 36
Create a macro to do routine tasks for you in Microsoft Excel	"Automate Repetitive Tasks in Microsoft Excel," page 540
Create a macro to do routine tasks for you in Microsoft Access	"Automate Repetitive Tasks in Microsoft Access," page 553
Create a macro to do routine tasks for you in Word	"Automate Repetitive Tasks in Word," page 536

PART 2

Get Your Message Across

Letters, Mailings, and Other Business Communications

Contents

Write a Business Letter

Don't know how to get started writing a letter, or maybe you're working under a tight deadline? The Letter Wizard or the letter templates provide a fast and easy way to create a business or personal letter and matching envelope. You can choose from three professional designs, print on letterhead or plain paper, and even select a prewritten business letter, such as a request for payment.

Key Features

Letter Wizard

Letter Templates

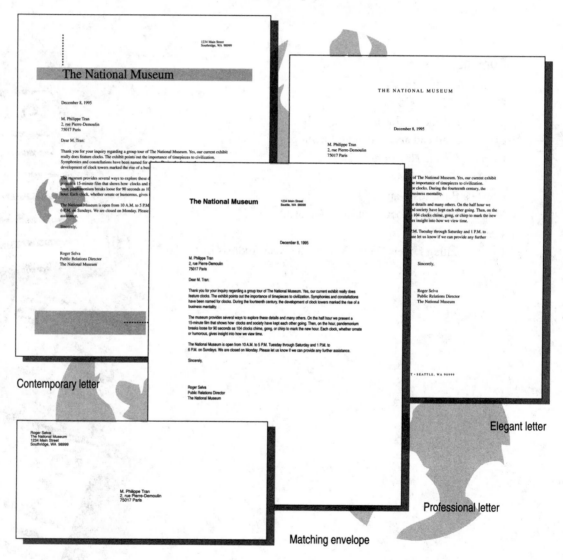

Contemporary letter

Matching envelope

Elegant letter

Professional letter

Use the Letter Wizard to Get Started

To start the Letter Wizard, click New (File menu), click the Letters & Faxes tab, and then double-click Letter Wizard.

The Letter Wizard "interviews" you and uses your answers to set up the letter's basic content and layout. The wizard also lets you try ready-to-use business letters and inserts addresses directly from your Microsoft Exchange personal address book or Schedule+ Contact List. When the wizard finishes, you can print a matching envelope (explained later in this topic) or start filling in the new letter right away.

For Help, double-click.
In the Word online index look up:
templates
wizards
address book

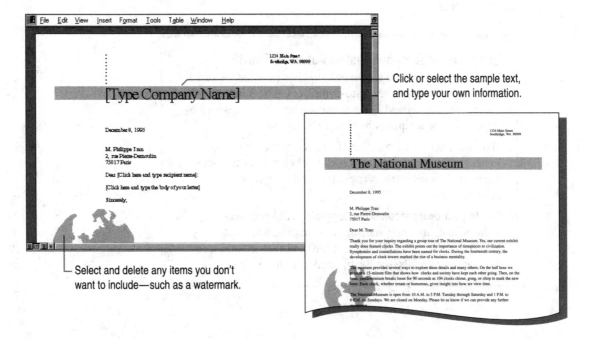

Click or select the sample text, and type your own information.

Select and delete any items you don't want to include—such as a watermark.

Is there a faster way to type your company name? You can store just about anything—company names, phone numbers, your scanned signature, or a logo—and insert it in your letter as you type. Select the item, click AutoCorrect (Tools menu), and type an abbreviation. To insert the item, type its abbreviation plus a space or other punctuation.

Try on a different letter design Click Style Gallery (Format menu), and then click a letter template (Contemporary, Elegant, or Professional).

Like the result—and want to use it to start your next letter? Delete any information you don't plan to include in future letters. Click Save As (File menu), and then click Document Template in the Save As Type box. Name and save the new template. Then select this template the next time you start a new letter.

Use a Letter Template Instead of the Wizard?

The Letter Wizard and the letter templates produce the same result—an attractive, ready-to-complete letter. Here's the difference: The wizard lets you choose layout options step by step, while the templates have a preset layout.

To use a letter template, click New (File menu), click the Letters & Faxes tab, and then double-click a letter template. Then, click or select the sample text and type your information.

Create your own personalized template Add your name, address, and any other standard information you want to include in each letter. Then, save the modified letter as a template (for details, see the tip earlier in this topic).

"Wordsmith" and Polish as You Work

The Letter Wizard takes care of most of the "finish work" for you, so what's left to polish? Word can act as your own personal editor—correcting typos and spelling mistakes, finding just the right word, and organizing information into lists.

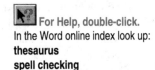 **For Help, double-click.**
In the Word online index look up:
thesaurus
spell checking

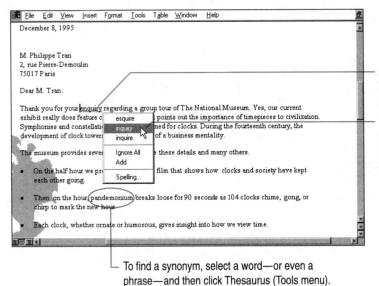

As you type, possible spelling mistakes or typos are marked with a wavy red underline.

To correct a mistake, point to it, click the right mouse button, and then select from the list.

To find a synonym, select a word—or even a phrase—and then click Thesaurus (Tools menu).

Don't see wavy red lines under spelling mistakes? Click Options (Tools menu), click the Spelling tab, and then click Automatic Spell Checking.

Are short letters scrunched up against the top of the page? To balance the letter on the page, click Page Setup (File menu), click the Layout tab, and then click Center in the Vertical Alignment box.

Create a bulleted or numbered list Type an asterisk (*) or the number **1.**, press the SPACEBAR, type the first item, and then press ENTER. Type the rest of the bulleted or numbered list, pressing ENTER after each item. To finish the list, press ENTER twice.

Want to show the date the letter was written instead of the current date? Select the date, click Date And Time (Insert menu), and then make sure that the Update Automatically (Insert As Field) check box is cleared.

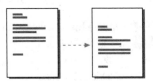

Before and after vertical alignment

Print an Envelope

If you selected Create An Envelope Or Mailing Label on the final step of the Letter Wizard, you're ready to start. If you didn't, it's not too late—with the letter on screen, click Envelopes And Labels (Tools menu). If necessary, edit the delivery and return addresses. Choose any options you want, insert the envelope into the printer as shown in the Feed box, and click Print.

For Help, double-click.
In the Word online index look up:
envelopes

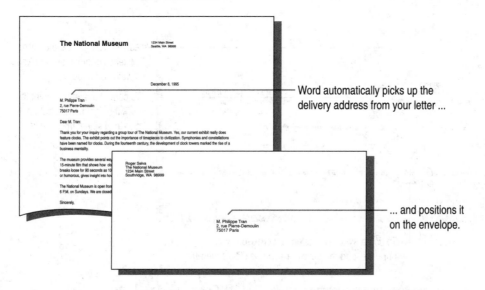

Word automatically picks up the delivery address from your letter ...

... and positions it on the envelope.

 Update the addresses in your personal address book To add, delete, or modify the addresses in your Microsoft Exchange personal address book or Schedule+ Contact List, click the Insert Address button and select the options you want.

Insert Address button

Next Steps

To	See
Design "electronic" or preprinted letterhead	"Create Letterhead and Matching Envelopes," page 133
Fax a copy of the letter	"Create a Fax Cover Sheet," page 129
Send form letters to people on your mailing list	"Create a Mailing," page 177

Create a Memo

If it's true that a memo is created more often than any other business document, then it pays to be able to create a memo quickly, and to create one that stands out from the crowd.

The Microsoft Word Memo Wizard is a quick and easy way to create a professional-looking memo. And because the wizard sets up the page, you can concentrate on composing the message.

Wizard-created memos come in three design families.

Key Features

 Memo Wizard

 Paste Microsoft Excel Information

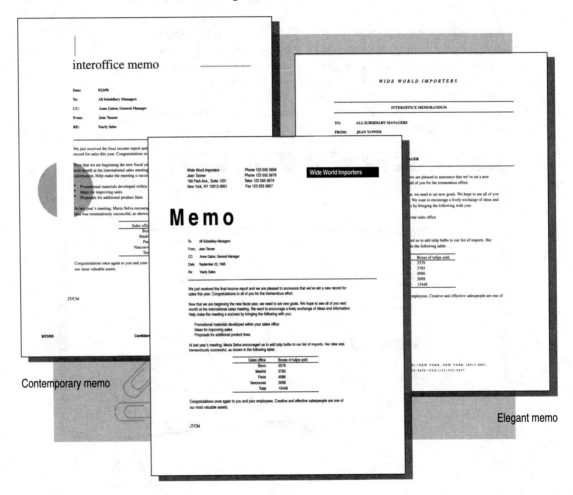

Contemporary memo

Professional memo

Elegant memo

Set Up the Page and Type the Standard Text

Start the Memo Wizard by clicking New (File menu). Click the Memos tab, and then double-click Memo Wizard.

The wizard asks you a few easy questions and then uses your answers to construct the memo.

Quickly insert names on the To or Cc line If you use an electronic personal address book, the Memo Wizard automatically provides access to it so you can insert one or more names on the To and Cc lines of your memo. If you don't have an address book, just type the names in the spaces provided.

Want to change the look of the memo? When the wizard finishes, change the formatting or layout just as you would in any other Word document. For example, to change one of the styles the wizard used, click Style (Format menu). Click the name of the style, and then modify the formatting of any part of the style you want, for instance, the paragraph formatting. For details, look up **styles** in the Word online index.

For Help, double-click. In the Word online index look up:
personal address book
styles

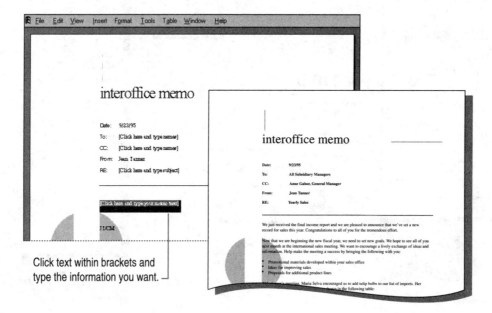

Click text within brackets and type the information you want.

Make a boilerplate memo   First, add items that will be the same in all memos. For example, you could add your company logo to the title line. Click Save As (File menu), and then click Document Template in the Save As Type box. Name and save the new template. For details, look up **templates** in the Word online index.

Word automatically checks spelling   Word marks misspellings with a wavy red underline as you work. To correct a misspelling, click the word with the right mouse button, and then select from the list. For details, look up **automatic spell checking** in the Word online index.

Highlight what's important   If you distribute your memo electronically, highlight sections you want to emphasize by selecting the text. Then click the Highlight button on the Formatting toolbar. For details, look up **highlighter pen** in the Word online index.

Highlight button

Use a Memo Template Instead of a Wizard?

The Memo Wizard and the memo templates produce an attractive, ready-to-complete memo. The difference between the two is that the wizard lets you choose layout options step by step while the templates have a preset layout.

To use a template, click New (File menu), click the Memos tab, and then double-click the memo template you want. Click or select the sample and instruction text, and then type the text you want.

Use the Style box on the Formatting toolbar to apply styles, or modify existing styles by using the Style command (Format menu). For details, look up **styles** in the Word online index.

Create your own personalized template   Add your name, address, and any other standard information you want to include in each memo. Then save the modified memo as a template. For details, see the tip on creating a boilerplate memo earlier in this topic.

Insert Information from Other Files

Want to include information from another document, for example, the latest corporate sales figures from a Microsoft Excel worksheet? Copy the information you want from the other document, and then paste it into your memo.

For Help, double-click. In the Word online index look up: **figures, copying and moving**

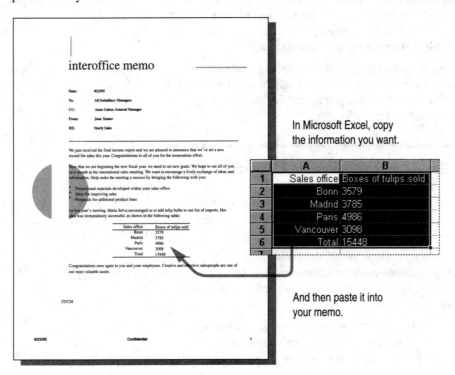

In Microsoft Excel, copy the information you want.

And then paste it into your memo.

Next Steps

To	See
Jazz up the memo	"Make Your Word Document Look Great," page 161
Send the memo electronically	"Share Documents Electronically," page 326

Create a Fax Cover Sheet

The Fax Wizard is a fast and easy way to create a fax cover sheet because the wizard builds it for you step by step. Just choose one of three professional designs and then fill in the blanks. For even more design choices, you can also use the fax templates.

Key Features

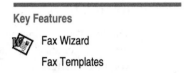

Fax Wizard

Fax Templates

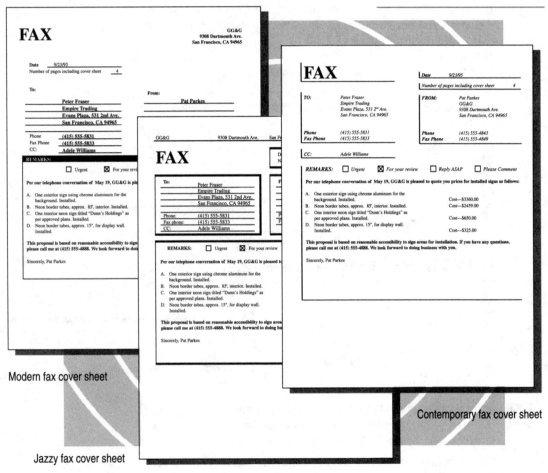

Modern fax cover sheet

Jazzy fax cover sheet

Contemporary fax cover sheet

Use the Fax Wizard to Get Started

To start the Fax Wizard, click New (File menu), click the Letters & Faxes tab, and then double-click Fax Wizard.

The Fax Wizard "interviews" you and uses your answers to set up the fax cover sheet's basic content and layout. The wizard also lets you insert names and addresses directly from your Microsoft Exchange personal address book or Schedule+ Contact List. When the wizard finishes, the new fax cover sheet appears—all you need to do is fill in the details.

 For Help, double-click.
In the Word online index look up:
wizards
templates
address book

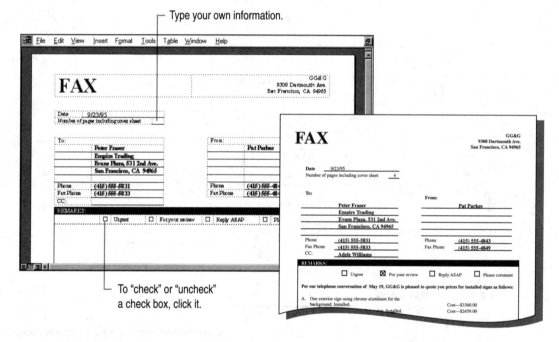

Type your own information.

To "check" or "uncheck" a check box, click it.

Add a confidentiality statement   Type it at the bottom of the page. If you plan to reuse the statement, save it as an AutoText entry. For details, look up **AutoText** in the Word online index.

Like the result—and want to use it to start your next fax cover sheet? Delete any information you don't plan to include in future fax cover sheets. Click Save As (File menu), and then click Document Template in the Save As Type box. Name and save the new template. Then select this template the next time you start a new fax cover sheet.

Use a Fax Template Instead of the Wizard?

If you want even more fax cover sheet design choices, use one of three attractive fax templates (Contemporary, Elegant, or Professional). They offer a fill-in-the-blanks "blueprint" that you can customize.

How to use a fax template Click New (File menu), click the Letters & Faxes tab, and then double-click a fax template. Click or select the sample text and type your own information. If you want to "check" or "uncheck" a check box, double-click it.

Try on a different fax design Click Style Gallery (Format menu), and then click a fax template.

Create your own personalized template Add your name, address, and any other standard information you want to include in each fax cover sheet. Click Save As (File menu), and then click Document Template in the Save As Type box. Name and save the new template. Then select this template the next time you start a fax cover sheet.

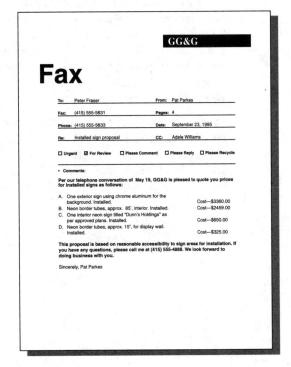

Professional fax cover sheet

Next Steps

To send the fax if you're using Microsoft At Work™ fax software   First, make sure you have a fax card installed. Next, create and save the fax cover sheet, and then insert it at the beginning of the document you're faxing. (For details, look up **inserting document into current document** in the Word online index.) Finally, click Send (File menu) and specify a fax address. For more information, see the Windows 95 online Help.

To send the fax if you're using a fax machine   Create and print the fax cover sheet, and then fax the cover sheet and document as usual. If you prefer to keep preprinted fax cover sheets on hand, leave the address and message areas blank. Then, print multiple copies and fill in the information by hand each time you're ready to send a fax.

Create Letterhead and Matching Envelopes

Word makes it easy to create letterhead that projects just the right personal or corporate image. To design letterhead, you can modify the three ready-to-use letter templates—which set up the design, sample text, an "automatic" date, and page numbers for you. If you want to get creative, use a complementary design for the second page, add a watermark, and create a matching envelope.

Key Features

Letter Templates

Headers and Footers

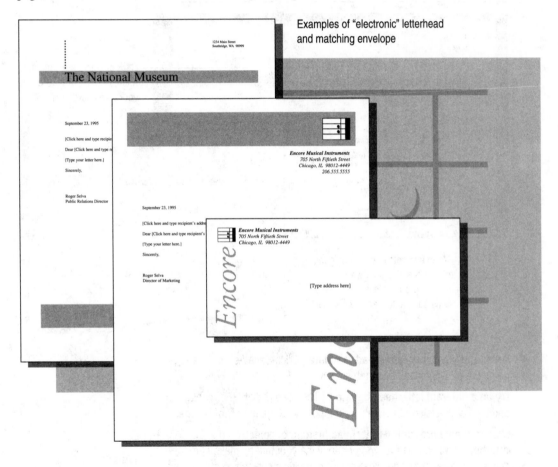

Examples of "electronic" letterhead and matching envelope

Start with an Existing Letterhead Design

For the fastest and easiest way to create letterhead, start with one of the ready-to-use letter templates. Just click Open (File menu), click the Document Templates file type, and then double-click a letter template in the Microsoft Office\Template\Letters & Faxes folder. (For illustrations of each template, see "Write a Business Letter," page 120.)

For Help, double-click. In the Word online index look up: **templates**

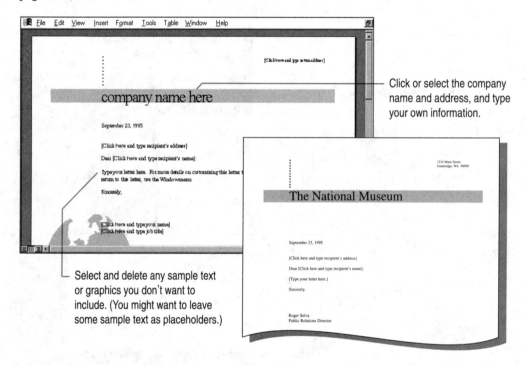

Click or select the company name and address, and type your own information.

Select and delete any sample text or graphics you don't want to include. (You might want to leave some sample text as placeholders.)

Name and save your letterhead template   Click Save As (File menu), name the new template, and then save it.

Try on a different letterhead design   Click Style Gallery (Format menu), and then click a letter template (Contemporary, Elegant, or Professional).

Want to create preprinted letterhead instead of "electronic" letterhead?   If you plan to type or handwrite your letters, make sure to delete all the sample body text. Then print multiple copies so you'll always have letterhead stock on hand.

Change the Text Design and Add a Logo

First, select and delete the existing company name, address, slogan, or any other elements you don't want to include in your letterhead. Then, click Header And Footer (View menu) and add your name, address, and logo as shown in the following illustration.

 For Help, double-click.
In the Word online index look up:
headers and footers
pictures, importing and inserting

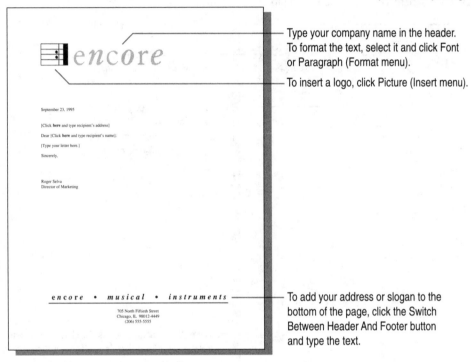

Type your company name in the header. To format the text, select it and click Font or Paragraph (Format menu).

To insert a logo, click Picture (Insert menu).

To add your address or slogan to the bottom of the page, click the Switch Between Header And Footer button and type the text.

 Want a quick way to switch between the header or footer and the main document? In page layout view, double-click the area you want to edit. When the main document is active, the headers and footers are dimmed—but they will appear in the printed document.

Add a rule or border Select a paragraph, click the Borders button, and then click a button on the Borders toolbar for the effect you want.

Insert dingbats such as • or ♦ to separate the parts of an address Click Symbol (Insert menu), select a font, and then double-click a symbol.

Switch Between Header And Footer button

Borders button

Add Visual Impact

To jazz up your letterhead, use various text effects such as fonts, colors, or WordArt. Include graphics from your company's collection of logos and scanned images or from the Microsoft Office ClipArt Gallery, or draw your own pictures. To position the elements just where you want them, use tables and frames.

 For Help, double-click.
In the Word online index look up:
tables
frames
WordArt
clip art

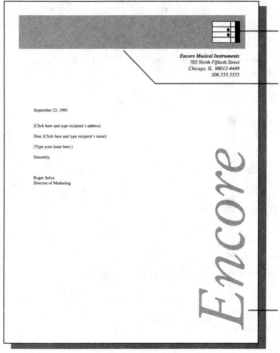

To position a logo on the page, use a frame (see the following tip).

To create a shaded area, use the Borders toolbar. Or, use the Drawing toolbar to draw a solid rectangle or other object.

To create text effects like this, click Object (Insert menu) and then click WordArt. To position the WordArt on the page, use a frame (see the following tip).

 Position your name or logo anywhere on the page   In page layout view, select the item and click Frame (Insert menu). You can now resize the framed item and drag it anywhere on the page.

Position your name, address, and logo side by side   Click in the header or footer, click the Insert Table button, and then drag to select the number of rows and columns. Drag the gridlines to adjust the cell sizes, and then insert your text or graphics into the cells.

Insert Table button

Need to adjust the margins so the letterhead design doesn't overwrite the letter text?   Click Page Layout (View menu), and drag the gray border on the horizontal or vertical ruler. For details, look up **margins** in the Word online index.

Create a Different Design for the Second Page

If you write multiple-page letters, you might want to create a simpler, complementary design for the second and subsequent pages of the letterhead.

 For Help, double-click. In the Word online index look up: **first page header or footer**

If your letterhead template doesn't already have two pages, insert a page break: Click Break (Insert menu), and then click Page Break. Then click Header And Footer (View menu). The header and/or footer for the second page already contains the date and page number, but you can modify the header or footer the way you want.

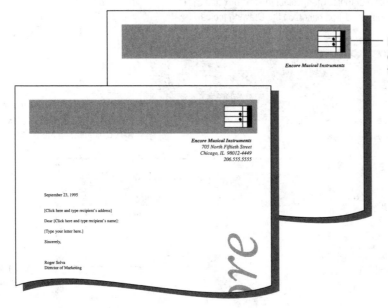

For example, copy some of the design elements from the first page header to the second page header.

 Need a faster way to switch between headers and footers? Click these buttons on the Header And Footer toolbar to switch between the header and footer on the same page, or between headers or footers on different pages.

What if the second page has the same header and footer as the first page? You probably started your letterhead from scratch, instead of from one of the ready-to-use letter templates. (The letter templates automatically set up a first-page header and footer that's different from the header and footer for subsequent pages.) To fix this problem, click Page Setup (File Menu), click the Layout tab, and then click Different First Page.

Header And Footer toolbar buttons

Add a Watermark

For a professional look, add a watermark—a logo, decorative graphic, or word (such as "draft" or "confidential") that appears to be stamped into the page.

Click Header And Footer (View menu), and then click the Drawing button. On the Drawing toolbar, click the Text Box button, and then drag to create a container for the watermark.

 For Help, double-click.
In the Word online index look up:
watermarks
text boxes

Drawing   Text Box   Send Behind Text
button   button   button

Type text in the box, or click Picture (Insert menu) and select a graphic. Then, select the text box and click the Send Behind Text button on the Drawing toolbar.

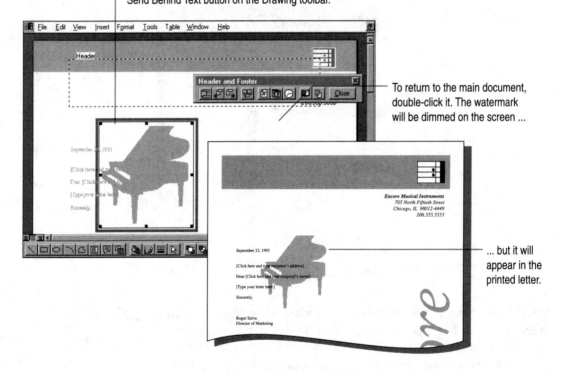

To return to the main document, double-click it. The watermark will be dimmed on the screen ...

... but it will appear in the printed letter.

Want to keep the document text out of your way while you're creating the watermark?   Click the Show/Hide Document Text button on the Header And Footer toolbar.

Show/Hide Document Text button

Want the watermark to appear on the second page?   If you want the watermark to appear on the second and subsequent pages, click Header And Footer (View menu), copy the watermark, switch to the header for the second page, and then paste the watermark.

Make sure the watermark doesn't obscure any text   Experiment with various shades of gray—or even colors, which print as shades of gray—to see which work best with your printer.

Create a Matching Envelope

Click Envelopes And Labels (Tools menu), and type some sample text for the delivery address—such as **[Type address here]**. Fill in your return address, and click Add To Document. Then, click Page Layout (View menu). To add a graphic, click Picture (Insert menu).

 For Help, double-click.
In the Word online index look up:
envelopes

To position the graphic, select it and then click Frame (Insert menu). Drag the graphic anywhere on the envelope.

Encore Musical Instruments
705 North Fiftieth Street
Chicago, IL 98012-4449

Encore

[Type address here]

Ready to print the envelope?   When you use the letterhead template to start a new letter, you can fill in the delivery address on the envelope and print it. To print just the envelope, click Print (File menu) and print page 0 (zero).

Plan to change other envelope options, such as envelope size?   If you open the Envelopes And Labels dialog box and make changes, Word won't preserve the graphic you added to the envelope. To solve this problem, save the graphic as an AutoText entry named "EnvelopeExtra1" or "EnvelopeExtra2." For details, see **AutoText** in the Word online index.

Next Steps

To	See
Add even more visual impact	"Make Your Word Document Look Great," page 161
Use the "electronic" letterhead to start a new letter	"Write a Business Letter," page 120
Fax a copy of the letter	"Create a Fax Cover Sheet," page 129

Create a Simple Newsletter

Whether you want to keep in regular contact with clients, update customers on what's new in your store for fall, or keep constituents informed of the latest legislation, a simple newsletter is a good way to do it.

If you want to produce a simple, attractive newsletter, create it using Word. But if you want to produce a complex newsletter or one with a very precise design, it's best to use a page layout program such as Microsoft Publisher.

Key Features

Columns

Frames

Do you want to keep your newsletter conservative and professional looking?

Or convey a light-hearted feeling?

What to Do First

Convert your articles   The first step is to convert the articles that will go into the newsletter. If you have stories written using other applications, just open and save them in Word's file format so that you can make editing and formatting changes in Word. Most or all of the original formatting will be retained.

What about changing formatting and styles?   The formatting or styles the story has now will be retained when you paste the text into the newsletter. If you want to change the formatting, do it now.

If the formatting changes are minimal, find and replace them. Click Find (Edit menu), click the Format or Special button, and choose what you want to find. Then click the Replace button, and repeat the process in the Replace dialog box.

To do more extensive reformatting, attach your own or one of Word's templates by clicking Templates (File menu). Then assign the styles you want from the template.

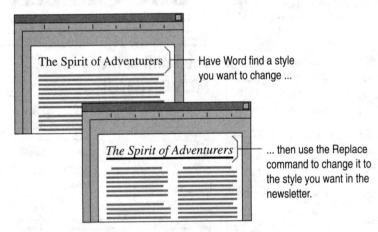

Have Word find a style
you want to change ...

... then use the Replace command to change it to the style you want in the newsletter.

For Help, double-click.
In the Word online index look up:
file formats
templates
styles
finding and replacing formatting

For Help on dialog box options, click this button.

Want to tell Word what to do when it converts files from other applications?   Click Options (Tools menu), and then click the Compatibility tab. Click the file format under Recommended Options For, and then select the options you want applied when you have Word convert documents from that format.

Need to know how long a story is?   Check the word count by clicking Word Count (Tools menu).

Create a Masthead

First, open a new document by clicking the New button. Then switch to page layout view and click the Show/Hide button on the Standard toolbar. Type the masthead text and format it.

To get the look you want, experiment with different font sizes. In the following example, the newsletter name is in 86-point Britannic Bold.

To set a right-aligned tab for the date, click here until you see this.

Then click on the ruler to insert a right-aligned tab stop for the date.

To choose the width and placement of a rule, use these buttons.

To insert a rule above and below the masthead, click the Borders button.

For Help, double-click. In the Word online index look up:
fonts
borders

 Speed up your work Display the Borders toolbar and the Drawing toolbar by clicking the Borders button and the Drawing button.

Borders button   Drawing button

Make formatting easier Add a few empty paragraph marks to your document. Otherwise, every time you press ENTER, the most recent formatting is applied to the new paragraph—something you may not want. With empty, normal paragraph marks available, you can just move the insertion point to one of them and begin new formatting. Later, select and delete any extra empty paragraphs.

Add a professional touch If you used a TrueType® font for the masthead, you can improve its appearance with kerning. To set kerning options, select the text, click Font (Format menu), and then click the Character Spacing tab.

Add Columns

Now, add and format the columns. Move the insertion point to an empty paragraph below the masthead.

First, add a section break. Click Break (Insert menu), and then click Continuous.

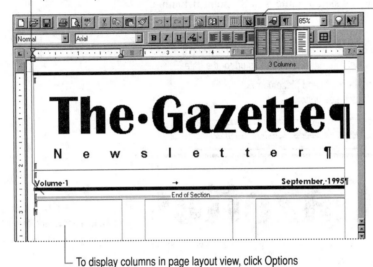

 For Help, double-click.
In the Word online index look up:
columns (newspaper)
rules (borders)

Then click the Columns button and drag to select the number of columns.

To display columns in page layout view, click Options (Tools menu). On the View tab, turn on Text Boundaries.

Want to tinker with the appearance of columns? You can make your newsletter look more compact by reducing the space between columns. To adjust the space between columns, add lines between columns, or make columns of unequal widths, click Columns (Format menu), and then make the changes you want.

Get the Help You Need While You Work

Expanded and improved online assistance is just a click away. It's the fastest way to get information so you can keep working.

Ask the Answer Wizard   Type a question in your own words. The Answer Wizard lists online Help topics related to your question. Double-click the Help button and then click the Answer Wizard tab.

Look it up in the online index   Instead of typing a question, use index entries provided in this book to find online topics related to your task. Double-click the Help button and then click the Index tab.

For details, see "Get Assistance While You Work," page 30. Or look up **Help** in the Word online index.

Add Stories and Headlines

Adding a story is a simple matter of copying the story you want and then pasting it into the newsletter.

For Help, double-click.
In the Word online index look up:
copying text and graphics

Type and format headlines and subheads as you would any other text. To place headlines anywhere on the page, see the next section.

The Gazette
N e w s l e t t e r

Volume 1   September, 1995

The Spirit of the Adventurer

An adventure is a dare you take personally. It's an opportunity that also involves some risk. It is inspired by an age-old sort of challenge, and the tools it involves—boats, planes, or snow shoes—are only incidental. Few of us accept such a challenge, although many of us dreamed of adventure during childhood. What is so different about adults who live out their dreams?

For an answer, we gathered together four modern-day adventurers. Jean Herder is famous for solo air speed and distance records. P. T. Lopez is known for daring sea voyages. Dieter Rauh travels the jungle in search of forgotten tribes, and Lucie Caselli is a mountain climber who scales peaks that others find impossible.

Panel moderator: *Each of you has done something that the average person would never try. Can you explain why you did?*

Dieter: I am intensely curious. I love a physical challenge. And, in a way, I like to test my luck.

Jean: The explorers we read about in school were different from us. They risked their lives for money or royal favor. There's no money in what we do ... although P. T. made a film about his voyage. I do it for the thrill of it.

Lucie: I think it was curiosity that set me apart from other kids. Kids are naturally curious, but my curiosity was more focused than most. I was absolutely obsessed

Jean: I thought of *nothing* but airplanes. I built intricate models in the evenings. And on Saturday nights, my parents and I would sit at the airport and watch the planes come and go.

P. T.: My parents bought me a kit for a row boat when I was twelve. I'd always loved the sea, but that gift marked a turning point.

"...And on Saturday nights, my parents and I would sit at the airport and watch the planes come and go."

Panel moderator: *What were you like as children?*

with heights. I'd climb anything that stood still long enough.

CONTINUED ➡

Word pastes text into the columns in sequence starting from the insertion point.

Page 2

Panel moderator: *Tell me what inspired your last adventure.*

Lucie: I'd dreamed of climbing that particular peak since childhood. I saw a picture of it in a book.

How to spot a future adventurer

The following traits are common to those we interviewed. Spot these traits in a child, and you may be looking at the next generation's adventurer.

* Resourceful and self-reliant
* Fascinated with a particular dream
* Driven by curiosity
* Very lucky
* Meticulous in their work, but daring

P. T.: The dream aspect is a very important part of the adventure, isn't it? It's what drives you to accomplish whatever it is you want to do.

Dieter: And once you start talking to other people about your dream, the dream holds you hostage.

Jean: Yes! You become a captive of your own expectations. You feel like you can't back out even though you aren't sure you can follow through on your plans.

Panel moderator: *So you've had doubts?*

Lucie: You have doubts, but you do it anyway because you can't resist the adventure.

Panel moderator: *I expected to meet four outgoing, boisterous*

people. Some of you seem fairly reserved. How would you describe your personalities?

P. T.: I'm frightfully shy. Showing up today was harder for me than sailing around the world. I thrive on solitude.

Jean: When I was in medical school, I was a nervous wreck with all the pressures and deadlines. I love the simplicity of the sky in good weather. And, like P. T., I enjoy solitude.

Dieter: I love to be around people, and I like the city ... but I enjoy the

dramatic change of going to the jungle. I think I'm very unusual in that I seek out situations that force me to adjust.

In closing
All but one of the explorers we interviewed describe their lives as fulfilling their childhood fantasies. All but one believe that seeking

out adventure is somehow part of their destiny. The one dissenter, Dieter, insisted that his first jungle adventure was born of a warm summer day and a cold drink. He told us the idea came to him during one of those lovely moments in life when anything seems possible.

Upcoming EuroClimb Adventure

Exotic Excursions welcomes your participation in the travel event of the year!

EuroClimb is an adventure that combines a European vacation with the thrill of climbing some of the world's most beautiful and challenging mountains. This year's excursion covers the French, Swiss, and Italian Alps

Climb with a small group for two months and forge friendships that will last a lifetime.

TRIVIAL PURSUIT
Here's a little exercise just for fun. Use the following formula to calculate the volume of one of the peaks that we will climb. $v=1/3 (t) (r, z h)$ For tips on calculating the volume, turn to page 3.

As explained in our brochure, the Exotic Excursions EuroClimb package includes all climbing and camping equipment, meals and accommodations, round-trip first-class air travel to Paris, and flights and ground travel throughout Europe.

We've already mailed you several complimentary resource books. Our clients tell us these materials are useful before and during the trip. Watch your mailbox for:

To even out columns of text, place the insertion point at the end of the story, click Break (Insert menu), and then click Continuous.

Where do you do your writing? If your story is short, you can type it directly into the newsletter columns, or switch to normal view to write. For longer stories, however, you may work faster if you write in a separate Word document and then paste the story into the newsletter.

Better copy-fitting Make text fit neatly within columns by clicking Hyphenation (Tools menu).

Need a banner headline? To create a banner headline that spans all columns, type the text and press ENTER. Select the headline text, click the Columns button, and then select a single column. While the text is selected, format it or apply a heading style.

Add Interest with Graphics and Illustrations

You can insert and move graphics or text anywhere on the page by putting it in a *frame*. To insert a frame, click Frame (Insert menu). Select the frame and drag the handles to the size you want.

For Help, double-click.
In the Word online index look up:
frames
pictures

To put a graphic inside the frame, click Picture or Object (Insert menu), and choose the filename of the picture or the type of object you want to insert. Or, to put text in the frame, either copy and paste existing text into the frame, or type the text in the frame, and then format it.

The frame and the graphic can be sized to fit within a column, to cover multiple columns, or to cover all of one and part of other columns. Word adjusts any surrounding text or other objects to accommodate the new frame size.

To keep a graphic with related text, select the frame, and then move the anchor to the text. Click Frame (Format menu), and then click Lock Anchor.

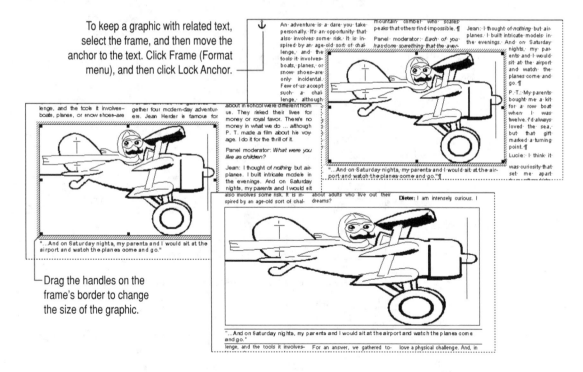

Drag the handles on the frame's border to change the size of the graphic.

Try Out the Newsletter Wizard or Template

Instead of creating a newsletter from scratch, you can create a newsletter using the Newsletter Wizard or Word's newsletter template.

To start the Newsletter Wizard or use the template, click New (File menu), click the Publications tab, and then click the Newsletter Wizard or template.

You can copy and paste text into the newsletter, change the formatting, move framed objects to any location on the page, and select and delete text or an object.

To replace a graphic, select it and click Picture (Insert menu). When you choose and paste the graphic, it will replace the existing one.

Newsletter template

Modern newsletter wizard

Classic newsletter wizard

Next Steps

To	See
Create an envelope	"Create a Resume and Cover Letter," page 508
Add formatting	"Make Your Word Document Look Great," page 161
Create labels	"Create a Mailing," page 177
Linking the original story to the newsletter	"Use Office Applications Together," page 103

Create a Flyer

Whether you want to announce a sale, advertise the opening of a
new branch office, or announce the company holiday party, you can
use Microsoft Word to create an attractive, attention-getting flyer.

First, create a jazzy page layout, then combine special text effects,
borders, and clip art to finish the project.

Key Features

 Tables

Inserting Graphics

New for Spring

The Latest Spr
from top-name

Come to a show on
Sunday, May 8
1223 Main St.

Please accept our invitati
any purchase with this co

Choose a distinctive typeface to
help set the tone of the flyer.

Smith's
Coffee Shop
2343 South 2nd Avenue

Wednesday Special:

Free cup of coffee wit
of any sandwich.

Open 6 a.m. - 4 p.m.

Vintage Fixer-Upper

Great Buy

• New on the
  market
• 3 bedrooms
• Detached garage
• Mountain view
• Schools close by

Open House
Saturday 1-5pm
Call for directions
555-3242

Hurry, this one won't last!
Owner will carry the loan.

Mix a graphic text effect
with clip art.

Use clip art to grab the reader's attention.

Lay It Out

When you know what you want the flyer to say and what graphics you want to include, draw a simple sketch that shows how you want to arrange the text and graphics on the page.

Now transfer your sketch from paper to Word. First open a new document by clicking the New button, and then switch to page layout view (View menu).

To establish the overall page area you'll use for text and graphics, set the page margins. Then insert one or more tables to match the layout you sketched by clicking the Insert Table button.

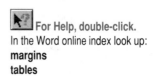 **For Help, double-click.**
In the Word online index look up:
margins
tables

Insert Table button

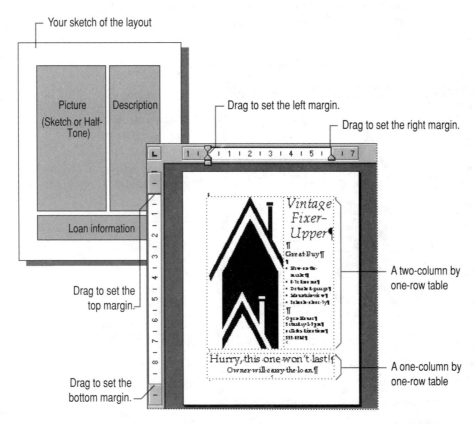

- Your sketch of the layout

Picture (Sketch or Half-Tone)

Description

Loan information

- Drag to set the left margin.

- Drag to set the right margin.

Drag to set the top margin.

Drag to set the bottom margin.

A two-column by one-row table

A one-column by one-row table

 Want the page to have a horizontal orientation? To create a flyer with a horizontal or landscape orientation, click Page Setup (File menu), and then click the Paper Size tab. For details, look up **orientation, page** in the Word online index.

Horizontal orientation

Add rows or columns quickly   Select the same number of existing rows or columns you want to add, and then click the Insert Table button.

Want to include newspaper-style columns?   If you want text to flow from the bottom of one column to the top of the next, use newspaper-style columns. For details, see "Create a Simple Newsletter," page 141.

Add the Art and Text

Insert the graphic you want by clicking Picture (Insert menu). Or, to insert clip art, click Object (Insert menu), and then click the type of object you want.

Next, type the text you want in each column. Format text using the Font and Font Size boxes. To create a graphic text effect, use WordArt by clicking Object (Insert menu).

For Help, double-click. In the Word online index look up:
WordArt
borders

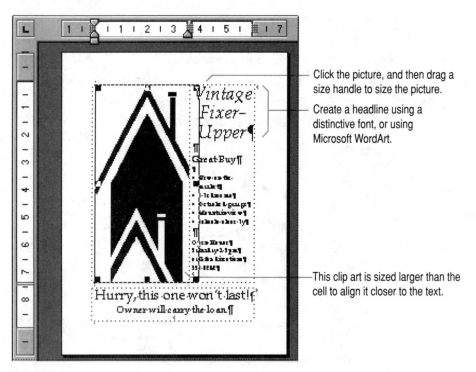

Click the picture, and then drag a size handle to size the picture.

Create a headline using a distinctive font, or using Microsoft WordArt.

This clip art is sized larger than the cell to align it closer to the text.

Want to exclude part of a picture?   Crop the picture by holding down the SHIFT key as you drag a size handle.

Need to add a border quickly?   Click the Borders button, and then on the Borders toolbar choose the line style, the kind of shading, and the kind of border you want.

Borders button

Position Text and Graphics Anywhere on the Page

By placing text, a graphic, or a table into a frame, you can position it anywhere on the page you want, and, if you drag the frame within a paragraph of text, Word wraps text around it.

To insert an empty frame, click Frame (Insert menu), and then drag the crosshair to the size you want. To put a frame around an existing object, in page layout view select the item, and then click Frame (Insert menu).

Mary Cabor believes she was destined to be a postage stamp designer. "I remember when I was very small, my mother would give us kids some chalk and then assign us each a square of the front walk to decorate. I always took the longest time because I filled every inch of the space, trying to capture the scene in my mind in perfect detail, but without leaving the square my mom had given me. My brother, Thomas, paints murals for an interior design firm. He never could keep his drawings inside the one square."

Cabor is convinced that she has found the one career she always wanted, however, the road to designing postage stamps was circuitous, to say the least. She spent time on a hay crew and then switched to herding sheep. Next she took a detour to Thailand, where she taught school in a remote village. After three years there, Mary says she "just traveled everywhere." In 1975, she stayed at home to care for her mother, who was convalescing after breaking a hip. "She couldn't get out and I hated to just leave her home alone. So I spent a lot of time in the house, going crazy." She happened to see an advertisement calling for designs for a postage stamp commemorating the 75th anniversary of the first successful airplane flight.

"I was stir-crazy and looking for anything to keep my mind occupied. I went to the library and got a lot of books out. I'd sit and read to my mother in the afternoons. And then, in the evenings, I'd make sketches. I'm afraid I didn't really know what I was doing, but maybe my enthusiasm for the subject came through, or maybe it was just beginner's luck."

Her design was chosen as a finalist, and she's never looked back. "I love the research and I've met people from all over and done work for exotic countries I at least twelve countries."

Next Steps

To	See
Jazz up the appearance of your flyer	"Make Your Word Document Look Great," page 161
Mail the flyer to customers	"Create a Mailing," page 177

Create a Business Plan

Write a Report Using Word and Link Information from Microsoft Excel

Whether you are starting a new business or expanding an existing one, a business plan helps you chart a clear direction and communicate your objectives to employees, potential investors, lending institutions, suppliers, and other vendors.

You can write the plan using Microsoft Word. If you have financial information in a Microsoft Excel worksheet, you can include it by linking it to your Word document. Then, if financial information changes, your Word document can be automatically updated.

To create a business plan like the one in this example, you can use workbooks created in Microsoft Excel for Windows 95 that contain financial estimates and summaries.

Key Features

 Link or Embed a Microsoft Excel Worksheet

 Table of Contents

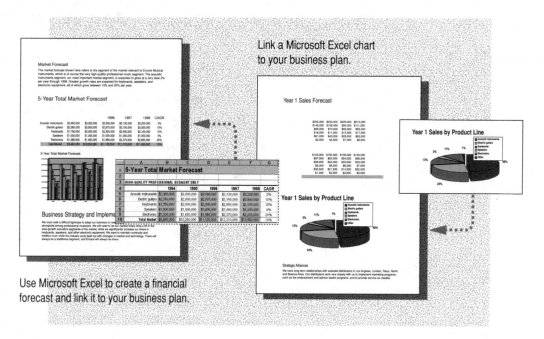

Link a Microsoft Excel chart to your business plan.

Use Microsoft Excel to create a financial forecast and link it to your business plan.

Write the Business Plan

A good way to begin is to organize your ideas in an outline. Or, if you prefer not to do an outline, simply apply Word's built-in heading styles to your headings as you write. Either way, you'll be able to quickly create a table of contents when you finish.

First create a new document by clicking the New button.

If you want to create an outline Switch to outline view (View menu) and compose the outline. When you are ready, you'll probably find it easier to write the details of the plan if you switch to normal view (View menu).

If you don't want to create an outline Just start writing. If you want to include a table of contents, make sure you use the Style box to apply heading styles (Heading 1, Heading 2, and so on).

For Help, double-click.
In the Word online index look up:
outlines
styles

New button

Heading 1
Style box

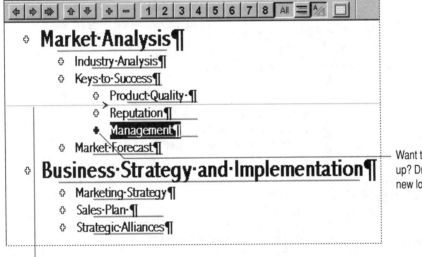

Want to move this section up? Drag the icon to the new location.

Word shows where the section you're moving will be placed.

The quickest way to create a business plan Use the business plan in the Microsoft Small Business Pack for Microsoft Office. It provides a business plan template with headings and links to Microsoft Excel financial and analysis worksheets. The Small Business Pack, which offers a collection of templates designed especially for small businesses, is sold separately in software stores nationwide.

Want to change the look of Word's built-in heading styles? Click Style (Format menu), and then choose the heading style you want to change. Click the Modify button, and make the changes you want.

Insert and Update Financial Information Automatically

Financial projections show how your business will make money or how you will finance a new venture. To insert financial information, open your financial workbooks in Microsoft Excel. If the numbers are likely to change as you refine your plan, link the Microsoft Excel information so that the numbers in your Word document can be updated automatically.

For Help, double-click.
In the Word online index look up:
linked objects, overview
figures, copying and moving

If the numbers won't change, select and copy the information in Microsoft Excel that you want to include, and then paste it into your Word document.

To make financial information more persuasive, include charts. You can either link or paste a Microsoft Excel chart into your document. For details, see "Add a Chart to a Document or Presentation," page 223, and "Customize the Look of a Chart," page 236.

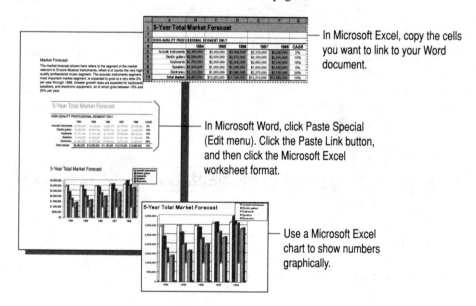

In Microsoft Excel, copy the cells you want to link to your Word document.

In Microsoft Word, click Paste Special (Edit menu). Click the Paste Link button, and then click the Microsoft Excel worksheet format.

Use a Microsoft Excel chart to show numbers graphically.

Add a Cover Page and Running Titles

Create a cover page   Move the insertion point to the beginning of the document and type the cover page text. To put the cover page text on a separate page, click Break (Insert menu), and then make sure Page Break is selected.

Create running titles at the top or bottom of the page   Click Header And Footer (View menu), and then type the text you want. To add page numbers, the date, or the time, click the appropriate button on the Header And Footer toolbar.

Change or delete the running title on the cover page   Click the Page Setup button on the Header And Footer toolbar. On the Layout tab, click Different First Page. Then, in the First Page Header or Footer window, type the text you want, or leave it blank entirely.

For Help, double-click.
In the Word online index look up:
headers and footers
page numbers
hiding first page number

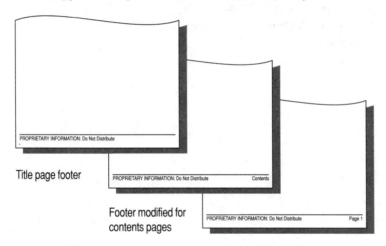

PROPRIETARY INFORMATION: Do Not Distribute

Title page footer

PROPRIETARY INFORMATION: Do Not Distribute   Contents

Footer modified for contents pages

PROPRIETARY INFORMATION: Do Not Distribute   Page 1

Footer with page number added

Switch between headers and footers quickly   Click these buttons on the Header And Footer toolbar to switch quickly between the header and footer on the same page, or between headers or footers on different pages.

Header And Footer toolbar buttons

Add Polish to Your Header or Footer

You can format header and footer text just as you would any other text in Word. Try experimenting with different fonts, font sizes and styles, and borders and shading.

For example, you can have the word "Confidential" appear in light gray in every footer. Just type the text in the footer window, select it, and then click Font (Format menu). On the Font tab, choose the text color you want.

Or, perhaps you want your company's logo to appear at the top of every page. In the Header window, place the insertion point where you want the logo, click Object (Insert menu), and then click the object you want.

Finish by Adding a Table of Contents

If you created an outline or used Word's built-in heading styles (Heading 1, Heading 2, and so on), it's easy to create a table of contents. If you didn't use the built-in heading styles, just select headings in your document, and then click the name of the heading style you want in the Style box.

Move the insertion point to where you want to insert the table of contents. Click Index And Tables (Insert menu), and then on the Table of Contents tab, click the format you want.

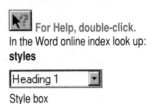

For Help, double-click.
In the Word online index look up:
styles

Heading 1

Style box

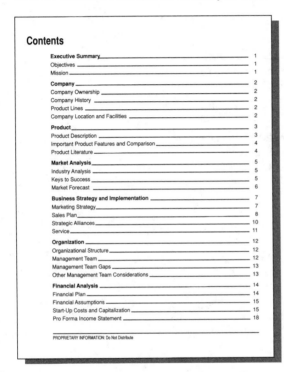

Contents

PROPRIETARY INFORMATION: Do Not Distribute

Word automatically includes the page number for each heading.

Last minute changes after you created the table of contents? If you add text and the page breaks change, or you change the wording of a heading, you'll want to update the table of contents. Just place the insertion point in the table of contents, click the right mouse button, and then click Update Field. You can have Word update only page numbers or the entire table of contents.

Need to Create a Top-Quality Presentation Quickly?

Are you scheduled to present your business plan to potential investors or associates? If you used Word's built-in heading styles, you can quickly create a PowerPoint slide presentation.

When you open your Word document in PowerPoint, PowerPoint uses the heading styles to create presentation slides. Each Heading 1 becomes the title of a slide, and Heading 2 through Heading 5 are successive levels of indented text. For details, see "Transfer Information Between PowerPoint and Other Applications," page 268.

Next Steps

To	See
Route a Word document for review	"Have Your Team Review a Word Document," page 333
Fax a copy of the business plan	"Create a Fax Cover Sheet," page 129
Create a slide presentation	"Transfer Information Between PowerPoint and Other Applications," page 268

Make Your Word Document Look Great

If you've started with a wizard or template, you're well on your way to creating a great-looking document. But if you want to experiment with the wide variety of formatting options in Word, just browse through this topic to see which effects you'd like to try. You'll get quick "how to" information and lots of tips and shortcuts for adding polish and pizzazz.

Include running headers and footers with automatically updated page numbers, dates, and so on.

Set extra-wide margins for notes and side heads.

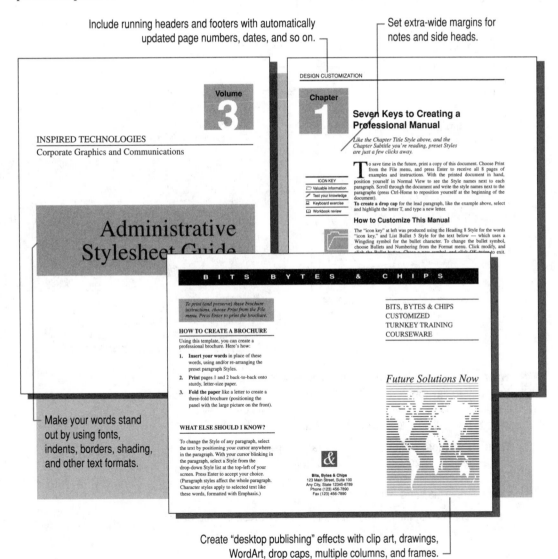

Make your words stand out by using fonts, indents, borders, shading, and other text formats.

Create "desktop publishing" effects with clip art, drawings, WordArt, drop caps, multiple columns, and frames.

Fonts, Bold, Italic, and Other Text Enhancements

Word offers a wide range of character formats, such as fonts, font sizes, bold, italic, all caps, superscript, kerning, color, and so on.

To make your words stand out   For the quickest and easiest way to apply fonts, font sizes, bold, italic, and underline, use the toolbar buttons. (For details, see "Create Your First Word Document," page 57.) Or, apply any number of character formats by selecting the text and then clicking Font (Format menu).

For Help, double-click.
In the Word online index look up:
character formatting
case of text

Use all caps or small caps to emphasize short titles or headings.

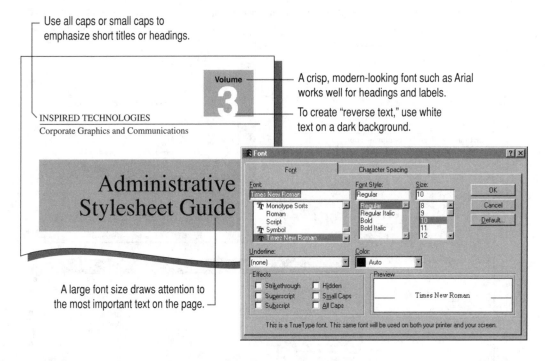

A crisp, modern-looking font such as Arial works well for headings and labels.

To create "reverse text," use white text on a dark background.

A large font size draws attention to the most important text on the page.

 Want to use something other than Times New Roman® 10-point for your day-to-day font?   Just click Font (Format menu), select your favorite font, click Default, and then click Yes. (If you use a different template, you'll need to repeat these steps to reset the default font for that template.)

What are all those options on the Character Spacing tab?   If you want to fine-tune the horizontal or vertical spacing of text, use the Spacing, Position, and Kerning options. For details, look up **spacing between characters** in the Word online index.

Quickly change capitalization, such as to UPPERCASE or Title Case   Click Change Case (Format menu).

Examples of character spacing

Text Spacing and Alignment

This section describes how to set the following paragraph formats: alignment, indents, line spacing, and spacing between paragraphs.

To position text on the page   You can use toolbar buttons to quickly align or indent text. Just select the text, and click a button. (For details, see "Create Your First Word Document," page 57.) Or, apply any number of paragraph formats by selecting one or more paragraphs, and then clicking Paragraph (Format menu).

For Help, double-click. In the Word online index look up: **paragraph formatting**

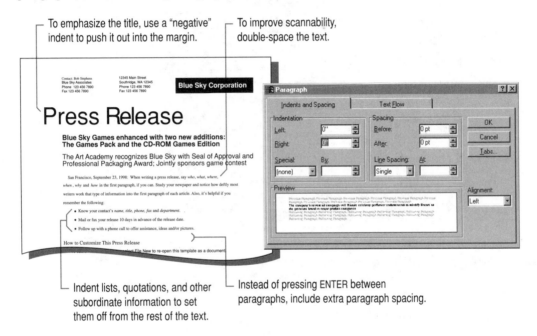

To emphasize the title, use a "negative" indent to push it out into the margin.

To improve scannability, double-space the text.

Indent lists, quotations, and other subordinate information to set them off from the rest of the text.

Instead of pressing ENTER between paragraphs, include extra paragraph spacing.

Apply formats without selecting an entire paragraph   Just click in the paragraph, or select any part of it, and then apply the formats you want.

Quick and easy indents   If you don't need to set an indent at exactly .38 inches, use the indent markers on the ruler. For example, instead of pressing TAB to indent the first line of each paragraph, set a first-line indent. For details, look up **indenting paragraphs** in the Word online index. (By the way, don't confuse indents with margins; indents are the distance that individual paragraphs are pushed in or out from the margin.)

Help! Your paragraph lost its formatting and merged with the next paragraph   You probably deleted the hidden paragraph mark (¶) at the end of the paragraph. This ¶ controls the paragraph's alignment, indents, and other paragraph formats. To restore the ¶—and your paragraph's original formatting—click the Undo button.

First-line indent

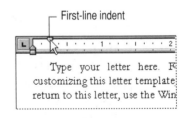

Undo button

Custom Margins

You can narrow the margins to fit more text on the page, or widen them to create a custom design for letterhead or a publication.

To set margins   Click Print Preview (File menu) or Page Layout (View menu), and then drag the gray margin boundaries on the horizontal and vertical rulers.

 For Help, double-click.
In the Word online index look up:
margins

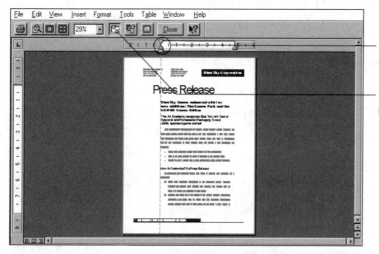

For example, in print preview, drag this boundary to set the left margin.

If you don't see the rulers, click this button.

 Having trouble getting a grip on the margin boundary?   When you drag the left margin, it's easy to grab the indent markers by mistake. Make sure the pointer looks like this ↔ before you start dragging.

Pointer when dragging margin boundary

Need to set precise margins?   Click Page Setup (File menu), and then select options on the Margins tab.

Need to Fix an Awkward Page Break?

Click where you want to break the page, and then press CTRL+ENTER to insert a hard page break. Or, to avoid having to manually rebreak pages as you edit, use "intelligent" pagination options instead. For example, use the Keep With Next option to attach a heading to the following paragraph, so that a page break can never come between them. For details, look up **page breaks** in the Word online index.

Page Numbers, Headers, and Footers

A header or footer is text—such as a page number, chapter title, or date—that appears at the top or bottom of every page.

To add headers and footers Click Header And Footer (View menu). You'll see boxes for entering the headers and footers.

 For Help, double-click.
In the Word online index look up:
headers and footers
page numbers

Type your header here.   To add a date, press TAB and click the Date button.

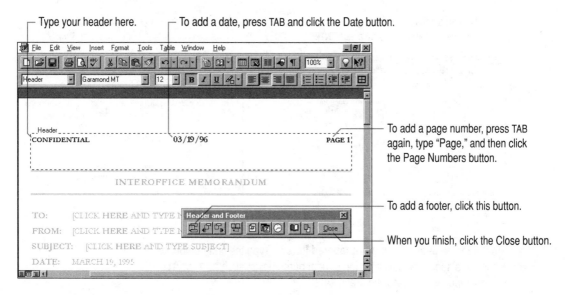

To add a page number, press TAB again, type "Page," and then click the Page Numbers button.

To add a footer, click this button.

When you finish, click the Close button.

Don't see your headers and footers? Click Page Layout (View menu).

Add the time, filename, author's name, or running page numbers (such as page 2 of 5) To add the time, click the Time button. Or, click Field (Insert menu), and then insert the FILENAME, AUTHOR, or NUMPAGES field. For details, look up **fields** in the Word online index.

Want to leave the header and footer off the first page? Click the Page Setup button, and then click Different First Page on the Layout tab.

Page Numbers, Date, Time, and Page Setup buttons

? For Help on dialog box options, click this button.

A Shortcut for Inserting Page Numbers

Click Page Numbers (Insert menu), and then select the options you want.

What if you end up with two sets of page numbers? For example, your template might already have preset page numbers. To fix this problem, click Header And Footer (View menu), and then delete the unwanted page number.

Bulleted and Numbered Lists

To organize your information, you can add a simple bulleted list or create a numbered list like this: 1, 2, 3; or a), b), c); or i., ii., iii.

To create a bulleted list For the speediest bullets, just start typing the list; Word automatically "bullets" the list as you go.

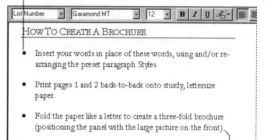

For Help, double-click.
In the Word online index look up:
applying bullets and numbers

┌ Type an asterisk (*), press the SPACEBAR, type the first item, and then press ENTER.

┌ Word "bullets" the item and inserts another bullet so you can continue typing the list.

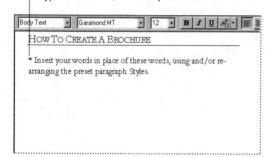

To end the list, press ENTER twice. ┘

What's the easiest way to do numbered lists? Type the first number or letter in the sequence plus a period or right parenthesis, such as **1.** or **A)** or **i.** Then, type the first item and press ENTER.

You pressed ENTER, but nothing happened Click Options (Tools menu), click the AutoFormat tab, click AutoFormat As You Type, and then click Automatic Bulleted Lists and Automatic Numbered Lists.

Need to "unnumber" or "unbullet" a list? Select the list, and then click the Numbering or Bullets button.

Use a different bullet style, say, ⊃ or ☞ Click Bullets And Numbering (Format menu). On the Bulleted tab, click one of the preset bullet styles, or click the Modify button and select a custom bullet.

Numbering and Bullets buttons

Need More Numbering Options?

If you're writing a legal contract, scientific paper, or script, you can number the headings, paragraphs, or individual lines in your document. For details, look up **headings, numbering**; **multilevel lists**; or **numbering lines** in the Word online index.

Tables for Side-by-Side Information

To create side-by-side columns (think of a spreadsheet or phone list), use a table. The table's cells keep your information neatly lined up, no matter how often you edit the text.

To insert a table For the nuts and bolts of inserting and formatting a table, see the following illustration. For more details on modifying a table—such as inserting rows, changing column widths, or centering the table—use Word online assistance.

 For Help, double-click.
In the Word online index look up:
tables

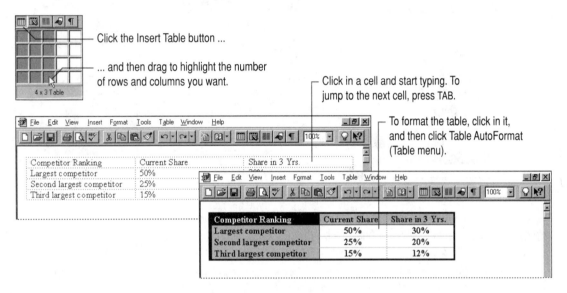

Click the Insert Table button ...

... and then drag to highlight the number of rows and columns you want.

Click in a cell and start typing. To jump to the next cell, press TAB.

To format the table, click in it, and then click Table AutoFormat (Table menu).

Competitor Ranking	Current Share	Share in 3 Yrs.
Largest competitor	50%	30%
Second largest competitor	25%	20%
Third largest competitor	15%	12%

Tables aren't just for facts and figures Use them to create "desktop publishing" effects such as sidebars, mastheads, or pictures and captions. Or, set up a "grid" for the entire document, for example, a resume, phone list, invoice, catalog, questionnaire, or annual report.

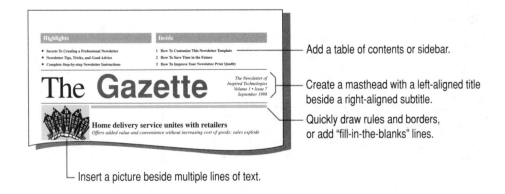

Add a table of contents or sidebar.

Create a masthead with a left-aligned title beside a right-aligned subtitle.

Quickly draw rules and borders, or add "fill-in-the-blanks" lines.

Insert a picture beside multiple lines of text.

Clip Art, Graphics, and Drawings

To illustrate your points, browse the Word ready-to-use clip art, import graphics from other programs, or draw your own pictures.

To add clip art or another graphic   Click Picture (Insert menu), and then select the picture you want.

 **For Help, double-click.** In the Word online index look up:
graphics
clip art

For example, insert a piece of clip art.

To resize the picture, click it, and then drag one of the corner handles.

To "crop" or hide part of the picture, click it, press SHIFT, and drag one of the handles.

Want to change the clip art color?   Double-click the clip art and use the Line Color and Fill Color buttons on the Drawing toolbar. For example, use lighter or darker shades of gray to optimize the clip art for your printer.

Need a simple, crisp-looking graphic?   Click Symbol (Insert menu), double-click the symbol you want, and then give it a large font size. To create a "reverse" symbol, change the symbol's text color to white and shade the paragraph with black or gray. To "crop" the shading around the symbol, adjust the indents or insert it into a frame.

Regular and "reverse" symbols

Create Your Own Drawings

Use tools on the Drawing toolbar to create diagrams, maps, logos, arrows, or other shapes. To focus attention on key parts of the drawing, use callouts or captions. For details, look up **drawing objects** in the Word online index.

Drawing toolbar

Lines, Boxes, and Shaded Backgrounds

You can add lines, boxes, or shaded backgrounds to paragraphs, tables, pictures, and frames. For example, include a line under the header, shade sidebar text, or create a heading with "reverse" text.

To add borders or shading Select an item, click the Borders button, and then click options on the Borders toolbar.

 For Help, double-click.
In the Word online index look up:
borders
shading

Borders button

To adjust the width of the border or shading, drag the square left indent marker ...

... or the right indent marker.

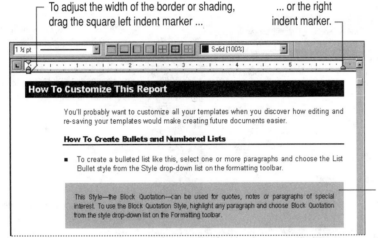

To change the spacing between the text and the border, see the following tip.

 Adjust the distance from the text to the edge of the border or shaded area If you're working with a shaded area, first apply a border. (If you don't want the border to show, color it white.) Then, click Borders And Shading (Format menu), and set the From Text option on the Borders tab.

Quick and easy lines At the start of a new paragraph, type three dashes (---) and press ENTER; Word automatically adds a line below that paragraph. If you don't see the line, click Options (Tools menu), click the AutoFormat tab, click AutoFormat As You Type, and then click Borders.

Want to remove the borders or shading? Select the item, and then select the appropriate option on the Borders toolbar.

Use WordArt for Special Text Effects
You can use WordArt to rotate or curve text, create 3-D effects, add drop shadows, and so on. For example, create banner headings, logos, or drop caps. For details, look up **WordArt** in the Word online index.

Example of WordArt

Multiple Columns

Word makes it easy to create newspaper-style columns for catalogs, newsletters, or other documents with multiple-column layouts.

To create multiple columns   First, switch to page layout view. If you want to format only part of the document in columns—say, just the glossary—select that text. Then, click the Columns button, and drag to highlight the number of columns you want.

 For Help, double-click.
In the Word online index look up:
multiple columns

Columns button

To adjust the column widths, drag the column boundaries on the ruler.

To create a banner heading that spans the columns, see the following tip.

To force one column to end and start a new one, click Break (Insert menu), and then click Column Break.

See only one column?   Switch to page layout view or print preview.

Create a banner heading   At the beginning of the leftmost column, type your heading and press ENTER. Then, select the heading, click the Columns button, and then click the single-column layout.

Create columns of unequal width   Click Columns (Format menu), and then click the Left or Right preset option. For details, look up **multiple columns** in the Word online index.

Columns of unequal width

Create a "Document Within a Document"

You may have noticed the dotted section breaks (visible in normal view) that separate a banner heading from the multiple-column layout. In Word, you can use section breaks to create different layouts within an individual document. For example, from section to section you can modify the margins, headers and footers, page numbers, page orientation, and so on. For details, look up **sections** in the Word online index.

Frames for "Desktop Publishing" Effects

A frame is a box of text or graphics that you can position anywhere on the page. For example, use frames to wrap text around a picture or to position side heads in the margin.

To insert a frame First, switch to page layout view. If you want to frame existing text or graphics, select the item and click Frame (Insert menu). Or, insert an empty frame and fill it in as shown in the following illustration.

For Help, double-click.
In the Word online index look up:
frames
hyphenation
drop caps

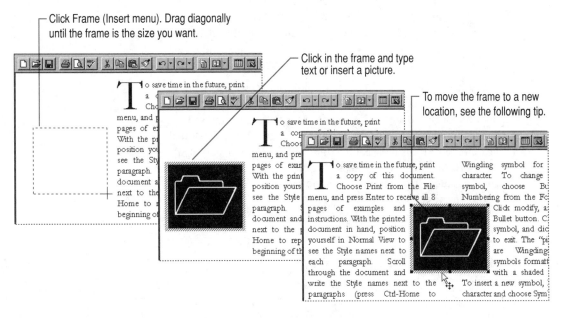

Click Frame (Insert menu). Drag diagonally until the frame is the size you want.

Click in the frame and type text or insert a picture.

To move the frame to a new location, see the following tip.

Want to move a frame? Select the frame by clicking its cross-hatched border. Then point to the frame; when the pointer looks like a four-headed arrow, drag the frame to a new location. If you want to position the frame in a precise location, select it and click Frame (Format menu).

Planning to wrap text around a frame? To create crisp, "squared off" text edges around the frame, apply justified alignment to the text. To tighten up spacing beween words, click Hyphenation (Tools menu).

Create a Drop Cap
To start any paragraph with a large, decorative letter, click in the paragraph, and then click Drop Cap (Format menu).

To save time in the future, print a copy of this document. Chose Print from the File menu, and press

Let Word Do the Formatting for You

Wouldn't it be great if you could just sit back and let Word quickly cruise through your document and "clean up" its formatting? You can—with the AutoFormat feature. AutoFormat applies consistent styles to headings, body text, bulleted lists, and so on. AutoFormat also makes other minor fixes, such as turning straight quotation marks into "smart" quotes.

AutoFormat behind the scenes By default, AutoFormat is already "on." For example, if you've created a bulleted or numbered list, or typed three dashes to add a line, you've seen AutoFormat in action. To control which "behind the scenes" changes AutoFormat makes, click Options (Tools menu), click the AutoFormat tab, and then make sure AutoFormat As You Type is "checked."

AutoFormat on demand To have AutoFormat "clean up" your document all at once, click the AutoFormat button. Or, click AutoFormat (Format menu) to accept or reject each proposed change. To control which "on demand" changes AutoFormat makes, click Options (Tools menu), click the AutoFormat tab, and then make sure AutoFormat is "checked." Once your document has been "autoformatted," you can use the Style Gallery to quickly switch between professional document designs.

For Help, double-click.
In the Word online index look up:
AutoFormat
Style Gallery

AutoFormat button

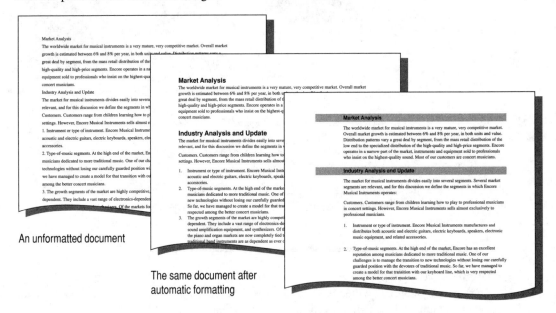

An unformatted document

The same document after automatic formatting

The document after applying the contemporary report template in the Style Gallery

Reuse Your Custom Formatting

You've probably already created custom formatting, say, a heading with white text on a black background. Instead of recreating this formatting each time you want to add another heading, just save the formats as a *style*. Then, you can apply the style to other text with a few mouse clicks.

 For Help, double-click.
In the Word online index look up:
styles
copying formatting

To create a style, format a paragraph the way you want, click in it ...

... click in the Style box, type a new name for the style, and then press ENTER.

To apply the style to another paragraph, select it, and then click the style in the Style box.

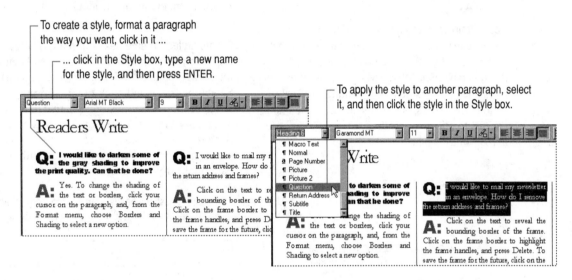

 Want to reformat a style? First, select a paragraph that has the style you want to change. Then, apply the new formats. Double-click in the Style box and press ENTER. Word automatically reformats all other text that has the same style.

Copy Formatting in a Flash

If you don't want to bother with creating styles, you can copy character formats from one area of text to another. Just select text with the formats you want to copy, click the Format Painter button, and then drag over the destination text to "paint" the formats onto it.

Format Painter button

Want to copy formatting to more than one area of text?

Double-click the Format Painter button, and then drag over each area of text you want. When you finish copying formats, click the Format Painter button.

Put It All Together: Design a "Facing Pages" Layout

Do you plan to print a document, such as a handbook, on both sides of the page and then bind it? If so, you might want to optimize the design for a "facing pages" layout (also called a "two-page spread").

Create "mirror" margins That is, the margins on the left page exactly mirror the margins on the right page. Click Page Setup (File menu), click the Margins tab, click Mirror Margins, and then set the inside and outside margin values. To include a "gutter," or extra space that's added to the inside margins to allow for binding, set the gutter value on the Margins tab.

Specify different headers and footers for odd and even pages Click Header And Footer (View menu), click the Page Setup button, click the Layout tab, and then click Different Odd And Even. Then, create the headers and footers as usual.

Create styles for side heads or margin notes First, format a paragraph the way you want. Then, select the paragraph and click Frame (Insert menu). Select the frame and click Frame (Format menu). Set a left horizontal position relative to the page, and then set the distance from text to .25 inches. Set a 0 (zero) vertical position relative to the paragraph, and then move the frame with the paragraph. If you want, set an exact frame width.

Use "negative" indents to push the headers out into the margins, and then align the even header on the left and the odd header on the right.

Include the part title in the even-page header and the chapter title in the odd-page header.

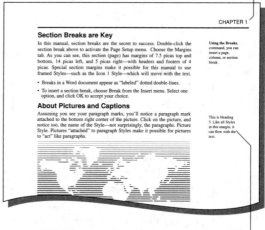

With mirror margins, you can create extra-wide outside margins and position side heads, pictures, and margin notes in them.

Next Steps

To	See
Insert symbols and special characters, such as ® or an em dash (—)	**symbols** or **special characters** in the Word online index
Set tab stops	**tabs** in the Word online index
Find out more about multiple columns and framed graphics	"Create a Simple Newsletter," page 141
Include a chart	"Add a Chart to a Document or Presentation," page 223
Add fractions, exponents, integrals, and other mathematical elements	**Equation Editor** in the Word online index
Add a watermark	"Create Letterhead and Matching Envelopes," page 133
Learn about formatting text for viewing online	"Create an Online Manual," page 342

Create a Mailing

Send a Form Letter to People on Your Mailing List

You probably need to send out lots of letters to promote your products or services, raise funds, collect payments, keep club members or employees informed, and so on. You don't have time to type a personalized letter for each person—but you don't want to send out a generic "Dear Valued Customer" letter either.

Word has the solution: It's a snap to use the Mail Merge Helper to set up and print form letters and matching mailing labels in a matter of minutes.

Key Features

 Mail Merge Helper

Get addresses from these sources, or create a simple mailing list.

Write a generic letter, and then merge the addresses to create personalized form letters—one for each person.

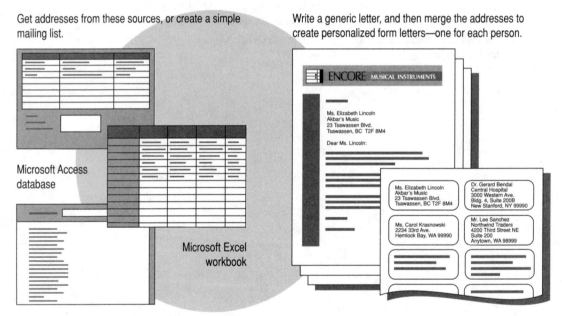

Microsoft Access database

Microsoft Excel workbook

Electronic personal address book

You can also merge the addresses to create a mailing label for each letter.

Write the Form Letter

Start by writing the basic form letter—the generic text you want to send to each person on your mailing list. Don't include names and addresses, since they'll be inserted automatically from the mailing list. To write the letter, you can use the Letter Wizard, a letter template, or start from scratch. For details, see "Write a Business Letter," page 120.

Then, click Mail Merge (Tools menu) to use the Mail Merge Helper to start the mail merge.

For Help, double-click.
In the Word online index look up:
form letters
mail merge

With the form letter on the screen ...

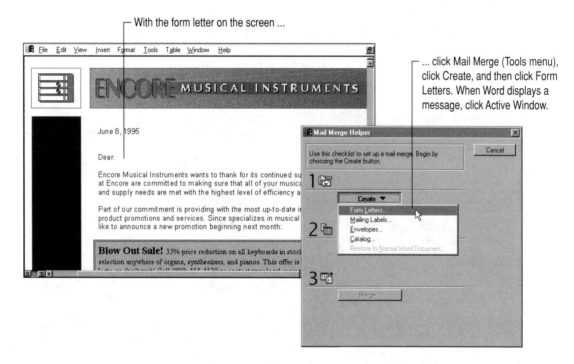

... click Mail Merge (Tools menu), click Create, and then click Form Letters. When Word displays a message, click Active Window.

Specify or Create the Mailing List

Where should you store the mailing list?   If your list is short and you don't plan to update it frequently, you might want to create the list in Word (as explained in this section). For longer lists that require frequent updates, use your Microsoft Exchange personal address book or Schedule+ Contact List, or Microsoft Excel. For full relational database capabilities, use Microsoft Access. For details, see "Next Steps" later in this topic.

For Help, double-click. In the Word online index look up: **data source for mail merging**

Here's how to specify or create the mailing list   In the Mail Merge Helper dialog box, click Get Data.

- If you already have addresses in your Microsoft Exchange personal address book or Schedule+ Contact List, click Use Address Book, select the item you want, and then skip ahead to the next section.

- If you already have a mailing list in Microsoft Excel, Microsoft Access, or another data source, click Open Data Source, select the mailing list, and then skip ahead to the next section.

- If you want to create the mailing list from scratch using Word, click Create Data Source and follow these instructions.

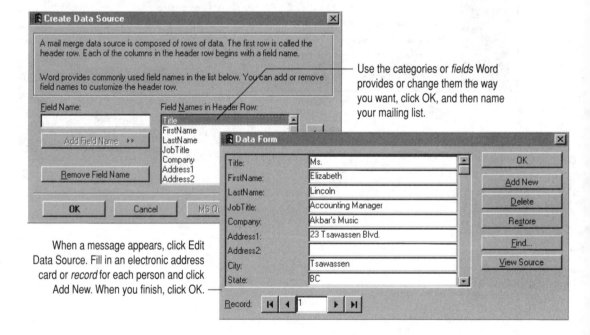

Use the categories or *fields* Word provides or change them the way you want, click OK, and then name your mailing list.

When a message appears, click Edit Data Source. Fill in an electronic address card or *record* for each person and click Add New. When you finish, click OK.

What should your mailing list contain? Don't stop at using just names and addresses to personalize form letters. You can include other types of customer data, such as phone numbers, products purchased, sales representative to contact, and so on.

Need to update the mailing list? For example, you might want to add the names and addresses of new customers, or add another field, such as fax number or purchase order number. If you've stored the mailing list in Word, look up **editing mail merge data source** in the Word online index. If you've stored the mailing list in your Microsoft Exchange personal address book or Schedule+ Contact List, Microsoft Excel, or Microsoft Access, see "Next Steps" later in this topic.

Insert Merge Fields into the Form Letter

Now that you've created the generic form letter and specified a mailing list, you'll insert *merge fields* or placeholders that tell Word where to put the names, addresses, and other personalized information.

For Help, double-click.
In the Word online index look up:
merge fields

Click where you want to insert a merge field. Then click the Insert Merge Field button and click a field.

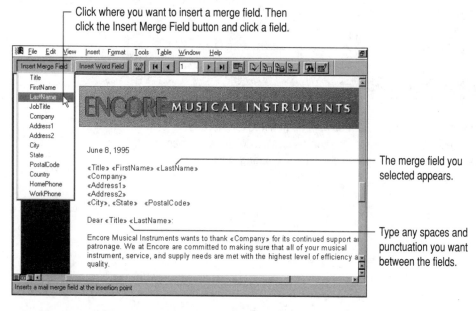

The merge field you selected appears.

Type any spaces and punctuation you want between the fields.

 Want to emphasize the personalized information? Select a merge field and apply bold, italic, or any other format.

Save the generic form letter for future use When you've inserted all the merge fields—and added any text and graphics you want to include in each letter—save the form letter.

Target the Form Letter Recipients

To get the best response at the lowest cost, you probably don't want to send a form letter to everyone on your mailing list. For example, you might want to zero in on just your Canadian customers.

You can set up a simple *query*—or set of criteria—that tells Word to find and separate out just the address cards you want to merge. Here's how: After you insert the merge fields, click the Mail Merge button on the Mail Merge toolbar, and then click Query Options. On the Filter Records tab, set up your query. For details, look up **filtering records** in the Word online index.

 For Help, double-click.
In the Word online index look up:
filtering records

Mail Merge button

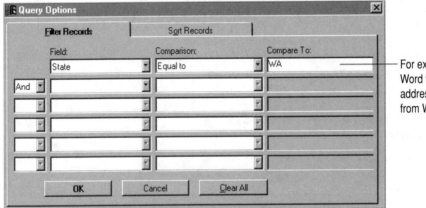

For example, this query tells Word to merge only the address cards of customers from Washington state.

 Want to use a query you've already set up in Microsoft Access?
When you open the data source, you can select Microsoft Access tables or queries. For details, look up **queries** or **tables, creating** in the Microsoft Access online index.

Merge the Mailing List with the Form Letter

To preview a few letters To make sure the information is merged correctly, click the View Merged Data button on the Mail Merge toolbar. Then, click the Next Record button to preview each letter.

To start the merge Click the Merge To Printer button on the Mail Merge toolbar. Word prints one personalized letter for each name and address retrieved from the mailing list. For more mail merge options, you can return to the Mail Merge Helper instead of clicking the Merge To Printer button; just click Mail Merge (Tools menu), and then click the Merge button.

 For Help, double-click.
In the Word online index look up:
merging documents (mail merge)

Merge To Printer button

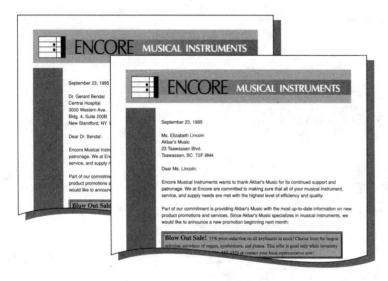

 Want to merge the letters to a document instead of directly to the printer? Click the Merge To New Document button on the Mail Merge toolbar. Word places the resulting letters in a single document, separating the letters with section breaks. Then, you can review the letters before you print, or save a permanent copy of them. To print an individual letter, specify its section number in the Pages box in the Print dialog box (for example, type **s3** to print the third letter).

Why isn't the first address merged from your Microsoft Excel worksheet? Word doesn't merge data from the first row in the worksheet because it assumes that this row contains the field names (FirstName, City, and so on). To fix this problem, add column labels to the worksheet and then repeat the merge.

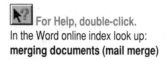

Merge To New Document button

Print Addresses on Mailing Labels

You can merge names and addresses from your mailing list and print them on Avery® labels or other types of mailing labels using a dot-matrix or laser printer. The procedure is similar to merging into form letters, so here's just a quick check list to follow.

First, set up a "form" for the mailing labels: Open a new document, click Mail Merge (Tools menu), click Create, and then click Mailing Labels. When a message appears, click Active Window. Click Get Data and select the data source: your mailing list or address book. When a message appears, click Set Up Main Document.

Select the label options you want, and click OK.

For Help, double-click. In the Word online index look up: **mailing labels**

Insert merge fields to put information where you want it on the labels, and then click OK.

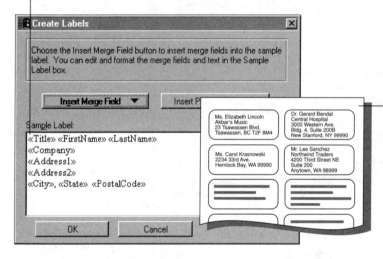

Check that your printer is ready to print the labels. Then click Merge, select any options, and click Merge.

 Want to print addresses on envelopes instead?   Look up **envelopes** in the Word online index.

Have you stored names and addresses in a Microsoft Excel list? From your Microsoft Excel list, you can run the Microsoft Access Report Wizard to create mailing labels. For details, see "Create Mailing Labels from a Microsoft Excel Address List," page 185.

Use Microsoft Access to Start the Merge

If you've stored your mailing list in Microsoft Access, you can start the mail merge from Microsoft Access instead of from Word.

Use Microsoft Access to create a query and start the merge To target the exact audience for the form letter, design a query that retrieves only the names and addresses you want. (For details, see "Evaluate Sales Performance in a Microsoft Access Database," page 458.) Then, in the Database window, select the query you just created. Click the OfficeLinks button, select Merge It, and follow the instructions on the screen.

Next, use Microsoft Word to create the form letter and complete the merge First, write the generic form letter. Then, insert the merge fields (see "Insert Merge Fields into the Form Letter" earlier in this topic). Finally, complete the merge (see "Merge the Mailing List with the Form Letter" earlier in this topic).

Then, use Microsoft Access to print matching mailing labels Select a query in the Database window, click the New Object button, click New Report, start the Label Wizard, and then follow the instructions on the screen.

Create a query to select the form letter recipients from your database.

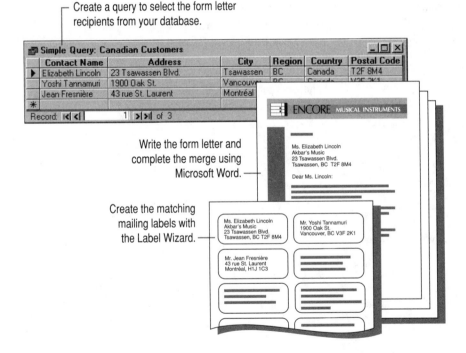

Write the form letter and complete the merge using Microsoft Word.

Create the matching mailing labels with the Label Wizard.

Next Steps

To	See
Print mailing labels using names and addresses stored in a Microsoft Excel list	"Create Mailing Labels from a Microsoft Excel Address List," page 185
Manage contacts with customers, including updating the mailing list and tracking responses from the form letter	"Manage Contacts with Schedule+," page 296
	"Create a Business Contact List in Microsoft Excel," page 300
	"Track Your Business Contacts in Microsoft Access," page 306
Schedule follow-up calls, sales visits, and demos	"Schedule an Appointment," page 314
Prepare a bid or quote (if your customers request it)	"Prepare a Customer Quote," page 427
Track new orders (if your form letter results in orders)	"Track Orders in a Shared Database," page 355
Print a report that summarizes how many new orders your form letter generated	"Create a Sales Summary," page 446
	"Create an Executive Sales Summary," page 473

Create Mailing Labels from a Microsoft Excel Address List

Use the Microsoft Access Label Wizard to Print Mailing Labels

Do you have a letter or promotional material that you'd like to send to your customers? If you have a list of names and addresses in a Microsoft Excel worksheet, you can use that information to quickly print mailing labels with Microsoft Access.

Key Features

- List
- Link Spreadsheet Wizard
- Label Wizard

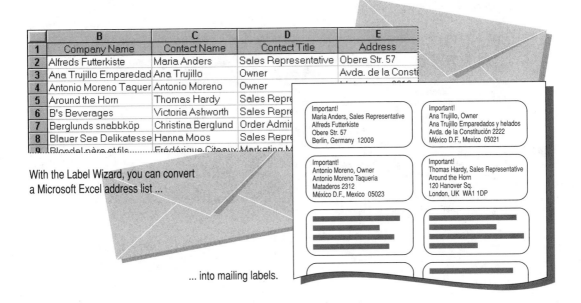

With the Label Wizard, you can convert a Microsoft Excel address list ...

... into mailing labels.

To complete the steps in this topic   You need to have either Microsoft Office Professional for Windows 95 or individual copies of Microsoft Access for Windows 95 and Microsoft Excel for Windows 95 installed. And, your Microsoft Excel worksheet must be set up as a list. For list format guidelines, look up **lists, creating** in the Microsoft Excel online index.

You can also create mailing labels using Word   For details, see "Create a Mailing," page 176.

Link Your Worksheet to a Microsoft Access Database

First, link your name and address worksheet into a Microsoft Access database.

Create an empty database   Start Microsoft Access, displaying the Microsoft Access dialog box. Click Blank Database, and then click OK. In the File New Database dialog box, type a name for the database, and then click Create.

Run the Link Spreadsheet Wizard   In the new database, click Link Tables (File menu, Get External Data submenu). In the Files Of Type list box, click Microsoft Excel, and browse to find your worksheet. Double-click the filename, and then follow the instructions that appear on your screen. Be sure to check Include Field Names On First Row. When the wizard finishes, click Open to view the linked table.

The Link Spreadsheet Wizard makes your Microsoft Excel list available as a Microsoft Access table.

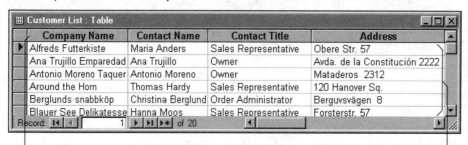

Company Name	Contact Name	Contact Title	Address
Alfreds Futterkiste	Maria Anders	Sales Representative	Obere Str. 57
Ana Trujillo Emparedad	Ana Trujillo	Owner	Avda. de la Constitución 2222
Antonio Moreno Taquer	Antonio Moreno	Owner	Mataderos 2312
Around the Horn	Thomas Hardy	Sales Representative	120 Hanover Sq.
Berglunds snabbköp	Christina Berglund	Order Administrator	Berguvsvägen 8
Blauer See Delikatesse	Hanna Moos	Sales Representative	Forsterstr. 57

The column headings in your worksheet become the field names in the table.

Each row of your list becomes a record.

Create the Mailing Labels

To create mailing labels, click the arrow next to the New Object button, and then click New Report. Double-click Label Wizard, and follow the wizard's instructions.

New Object button

— The fields are the column headings from your list.

— Select each field you want, and then click here.

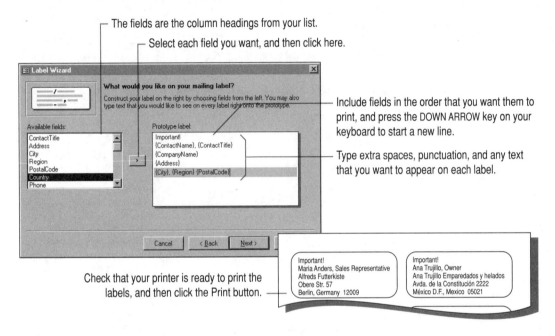

Include fields in the order that you want them to print, and press the DOWN ARROW key on your keyboard to start a new line.

Type extra spaces, punctuation, and any text that you want to appear on each label.

Check that your printer is ready to print the labels, and then click the Print button.

What if the labels don't print properly? Get troubleshooting assistance by looking up **troubleshooting, printing** in the Microsoft Access online index.

Include new customers in your next mailing When you update your linked worksheet, your changes are reflected in the database. To include new customers, just open the mailing label report.

Next Steps

To	See
Write a form letter to send to the people on your address list	"Create a Mailing," page 176

PART 3

In Triplicate

Printed and Online Business Forms

Contents

What's the Best Way to Create a Form?

With the Office applications, you can create many different *forms* and use them in widely varying ways. A form is a framework for a document you use repeatedly, for example, an expense report or an order form. In a database, a form is a view you can use to enter, edit, or browse data.

You may use paper forms, or you may already be creating your own, although chances are you call them something different. If you open an existing document, save it with a different filename, and fill in information such as expenses or customer data, you are using the document as a form.

There are several topics in this book that discuss creating and using forms. Use the following table to decide which topic, and which use of forms, is closest to the work you want to do.

If you want to	Use this application	See
Create a form to be filled out on paper or online, which does not require calculation or entry into a database	Microsoft Word	"Create a Printed or Online Form in Word," page 191
Create a form for entering and calculating worksheet data, which can be sent automatically to a database	Microsoft Excel	"Create a Form for Online Customer Quotes," page 198
Create a form for entering, editing, and storing data, or for browsing data in a database	Microsoft Access	"Create a Great Looking Product Form," page 400

Create a Printed or Online Form in Word

Your company doesn't have to live with poorly designed forms, and you don't have to type and retype information as the form is processed. Instead, create your own online or printed form that meets your company's specific needs. Then, if those needs change, you can quickly update or modify the form. And if your form is online, users can process the form by routing it electronically.

You can create the form so that it automatically verifies and updates entries, offers custom Help instructions to users, and allows users to change only specific parts of the form.

Key Features

 Forms

Tables

Author creates online form.

Users fill in and share the form electronically, or they can print it and complete it manually.

Build the Form

Design and create the form   Sketch a layout for the form first, or use an existing form as a guide for designing the new form. You might want to note the parts of the form you want to protect from changes. (Form protection is covered later in this topic.)

Start by clicking the New button.

Build the form using tables   Click the Insert Table button to insert a table that has the same number of rows and columns as your sketch or example. If your information requires several tables with different numbers of columns and rows, separate individual tables with blank paragraphs. Later, if you want to join the tables, just select and delete the paragraph mark between them by pressing DELETE.

 For Help, double-click.
In the Word online index look up:
tables
splitting tables

New button

Insert Table button

To choose a line style, click here.

To add a border to all or part of the active cell, click one of these border buttons.

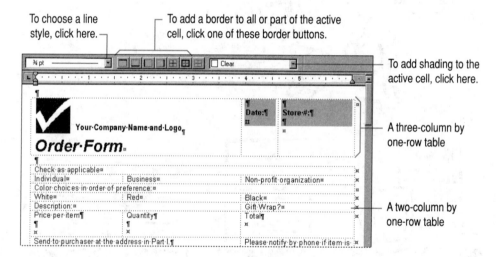

To add shading to the active cell, click here.

A three-column by one-row table

A two-column by one-row table

 Need to break up an existing table?   Select where you want to break the table, and then click Split Table (Table menu). To join or split existing cells, select the cells you want to change, and then click Merge Cells or Split Cells (Table menu).

Want to change the orientation for part of the form?   Select the part of the form you want to change, click Page Setup (File menu), click the Paper Size tab, and then click Landscape.

So that others can use the form online   Make sure that you save the form as a template. To do so, click Document Template in the Save As Type box. For details, look up **templates** in the Word online index.

Make the form visually easy to follow   Add shading and borders to key elements in the form. To apply either shading or borders, select the item you want to emphasize, click the Borders button, and choose the options you want. For details, look up **shading** or **borders** in the Word online index.

Borders button

Add Fill-Ins, Drop-Down Lists, and Check Boxes

Now add fill-ins (also called text form fields), drop-down lists, and check boxes to your form. You can insert any of these items, or fields, within text or tables.

To quickly insert a field, use the Forms toolbar and click the button you want. To display the Forms toolbar, click Toolbars (View menu), and then click Forms.

For Help, double-click.
In the Word online index look up:
check boxes
drop-down form fields
form fields

Use the Forms toolbar to quickly add fill-ins,
check boxes, and drop-down lists.

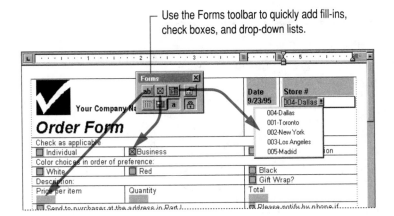

Want to test fields, such as drop-downs, that users will fill in online? First protect your document by clicking the Protect Form button on the Forms toolbar, and then test the fields. When you want to go back to writing or editing the form, click the Protect Form button again to unprotect the form. Once you unprotect the form, any data you entered to test fields will be cleared.

Need to calculate numbers in fields? To add a row or column of numbers, or to complete another calculation, use a calculation field. Click Form Field (Insert menu), and then click the Options button. If your form contains mostly numbers, such as financial information, it may be best to create the form in Microsoft Excel. For details on creating an online Microsoft Excel form, see "Create a Form for Online Customer Quotes," page 198.

Want to quickly change field settings? If you want to change, for example, the size of a check box or the maximum number of characters in a text form field, double-click any field on your form. Word displays the appropriate options dialog box in which you can make changes.

Control What Users Enter on the Form

Use text fields to determine the kind of information you want users to enter. Following are brief descriptions of the different kinds of text form fields. For details, look up **form fields** in the Word online index.

Regular Text Use when you want the user to enter any type of text—text, numbers, or symbols.

Number Use when you want the user to enter a number in the field.

Date Use when you want the user to enter a date.

Current Date and Current Time Use when you want Word to automatically supply the current date or time.

Calculation Use when you want Word to sum a column or row of numbers or complete another calculation. Word uses the =(Formula) field to perform calculations. Type the expression for the calculation in the Expression box.

In Case Your Users Need Help

You can make it easier for your users to fill in the form by adding Help text for one or all of the fields on your form.

To include Help text for a text form field, for example, double-click the field, and then, in the Text Form Field Options dialog box, click the Add Help Text button. Click the Status Bar or Help Key (F1) tab, and then type the instructions.

For Help, double-click.
In the Word online index look up:
filling in online forms
online forms, Help text

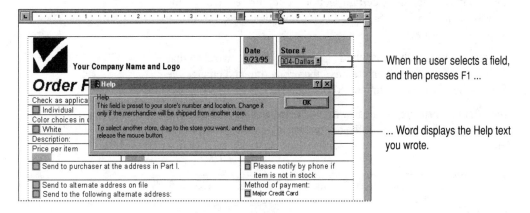

When the user selects a field, and then presses F1 ...

... Word displays the Help text you wrote.

Additional instructions for users Be sure to tell users that when they use the form online they can name and save it just as they would any other Word document.

Protect the Form from Changes

Protect the whole form Before you make an online form available to users, protect it. Protection allows users to fill in the form, but also prevents them from changing the form's layout and its standard elements. To protect the form, click the Protect Form button on the Forms toolbar.

Protect sections in a form If you inserted sections within the form and want to protect only certain sections, click Protect Document (Tools menu), click the Sections button, and then click the sections you want to protect.

Protect the form with a password You can add a password so that only users who know it can remove the protection and change the form. Click Protect Document (Tools menu).

Important Be sure to use a password you will remember because if you forget it, you will not be able to remove protection from the form to make changes.

For Help, double-click. In the Word online index look up: **protecting online forms**

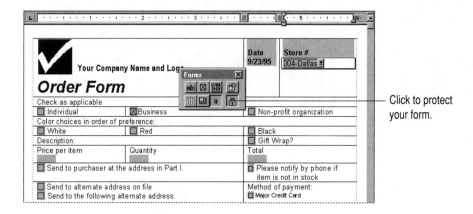

Click to protect your form.

Automate Your Form

Macros can help validate information that users enter into the form. For example, you can assign a macro to check the information a user types, or to update fields when the field is activated or when the user moves to another field. For details, look up **macros, online forms** in the Word online index.

For example, if your form includes a field for Marital Status, you could insert two check box form fields—"Married" and "Single." Then, for the "Married" field you could assign an exit macro to see if the box is selected. If it is, the macro could activate a "Name of Spouse" field.

For details on writing macros, see "Automate Repetitive Tasks in Word," page 536. Also see

Chapter 9, "More WordBasic Techniques," in the *Microsoft Word Developer's Kit*. (Available wherever computer books are sold and directly from Microsoft Press.)

Once you've created a macro for your form, double-click the field to which you want to assign it. Select the macro from the list in the Run Macro On boxes, and then select any other options you want.

Make sure you save the form as a template. This ensures that any macros you add will automatically run or be available when your users fill in the form. Click Save As (File menu), and then click Document Template in the Save As Type box.

Next Steps

To	See
Send the completed form to others for approval or review	"Have Your Team Review a Word Document," page 333
Send or route a document through e-mail	"Share Documents Electronically," page 326
Format the form	"Make Your Word Document Look Great," page 161
Write a macro	"Automate Repetitive Tasks in Word," page 536

Create a Form for Online Customer Quotes

Track Data from Microsoft Excel Workbooks to the Database of Your Choice

When you have data that you routinely enter into forms in Microsoft Excel, you can collect the data and store it in a database automatically, without rekeying. The Template Wizard With Data Tracking transforms a workbook into an online template or form and links it to a designated database. Then, each time the form is filled out and saved as a separate workbook, its data can be automatically entered into the database where you can create reports, filter, and summarize the compiled data, to make the best use of it.

Key Features

 Template Wizard
With Data Tracking

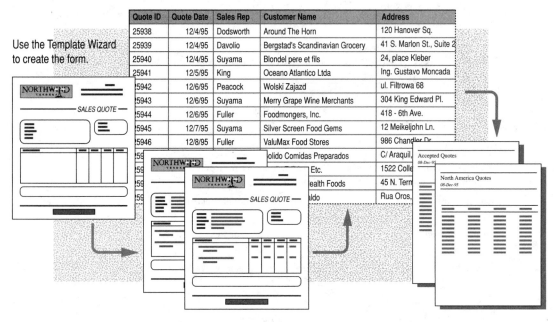

Use the Template Wizard to create the form.

Collect data from Microsoft Excel workbooks in a database.

Then generate reports and PivotTables from the database.

Important   You must have the Template Wizard installed to complete the tasks in this topic. To link templates to databases other than Microsoft Excel, you must have Data Access Objects (DAO) and the appropriate ODBC driver installed. If you need to install the Template Wizard, DAO or an ODBC driver, rerun Setup. To load the Template Wizard or DOA add-in, click Add-Ins (Tools menu). For details, look up **installing add-in programs** or **loading an add-in** in the Microsoft Excel online index.

Turn Your Form into a Data-Tracking Template

Open the workbook that contains the form you want to base your template on. If you have not created the workbook yet, do so before using the Template Wizard With Data Tracking.

Once your workbook is ready, click Template Wizard (Data menu) to start the Template Wizard. In step 1, give the template a name. In step 2, specify the database you want to link to and its location. If the database does not exist yet, the wizard creates it in the file type and location you specify.

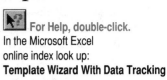 **For Help, double-click.** In the Microsoft Excel online index look up: **Template Wizard With Data Tracking**

An existing workbook can be the basis ...

... for the form you create with the Template Wizard.

Delete data you don't want included in the standard form.

Which database file types can you link to? The Template Wizard can link forms to databases in Microsoft Excel, Microsoft Access, FoxPro®, Paradox®, dBASE®, and SQL Server. When necessary, new databases can be created in these applications, except SQL Server. For details, look up **Template Wizard** and **ODBC drivers** in the Microsoft Excel online index.

Prevent unwanted changes to the form If coworkers will be adding data to the form and you want to make sure certain information cannot be changed, you can protect those cells that should not be changed. For example, protect cells containing formulas so that all calculations are correct and consistent. For details, look up **cells, protecting** in the Microsoft Excel online index.

Make the form attractive and easy to read Use formatting to emphasize important information and make the form easy to fill out. For example, add borders, pictures, or shading; change the font, style, and size of text; and format the numbers. For details, see "Make Your Microsoft Excel Worksheet Look Great," page 206.

Save time by using a built-in template Microsoft Excel provides a set of built-in templates intended for small businesses. Some of these templates are already linked to companion databases; just use the Template Wizard to adapt them if necessary. For details, see "The Template You Need May Already Exist," later in this topic.

Link Template Cells to Database Fields

In step 3 of the Template Wizard, specify which worksheet cells map to particular database fields. The wizard looks for labels in the worksheet and proposes database field names. You can accept the proposed field names or change them as needed.

For Help, double-click.
In the Microsoft Excel
online index look up:
cells, linking to database fields

You specify the cells in the form that link to database fields.

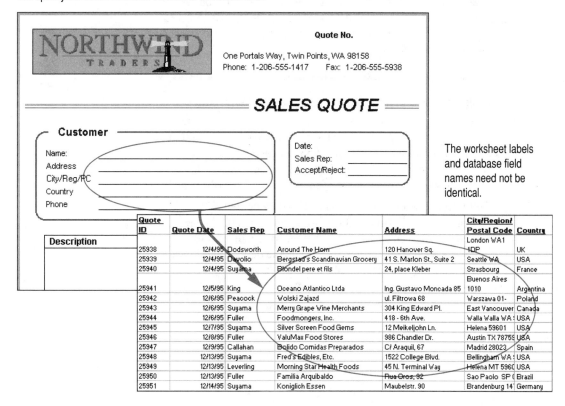

The worksheet labels and database field names need not be identical.

Add a routing slip for distributing the form   If you want to route the form electronically, you have the option of adding a routing slip in step 5 of the Template Wizard. Other ways you can distribute the form include sending it through electronic mail and posting it on the network. For details, see "Share Documents Electronically," page 326.

Need to make changes to your template?   To modify a template you've created, open the template workbook (in the Open dialog box, hold down SHIFT while you click OK and then start the Template Wizard.) You can change the template's name, the database location, cell-to-database field linking, and the routing slip. However, you cannot add fields to a template you've already created.

Link Data from Other Workbooks to the Database

If you have other workbooks whose data corresponds to the workbook you are basing your template on, you can link them all to one database. The data must be arranged in the same way as the workbook the template is based on. Specify the duplicate workbooks in step 4 of the Template Wizard.

This option is useful when you have already copied an existing workbook (in effect using it as a template), changed the data, and saved each copy with a new filename. Using the Template Wizard allows you to compile the data from all the workbooks into the same database.

Help Others Use the Form to Add Database Records

Now that the template is created and ready to use, others can fill out the form, save each completed form as a workbook, and send the data to the database. To fill out the form, click New (File menu), select the tab containing the template, and double-click the template name.

The next step is to add data to the template fields, and then save the workbook. Next, specify whether to create a new record in the database or close the workbook without updating the database. If the workbook has been saved previously, specify whether to update the existing record, create a new record, or close without updating.

Quote ID	Quote Date	Sales Rep	Customer Name	Address
25938	12/4/95	Dodsworth	Around The Horn	120 Hanover Sq.
25939	12/4/95	Davolio	Bergstad's Scandinavian Grocery	41 S. Marlon St., Suite 2
25940	12/4/95	Suyama	Blondel pere et fils	24, place Kleber
25941	12/5/95	King	Oceano Atlantico Ltda	Ing. Gustavo Moncada
25942	12/6/95	Peacock	Wolski Zajazd	ul. Filtrowa 68
25943	12/6/95	Suyama	Merry Grape Wine Merchants	304 King Edward Pl.
25944	12/6/95	Fuller	Foodmongers, Inc.	418 - 6th Ave.
25945	12/7/95	Suyama	Silver Screen Food Gems	12 Meikeljohn Ln.
25946	12/8/95	Fuller	ValuMax Food Stores	986 Chandler Dr.
25947	12/9/95	Callahan	Bolido Comidas Preparados	C/ Araquil, 67
25948	12/10/95	Suyama	Fred's Edibles, Etc.	1522 College Blvd.
25949	12/10/95	Leverling	Morning Star Health Foods	45 N. Terminal Way
25950	12/10/95	Fuller	Familia Arquibaldo	Rua Oros, 92

Open the template and fill out the form to enter data in the database.

Find and calculate the data you need Use the Microsoft Excel lookup functions and advanced filtering to pull together quickly the information needed for a customer quote or similar form. For details, see "Prepare a Customer Quote," page 427.

How do you delete a record from the database? Once you have sent a record to the database, you can delete it anytime you are working in the database. However, you cannot delete records while using the Template Wizard.

If sending or updating a record in the database is interrupted There is no change to the information in the database; this prevents entry of incomplete records. Try again later to send or update the record.

Create Reports from the Database

Summarize and analyze the data entered from forms into your database by creating reports. In Office, you can also create PivotTables. For example, you might want to see only the customer quotes that have been accepted, or look at the quote data by product, by salesperson, or by country.

 For Help, double-click.
In the Microsoft Excel online index look up:
creating PivotTables

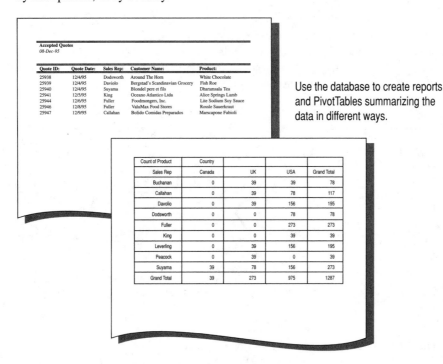

Use the database to create reports and PivotTables summarizing the data in different ways.

Learn more about creating reports and working in databases To find out what kinds of reports you can create, see the documentation for your database application. For examples of reports created in Microsoft Excel, see "Create a Detailed Sales Report," page 439, and "Create a Sales Summary," page 446. For an example of creating a report in Microsoft Access, see "Create a Price List," page 420.

What's a PivotTable? In Microsoft Excel, a PivotTable is an interactive worksheet table that quickly summarizes large amounts of data using a format and calculation methods you choose. For details, see "Create a Sales Summary," page 446.

The Template You Need May Already Exist

Microsoft Excel provides a set of flexible, attractive, and easy-to-use templates that you may be able to use to create workbooks you need, quickly and easily.

The built-in templates are designed with small businesses in mind, and they are easily customizable for a variety of purposes.

The following templates have already been created with the Template Wizard With Data Tracking. They are linked to companion databases located in the Library folder within the Microsoft Excel folder.

- Invoice
- Purchase Order
- Timecard
- Expense Statement
- Sales Quote
- Change Request

Use these templates as they are, or run the Template Wizard to adapt them as needed, for example, to link to different fields.

In addition to linked templates, the following built-in templates are provided.

- Financial Planner
- Personal Budget Planner
- Loan Manager
- Car Leasing Manager

To use built-in templates, you may need to install them first by running Microsoft Excel Setup. To work with a template, click New (File menu), click the Spreadsheet Solutions tab; and then select the template you want.

For details on working with templates in Office, see "About Creating and Opening Documents and Databases," page 46.

Next Steps

To	See
Find out about different types of forms you can create with Office applications	"What's the Best Way to Create a Form?" page 190
Learn more about alternative ways to store data	"Where Should You Store Your Contact Information?" page 294

Make Your Microsoft Excel Worksheet Look Great

Plain text and numbers on a worksheet do the job, but additional formatting can greatly enhance your worksheet's presentability. There are many ways you can change the way a worksheet looks, including:

- Format text, numbers, spacing, and alignment in cells for increased readability.

- Format cell colors, patterns, and borders for better organization.

- Copy formatting from one range of cells to another to reduce repetitive work.

- Save your custom formatting to apply to other worksheets for consistency.

- Apply an *autoformat* for utmost efficiency.

Key Features

Formatting

Format Painter

Styles

	A	B	C	D	E
1	1995 Book Tour Results				
2	City	Date	Fee		
3	New York	1/23/95			
4	Boston	1/25/95			
5	Washingto	1/27/95			
6	January Total				
7	Miami	2/4/95			
8	Memphis	2/6/95			
9	Atlanta	2/8/95			
10	February Total				
11	Los Angele	3/5/95			
12	San Franc	3/7/95			
13	Seattle	3/11/95			
14	March Total				

	A	B	C	D	E
1	**1995 Book Tour Results**				
3	**City**	**Date**	**Fee**	**Attendance**	**Books Sold**
4	New York	23-Jan-95	$ 1,180	205	147
5	Boston	25-Jan-95	$ 821	385	146
6	Washington, D.C.	27-Jan-95	$ 1,724	499	151
7	*January Total*		$ 3,725	1089	444
8	Miami	4-Feb-95	$ 757	221	41
9	Memphis	6-Feb-95	$ 910	93	45
10	Atlanta	8-Feb-95	$ 1,880	149	95
11	*February Total*		$ 3,547	463	181
12	Los Angeles	5-Mar-95	$ 941	265	47
13	San Francisco	7-Mar-95	$ 904	171	145
14	Seattle	11-Mar-95	$ 936	279	109
15	*March Total*		$ 2,781	715	301
16	**Tour Grand Totals**		**$ 10,053**	**2267**	**926**

A formatted worksheet communicates more clearly.

Use the Best Number Format

There are two ways to apply specific formats to numbers in Microsoft Excel.

 For Help, double-click. In the Microsoft Excel online index look up: **numbers, formatting**

- **Cells command** To select a number format to apply to the selection, select a cell or range of cells, click Cells (Format menu), and click the Number tab.

- **Formatting in place** When you enter a number or date, type it in the format you want, including numeric punctuation. Microsoft Excel will then automatically apply the built-in number format, if one exists, that corresponds to what you have typed to the selected cell or cells.

― Abbreviated months date format

	A	B	C	D	E
1	1995 Book Tour Results				
2	City	Date	Fee	Attendanc	Books Sold
3	New York	23-Jan-95	$ 1,180	205	147
4	Boston	25-Jan-95	$ 821	385	146
5	Washingto	27-Jan-95	$ 1,724	499	151
6	January Total		$ 3,725	1089	444
7	Miami	4-Feb-95	$ 757	221	41
8	Memphis	6-Feb-95	$ 910	93	45
9	Atlanta	8-Feb-95	$ 1,880	149	95
10	February Total		$ 3,547	463	181
11	Los Angele	5-Mar-95	$ 941	265	47
12	San Franc	7-Mar-95	$ 904	171	145
13	Seattle	11-Mar-95	$ 936	279	109
14	March Total		$ 2,781	715	301

― Currency format without decimals

― General format (no specific number format applied)

 Number too wide for cell? If you see #### in a cell, this means the cell contains a number that is too long to display. Instead of changing to a smaller font size or decreasing the number of decimal places, you can widen the column by dragging the border in the column heading. See "Adjust the Spacing and Alignment of Data," later in this topic.

Decrease Decimal button

Custom number formats You can create your own custom number formats using special formatting codes. For information about number formatting codes, see **custom number formats** in the Microsoft Excel online index.

Common list formats If you need to format cells to display ZIP Codes®, phone numbers, or social security numbers, click the Number tab (Cells command, Format menu), and select the Special category.

Make Data and Text Clear and Readable

You have complete control over the fonts used in your worksheets. The Formatting toolbar contains most of the tools you need to apply font styles to selected cells. For more options, click Cells (Format menu), and click the Font tab.

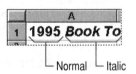 **For Help, double-click.** In the Microsoft Excel online index look up: **formatting cells** **formatting text**

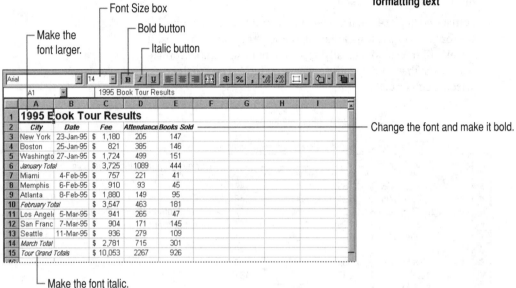

Font Size box

Bold button

Italic button

Make the font larger.

Change the font and make it bold.

Make the font italic.

 Formatting individual characters You can format selected characters within a cell. Just select characters in the cell and make the changes you want using the toolbar or the Cells command.

Subtotals and outlines You can use the Subtotals command (Data menu) to help you automatically insert rows for subtotals, add subtotal formulas, and create an outline of your worksheet. For more information, see "Create a Detailed Sales Report," page 439.

Normal   Italic

Adjust the Spacing and Alignment of Data

To help distinguish different types of information in cells, adjust the alignment of cell contents using the alignment buttons on the Formatting toolbar. Insert rows and columns to set data or labels apart using the Rows or Columns commands (Insert menu). Adjust the width and height of rows and columns by dragging or double-clicking the line to the right of the column letter or below the row number in the header.

For Help, double-click.
In the Microsoft Excel online index look up:
aligning cell contents
cells, inserting and deleting

Heading in cell A1 centered across columns A through E

Text center aligned

Double-click to adjust the width of column to fit its widest entry.

	City	Date	Fee	Attendance	Books Sold
1	**1995 Book Tour Results**				
3	*City*	*Date*	*Fee*	*Attendance*	*Books Sold*
4	New York	23-Jan-95	$ 1,180	205	147
5	Boston	25-Jan-95	$ 821	385	146
6	Washington, D.C.	27-Jan-95	$ 1,724	499	151
7	*January Total*		$ 3,725	1089	444
8	Miami	4-Feb-95	$ 757	221	41
9	Memphis	6-Feb-95	$ 910	93	45
10	Atlanta	8-Feb-95	$ 1,880	149	95
11	*February Total*		$ 3,547	463	181
12	Los Angeles	5-Mar-95	$ 941	265	47
13	San Francisco	7-Mar-95	$ 904	171	145
14	Seattle	11-Mar-95	$ 936	279	109
15	*March Total*		$ 2,781	715	301
16	*Tour Grand Totals*		$ 10,053	2267	926

New row inserted

Text right-aligned

Centering across columns You can easily align titles across the top of a range of cells. Type the title in the leftmost cell in the range, select that range, and click the Center Across Columns button. The title is still in the leftmost cell, although it might not look like it.

Getting vertical You can rotate text or data to fit. Select the cell, click Cells (Format menu), and select orientation options on the Alignment tab.

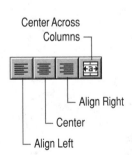

Center Across Columns

Align Right

Center

Align Left

Mock Indents

You can use narrow columns to create an "indented" effect.
Use shallow rows for similar spacing flexibility.

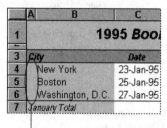

Use a narrow column to
create an indented effect.

Organize with Colors and Borders

Adding borders can greatly enhance the readability of your worksheet. Adding colors, patterns, and shading to cells improves readability and, at the same time, enhances the visual appeal of worksheets for presentation to others.

Apply borders and colors using buttons on the Formatting toolbar, or click Cells (Format menu), and then click the Border or Patterns tab.

For Help, double-click. In the Microsoft Excel online index look up:
borders
shading

	A	B	C	D	E
1	1995 *Book Tour Results*				
3	*City*	*Date*	*Fee*	*Attendance*	*Books Sold*
4	New York	23-Jan-95	$ 1,180	205	147
5	Boston	25-Jan-95	$ 821	385	146
6	Washington, D.C.	27-Jan-95	$ 1,724	499	151
7	*January Total*		$ 3,725	1089	444
8	Miami	4-Feb-95	$ 757	221	41
9	Memphis	6-Feb-95	$ 910	93	45
10	Atlanta	8-Feb-95	$ 1,880	149	95
11	*February Total*		$ 3,547	463	181
12	Los Angeles	5-Mar-95	$ 941	265	47
13	San Francisco	7-Mar-95	$ 904	171	145
14	Seattle	11-Mar-95	$ 936	279	109
15	*March Total*		$ 2,781	715	301
16	*Tour Grand Totals*		$ 10,053	2267	926

For emphasis, apply colors to cells.

Use borders to make the sheet more readable.

Turning off gridlines The gridlines on your screen are different than borders. Gridlines make it easier to distinguish individual cells on screen, but you can turn them off by clicking Options (Tools menu), clicking the View tab, and clearing the Gridlines box.

Printing gridlines Gridlines are normally turned off for printing. If you want to see gridlines in your printouts, click Page Setup (File menu), and select the Gridlines option on the Sheet tab.

Get Attention with Arrows and Shapes

Call attention to key information on your worksheet. With the Microsoft Excel drawing tools you can draw and format lines, boxes, circles, and text boxes that "float" over the worksheet. Draw ovals with no fill color to "circle" worksheet items you want to highlight.

To make the drawing tools available, click the Drawing button on the Standard toolbar to display the Drawing toolbar.

 For Help, double-click.
In the Microsoft Excel online index look up:
drawing objects, with Drawing tools

Drawing button

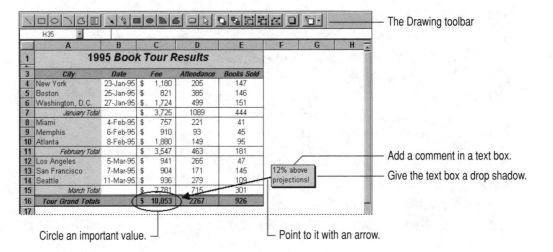

The Drawing toolbar

Add a comment in a text box.

Give the text box a drop shadow.

Circle an important value.

Point to it with an arrow.

 Formatting graphic objects Using buttons on the Drawing and Formatting toolbars, you can format graphic objects you have created, or select the object you want to format and click Object (Format menu).

Moving objects with cells Objects you draw can be "attached" to their underlying cells. If you want an object to respond to changes such as moving cells or changing the size of rows or columns, click Object (Format menu), available only when an object is selected. Click the Properties tab, and select one of the Object Positioning options.

Reuse Your Custom Formatting

There are at least two ways you can take advantage of the formatting work you've done.

- Copy the formatting from one cell or range to another using the Format Painter button. The Format Painter allows you to copy any number of different cell formats at once. You can select a range of cells with different formats, and the Format Painter will apply identical formats to another range without disturbing the actual contents of the cells.

- Define the formatting of a cell as a *style*. Select the cell, click Style (Format menu), and give the style a name. To apply a style, select a cell, click Style (Format menu), and select the style name.

 For Help, double-click.
In the Microsoft Excel online index look up:
**Format Painter
styles**

Format Painter button

City	Date	Fee	Attendance	Books Sold
New York	23-Jan-95	$ 1,180	205	147
Boston	25-Jan-95	$ 821	385	146
Washington, D.C.	27-Jan-95	$ 1,724	499	151
January Total		$ 3,725	1089	444
Miami	2/4/95	757	221	41
Memphis	2/6/95	910	93	45
Atlanta	2/8/95	1880	149	95
February Total		3547	463	181

Select a range you want to copy formats from.

Click the Format Painter button, and then select the area you want to format.

 Reuse custom cell styles Save yourself from doing all this formatting again. You can use your custom styles in other workbooks. In the Style dialog box, click the Merge button to select another workbook and copy its style definitions to the current workbook.

If You Don't Want to Spend Time Formatting Manually

The AutoFormat command provides access to "smart" sets of predesigned worksheet formats. When you apply an autoformat, Microsoft Excel analyzes the current region of the worksheet and automatically applies formatting based on position of headers, formulas, and data. Apply an

autoformat by selecting any cell in the current region, clicking AutoFormat (Format menu), and selecting the style you want from the list.

For information about using and customizing autoformats, look up **autoformat** in the Microsoft Excel online index.

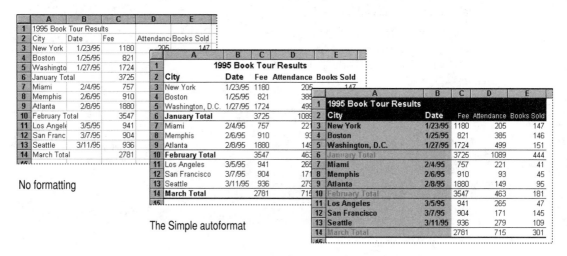

No formatting

The Simple autoformat

The Classic 2 autoformat

Next Steps

To	See
Create a chart	"Create a Chart From Worksheet Data," page 216
Create macros to speed up your work	"Automate Repetitive Tasks in Microsoft Excel," page 540

PART 4

Your Numbers Take Shape

Show Data in Charts and Maps

Contents

Create a Chart from Worksheet Data

Display Microsoft Excel Data Graphically

What can you do with Microsoft Excel data besides arrange it in rows and columns? Display it graphically in a chart. Show the values as lines, bars, columns, pie slices, and other markers, and even combine different markers in the same chart.

When it's best to display the chart along with the associated data, create an *embedded chart* directly on the worksheet. When the chart itself is all you need, create a separate *chart sheet*. In either case, the values in the chart are updated whenever the source worksheet data changes.

Key Features

ChartWizard

Chart Types

Chart Autoformats

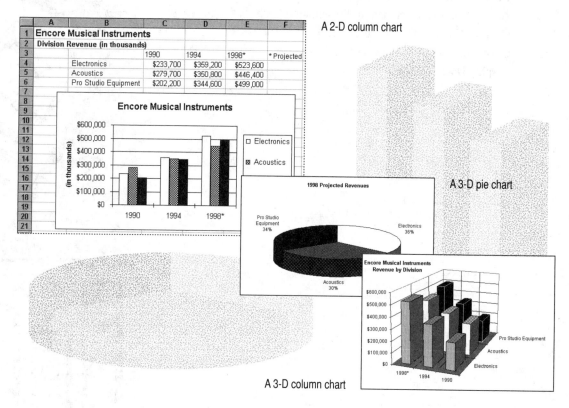

A 2-D column chart

A 3-D pie chart

A 3-D column chart

Create the Chart

Begin by selecting the range of worksheet data you want to include in the chart. To create a chart sheet, click Chart (Insert menu) and then click As New Sheet. Follow the steps in the ChartWizard to specify the chart you want.

To create an embedded chart on the worksheet, select the data and click the ChartWizard button. Drag to indicate the area on the sheet where you want the chart, or just click on the sheet to position the chart automatically.

 For Help, double-click. In the Microsoft Excel online index look up: **charts in Excel, creating**

ChartWizard button

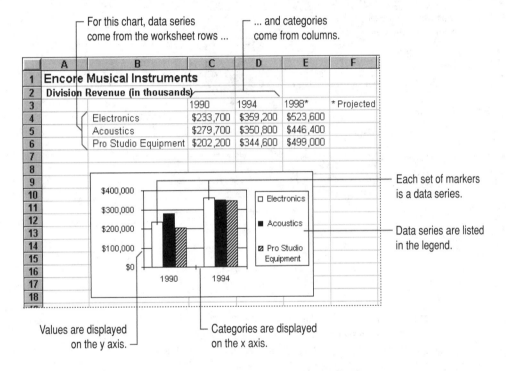

For this chart, data series come from the worksheet rows ...

... and categories come from columns.

Each set of markers is a data series.

Data series are listed in the legend.

Values are displayed on the y axis.

Categories are displayed on the x axis.

 How do you indicate whether rows or columns are the data series? Specify this in step 4 of the ChartWizard when you are creating the chart. Microsoft Excel proposes data series in rows or columns based on the shape of the range you selected. Check the sample to make sure the setting is right, and if necessary try it the other way.

Once it's created, how do you work with a chart? You need to *activate* a chart to make changes to it. Double-click an embedded chart; when active, its border becomes thicker, with a pattern. To activate a chart sheet, click its tab at the bottom of the workbook. When either kind of chart is active, the charting commands and toolbar buttons are available for use.

Add Data to the Chart

Data seems to be constantly changing, and sometimes you'll need to revise a chart you've already created. For example, add data points to show another revenue value for each division in the company. Or you might add a data series, such as another division.

For an embedded chart, just select the new data and drag it onto the chart. If you're working with a chart sheet, use the Copy and Paste commands (Edit menu) to add the data.

 For Help, double-click.
In the Microsoft Excel
online index look up:
charts in Excel, source data

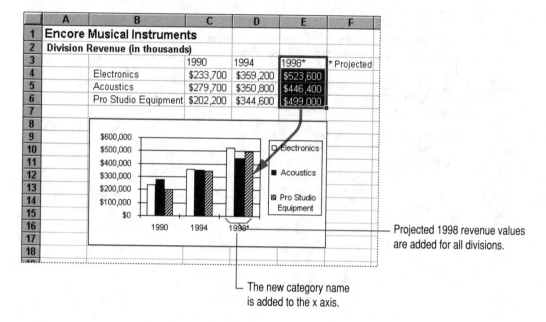

Projected 1998 revenue values
are added for all divisions.

The new category name
is added to the x axis.

Note   When you add data, Microsoft Excel examines the selection and places it according to how the existing data is plotted on the chart. If necessary, you're asked to specify in the Paste Special dialog box whether the new values are data series or data points.

What if you make a mistake?   If you add data incorrectly, you can remove it using the Undo command on the Edit menu. You can also undo many other tasks using this command.

How can you remove data from the chart?   To delete a data series, select the series on the chart and press DELETE. To delete one data point, just delete the value on the worksheet.

Find the Best Chart Type for Your Data

There are 14 chart types to choose from, and many offer variations; experiment to find the one that presents your data most effectively. Sometimes combining chart types, such as columns and lines, can help provide clarity and emphasis.

Change the chart type by clicking the Chart Type button on the Chart toolbar and selecting the type you want from the palette. If you need to display the Chart toolbar, click Toolbars (View menu). To change the chart type for one data series, select the series before clicking the Chart Type button.

 For Help, double-click. In the Microsoft Excel online index look up: **choosing chart type**

Chart Type button

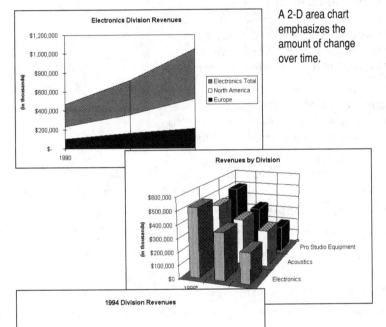

A 2-D area chart emphasizes the amount of change over time.

A 3-D column chart allows comparison of values within data series and by category.

A 3-D pie chart displays one data series, showing the relationship of parts to the whole.

When the chart shows different kinds of data   In addition to varying the chart types, you can display a *secondary value axis* and associate some of the data series with that value axis. For example, show price along one value axis, and volume along the other. For details, look up **secondary value axis** in the Microsoft Excel online index.

When the data is sets of values without categories   Use the xy (scatter) chart, which displays values along both the x and y axes and is often used for scientific data. For details, see "Display Scientific Data in a Chart," page 483.

Change a Chart's Look Automatically

Want a finished chart in a hurry? Change the way your chart looks all at once, without changing individual items, by applying an *autoformat*. Similar to a template or style, an autoformat changes the look but does not affect the chart's data.

For example, you can apply an autoformat to quickly get a chart combining column and line data markers, an xy (scatter) chart with logarithmic gridlines, or a line chart with curve smoothing.

To apply an autoformat, activate the chart and click AutoFormat (Format menu).

Create a custom look for a chart and reuse it later   If you want to manually format your chart instead of using an autoformat, you can save your custom formatting and apply it to other charts just like you would a built-in autoformat. For details on working with autoformats, look up **charts in Excel, AutoFormat** in the Microsoft Excel online index.

When Your Data Is More Complex

When necessary, your chart can show more than one level of categories. For example, you might need to show divisions within regions for your company. Or you might be creating a chart from a filtered list or from data with subtotals. Like other charts, the chart is updated when the source data changes.

For details, look up **axes in Excel charts, multilevel chart categories** in the Microsoft Excel online index.

Create a chart from a PivotTable Some of your worksheet data may be in the form of a *PivotTable*—an interactive worksheet table that summarizes large amounts of data. You can use a PivotTable as the source data for a chart. For details about PivotTables, see "Create a Sales Summary," page 446. Or look up **PivotTable** in the Microsoft Excel online index.

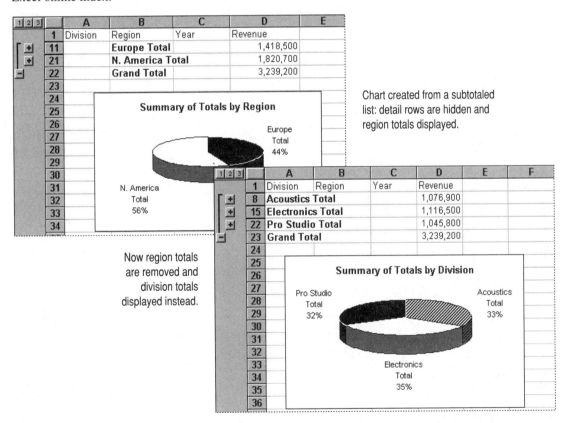

Chart created from a subtotaled list: detail rows are hidden and region totals displayed.

Now region totals are removed and division totals displayed instead.

Next Steps

To	In the Microsoft Excel online index look up
Add text to a chart	**adding chart text**
Change the worksheet cells included in the chart	**editing cell contents**
Change chart values	**charts in Excel, source data**

Add a Chart to a Document or Presentation

Create a Link to a Microsoft Excel Chart

Don't let too many numbers make your document or presentation dull: show data in chart form. Charts add visual interest along with useful information. Numeric data can be represented as lines, bars, columns, pie slices, or other markers. Colors, patterns, and explanatory text help make your point quickly and clearly.

A chart you create in Microsoft Excel can be kept up-to-date automatically. Microsoft Graph offers an alternative way to create charts. However you create it, you can modify the chart while working in your document or presentation.

Key Features

 Linked Charts
Microsoft Graph

 Linked Charts
Microsoft Graph

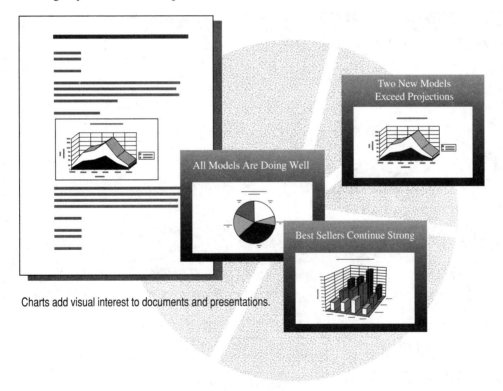

Charts add visual interest to documents and presentations.

Add a Chart That Stays Up To Date

Creating a *link* directly to a chart in a Microsoft Excel workbook
ensures that the chart displays the most recent data. The chart you
see in your document or presentation is actually a representation of
the chart that exists in the workbook. That chart is updated
whenever its source data changes, and the linked representation is
updated accordingly.

Important For updating, the workbook containing the chart must be
available. The surest way to maintain the link is to save the Microsoft Excel
workbook and the document or presentation file together in the same folder,
such as a project folder.

First open the Microsoft Excel workbook containing the chart.

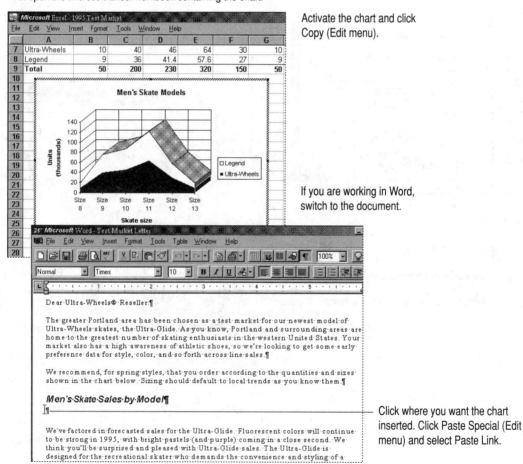

Activate the chart and click
Copy (Edit menu).

If you are working in Word,
switch to the document.

Click where you want the chart
inserted. Click Paste Special (Edit
menu) and select Paste Link.

If you are adding a chart to a slide in PowerPoint After copying the chart in Microsoft Excel, switch to PowerPoint and display the slide you want to add the chart to. Then click Paste Special (Edit menu).

If you haven't created the chart yet See "Create a Chart from Worksheet Data," page 216.

What if your data is in a table in Word? You don't have to copy the data into Microsoft Excel. Instead, use Microsoft Graph to create the chart. For more information, see "Microsoft Graph: Another Way to Work with Charts," later in this topic.

If Updating the Chart Won't be Necessary

When you want a chart to be part of your document or presentation instead of a representation of a chart that exists elsewhere, *embed* the chart.

For example, you might be submitting a final report, so that updating won't be important. Or the source data might not be available later for updating. The chart looks the same whether it is linked or embedded, and in either case you can activate, modify, and format the chart.

Embedding a chart works just like linking one, except that after copying the chart, you select Paste instead of Paste Link in the Paste Special dialog box.

Modify the Chart

After you have added a chart, you sometimes need to modify it. For example, you might change the chart type from pie to column, make the text larger, or use different colors.

Double-click the chart on your document or presentation to start Microsoft Excel. If the chart is embedded on a worksheet, double-click the chart to *activate* it. The charting commands and toolbars become available, and you can make the changes you want. To resume work in your application, close the workbook by clicking the Close (X) button.

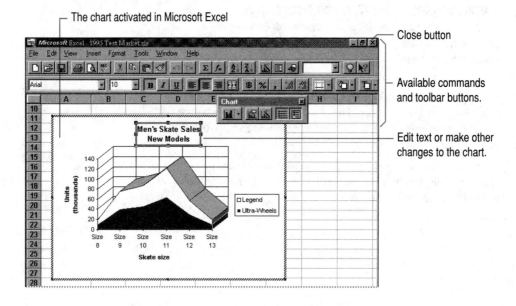

The chart activated in Microsoft Excel

Close button

Available commands and toolbar buttons.

Edit text or make other changes to the chart.

Give the chart a new look, automatically The easiest way to change the look of a chart is to apply a built-in *autoformat*. Doing so changes the chart's formatting but does not affect its data. After activating the chart, click AutoFormat (Format menu). Then select the look you want.

Create your own formats and use them for other charts After manually formatting a chart, save your custom formatting and apply the same look to other charts. You can even use pictures for data markers. For more information, see "Customize the Look of a Chart," page 236.

Modify the link Once you have created a link to a chart, there are several ways you can modify it; for example, link to a different chart, specify manual or automatic updating, or lock the link to prevent changes. To modify a link, click Links (Edit menu).

Microsoft Graph: Another Way to Work with Charts

If Microsoft Excel is not available, or if you have data in a table in your Word document, you can create charts with Microsoft Graph. Graph is available from Word and PowerPoint.

A chart you create in Graph looks like a Microsoft Excel chart, and the same formatting options are provided. Graph does not allow calculation, but you can enter, import, and edit data in the Graph datasheet.

Use Graph to create a chart in Word   Place the insertion point where you want to insert the chart in the document. Or, if you want to base the chart on a table of data, select the table. Click Object (Insert menu) and specify Microsoft Graph 5.0 Chart.

Use Graph to create a chart in PowerPoint   Display the slide you want to add a chart to. Then click the Insert Graph button on the Standard toolbar.

If you are creating a new slide in a presentation
In the AutoLayout window, pick a layout that includes a chart. After creating the slide, double-click the chart icon to activate Graph.

Modifying a chart created in Graph   Double-click the chart to activate it. Then make the changes you want using the Graph commands and toolbars.

Getting information about Graph   While you are working in Microsoft Graph, you can get information on Graph by using the commands on the Help menu. For details on working with Graph, see the Graph online index. Click Search For Help On (Graph Help menu).

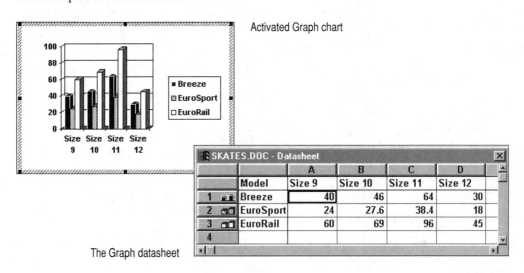

Activated Graph chart

The Graph datasheet

		A	B	C	D
	Model	Size 9	Size 10	Size 11	Size 12
1	Breeze	40	46	64	30
2	EuroSport	24	27.6	38.4	18
3	EuroRail	60	69	96	45
4					

SKATES.DOC - Datasheet

Next Steps

To	See
Add data labels, titles, and other items to a chart	"Customize the Look of a Chart," Page 236
Change the format of a Chart	"Customize the Look of a Chart," Page 236

Create a Chart from a Database

Use Microsoft Graph to Analyze Your Data Visually

When you browse through your database, do you want to see at a glance, for example, how many orders are coming in for each product? With Microsoft Access, you can represent your data graphically with a chart on a database form or report. Microsoft Access provides a Chart Wizard that makes charting easy.

Key Features

Chart Wizard

Microsoft Graph

Create a chart that reflects orders for each product as you move from record to record ...

... or summarize your data to see the overall order picture.

To create a chart that changes as you browse through records   You need a Microsoft Access form. You can also create charts on Microsoft Access reports. For details about forms, see "Create a Great Looking Product Form," page 400.

Choose a Microsoft Access Form for the Chart

When you look up pricing and quantity in stock for a product, you might also want to see a chart comparing the volume of orders for the product. You can add a chart to your Product Form that shows the total orders during each of the past few months.

To create this chart Run the Chart Wizard and follow its instructions. Your chart will count the number of orders for the current product by counting the order IDs. The chart will use the order dates to group the orders by month, displaying a column for each month's total orders. You'll specify the OrderID, OrderDate, and ProductName fields from a query in your database. You'll link the ProductName field in the chart with the Product Name field on the form so that the chart displays information for one product at a time.

To run the Chart Wizard Open your database. Click the Forms tab, and click the form you want. Click Design, and then click Chart (Insert menu). The first thing you do is draw a box where you want the chart to appear.

For Help, double-click. In the Microsoft Access online index look up:
forms, creating
adding charts

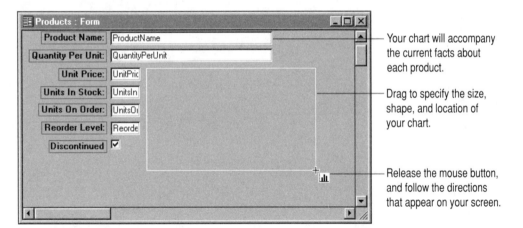

Your chart will accompany the current facts about each product.

Drag to specify the size, shape, and location of your chart.

Release the mouse button, and follow the directions that appear on your screen.

Do you want to chart a specific part of your data?   You can create a query that retrieves only the records you want to chart. For example, you could include only the products sold in a particular region. You would then specify your query when the wizard asks you to select a source for the chart's data. For details, look up **queries, creating** in the Microsoft Access online index.

You Can Add Charts to Reports as Well as Forms

Consider how your report groups your data when you add a chart. If your chart will summarize information from several records, you'll want to place the chart in the group header. For details, look up **adding charts** in the Microsoft Access online index.

View the Results

When you're finished, the wizard returns you to the Form Design view. Click Form (View menu) to see the chart. When you browse through your product records with the Products form, the chart changes to show information for each product that you view.

 For Help, double-click.
In the Microsoft Access online index look up:
forms, saving
forms, opening

Your form shows the record for each product in your database.

The chart shows order totals for the product you're currently viewing.

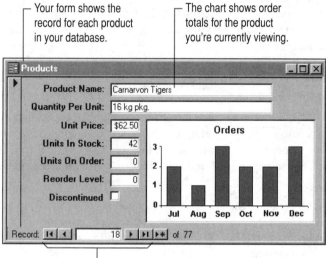

Browse through the records and watch the chart change as you display the record for each product.

Make your chart look great Open the form in Design view again, and double-click the chart to edit and format it. For details, see "Customize the Look of a Chart," page 236.

Create a Chart Report

What if, for example, you want a single chart that compares the total orders of several products over a period of time?

You can create a chart that draws information from many records in your database instead of linking the chart to the current record on a form or report. This kind of chart is updated all at once, when you view the form or run the report. The process you'll follow is similar to the one you just completed, except that you create a new form or report for this type of chart.

Create a new chart report   In your database, click the Reports tab, and then click New. Choose the table or query that contains the data to chart, and then double-click Chart Wizard.

Follow the instructions that appear on your screen. The example below and on the first page of this topic charts the total number of orders by month for all product categories, so it uses a query that

includes three fields: OrderID, OrderDate, and CategoryName. A line chart like this is useful when you want to compare results for several products simultaneously.

To see the chart, preview the report   When you finish the Chart Wizard, click the Print Preview button.

 Print Preview button

Add the chart report to your application   If you've set up your database as an application, you can add the chart to your main *Switchboard* screen. For details, look up **switchboards, changing** in the Microsoft Access online index.

For more information about Microsoft Access reports, look up **reports, overview** in the Microsoft Access online index.

Print Preview lets you view the chart report before printing.

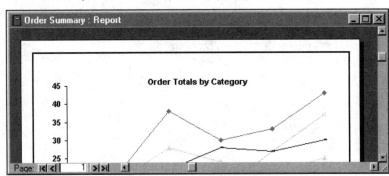

Next Steps

To	See
Further customize the chart: change the chart type, layout, colors, scale, or other aspects of its appearance	"Customize the Look of a Chart," page 236
Use a chart in another document	"Add a Chart to a Document or Presentation," page 223

Customize the Look of a Chart

Format the Items in a Chart

There are many ways you can change, or *format*, a chart to get the look you want. Each item in the chart has characteristics you can alter, such as color, pattern, line style, text or number appearance, and placement. To see a dialog box with the formatting options available for an item, double-click the item.

Key Features

Microsoft Graph

Format (Selected Chart Item)

Format 3-D View

Charts with custom formatting

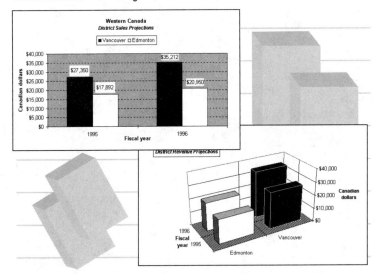

When you want to work with a chart   To make chart items, commands, and toolbar buttons available, *activate* the chart. Double-click the chart object. The border changes to a thick, patterned line when the chart is active. To display and activate a chart sheet, click the sheet's tab in the workbook.

For more information, see "Create a Chart from Worksheet Data," page 216, "Add a Chart to a Document or Presentation," page 223, or "Create a Chart from a Database," page 230.

Change the Data Markers

The graphic elements that indicate numeric values in a chart, such as lines, bars, columns, and pie slices, are *data markers*. To change the color and patterns for one data series, double-click one of the markers and make changes on the Patterns tab. To change only one marker, after selecting the series, click again to select the individual marker. Then double-click the marker to display the Patterns tab.

For Help, double-click. In the Microsoft Excel online index look up: **data markers in Excel charts**

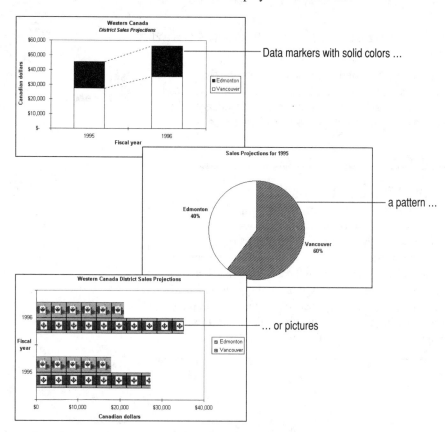

Data markers with solid colors ...

a pattern ...

... or pictures

Important The online index references in this topic refer to the Microsoft Excel online index only. If you are using Graph to create your chart, you must use Graph Help to find additional information. To see Graph Help, click Search For Help On (Graph Help menu) in Microsoft Graph.

Line and xy (scatter) charts can have both markers and lines These chart types give you the option of displaying data markers connected by lines. When you double-click a data series, you can specify in the Patterns tab which one (or both) to display, and how you want them to look. For information on xy (scatter) charts, see "Display Scientific Data in a Chart," page 483.

To add picture markers Copy the picture or graphic object, select the data series or a single data marker where you want to place the image, and click Paste (Edit menu).

To emphasize one slice of a pie or doughnut chart Select the slice and drag it away from the rest of the pie or doughnut.

To change to a different kind of data marker Change the chart type; for example, change columns to lines or pie slices. On the Chart toolbar, click the Chart Type button and select the type you want. For information about chart types, look up **changing chart type** in the Microsoft Excel online index.

Chart Type button

Combine Chart Types on One Chart

You can mix chart types—for example, combine lines and columns in the same chart to show data clearly. Select an individual data series and apply a different chart type; only that series changes. All data series that share the same chart type make up a *chart type group*, and each group is listed on the Format menu. You can work with a chart type group as a unit; for example, change the spacing of columns for all data series displayed as columns. For details, look up **combination charts** in the Microsoft Excel online index.

Label the Data Markers

Data labels are optional text or values, associated with data markers, that provide additional information. The information comes from the associated source data, for example, the value from the worksheet cell or the percentage of the whole that one marker represents. You can add data labels to individual data markers, one data series, or all the markers in a chart.

Add data labels To add labels to all markers in a chart, click Data Labels (Insert menu), and then select the type of label you want. To add labels to one data series, or to only one data point, select the series or the individual marker.

Modify data labels To change the font, number format, or other characteristics, double-click a label for a data series. The selections you make in the Format Data Labels dialog box apply to all labels for the series. To modify only one label, after selecting the labels for the series, click the individual label, and then double-click it.

For Help, double-click. In the Microsoft Excel online index look up: **data labels in Excel charts**

? For Help on dialog box options, click this button.

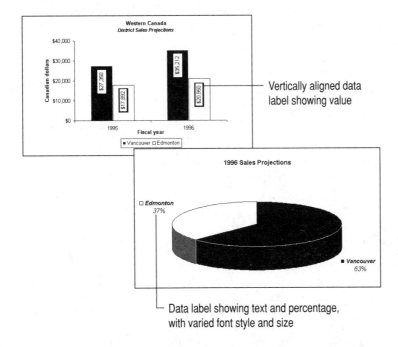

Vertically aligned data label showing value

Data label showing text and percentage, with varied font style and size

Edit data label text You can edit a data label by clicking it and typing. However, this breaks the link between the label and the source data. If you want to restore the link, double-click the data marker (not the label itself) and select the Automatic Text check box on the Data Labels tab.

If data labels are too long or awkwardly placed   You can move or rotate labels, or change the font. To move labels, select and drag them. Make other changes by double-clicking a label: Rotate labels by changing the alignment on the Alignment tab, and change the font on the Font tab.

Title the Chart and Its Axes

To convey a chart's purpose and clarify the kind of data it shows, add titles. If you did not add titles to the chart and its axes when you created the chart, you can add them at any time.

 For Help, double-click. In the Microsoft Excel online index look up: **titles, chart titles**

Add titles   Click Titles (Insert menu) and indicate which titles you want. For each one, a placeholder appears on the chart; to replace it with text, select and type. If you want a title to contain two lines, press ENTER where you want the line break. You can select and format the two lines separately; for example, make the lower line of text a smaller font size.

Modify titles   Double-click a title to make selections on the Patterns, Font, and Alignment tabs. You can move titles by dragging them, though their size is determined by the amount of text and the font size.

For Help on dialog box options, click this button.

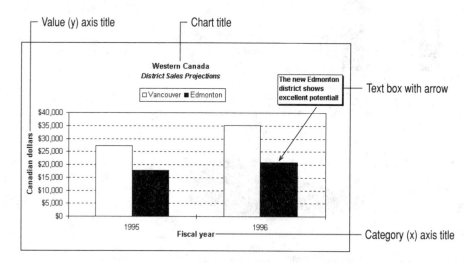

Add other text to a chart   When you want to add explanatory text that is not attached to a chart item, create a text box. Click the Text Box button on the Drawing toolbar, and then click where you want the text and type it. To format the text box, for example, to add a border or change the font, double-click to see the available formatting options.

Text Box button

Add an arrow or other graphic object Arrows are useful for pointing out important information or connecting text to items in the chart. Ovals and rectangles can also add visual interest. Click the Drawing button to display a toolbar of buttons you can use to create arrows, rectangles, and other objects. For information on working with graphic objects, see **graphic objects in Excel** in the Microsoft Excel online index.

Drawing button

Format the Axes and Gridlines

The *axes* show the range of values, the categories, or, for some 3-D charts, the data series in a chart. You can change the color, line pattern, tick marks, and labels of an axis. You can also adjust the *scale*, or the range of values, shown along the axis. *Gridlines* extend from an axis across the plot area, and may be turned on or off; you can also format their color and line style.

Format an axis Double-click the axis and make the changes you want on the Patterns, Scale, Font, Number, and Alignment tabs. Axes are displayed by default, but if you want to hide them, click Axes (Insert menu).

Add and format gridlines Click Gridlines (Insert menu) and specify which axes you want them to appear on, and at what intervals. To format gridlines for an axis, double-click one and specify the look you want on the Patterns tab. You can also change the axis scale on the Scale tab while formatting gridlines.

For Help, double-click. In the Microsoft Excel online index look up: **axes in Excel charts, formatting gridlines in charts**

? For Help on dialog box options, click this button.

— Tick-mark labels shown as currency along axis

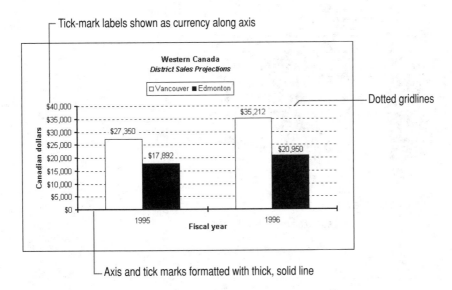

— Dotted gridlines

Axis and tick marks formatted with thick, solid line

If category axis labels are too long   Double-click the axis. Rotate the labels on the Alignment tab, or change the font size on the Font tab. Another option is to display fewer labels: on the Scale tab, adjust the number of categories displayed.

Add a secondary value axis   When values for different data series vary widely, or when you have different types of values, such as price and volume, switch one or more data series to a secondary axis. Double-click the series and select the Secondary Axis option on the Axis tab. For more information, look up **secondary value axis** in the Microsoft Excel online index.

Format and Position the Legend

The *legend* in a chart identifies the data series. You can add a legend while creating the chart, or add it later by choosing Legend (Insert menu). You can move the legend, change its shape and size, and format individual entries and keys within the legend. Changing an entry's color or pattern also changes the markers in the associated data series.

To work with the legend   Double-click the legend to display the Format Legend dialog box with the available formatting options. To move or resize the legend, just select and drag it. Dotted lines show the shape and placement of entries as you drag.

For Help, double-click. In the Microsoft Excel online index look up: **legends in Excel charts**

? For Help on dialog box options, click this button.

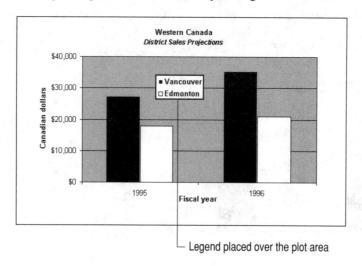

Legend placed over the plot area

To change an individual entry or key After selecting the legend, click the entry or key and then double-click it to display the available formatting options.

Position the legend automatically Instead of dragging, you can automatically place the legend at the top, bottom, right, left, or corner of the chart. Double-click the legend and select the position you want on the Placement tab. Because automatic positioning sets the legend to the default size and adjusts the plot area accordingly, it's best to position the legend first, and then resize it and the plot area manually if necessary.

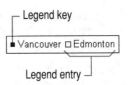

Format the Background and Size the Chart for Printing

There are two background areas in a chart that you can format with colors and patterns: the entire chart area, or the plot area, which is contained within the axes. When formatting the chart area, you can also change the font for the entire chart. Double-click the chart area and make changes on the Patterns tab and the Font tab. To format the plot area, double-click and specify your choices on the Patterns tab.

For Help, double-click. In the Microsoft Excel online index look up:
chart area, formatting
plot area in Excel charts, formatting

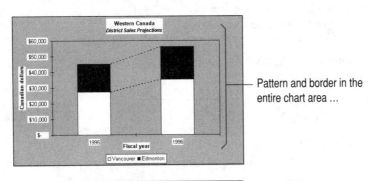

Pattern and border in the entire chart area ...

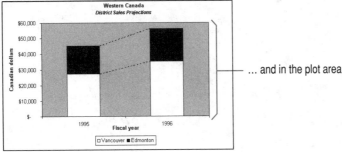

... and in the plot area

Resize the plot area   When you have moved the legend, or added a title or a text box, resizing the plot area can help make all the chart items fit together well. Select the plot area and drag until it's the size you want.

Control an embedded chart's position on a worksheet   You can set whether the chart is moved, sized, or both when worksheet cell widths and heights change. Change this setting by selecting the chart, clicking Object (Format menu), and selecting the Properties tab.

Get the Help You Need While You Work

Expanded and improved online assistance is just a click away. It's the fastest way to get information so you can keep working.

Ask the Answer Wizard   Type a question in your own words. The Answer Wizard lists online Help topics related to your question. Double-click the Help button and then click the Answer Wizard tab.

Look it up in the online index   Instead of typing a question, use index entries provided in this book to find online topics related to your task. Double-click the Help button and then click the Index tab.

For details, see "Get Assistance While You Work," page 30. Or look up **Help** in the online index.

Formatting a 3-D Chart

In addition to the chart formatting options discussed earlier in this topic, there are several more ways you can change the look of a 3-D chart.

When a 3-D chart has three axes You can adjust the rotation, elevation, and perspective. By doing so, you can find the best arrangement for clearly displaying the values and axes in the chart.

Change the rotation and elevation Click a corner and drag. To see outlines of the markers while you drag, hold down CTRL.

For more formatting options Click 3-D View (Format menu) to adjust the chart's perspective. Click 3-D Column Group (Format menu) to adjust the chart depth and the gaps between markers.

Change the color and pattern of the walls and floor The walls are formatted together as a unit. The floor is always opaque, unless you have rotated it to view the chart from below; in this case, the floor is transparent. Double-click a wall or the floor to make your formatting selections.

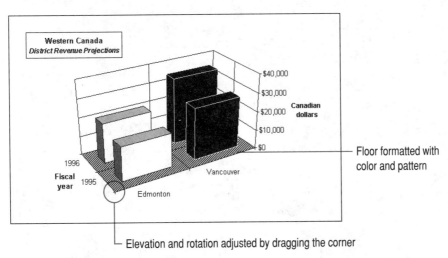

Floor formatted with color and pattern

Elevation and rotation adjusted by dragging the corner

Next Steps

To	See
Add a trendline to a chart	"Display Scientific Data in a Chart," page 483
Add error bars to a chart	"Display Scientific Data in a Chart," page 483
Show a moving average on a chart	"Create a Sales Forecast," page 453

Display Data on a Map

Use Microsoft Data Map to Give Information a Geographical Context

When you work with data that is associated with geographic regions, the most meaningful way to display it may be on a map. Use Microsoft Data Map for appealing presentation, for effective analysis and decision support, or for a combination of these purposes. Plot your own data on one or more maps, or use demographic data provided with Data Map. There are several display formats, a selection of maps to choose from, and features that you can add to maximize your maps' usefulness.

Key Features

 Microsoft Data Map

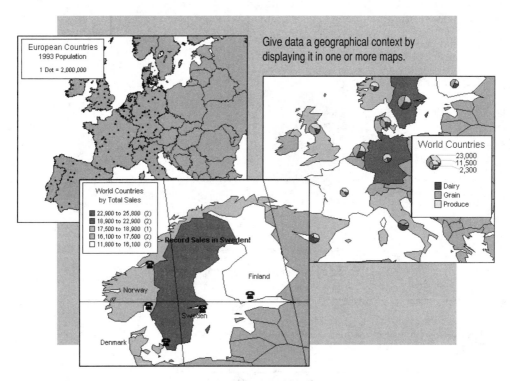

Give data a geographical context by displaying it in one or more maps.

Important You must have Data Map installed before you begin creating a map. To install Data Map, run Microsoft Excel Setup. For details, look up **installing Microsoft Office components** and **installing add-in programs** in the Microsoft Excel online index.

Create the Map

The first step in creating a map is selecting the data you want displayed. The selection must contain a column of data that identifies geographical regions, such as states or countries, as well as the columns of data you want to show on the map. You can display and hide these columns when you need to, as described in a section later in this topic.

Click the Data Map button. Drag on the worksheet to indicate the size and location of the map you want to create. After the default map is created, you can modify it. For details, see "Change the Data Display and Format" and "Add Emphasis and Detail," later in this topic.

Data Map button

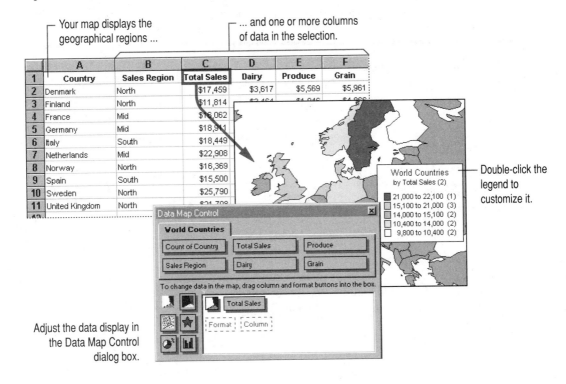

Your map displays the geographical regions ...

... and one or more columns of data in the selection.

	A	B	C	D	E	F
1	Country	Sales Region	Total Sales	Dairy	Produce	Grain
2	Denmark	North	$17,459	$3,617	$5,569	$5,961
3	Finland	North	$11,814			
4	France	Mid	$16,062			
5	Germany	Mid	$18,911			
6	Italy	South	$18,449			
7	Netherlands	Mid	$22,908			
8	Norway	North	$16,369			
9	Spain	South	$15,500			
10	Sweden	North	$25,790			
11	United Kingdom	North				

World Countries
by Total Sales (2)

- 21,000 to 22,100 (1)
- 15,100 to 21,000 (3)
- 14,000 to 15,100 (2)
- 10,400 to 14,000 (2)
- 9,800 to 10,400 (2)

Double-click the legend to customize it.

Data Map Control

World Countries

| Count of Country | Total Sales | Produce |
| Sales Region | Dairy | Grain |

To change data in the map, drag column and format buttons into the box.

Total Sales

Format | Column

Adjust the data display in the Data Map Control dialog box.

Data Map checks for mismatched or misspelled geographical regions
If some regions in your selection don't match Data Map's geographical data,
Data Map displays a dialog box in which you can correct the information.

Do you have to select data first?   No, you can start working with Data
Map with no data selected. This displays a blank map, to which you can
then add data. For details on inserting data, see "Change the Data Display
and Format" later in this topic.

Another way to create a map is by copying it   If you already have a
map, you can create another by copying and pasting the existing one. After
pasting, you can add data, change the way it's displayed, and make other
modifications.

Get Help while you use Data Map   Data Map has online Help built in for
you to use while you are working with your maps. With Data Map activated,
click the commands on the Help menu to find the information you need.

What Maps Can You Use?

The following maps are installed with Microsoft Data Map.

- World Countries

- United States

- Canadian Provinces

- European Countries

- United Kingdom

- Australian States

- Mexican States

You can obtain additional maps to use with Data Map. For
more information, look up "Where Can I Obtain More
Maps?" in the Data Map online Help table of contents. To
access this Help, Data Map must be activated.

Change the Way You View the Map

While you work, it's helpful to display precisely the area you need to see: Zoom in for more detail and zoom out to see the bigger picture. Adjust the area currently displayed in the window by *panning*.

To zoom, click the Zoom In or Zoom Out button on the Data Map toolbar, and then click a point on which you want the map centered. To pan, click the Grabber button and then drag the map until you see the area you want.

Zoom In   Zoom Out   Grabber
button   button   button

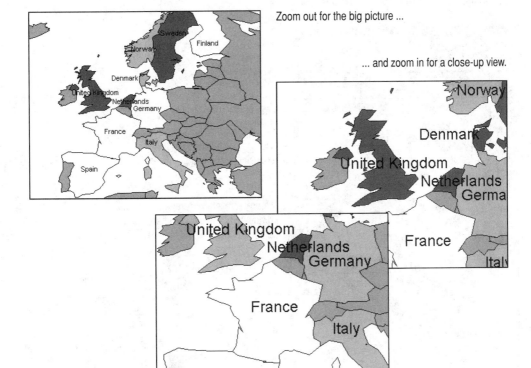

Zoom out for the big picture ...

... and zoom in for a close-up view.

Pan to change the area currently displayed.

 Can't find the Data Map toolbar buttons? Double-click the map to activate it on your worksheet. When activated, your map is surrounded by a thick border.

Change the Data Display and Format

When you first create a map, the Data Map Control dialog box appears and your map is activated. Each column of data in the selection appears as a button in the Data Map Control dialog box. The buttons in the lower-left corner of the dialog box represent available formats.

To add data, drag a format button into the box at the lower right, and then drag a data button beside it. To change formats, drag a different format button to a data button. Experiment to find the combination of data and formats that suits your purpose.

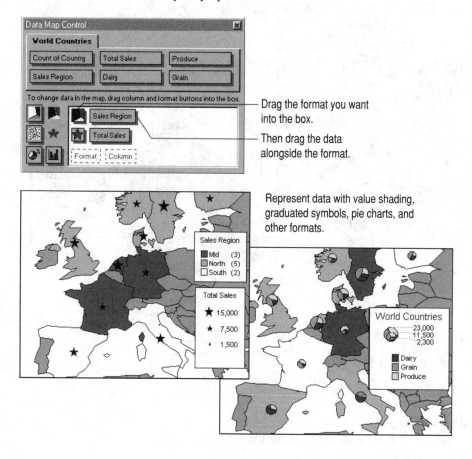

Drag the format you want into the box.

Then drag the data alongside the format.

Represent data with value shading, graduated symbols, pie charts, and other formats.

How do you display the Data Map Control dialog box when you need it? When you want to change the data displayed or its format, click the Show/Hide Data Map Control button on the Data Map toolbar. If you can't see the Data Map toolbar, make sure your map is activated.

Show/Hide Data Map Control button

Not seeing the legend you want? Double-click the legend to change its default text and appearance. To display a full legend, clear the Use Compact Format check box in the Edit Legend dialog box. This enables you to change the legend title text, and individual legend entries.

Add pie charts or column charts for more detail Use these charts to compare two or more columns of data, for example, individual product information for each region. You can display one of these chart types at a time on your map. In the Data Map Control dialog box, drag the Pie Chart or the Column Chart format button into the box, and then drag the data columns that you want displayed beside the format button.

Change the way data is displayed To modify the way a column of data is displayed, double-click it in the box inside the Data Map Control dialog box. Then, make the formatting changes you want, such as changing the color or the symbol.

Remove data from the map To hide a column of data, drag the column button outside the dialog box. If you want to add the column again later, drag its column heading into the box alongside a format button.

Add Emphasis and Detail

There are several ways you can provide orientation, highlight specific data, or otherwise make your map more informative. One way is to show highways, cities, airports, lakes, or a combination of these. This information is provided with Microsoft Data Map. To add these features, click Features (Map menu), and select the ones you want.

Display labels to identify countries, regions, or cities. Click the Map Labels button, choose the options you want, and then click each point at which you want a label. To add a text box with a comment or explanation, click the Add Text button, and type the text. Click the Custom Pin Map button to add custom labels, or symbols, to the map, identifying points of interest. To return to normal selection, click the Select Objects button.

Map Labels   Add Text   Custom
button   button   Pin Map
                          button

Select Objects button

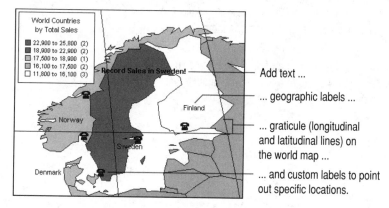

Add text ...

... geographic labels ...

... graticule (longitudinal and latitudinal lines) on the world map ...

... and custom labels to point out specific locations.

 By default, your map has a title and one or more legends   Initially, the title and the content of the legends are determined by the map and data you are working with. You can edit, move, format, resize, or delete these items as needed.

Format and edit text and other map elements   Double-click legends and symbols to display a dialog box in which you can make changes. The available options depend on the item you are working with. Click to select a text box or title, and then double-click to display the dialog box. To edit the text in place, double-click the text. For details on formatting and editing map elements, see Data Map online Help.

Update the Data or Add to It

Once you've created a map, you can adjust the data it displays. You might need to add more data than you initially plotted, change the source data you're working with, or import data from an external source. You can also hide data you no longer want displayed.

To add a column of data from the same source, click Data (Insert menu). To add data from an external source, click External Data (Insert menu). To hide data currently displayed, click the Show/Hide Data Map Control button. In the Data Map Control dialog box, drag the button representing the data you want to hide out of the dialog box.

Show/Hide Data Map Control button

The Beverages column is added to the source data ...

	A	B
	Country	Beverages
	Denmark	$2,312
	Finland	$1,538
	France	$6,222
	Germany	$8,472
	Italy	$3,464
	Netherlands	$1,946
	Norway	$4,866
	Spain	$1,474
	Sweden	$3,768
	United Kingdom	$4,598

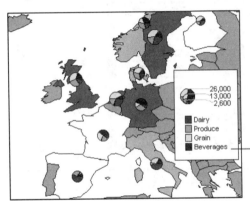

... and displayed in the updated map.

Select geographic regions along with new data   When you add a column of data, select that column along with the column containing the geographic regions you originally used to create your map (the new data column must be contiguous with the geographic region column). By doing this, you provide the information Data Map needs to plot the new data.

Look for a cue that it's time to refresh the map   When source data changes, the Map Refresh button appears in the upper-left corner of your map to alert you that the map needs to be refreshed. Click this button to update the data displayed in the map.

Adding a row instead of a column?   If you are adding a new row (such as another country's data) to the map, insert the row between existing rows. Then use the Map Refresh button to update your map with the new data.

The Map Refresh button alerts you when data has changed.

Insert the Map in Other Applications

Once you've created a map, you can add it to documents in other applications by dragging and dropping across application windows or by using the Copy and Paste commands (Edit menu).

To insert a new map in another application click Object (Insert menu) in the application where you want to insert the map, and select Microsoft Data Map from the list.

For details, look up **inserting linked objects** and **inserting embedded objects** in the online index for the application you're using.

Add data maps to documents, presentations, and database forms and reports.

Worldwide Sales

Next Steps

To	See
Use mapping data from an outside source	Data Map online Help

Your Ideas Take the Stage

Create Informative and Entertaining Presentations

Contents

Quickly Prepare a Black & White Presentation

PowerPoint Provides Special Tools

If you don't have the equipment for an electronic presentation, can't use 35mm slides, or you don't have time to get high-quality color overheads, black and white overheads are your best option. Perhaps your presentation must do double duty as great black and white overheads and still look good in color later.

Key Features

Black & White View

Color Scheme

Black and white view helps you put together a great high-contrast presentation.

Guidelines for Using Color Presentations in Black and White

- Use the B&W View button to show you what a color presentation will look like in black and white.

B&W View button

- Use Slide Color Scheme (Format menu) to change to a different color scheme, a black and white scheme, or to modify problematic colors within a color scheme.

- Control how individual objects look when printed. In black & white view, select an object, click the right mouse button, and then click the Black and White command. Choose an option to modify the selected object.

Work in outline view   Nothing beats outline view for putting a presentation together quickly. Even if your presentation consists largely of text, you can manipulate and organize it faster in outline view. For more information, see "Create Your First PowerPoint Presentation," page 82.

Get the Help You Need While You Work

Expanded and improved online assistance is just a click away. It's the fastest way to get information so you can keep working.

Ask the Answer Wizard   Type a question in your own words. The Answer Wizard lists online Help topics related to your question. Double-click the Help button and then click the Answer Wizard tab.

Look it up in the online index   Instead of typing a question, use index entries provided in this book to find online topics related to your task. Double-click the Help button and then click the Index tab.

For details, see "Get Assistance While You Work," page 30. Or look up **Help** in the online index.

Give a Great Presentation on Paper

PowerPoint is the best application to use when putting a presentation together, even if you aren't using a projector or a computer to display it. Along with its black and white-specific features, PowerPoint has graphic design and output muscle that help create great-looking printed handouts for your audience.

After making sure everything will look good on your printer, you can employ one of these output options:

- Print your slides full page, or 2, 3, or 6 slides per page.

- Print one slide per page along with notes or a blank note-taking area.

- Export your notes and graphic images of slides to Word, where you can edit and format using all of Word's features.

- Export the text of slides as an outline to Word, where you can create an expanded report.

For information about printing options, see "Create Presentation Handouts and Speaker's Notes," page 259. For further details, see **printing** and **notes** in the PowerPoint online index.

Next Steps

To	See
Create printed handouts	"Create Presentation Handouts and Speaker's Notes," page 259.
Add graphics	"Get Your Point Across with Graphics," page 271.

Create Presentation Handouts and Speaker's Notes

Generate Supporting Materials for You and Your Audience

Once you've put your presentation together in PowerPoint, you needn't duplicate the effort in another application just to create supporting materials for your presentation. Each slide in a presentation has a place called Notes View where you can type information to accompany your slides in order to create handouts or speaker's notes. Your presentation slides can be automatically turned into handouts.

Key Features

Handouts

Notes Pages

Write-Up

- Use Handouts when you want to show only the content of the slides themselves, or when you want to squeeze more slides onto a page.

- Use Notes Pages when you want to include additional content beyond the slides themselves.

Speaker's notes include slide images and text

Handouts show slide images only

Create Notes for the Presenter

Half of your job as a presenter is to create slides with precise, concise messages, so that the communication is very clear. The other half of your job is to communicate verbally, putting each slide's message in perspective. Sometimes you need to do a lot of talking to support your bullet list on the slide, so keeping some notes handy is a good idea.

 For Help, double-click.
In the PowerPoint online index look up:
notes
Meeting Minder

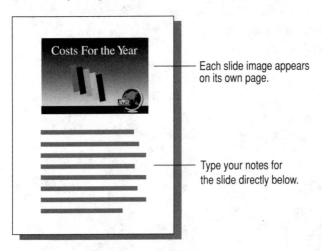

Each slide image appears on its own page.

Type your notes for the slide directly below.

 Get a closer look   The Zoom Control box gets you up close to your work, no matter what view you are in at the moment. Just click the arrow and select a percentage from the list, or click in the edit box and type the exact percentage you want, even if it isn't on the list.

Zoom Control box

View notes during a presentation   Most of the time, you'll print out your notes pages so you can refer to them while speaking. You can also view notes pages on screen while a slide show is in progress, using the Meeting Minder feature. This is particularly useful if you are giving an on-screen presentation using two computers. You can also record notes during an on-screen presentation that you can later add to your notes pages or export to a Word document. For more information, see "Give an Electronic Presentation," page 288.

Fit more notes on a page   If you need more room for text, you can change the size of the slide image on the notes page by dragging to resize and reposition the slide image. You can do this on the Notes Master to apply it to all notes pages at once. Click Notes Master (Master command, View menu).

Create Audience Handouts

PowerPoint provides three different built-in layouts for handouts, giving you several ways to put your presentation in the hands of the audience. When you print, choose one of the Handout options to create paper versions of your slides.

 For Help, double-click.
In the PowerPoint online index look up:
handouts
headers and footers

Two slides per page

Three slides per page

Six slides per page

 Share your notes? When making notes for yourself, your writing style can be as casual as you like. But if it makes sense to provide some of this information to the audience, you can employ a more formal writing style and print copies of your notes pages instead of using the Handouts feature.

Add headers and footers When you print handouts and notes, you can add information such as page numbers and dates at the top and bottom of each page with the Headers and Footers command (Format menu).

Handouts and Build Slides

If your on-screen presentation uses "build slides," in which items on a slide are revealed one at a time, you have a decision to make when you print your handouts. You can either print each first-bullet-level step of the build as a separate slide on your handouts, or just print the whole slide with all the bullets visible. If any slide in your presentation is set up as a build slide, you can select the Slides With Builds option when you print. For information about build slides, see "Prepare for an Electronic Presentation," page 280.

Does Your Audience Need a Book?

Suppose you need to provide your audience with more than just printouts of your slides; for example, comb-bound training books, seminar notebooks, or other presentation reference materials. With the Write-Up command (Tools menu), you can export your slides and notes to Word where they can become the starting point for a more exhaustive handout.

 **For Help, double-click.**
In the PowerPoint online index look up:
Write-Up

- After transferring slide images and notes to Word, you can use Word features to enhance the appearance, add an index and table of contents, and so on.

- If you want, the slide images transferred to Word can be linked to the original slides in PowerPoint. Then, if you make changes to a slide in the presentation, those changes are automatically reflected in the linked slide image in Word.

- The note text associated with each slide is also transferred to Word from PowerPoint, but is not linked to the original text, so you can freely edit it, add to it, and format it in Word.

When you export your PowerPoint notes pages ...

... the contents appear in Word tables.

Note text is placed next to slide images,
or below them for multi-page notes.

The Handout Binder

If your audience-education needs include multiple pages of output from more than one application, perhaps the Office Binder would be the best tool for you. The Office Binder is an application supplied with Office that you can use to keep together various documents you create with Office applications.

For example, suppose you want to print several worksheets and charts from Microsoft Excel and a couple of reports from Word, and then combine them into a single package to distribute to your audience. Instead of separately printing everything, and then collating and stapling by hand, use the Office Binder to assemble exactly what you need, and then just print the whole thing at once. It's also a handy way to keep related files together in one place.

For more information, see "Use Office Applications Together," page 103.

Bring Microsoft Excel, Word, and PowerPoint documents together with the Office Binder.

Next Steps

To	See
Format a report in Word	"Make Your Word Document Look Great," page 161
Print out your slides	"Create Your First PowerPoint Presentation," page 82
Link or embed objects	"Use Office Applications Together," page 103

Customize the Appearance of Your Presentation

You want your presentation to have a distinctive appearance that works well for the type of material you need to present and also communicates your points to your audience.

Perhaps you want to create a presentation that you can use repeatedly as the basis for other presentations with a common theme—using company colors and logo in the same location, and so on.

PowerPoint templates and masters can help you create an effective presentation you can use once or many times.

- *Design templates* are sets of predesigned master formats and graphics you can apply to any presentation. They change the appearance, but not the content of your slides and notes.

- *Masters* are special views where you can add repeated elements and define the general appearance of all slides and pages at once.

- *Templates* are predesigned presentations that contain formatted masters plus slides that contain formatting, text, and graphics.

Key Features

 Design Templates

Masters

Templates

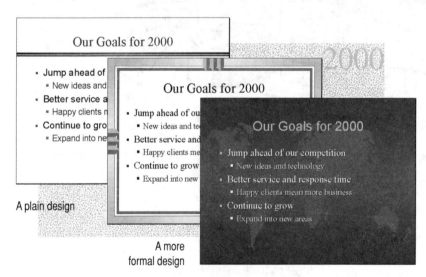

A plain design

A more formal design

A highly graphical design

Determine the Overall Appearance of Your Presentation

Design templates are presentations with formatting and graphic elements in master views only. Click Apply Design Template (Format menu) to determine most of the formatting in your presentation.

If you are working on an individual slide and you like what you see, you can change all the slides in that presentation at once without applying a design template or changing to the master view. Use the Apply To All button that appears in applicable dialog boxes.

 For Help, double-click.
In the PowerPoint online index look up:
Design Templates
master views

When you apply a Design Template ...

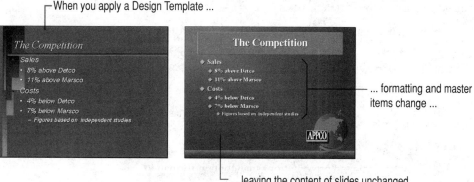

... formatting and master items change ...

... leaving the content of slides unchanged.

Customize individual slides The overall appearance you choose might not be the best way to present the information on every slide in your presentation. Particular slides might communicate better using a different layout or color scheme. You can make changes to a slide using commands on the Format menu to override the master formatting.

Headers and footers Use headers and footers to include information, such as date or company name, that you would like to appear on all slides or pages. For details, see **headers and footers** in the PowerPoint online index.

Multiple color schemes Each design template includes a number of different color schemes you can use, and you can also create your own. Click Slide Color Scheme (Format menu) and click the Custom tab. Notes pages have separate color schemes you control using the Notes Color Scheme command (Format menu), which appears when notes pages view is active.

Mastering Masters

Using the Master command (View menu), you determine the default appearance for each key component in a presentation: slides, notes pages, and audience handouts. For slides, there are two masters. The *Title Master* determines the appearance of special "title slides" you can use at the beginning of a presentation or wherever you want to set off distinct sections. The standard *Slide Master* controls the appearance of all other slides in your presentation.

Text and graphics you include on the masters will appear on every slide or page. When you format a master, all other slides or pages automatically display the same formats.

- Use Format menu commands to change the design of masters.
- Use drawing tools or Insert menu commands to add graphic elements to masters.

For Help, double-click.
In the PowerPoint online index look up:
master views
custom backgrounds

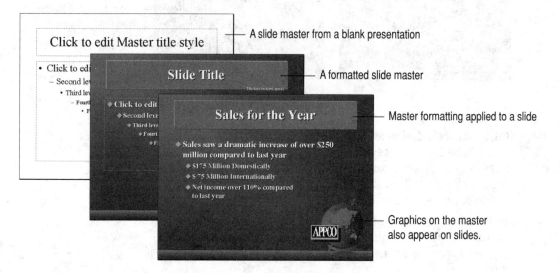

A slide master from a blank presentation

A formatted slide master

Master formatting applied to a slide

Graphics on the master also appear on slides.

Disobeying the master   What if you don't want background items that appear on the Slide Master, such as your company name and logo, to appear on one of the slides? While the slide is displayed, click Custom Background (Format menu) and click the Hide Objects From Master check box. You can also manually change individual slide or page formatting, overriding the master formats for that slide or page.

Understanding Templates

Templates are professionally designed presentations you can use as the basis for your own presentations. PowerPoint uses two kinds: templates and design templates.

Templates are like cookie-cutter presentations that give you a head start with content and organization, as well as formatting and design.

Design templates are a specific kind of template that includes master elements and formatting, but no slides. You can apply design templates to any presentation without changing the existing content of slides or notes. Only the content and appearance of the masters are changed, in turn determining the default appearance of the rest of the presentation.

Why use templates? If you want, you can start with a blank presentation and create your own from scratch. But the advantage of using templates, besides saving time, is that the way in which fonts, colors, and layout work together has been carefully considered for you.

No color? If you are limited to black and white output, each of the PowerPoint design templates is optimized for black and white printing. For more information, see "Quickly Prepare a Black & White Presentation," page 256.

Saving templates You can save any presentation as a template. Click Save (File menu) and select Template from the File Type list. To save a design template, first delete all the slides in slide sorter view, so that only the content and design of the masters remain. Then click Save As (File menu), and select Template from the File Type list.

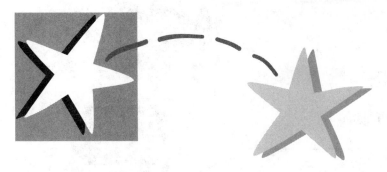

Next Steps

To	See
Add graphics	"Get Your Point Across with Graphics," page 271
Add effects especially designed for electronic presentations	"Prepare for an Electronic Presentation," page 280

Transfer Information Between PowerPoint and Other Applications

You Needn't Do Any Unnecessary Retyping

You need to prepare slides to accompany a report. Or, you need to prepare a report to accompany a presentation. Don't panic. You can easily exchange outlines between PowerPoint and Word.

In addition to Word documents, PowerPoint also reads many other file formats, including Microsoft Write, Harvard Graphics®, Freelance Graphics® for MS-DOS® and Windows, Rich Text Format, and plain text.

Key Features

 Slides From Outline Command

Open Command

Report It

 AutoFormat

PowerPoint and Word can share outlines.

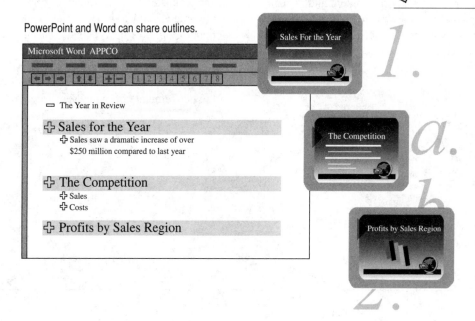

Insert a Word Outline

When you use an outline from Word, PowerPoint picks up the outline structure from:

 For Help, double-click.
In the PowerPoint online index look up:
slides from outline
slides from file

- Styles—Heading 1 becomes the slide title, Heading 2 becomes the first level of text, and so on, up to five levels of subhead text. When you import an outline, levels six and below are all imported as level 5 text in PowerPoint. Only heading styles are used to create slides; additional body text is ignored.

- Paragraph indents—if there are no styles

- Tabs—at the beginning of paragraphs in plain text files

Insert outlines from Word or another application into an open PowerPoint presentation by clicking Slides From Outline (Insert menu).

Insert the contents of a Word document in a presentation.   Slides are created using the outline structure.

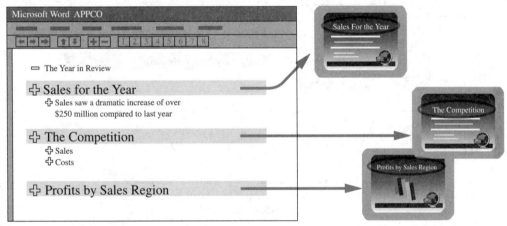

 Import an entire presentation Create a new presentation from an outline in any file format that PowerPoint reads. Click Open (File menu) and select Outlines in the File Types list.

Create headings quickly with AutoFormat If the Word document you are using isn't formatted or doesn't use standard heading styles, use the Word AutoFormat to apply standard styles to the whole document before you import it. PowerPoint can then use these styles to more efficiently create slides.

AutoFormat button (Word)

Insert slides from a file You can insert entire slides from another presentation (or another application) by clicking Slides From File (Insert menu).

Export a Presentation to Word

Export everything from PowerPoint   You can export an entire presentation to Word, including slide images and notes pages, by clicking Write-Up (Tools menu).

Start a report from PowerPoint   Perhaps you created the presentation first, and now need to generate a more extensive document in Word. Use the Report It button to launch Word and export the text of your presentation without slide images.

Each slide title in PowerPoint becomes a Heading 1 in Word.

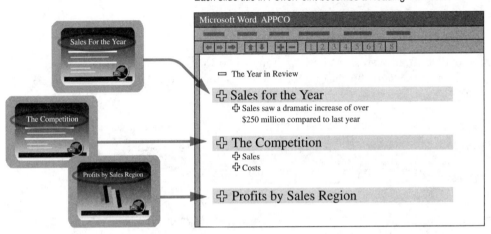

Next Steps

To	See
Format your presentation	"Customize the Appearance of Your Presentation," page 264
Export slide images and text to Word	"Create Presentation Handouts and Speaker's Notes," page 259

Get Your Point Across with Graphics

Let Your Audience See It While You Say It

You have a lot of complex information to present to a broad audience. Representing information graphically is often more effective than using text only. When it's necessary to reach a broad audience, some of whom might not be as familiar with your material, find ways to use visuals to help the overall comprehension level.

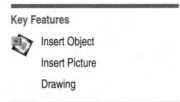

Key Features

Insert Object

Insert Picture

Drawing

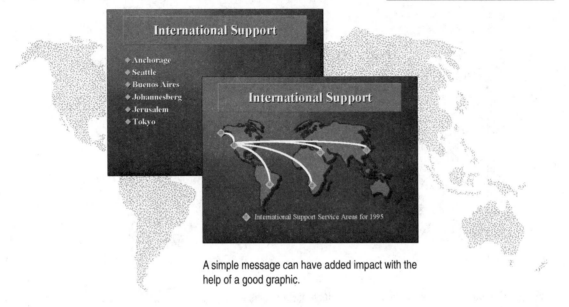

A simple message can have added impact with the help of a good graphic.

Note   In general, graphics are referred to as objects, whether the graphic is as simple as a line or as complex as a piece of clip art.

Use Graphic Effects

A well-placed graphic can transform a plain-looking slide into a compelling visual message. PowerPoint includes a full complement of tools you can use to draw simple line images or complex objects. The Drawing toolbar is normally visible on your screen. Additional drawing tools are available on the Drawing+ toolbar, which you activate by moving the cursor over any toolbar, pressing the right mouse button, and selecting Drawing+ from the menu.

For Help, double-click.
In the PowerPoint online index look up:
drawing
shadows
slide backgrounds

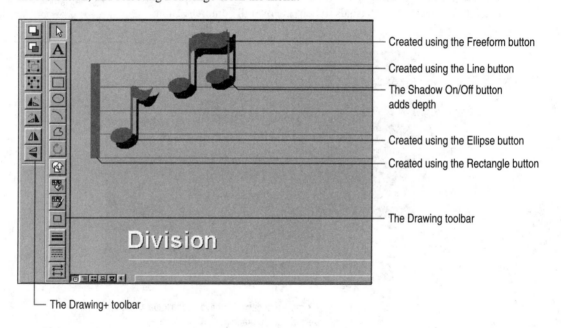

Created using the Freeform button

Created using the Line button

The Shadow On/Off button adds depth

Created using the Ellipse button

Created using the Rectangle button

The Drawing toolbar

The Drawing+ toolbar

 Selecting objects   With an object selected, Press Tab to move the selection to each object on the screen in succession. This is handy when trying to select stacked objects in close proximity to one another.

Shadow boxing   To apply a shadow to a slide's title box, you must first select the box and fill it with a color or pattern. To apply a shadow to the text only, click Font (Format menu).

Rotate and flip objects   Change the orientation of objects with the Flip and Rotate buttons on the Drawing and Drawing+ toolbars.

Rotate Left button

Fancy Fills

You can apply fills to slide backgrounds by clicking Custom Background (Format menu). Apply fills to text boxes and drawn objects by clicking Colors and Lines (Format menu).

PowerPoint includes a number of special patterns and textures you can use as fills. You can create shaded fills using one or two colors, and you can use pictures for slide backgrounds. For more information, see **fills** and **patterns** in the PowerPoint online index.

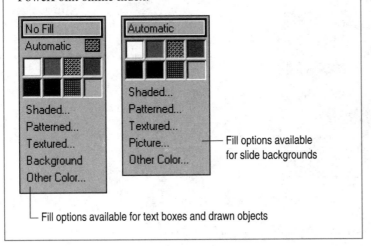

— Fill options available for slide backgrounds

└ Fill options available for text boxes and drawn objects

Add Clip Art

The ClipArt Gallery is your source for a variety of useful illustrations. In addition to providing a handy way to browse and select clip art, you can add your own clip art to the gallery, and you can reorganize and categorize your clip art using the ClipArt Gallery Options dialog box.

Activate the Microsoft ClipArt Gallery by clicking the Insert Clip Art button or by clicking Object (Insert menu) and selecting Microsoft ClipArt Gallery from the list.

 For Help, double-click.
In the PowerPoint online index look up:
clip art

If you want a complex graphic, check the ClipArt Gallery

 Insert pictures   If you know the exact filename and location of the artwork you need, click Picture (Insert menu) to place it in your presentation. Using the Picture command is useful when the art files are on floppy disks or in remote network locations that have not been indexed by the ClipArt Gallery.

Recoloring art   Many pieces of clip art are in color. If a particular color that is used in several places in the art doesn't work well, click Recolor (Tools menu) to select alternatives. All areas that are the same color are changed at the same time. To recolor a specific area of a piece of art, double-click the art and then click the Ungroup button on the Drawing+ toolbar. Select the area you want to recolor, and choose an alternative color using the Fill Color button on the Drawing toolbar.

Fill Color button

Insert Clip Art button

Add AutoShapes

The AutoShape button on the Drawing toolbar contains a number of useful shapes. Once you select an AutoShape, you can type text into it.

 For Help, double-click.
In the PowerPoint online index look up:
AutoShapes

AutoShapes with shadows and text

 Change objects' orientation Use the Flip buttons on the Drawing+ toolbar and the Rotate buttons on the Drawing toolbar to re-orient objects. Change the direction of AutoShape arrows, for example.

Flip Horizontal button

Auto-sizing AutoShapes To automatically fit an AutoShape to the text you type into it, select the shape, click Text Anchor (Format menu), and then click Adjust Object Size To Fit Text.

Free Rotate tool

Special handles Many AutoShapes have adjustment handles to adjust a unique dimension of the shape.

AutoShapes button

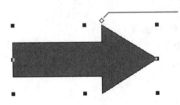

This adjustment handle changes the size of the arrowhead

Use Text Effects

You can make text more readable and more visually interesting using PowerPoint's text effects.

 For Help, double-click.
In the PowerPoint online index look up:
font attributes
WordArt

- Apply text shadow, color, font, and font size with buttons on the Formatting toolbar.

- Create subscript, superscript, and embossed effects by clicking Font (Format menu).

- Use the Change Case command (Format menu) to change the case of selected text.

- To create a special text effect, such as text in a circle, click Object (Insert menu) and select Microsoft WordArt in the Object Type list.

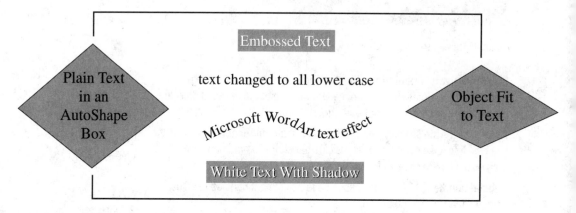

Text in shapes You can type text into any shape you draw with the Rectangle, Ellipse, or AutoShape buttons. The Text Anchor command (Format menu) gives you control over how text in shapes is positioned. The Adjust Object Size To Fit Text option automatically sizes any shape to fit the text it contains.

Add Graphics from Other Programs

You can use the PowerPoint drawing tools to create complex graphics, but sometimes you might need to use other graphics, such as a company logo created with an illustration program, or some charts. You can *embed* objects created by other programs using the Object and Picture commands (Insert menu).

 For Help, double-click.
In the PowerPoint online index look up:
embedded objects
charts

Note In PowerPoint, an embedded object is anything created by another program and inserted into your presentation. Charts, worksheets, and drawings are examples of information you can embed in a presentation. PowerPoint includes tools you can use to build embedded data charts and organizational charts.

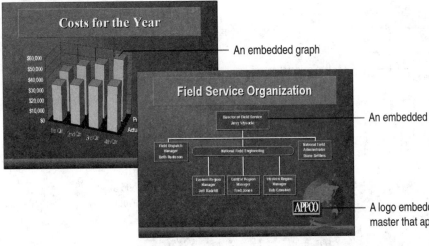

An embedded graph

An embedded organization chart

A logo embedded on the slide master that appears on every slide

 Drag from another application You can get existing data and graphics into your presentations without using any commands at all, simply by dragging. For example, you can drag a chart directly from Microsoft Excel to a PowerPoint slide. With both applications running, resize their windows so you can see both the slide in PowerPoint and the chart in Microsoft Excel. Then drag the chart to the slide.

Insert Graph button

For more information about Microsoft Excel worksheets, see "Create Your First Microsoft Excel Workbook," page 70; embedding objects, see "Use Office Applications Together," page 103; slide masters, see "Customize the Appearance of Your Presentation," page 264.

Special Objects in PowerPoint

Insert a Word table   The Insert Microsoft Word Table button creates an embedded Microsoft Word table on a slide. The table appears in a window with the Word ruler bars, and the menus and toolbars change to those of Word. You can use all of the Word features to complete the table. When you're finished, click anywhere on the slide outside the table window to return to PowerPoint. For more information, see **Word, tables** in the PowerPoint online index.

Insert an organizational chart   If you give presentations often, you've probably used organization charts from time to time. PowerPoint includes a special application to make creating organizational charts easier. Click Object (Insert menu) and choose Microsoft Organization Chart to add an organization chart to an existing slide. The colors in the organization chart are optimized to match the slide. For more information, see **Organization Chart** in the PowerPoint online index.

Create an organization chart slide   PowerPoint includes a special slide layout that makes it easy to create an organization chart. Click the Slide Layout button and select the Org Chart layout. For more information, see **slide layouts** in the PowerPoint online index.

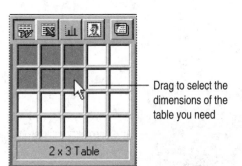

Drag to select the dimensions of the table you need

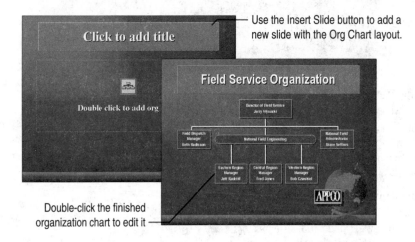

Use the Insert Slide button to add a new slide with the Org Chart layout.

Double-click the finished organization chart to edit it

Next Steps

To	See
Add multimedia elements and effects	"Prepare for an Electronic Presentation," page 280
Create charts	"Add a Chart to a Document or Presentation," page 223
Format text	"About Creating and Opening Documents and Databases," page 46

Prepare for an Electronic Presentation

Unleash the Full Power of PowerPoint

You are faced with the task of giving an important presentation electronically, using a computer instead of a slide projector. Using PowerPoint, you can prepare easily for many contingencies. You may need to display detailed data from Microsoft Excel. Your audience may have a reputation for asking tough questions. And, you might have the option of using a multimedia computer, so you want to add some multimedia dazzle, just in case.

Key Features

 Slide Transitions

Rehearsal

Media Clip

Why an Electronic Presentation?

- Make last-minute changes, literally, right up to the last minute.
- Slide transitions and builds provide more control over pacing.
- Color presentations look as good or better than 35mm slides.
- Multimedia!

Preparing Builds and Slide Transitions

If you'd like to keep your audience from getting ahead of you, you can create "builds." Each time you click the mouse, another item— a text item or a graphic object—appears. This is also known as "progressive disclosure."

For Help, double-click. In the PowerPoint online index look up:
build slides
transitions

- When you move to the next item in a build, previously displayed items can be dimmed or changed to a different color.

- You can set text items, including bullets and titles, to build one character at a time.

- You can create more than one build per slide, and determine the order in which they are activated.

You also plan to add special transition effects that occur between slides, including sound effects. Advancing to the next slide automatically activates any transition effects you apply.

Control what the audience sees with builds.

Transitions fade from one slide to the next.

Object builds   Besides building bulleted items on a slide, you can also use builds to disclose several graphic objects on a slide, one at a time. Select an object and click Animations Settings (Tools menu) to assign effects and to determine the order of appearance for each object.

Use the Animations Effects toolbar   Use handy buttons to apply builds to your slides. Click Toolbars (View menu) to display the Animations Effects toolbar.

Be Prepared with Hidden Slides

You want to have a slide or two ready with information that you'd rather not have to discuss unless absolutely necessary (when you get the dreaded awkward question). Click Hide Slide (Tools menu) to create hidden slides for information that you can choose to display or skip, at your discretion.

 For Help, double-click.
In the PowerPoint online index look up:
hidden slides
notes

   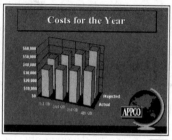

10

In Slide Sorter View, this icon
indicates a hidden slide.

 Provide additional information only in handouts   When printing slides, notes pages, or handouts, you can choose whether or not to include hidden slides. If you have information that you don't necessarily need to discuss but want to provide to your audience in a handout, you can put the information on hidden slides and print it, but skip it during the presentation.

Use hidden slides to add notes pages   If you use Notes Pages to produce your audience handouts, but you need more than one page of notes for a particular slide, copy it and paste a duplicate slide after it. Then hide the new slide, switch to notes view, delete the slide image, and continue typing in your notes.

Hide Slide button
(Slide Sorter toolbar)

Branching to Other Locations

Your presentation need not be limited to a single linear path. You can set up ways to branch from one slide to other slides or to activate other applications to display supporting data. To anticipate the needs of different audiences, you can also build contingency plans into your presentations.

Click Interactive Settings (Tools menu) to assign to any selected object an action that occurs when the object is clicked.

For Help, double-click.
In the PowerPoint online index look up:
branching
Interactive Settings
Insert Object

Clicking an object can jump to a particular slide ...

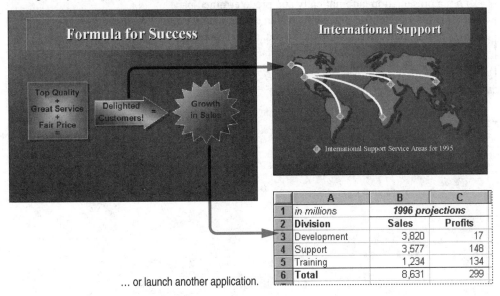

	A	B	C
1	*in millions*	*1996 projections*	
2	**Division**	**Sales**	**Profits**
3	Development	3,820	17
4	Support	3,577	148
5	Training	1,234	134
6	**Total**	**8,631**	**299**

... or launch another application.

Branching to hidden slides Perhaps a particular slide in your presentation could raise a question you don't want to address unless specifically asked. You can place an object on that slide that you can use as a "button" (but doesn't look like one) that, when clicked, jumps to a hidden slide containing information that addresses the question. With the object selected, click Interactive Settings (Tools menu) to specify the slide you want to activate. See "Be Prepared with Hidden Slides," earlier in this topic.

Presentation Kiosks

Computer kiosks with self-running presentations are a great way to provide information, one "audience member" at a time. If you want, attach media clips to play as each slide is displayed, with narration, music or sound effects.

For an interactive kiosk that a viewer can control, create objects such as "Next Slide" and "Previous Slide" buttons that appear on each slide. Then use the Interactive Settings command to assign the appropriate action to each object.

To run a presentation automatically at a predetermined pace, use slide timing. Set the slide show to run continuously until you press ESC. (Be sure to hide the keyboard and mouse to ensure an uninterrupted show.) For details, look up **kiosk** in the PowerPoint online index.

Time and Rehearse Your Presentation

You want to make sure that you're ready to go and that everything works correctly.

For Help, double-click.
In the PowerPoint online index look up:
rehearsal
Slide Meter

- First, do a "dress rehearsal" of your presentation with the Rehearsal dialog box displayed. Each time you advance to the next slide, the amount of time the slide was displayed is recorded.
- After running through the presentation, PowerPoint asks if you want to keep the timings and display them in Slide Sorter View. There you can check to see if you have too much or too little material and make necessary adjustments.

Select Rehearse New Timings (Slide Show command, View menu).

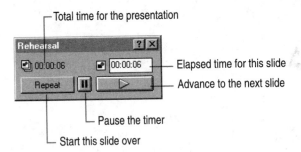

Total time for the presentation

Elapsed time for this slide

Advance to the next slide

Pause the timer

Start this slide over

 The Slide Meter As you rehearse a presentation, the Slide Meter keeps track of how you're doing compared to the slide timings you have entered for each slide. Click the right mouse button to display the shortcut menu while the slide show is running and click Slide Meter.

Rehearse Timings button
(Slide Sorter toolbar)

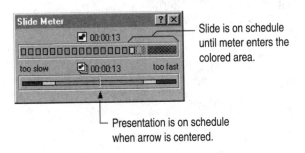

Slide is on schedule until meter enters the colored area.

Presentation is on schedule when arrow is centered.

Add Multimedia Effects

You're excited about presenting on a multimedia computer, and you've got some ideas. You want to add an animation clip for some comic relief. You want to add a sound effect to a slide that plays only if you click it with the mouse. You want to add a couple of sound effects to play automatically on certain slide transitions.

 For Help, double-click.
In the PowerPoint online index look up:
media clips
animations
multimedia

You can create special slides that play sounds when activated.

Inserting a Media Clip   The Media Player application allows you to embed a video clip, animation clip, MIDI (Musical Instrument Digital Interface) sequence, or sound clip in a presentation. Click Movie (Insert menu), Sound (Insert menu), or Media Clip (Object command, Insert menu).

Controlling playback   Click Animation Settings (Tools menu) to determine when a media clip will play: only when you click on it, as soon as the slide is displayed, or synched with any step of a build.

Use Slide Sorter View

You can apply builds and transitions and set slide timing using buttons on the Slide Sorter toolbar, which appears automatically when you activate Slide Sorter view. Icons appear below slide images if effects have been applied. For more information, look up **slide sorter view** in the PowerPoint online index.

Builds   Select a slide or slides and apply build effects.

Transitions   Select a slide or slides, apply transition effects, and specify the display time in seconds. Remove timing for selected slides by selecting Only On Mouse Click in the Transition dialog box.

Slide Timing   Click the Rehearse Timings button to start a slide show and record display time for each slide.

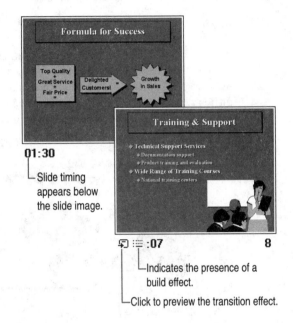

01:30

└ Slide timing appears below the slide image.

8

└ Indicates the presence of a build effect.

└ Click to preview the transition effect.

Next Steps

To	See
Take your electronic presentation on the road	"Give an Electronic Presentation," page 288

Give an Electronic Presentation

Use the Most Sophisticated "Slide Projector" Available—Your Computer

You've spent a lot of time putting together a great electronic presentation, and now it's time to actually make it happen. You are ready to go. You've anticipated the needs of the audience and the difficult questions that might arise. You've seeded your presentation with hidden information, effects, and detours you can employ at your discretion.

Key Features

 Slide Navigator

Meeting Minder

Stage Manager

 Packing for the road   When traveling to a far-away location to give an electronic presentation, it is essential that you bring all the files you need. The Pack And Go Wizard command (File menu) helps you bundle up all the essentials.

The Element of Surprise

You're at a crucial point in your presentation, and somebody asks a question about a previous slide. You need to find it without losing your place (and your credibility). You use the Slide Navigator to move directly to the slide without having to step through each slide in between. While the presentation is in progress, click the right mouse button and click Slide Navigator (Go To menu).

Following a few slides containing critical news you inserted hidden slides showing supporting information that you'd rather not have to discuss unless absolutely necessary. Sure enough, somebody asks an awkward question as a critical slide is being discussed. Using the Navigator, you display a hidden slide by selecting the title from the list. Hidden slides are indicated by parentheses around the slide number in the Slide Navigator dialog box.

You've attached some flashy effects to objects placed on slides. With the timing of a comedian, you click an object to play a sound effect. You click another object to open a Microsoft Excel workbook containing supporting data. You can return to the main presentation any time you want.

For Help, double-click.
In the PowerPoint online index look up:
Slide Navigator
hidden slides
sound effects

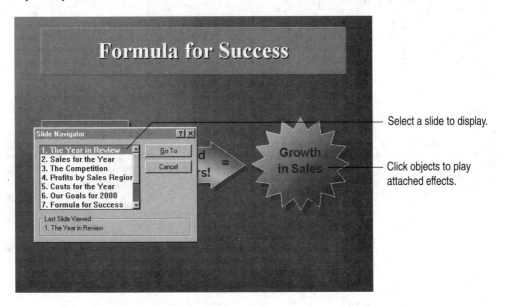

Select a slide to display.

Click objects to play attached effects.

Take Notes and Track Action Items on Screen

You want to keep track of some good ideas that came up during your presentation. You also want the audience to know you are earnestly interested in their comments. While the presentation is in progress, you can record "meeting minutes." Click the right mouse button during the slide show and click Meeting Minder.

Perhaps people in the audience will volunteer to do things and get back to you with the results. Track these action items with the Action Item tab in the Meeting Minder dialog box. The action item is displayed automatically on a new slide inserted at the end of the presentation.

Back in your office after the presentation, you can view and print your notes and action items. Click Meeting Minder (Tools menu).

 For Help, double-click.
In the PowerPoint online index look up:
**Meeting Minder
action items**

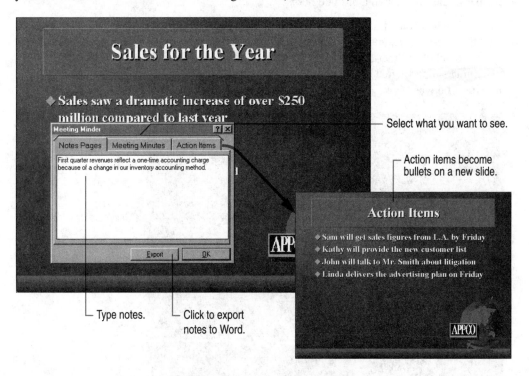

Select what you want to see.

Action items become bullets on a new slide.

Type notes.

Click to export notes to Word.

Draw attention to important facts   Like a coach drawing a play on the blackboard, use the Pen to draw on your slides to focus attention on important facts and figures. Don't worry about marking up your slides—Pen drawings are only temporary. Click the right mouse button while a slide show is running and click Pen.

Give a Presentation on a Remote Computer

"Pay no attention to the person behind the laptop!" If you have the hardware and the necessary network connections, use the PowerPoint capability to control another copy of PowerPoint on one or more remote computers. The controlling computer's screen can display behind-the-scenes tools that won't be displayed on the presentation screen. Click Presentation Conference (Tools Menu).

Network presentations You can run a presentation over a network on multiple computers using the Presentation Conferencing feature. You just need to know the names of the computers you need to connect. Click Presentation Conference (Tools menu).

For more information, see **presentation conferencing** in the PowerPoint online index.

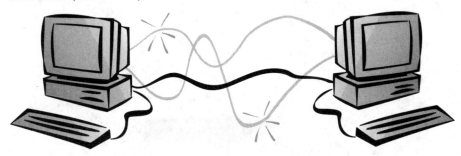

Next Steps

To	See
Create a report in Word using your presentation	"Transfer Information Between PowerPoint and Other Applications," page 268

PART 6

Beyond the Card File

Keeping Track of Contacts

Contents

Where Should You Store Your Contact Information?

You can use Schedule+, Microsoft Excel, or Microsoft Access to set up and maintain information about your customer contacts, and you easily can move information between applications. If you've started your contact list in Word, you'll benefit by moving the list to one of these three applications. (To store your data in Microsoft Access, you'll need either Microsoft Office Professional or an individual copy of Microsoft Access.)

Use the table on this page to decide which application best fits your needs. See the topics in the rest of this part of the book for details about how each application lends itself to contact management.

Should you use?	Ask yourself ...	If yes, consider that ...
Microsoft Schedule+	Do you just need to keep simple name, address, and phone number information for your personal contacts? Do you plan to use your list like a business card file?	Schedule+ lets you store and update your Contact List easily. You can sort your contacts and group them together.
	Are there a variety of types of information you'd like to include?	Schedule+ determines the storage categories for you. Make sure the categories provided meet your needs.
Microsoft Excel	Do you have a medium-sized list of contacts for which searching and filtering for particular types of contacts would be helpful?	Microsoft Excel stores up to 16,383 contact entries. You can search through your list, or filter it to display contacts that match criteria you specify.
	Do you need to set up custom categories, or analyze the data in your list?	In Microsoft Excel you can organize your data and display it in ways that allow you to analyze it. You can assign any column headings you need, then rearrange the columns or display a partial set of columns.
Microsoft Access	Is your contact list very large, or part of a larger multiuser database?	If your contact information feeds into sales quotes, packing lists, invoices, or other database applications, your department or company might want to make a multiuser Microsoft Access database the central focus for these activities.
	Do you want to keep extensive notes or other running commentary for each contact?	With Microsoft Access, you can add a record of each phone conversation or other interaction with your contacts and easily retrieve this kind of information.

Can I Move My Contact Data to Another Application?

You can easily move data among any of the Office applications, even if your data originates on a mainframe computer at corporate headquarters. You can export a list stored in any Office application, including Word, to any other Office application, in addition to copying and pasting data between applications. You can automatically create *delimited* plain-text files that make it easy to import (read) a list from one Office application into another. A delimited text file preserves information about how your data is organized when you move the data to another application.

Commas separate (delimit) the categories (columns) of information in each line of your list.

```
Borinski,Morris,Reggie's Wine and Cheese,208-555-9877
Dubois,Marie,Parisian Specialties,312-555-7002
Kumar,Hari,Seven Seas Imports,71-555-1717
Langford,Archibald,Richmond Sugar,71-555-1881
Martinez,Roberto,Silver Screen Food Gems,406-555-7699
```

With	You can read in data from ...	And you can move data out by ...
Microsoft Word	A delimited text file to a table.	Writing a table or other text to a delimited plain-text file.
Microsoft Schedule+	A delimited text file to your Contact List. You specify which text file column goes in which of the available categories.	Writing all or part of your contact information to a delimited text file.
Microsoft Excel	A delimited text file to a worksheet. The Text Import Wizard lets you specify how to set up the list. A dBASE .DBF file directly to a worksheet. External sources in any of the supported formats. You use Microsoft Query, a Microsoft Excel add-in that supports most popular database formats.	Exporting a list to a delimited text file. Creating and saving tables in any of the supported database formats.
Microsoft Access	A delimited text file to a new or existing database, by using the Text Import Wizard. A Microsoft Excel list to a new database, by using the Convert To Access command. External sources in any of the supported formats.	Outputting to a Microsoft Excel workbook file, a delimited text file, or a file in any supported database format.

Manage Contacts with Schedule+

Schedule+ makes it easy to store, update, organize, and retrieve names, phone numbers, and other important business and personal facts about your contacts. With Schedule+, you can quickly find the information you need, regardless of how many contacts you have, and you can locate information even when you can't remember a name, only a related fact, such as the name of the company where the contact works.

Key Features

 Contact List

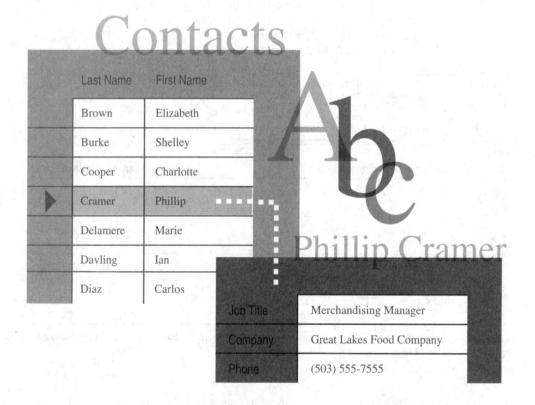

Create a Contact List

In the Schedule+ Contact List, you can list only names and phone numbers or you can include additional business information and personal facts. You may find the extra information you can store in your Contact List, such as job title or spouse's name, very handy when you need to call on a contact you haven't spoken to in a long time.

To create a Contact List, click the Contacts tab.

In the Schedule+ online index look up:
Contact List
importing

To display information about a contact, type the first few letters of the last name here.

To add a contact, type the last and first name, and press ENTER ...

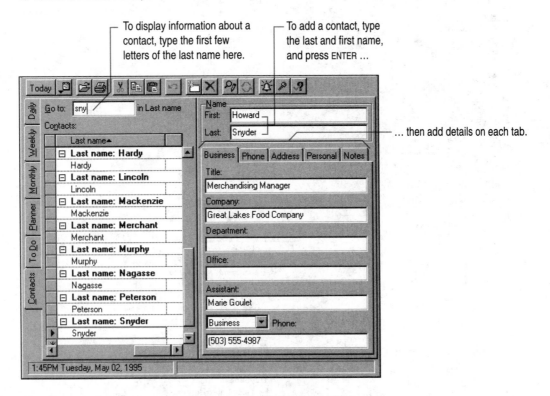

... then add details on each tab.

 Do you have a list of contacts in another application? Copy it into Schedule+ with the Text Import Wizard. To use the wizard, click Import (File menu). For more information, see "Where Should You Store Your Contact Information?," page 294.

Need to update contact information? Select the contact, and then change the information on the appropriate tab.

Organize Your Contact List

If you have many contacts, make it easier to find information by grouping related contacts and sorting your list alphabetically.

To organize your contacts by group, click Group By (View menu). To alphabetically sort the contents of any group in the Contact List, click the appropriate column heading.

In the Schedule+ online index look up:
grouping contacts
sorting, contacts

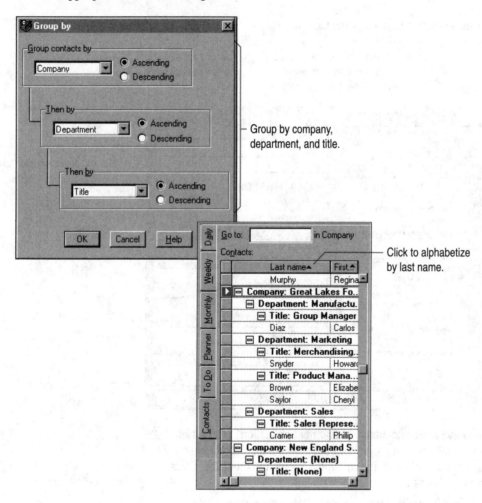

Group by company, department, and title.

Click to alphabetize by last name.

Get Assistance While You Work

Schedule+ for Windows 95 provides expanded and improved online assistance to help you get your work done faster. Step-by-step instructions and more help you perform your task.

When you need an answer to a Schedule+ question, click Microsoft Schedule+ Help Topics (Help menu).

Look up information in the online index Click the Index tab to look up index entries like those listed with the topics in this book.

Ask for help in your own words For more in-depth assistance, click the tab for the Answer Wizard. Ask the Answer Wizard questions in your own words, and then go quickly to the information you need.

Next Steps

To	See
Create mailing labels from your Contact List	"Create a Mailing," page 176

Create a Business Contact List in Microsoft Excel

Organize Names and Addresses

When you want help managing your expanding collection of customer contact information, turn to Microsoft Excel. Once entered in a list on a worksheet, your contact information is always at your fingertips. In a mouse click or two, you can zero in on the customers you need to call. Use the techniques in this topic to organize other similar lists for ready access.

Key Features

AutoComplete

Sort

AutoFill

AutoFilter

 Do you already have some names and addresses in a file? Microsoft Excel can read your text file. For details, look up **importing data** in the Microsoft Excel online index.

What Should Your List Contain?

Beyond name, address, and phone number, what do you want to know when you look up a contact? Think about how you organize your contact information now. Location? Size or type of account? Company name or contact name?

Assign a category for each item of information you want to keep.

 For Help, double-click. In the Microsoft Excel online index look up: **formatting characters wrapping text in a cell**

Type column headings to label your categories, then format the headings.

	A	B	C	D	E	F
	F1		f_x Address			
1	Company Name	First Name	Last Name	Phone	Product Line	Address
2						
3						
4						
5						
6						
7						
8						

Customer Contacts

Keep your column headings visible on screen Use the Freeze Panes command to keep the heading row at the top of the window while you enter and scroll through the rows of data. For details, look up **freezing panes** in the Microsoft Excel online index.

Guidelines

Label the columns with your categories   You'll enter one contact per row. The order of the columns isn't important—you can easily rearrange them or add more categories later.

Want to find people by their surnames?   Put first and last names in separate columns.

Make the column headings stand out   Format them bold, underlined, or a different color. From differently formatted headings, Microsoft Excel can detect that you're creating a list and help you manage its contents.

Bold button

Avoid blank lines, lines of dashes, and extra spaces   Use borders if you want to separate the column headings from the data. Use the alignment buttons to position text within cells.

Borders button   Alignment buttons

Get the Help You Need While You Work

Expanded and improved online assistance is just a click away. It's the fastest way to get information so you can keep working.

Ask the Answer Wizard   Type a question in your own words. The Answer Wizard lists online Help topics related to your question. Double-click the Help button and then click the Answer Wizard tab.

Look it up in the online index   Instead of typing a question, use index entries provided in this book to find online topics related to your task. Double-click the Help button and then click the Index tab.

For details, see "Get Assistance While You Work," page 30. Or look up **Help** in the online index.

Enter Your Contact Information

Now type the data for each contact under the headings you've established. Use the same formatting for all of your entries; just remember to make them different from the headings. When you need to make the same entry many times, Microsoft Excel learns what you want to type. With AutoComplete, Microsoft Excel finishes the entry for you—you only need to type a letter or two. Also, Microsoft Excel works behind the scenes, correcting typos.

 For Help, double-click.
In the Microsoft Excel
online index look up:
entering data
AutoComplete

Company Name	First Name	Last Name	Phone	Product Line
Richmond Sugar	Archibald	Langford	(71) 555-1181	Confections
Silver Screen Food Gems	Roberto	Martinez	(406) 555-7699	Confections
Parisian Specialties	Marie	Dubois	(312) 555-7002	Seafood
Reggie's Wine and Cheese	Morris	Borinski	(208) 555-9877	Beverages
Seven Seas Imports	Hari	Kumar	(71) 555-1717	
				Beverages
				Confections
				Seafood

Customer Contacts

Double-click a cell, and then press ALT+DOWN ARROW to pick from a list of your previous entries.

Don't worry about typing your contact entries in a particular order
After you key them in, you can reorder them with a couple of mouse clicks. For details, look up **sorting data, lists** in the Microsoft Excel online index.

Want to repeat an entry down a column? Drag the fill handle. For details, look up **AutoFill** in the Microsoft Excel online index.

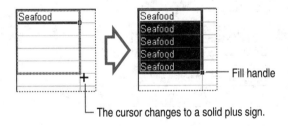

Fill handle

The cursor changes to a solid plus sign.

Zero In on the Contacts You Want

Once your list is entered, turn on AutoFilter by clicking AutoFilter (Data menu, Filter submenu). Now you're ready to find information fast.

Don't need to see some of the columns? Select them, click the right mouse button, and choose Hide.

 Alphabetize by any column. Just click a cell in the column, and then click the Sort Ascending button.

To see just the contacts who buy a particular product in a particular state, use AutoFilter. For example, display only the contacts in Washington who buy meat or poultry.

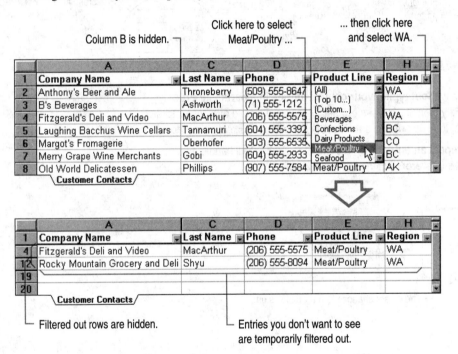 For Help, double-click. In the Microsoft Excel online index look up:
AutoFilter
columns, hidden
sorting data, lists

 Notice changes in how editing commands work? When you use AutoFilter, certain editing, formatting, and printing commands work differently.

Did You Know That You Can Use Microsoft Access Forms to Enter Contacts?

If you have Microsoft Access, you can create a custom form that makes it easy to enter and update your Microsoft Excel contact information. When you fill in the blanks in your form, the information is transferred to your Microsoft Excel worksheet.

You can easily specify the layout and appearance of the form, even reproduce familiar paper forms. Plus, a Microsoft Access form can help you enter data correctly, such as by checking to make sure postal codes have the right number of digits.

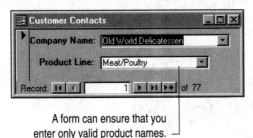

A form can ensure that you enter only valid product names.

For details, look up **Form Wizard (Microsoft Access)** in the Microsoft Excel online index.

Next Steps

To	See
Analyze your contacts: add up how many customers you have in each region, or find your top ten customers, for example	"Create a Sales Summary," page 446
Send a mailing to your contacts	"Create a Mailing," page 176

Track Your Business Contacts in Microsoft Access

Use a Database to Organize Business Contact Information

Is your collection of business contact information growing? Do you want to track details about phone calls to your contacts and about your follow-up activities?

The Microsoft Access Database Wizard can help you create a database to organize your contact information. Once you enter information into this database, you can find details about contacts instantly and can create quick summaries of phone calls and other contact information.

Key Features

 Database Wizard

Forms

Filter By Form

	First Name	Last Name	Company Name	Call Date	Call Time	Subject	Notes
	Jack	Tanner	LKXS Radiography	7/17/95	9:30 AM	Order of 6/4	Not delivered yet, investigating
	Jack	Tanner	LKXS Radiography	7/18/95	3:30 PM	Order of 6/4	Provided follow-up
	Jack	Tanner	LKXS Radiography	7/19/95	9:00 AM	Order of 6/4	Was delivered, missing some parts
▶	Jack	Tanner	LKXS Radiography	7/19/95	10:15 AM	Missing parts	Follow up: they will ship today
	Jack	Tanner	LKXS Radiography	7/23/95	9:00 AM	Missing parts	Follow up: delivered 7/22
	Irene	Mendel	ProElectron, Inc.	7/18/95	3:45 PM	New products	Sending her information about new
	Irene	Mendel	ProElectron, Inc.	7/23/95	1:30 PM	Order of 7/23	Ordering 3 electron microscopes

To complete the steps in this topic You need to have either Microsoft Office Professional or an individual copy of Microsoft Access for Windows 95 installed.

Create a Contact Management Database

From the Microsoft Access window, click New Database (File menu), and then double-click Contact Management to start the Database Wizard. Follow the instructions on the screen. Include all of the tables, and choose all of the fields from the Calls table and the First and Last Name fields from the Contacts table. When selecting fields, you can click the box to include sample data if you want to see examples of how to use the database.

For Help, double-click. In the Microsoft Access online index look up: **databases, creating**

The New dialog box lists the databases you can create automatically.

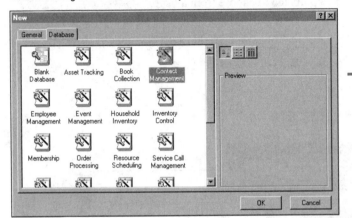

? For Help on dialog box options, click this button.

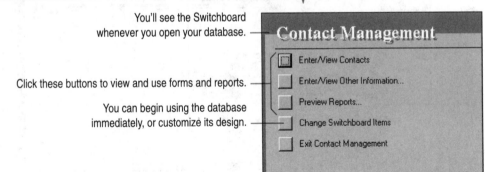

You'll see the Switchboard whenever you open your database.

Click these buttons to view and use forms and reports.

You can begin using the database immediately, or customize its design.

What's in Your New Database?

The Contact Management database contains a number of tables, forms, and reports ready for you to use. You have forms for entering and viewing contact names, addresses, telephone numbers, and notes, and a form that helps you log information about your calls to each contact. The reports in the database summarize information and include a weekly call summary and an alphabetic phone list.

Click the buttons on the Switchboard to explore the forms and reports in your database. Or, click the Database Window button, and then click the Tables, Forms, or Reports tab to choose from a list of objects.

 For Help, double-click.
In the Microsoft Access
online index look up:
forms, overview
reports, overview

Database Window button

Your Contact Management database includes everything you need
to store, retrieve, and summarize information about your contacts.

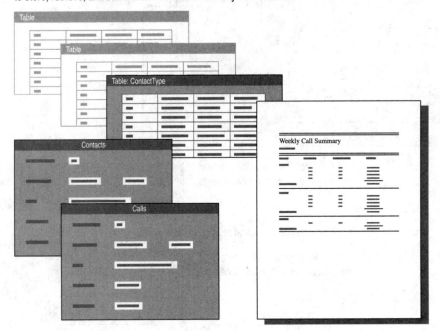

Enter Your Contact Information

Use the Contacts form to enter information about your contacts and to look up phone numbers when you make calls. On the Switchboard, click Enter/View Contacts. Then, as you interact with your contacts, click the Calls button to open the Calls form so you can enter information about each call.

If you included the sample data, you can view it as a guideline before entering your own data. Delete the sample data when you no longer want it.

For Help, double-click. In the Microsoft Access online index look up: **data, adding in Datasheet or Form view**

When you type details on the forms, Microsoft Access stores them for you.

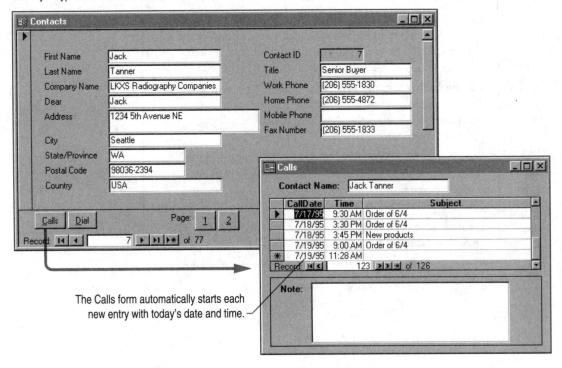

The Calls form automatically starts each new entry with today's date and time.

Want to include information about contacts that's stored elsewhere?
You can copy or import contact data from other Office applications or from
text files. For details, see "Where Should You Store Your Contact
Information?," page 294.

Use your contact data as a mailing list   You can create form letters and
mailing labels using the information in your Contact Management database.
For details, look up **queries, creating** in the Microsoft Access online index,
or see "Create a Mailing," page 176.

To view reports that summarize the information you've entered   Click
Preview Reports on the Switchboard.

Get the Help You Need While You Work

Expanded and improved online assistance is just a click away.
It's the fastest way to get information so that you can keep
working.

Ask the Answer Wizard   Type a question in your own words.
The Answer Wizard lists online Help topics related to your
question. Double-click the Help button, and then click the
Answer Wizard tab.

Look it up in the online index   Instead of typing a question, use
index entries provided in this book to find online topics
related to your task. Double-click the Help button, and then
click the Index tab.

For details, see "Get Assistance While You Work," page 30.
Or look up **Help** in the online index.

Get Critical Contact Information Fast

Once you've entered your data, you're in a position to find information fast. Filtering by form lets you find information in your database easily.

To find information about phone calls to a particular contact on a particular subject, open the Calls form, click the Filter By Form button, and then click the type of information you want to find.

 For Help, double-click.
In the Microsoft Access online index look up:
Filter By Form

Filter By
Form button

Apply Filter
button

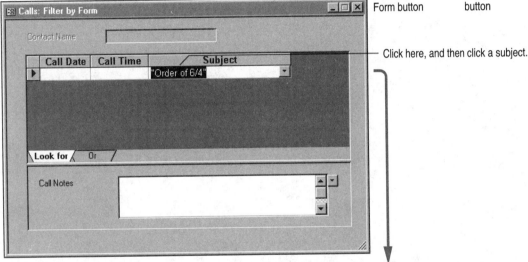

Click here, and then click a subject.

Click the Apply Filter button to see a list of the calls to the contact about the subject you chose.

CallDate	Time	Subject
7/17/95	9:30 AM	Order of 6/4
7/18/95	3:30 PM	Order of 6/4
7/19/95	9:00 AM	Order of 6/4

PART 7

Where Do You Need to Go Today?

Schedule Appointments, Tasks, and Meetings Electronically

Contents

Schedule an Appointment

Take control of your schedule by keeping all your appointments, including special events such as a friend's birthday, in the Schedule+ Appointment Book. Scheduling appointments, even recurring appointments, is a snap. And, keeping appointments online makes them easy to view and update. Whether you use your schedule online, print it, or download it to a Sharp Wizard or Timex Data Link wristwatch, it's always up to date.

Key Features

 Appointment Book

Printing Schedules

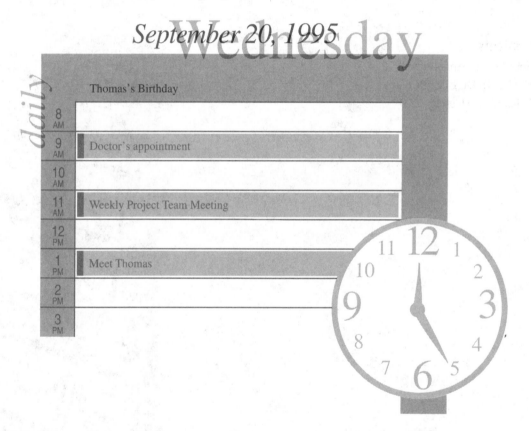

 Schedule new appointments quickly   Just click the Make An Appointment button on the Office Shortcut Bar. For details, look up **appointments** in the Schedule+ online index.

Make An Appointment

Enter an Appointment into Your Appointment Book

Keep your schedule up to date by entering all your appointments and special events, such as birthdays, in the Appointment Book. When you start Schedule+, you'll see the day's appointments first. Although you can check your schedule anytime during the day, you needn't—Schedule+ helps you arrive on time for each appointment by displaying a reminder shortly before you are due.

To enter an appointment into the Appointment Book, click the Daily tab.

In the Schedule+ online index look up:
Appointment Books
appointments, recurring

Type today's appointments in any open time slot.

To schedule a recurring appointment, click the Recurring button.

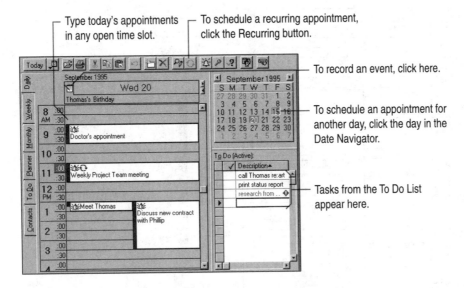

To record an event, click here.

To schedule an appointment for another day, click the day in the Date Navigator.

Tasks from the To Do List appear here.

 Need to reschedule an appointment? Drag it to another time slot. To move it to the same time on another day, drag it to the Date Navigator. Recurring appointments are automatically rescheduled for the new day and time.

Need more than 15 minutes to prepare for an appointment? Double-click the appointment, and then type the number of minutes you want.

Want to schedule two appointments at the same time? Click an existing appointment, and then click the Insert New Appointment button.

Have a Sharp Wizard or a Timex Data Link wristwatch? Download your schedule with the Export command (File menu). For details, look up **exporting** in the Schedule+ online index.

Insert New Appointment button

Print Your Schedule

If you'll be away from your desk for awhile, print your schedule and take it with you. Print daily, weekly, or monthly schedules in a choice of layouts that fit into your paper day planner.

To print your schedule, click Print (File menu), and then click a print layout.

By printing your daily, weekly, or monthly schedule, you can keep your appointments handy wherever you go.

In the Schedule+ online index look up:
schedules, printing

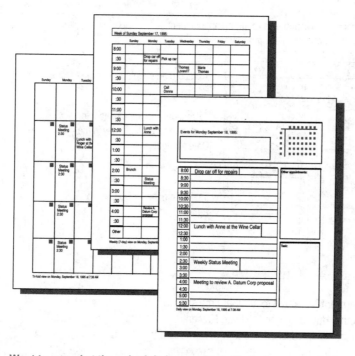

 Want to see what the schedule layouts look like before you print? Click Print (File menu), and then click the Preview button.

Next Steps

To	See
Set up a meeting	"Schedule a Meeting," page 320
Create a to do list	"Keep a To Do List," page 317

Keep a To Do List

Sometimes the hardest part of managing your time is keeping track of the tasks you need to accomplish to complete your assignments. By creating a To Do List in Schedule+, you keep a complete list of tasks in one place, where it's easy to find and update. And unlike a paper to do list, a Schedule+ To Do List will help you plan your work by allowing you to schedule time for tasks and by alerting you when a task is overdue.

Key Features

To Do List

Projects

September 25, 1995 Monday

Description	Priority	End Date	
Project: Monthly Report			
Write report	1	Fri 9/22/95	
Project: Trade Show			
Discuss new contract with Philip	3	Wed 9/27/95	
Project: Sales Meeting			
Weekly project team meeting	2	Mon 9/25/95	

✓ *tasks*

 Add tasks to your list whenever you think of them Just click the Add A Task button on the Office Shortcut Bar. For details, look up **tasks** in the Schedule+ online index.

Add A Task button

Create a To Do List

When you create a To Do List, you can add as much detail about a task as you need to help you manage your work. And although you can always switch to the To Do List to see which tasks you have yet to complete, you'll also see active tasks in the To Do List in your Appointment Book. That way, whenever you start Schedule+, you'll see what you need to do.

By adding some additional details when you enter a task in the To Do List, you can assure that tasks appear in your Appointment Book when you need them to. To have a task appear on a certain day, assign an end date. To provide early notification for a task, enter a duration and the task will appear in the Appointment Book that many days earlier.

In the Schedule+ online index look up:
To Do List
tasks

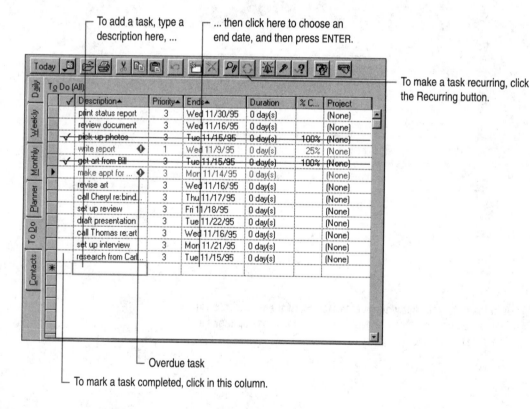

To add a task, type a description here, ...

... then click here to choose an end date, and then press ENTER.

To make a task recurring, click the Recurring button.

Overdue task

To mark a task completed, click in this column.

Do you have a to do list in another application?   Copy it into Schedule+ with the Text Import Wizard. Click Import (File menu).

Want to schedule time to work on a task?   Drag a task from the To Do List in the Appointment Book to a time slot in your Daily schedule.

Want to be reminded about an upcoming task? Assign the task an end date, select the task, and click the Reminder button.

Reminder button

Organize Tasks by Project

If you work on a number of projects at a time, you may find it useful to list and organize tasks by project. After typing project names, click Group By (View menu), and then choose the categories you want to group by.

In the Schedule+ online index look up:
projects
grouping projects
sorting, projects

To sort the projects by priority, click here.

To sort the projects by due date, click here.

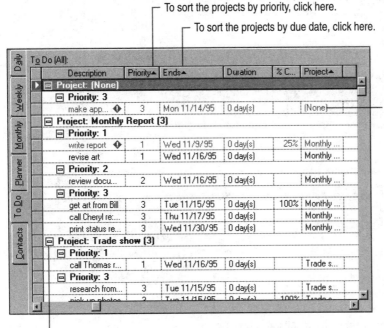

To assign a task to a project, click here and type a project name.

To hide a project's tasks, click the associated hide detail symbol.

Want to see only overdue tasks? Click Filter (View menu), and then point to Overdue Tasks.

Next Steps

To	See
Use your Schedule+ To Do List in another application	**exporting** in the Schedule+ online index
Keep track of names and addresses	"Manage Contacts with Schedule+," page 296

Schedule a Meeting

Does setting up a meeting have to include rounds of phone tag and rescheduling until you find a time that suits everyone? Not if you use Schedule+.

With Schedule+, you check your coworkers' schedules before you set a time, so you pick one that's convenient for everyone. Then, just send an invitation. Attendees won't forget about the meeting, since Schedule+ enters it in their Appointment Books when they accept the invitation.

Key Features

Meeting Wizard

Planner

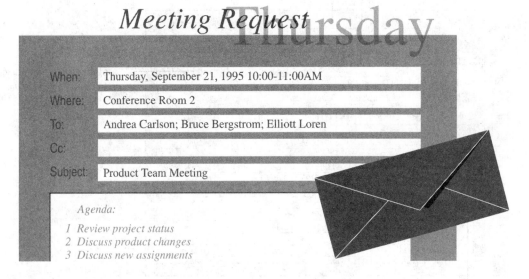

Meeting Request

When:	Thursday, September 21, 1995 10:00-11:00AM
Where:	Conference Room 2
To:	Andrea Carlson; Bruce Bergstrom; Elliott Loren
Cc:	
Subject:	Product Team Meeting

Agenda:

1 Review project status
2 Discuss product changes
3 Discuss new assignments

To schedule meetings, you need Microsoft Exchange client or a compatible electronic mail system.

Important The easiest way to schedule most meetings is with the Meeting Wizard. Just click the Meeting Wizard button. For scheduling a meeting with many busy people, the Schedule+ Planner provides more flexibility. For details, read the rest of this topic.

Meeting Wizard button

Find a Time to Meet

When you need to schedule a meeting with many busy people, use the Schedule+ Planner. First, list whom you want to invite. Schedule+ checks their schedules and displays the times when everyone is free and busy. Then, select a time when everyone can meet, and send a meeting request.

To display the Planner, click the Planner tab.

In the Schedule+ online index look up:
Planner

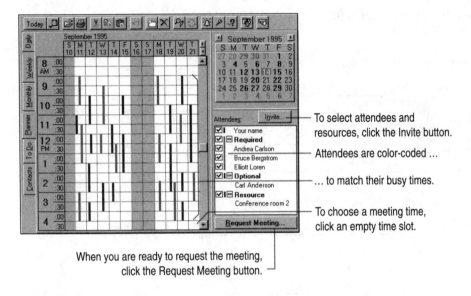

To select attendees and resources, click the Invite button.

Attendees are color-coded ...

... to match their busy times.

To choose a meeting time, click an empty time slot.

When you are ready to request the meeting, click the Request Meeting button.

 How can I tell who's busy at a given time? Click the right mouse button on a busy time to list the attendees who are busy then.

Having a hard time finding an available meeting time? To find the next time all attendees are free, click Auto Pick (Tools menu).

What if there are no free times? Remove all optional attendees from your list by clicking the check mark next to the Optional button. If there are no optional attendees or if you still can't find a free time, consider removing some required attendees by clicking the check marks next to their names.

Send a Meeting Request

Sending a meeting request gives each attendee the opportunity to accept or decline your invitation. When an attendee accepts, Schedule+ enters the appointment in his or her Appointment Book.

When you send the Meeting Request form, you can include a note, an agenda, and documents for attendees to review before the meeting.

To display the Meeting Request form, click the Request Meeting button on the Planner.

In the Schedule+ online index look up:
meeting requests
Appointment Books

To send the Meeting Request, click here.

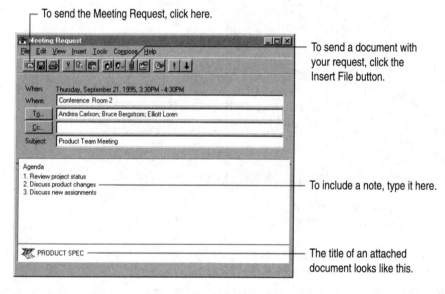

To send a document with your request, click the Insert File button.

To include a note, type it here.

The title of an attached document looks like this.

 Want to allow an associate to accept or decline your meeting requests?   Grant someone else permission to act as your delegate. For details, look up **delegates, for schedules** in the Schedule+ online index.

Get Assistance While You Work

Schedule+ for Windows 95 provides expanded and improved online assistance to help you get your work done faster. Step-by-step instructions and more help you perform your task.

When you need an answer to a Schedule+ question, click Microsoft Schedule+ Help Topics (Help menu).

Look up information in the online index Click the Index tab to look up index entries like those listed with the topics in this book.

Ask for help in your own words For more in-depth assistance, click the tab for the Answer Wizard. Ask the Answer Wizard questions in your own words, and then go quickly to the information you need.

Next Steps

To	In the Schedule+ online index look up
Set up recurring meetings	**meetings, recurring**
Change attendees or resources	**attendees** or **meetings, obtaining resources**
Track responses to your meeting request	**attendees, meeting request responses**
Reschedule or cancel a meeting	**rescheduling** or **canceling**
Manage another person's schedule	**opening, another user's schedule**

Working with the Team

Exchange Information with Others Over a Network

Contents

Share Documents Electronically

When you need to distribute your documents to coworkers, you want to do it in the most efficient way possible. You can easily distribute your documents online and get feedback from reviewers. Plus you can use Word to compose and reply to your messages.

You can share documents with other users over your network.

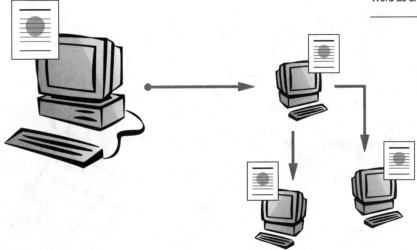

To send electronic mail   You must have Microsoft Exchange, Microsoft Mail, cc:Mail™, or another compatible electronic mail system installed on your computer. The examples in this topic use Microsoft Exchange.

 If you want to share Microsoft Access data   Send or route the data through electronic mail. For details, look up **sending** in the Microsoft Access online index. To post data, export it first. Look up **exporting** in the Microsoft Access online index.

Choose a Method for Sharing Documents

You have three options for sharing a document electronically.

Send a document Choose this method when you need to distribute a document quickly, you have a specific list of reviewers, and you want review comments quickly.

Route a document Choose this method when you have a longer review period, a short list of reviewers, and you want each reviewer to see the comments of previous reviewers.

Post a document Choose this method when you want to provide wide distribution of a document, such as a company policy manual, or when you're not sure who might need or want to review the document.

For Help, double-click.
In the online index look up:
sending
routing
posting

Send

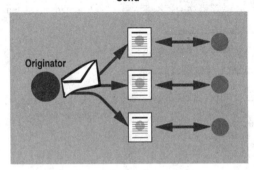

Route

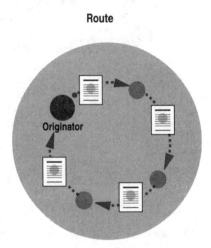

Post

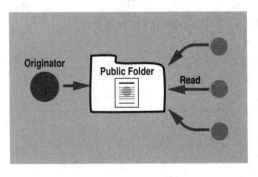

Send a Document

When you send a document, you have two options:

- Start from your electronic mail application, and then attach the document you want to send. For details, see the documentation for your electronic mail application.

- Click Send (File menu) to send a copy of the document you're working on. If you're sending from Microsoft Access, select a format for the document. This starts your electronic mail application, as shown in the example below.

For Help, double-click.
In the online index look up:
sending documents

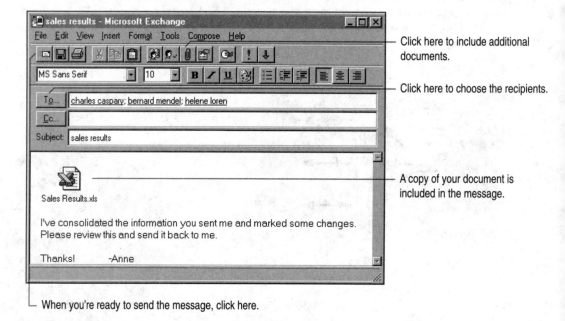

Click here to include additional documents.

Click here to choose the recipients.

A copy of your document is included in the message.

When you're ready to send the message, click here.

Want to use a better editor to write notes in the message form?   You can use Word. See "Using Word as Your Electronic Mail Editor," later in this topic.

Route a Document

When you route a document through electronic mail, you distribute a single copy of the review document to the reviewers in the order you specify. When a reviewer finishes reviewing the document and clicks Send (File menu), the document is automatically sent to the next reviewer. Each time the document is sent to another reviewer, you receive a status message letting you know who has the document. When the last reviewer clicks Send, the document is routed back to you.

For Help, double-click. In the online index look up: **routing**

To route a document, open it, and then click Add Routing Slip (File menu).

To choose recipients, click here.

Use these buttons to change the routing order.

To add a message, type here.

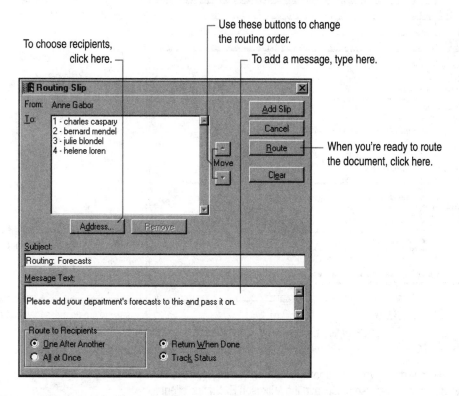

When you're ready to route the document, click here.

 How can I tell who made the comments in the review document?
Have the reviewers use revision marks or annotations to comment in the document. You can lock, or protect, the document so that reviewers can add only revision marks or annotations. Word then provides information about which reviewer made which comment. For details, see "Have Your Team Review a Word Document," page 333.

Using Word as Your Electronic Mail Editor

Instead of using the built-in message editor that comes with your electronic mail application, you can use Word to write, edit, and format your electronic mail messages. You can also use the Word reviewing options that make it easy to find and read the comments from an individual in long messages that include replies from many different people.

For Help, double-click.
In the Word online index look up:
email, mail editor

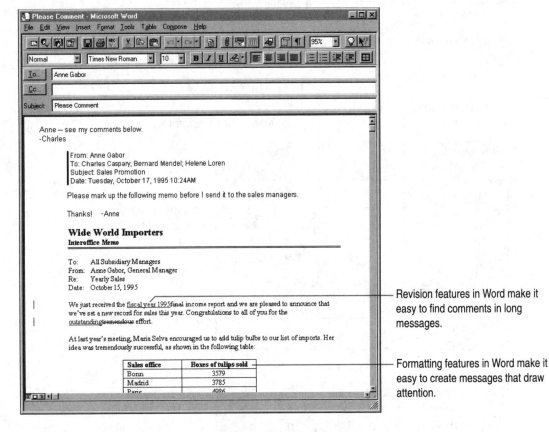

Revision features in Word make it easy to find comments in long messages.

Formatting features in Word make it easy to create messages that draw attention.

Important   To use Word as your electronic mail editor, you should have at least 12 MB of memory. You also must have the Microsoft Exchange client and Word installed on your machine, and you must have installed this capability when you first installed Office. To install the capability after you have installed Office, insert the Office Setup disk, and run the Setup program again. For details, look up **email, mail editor** in the Word online index.

Can I switch between electronic mail editors? In the message window, just click Word Mail Options (Compose menu). For details, look up **email, mail editor** in the Word online index.

Can I automatically include my signature in my electronic mail messages? Run Word, open your email.dot file, create an AutoText entry, and name it "signature." Your signature can include formatted text and graphics, such as a scanned image of your handwritten signature. Then whenever you send a message, Word automatically adds this signature to the message. For details, look up **signature, electronic mail** in the Word online index.

How can I make it easy for others to read long messages that include many replies? Use the Word Highlight button to mark sections that are particularly important. For details, look up **highlighter pen** in the Word online index.

Highlight button

Posting a Document

When you post a document, you deliver a copy of the document to a Microsoft Exchange public folder so that others can view the document over the network.

Important   To post a document, you must be connected to a network running Microsoft Exchange Server, and you must create a Public Folder Shortcut for the folder you want to use. For details, see your Microsoft Exchange documentation.

To post a document, click Post To Exchange Folder (File menu).

The Post Document dialog box lists the Microsoft Exchange public folders you currently have access to.

For Help, double-click. In the online index look up: **posting**

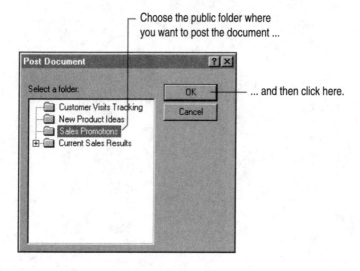

Choose the public folder where you want to post the document ...

... and then click here.

Next Steps

To	See
Get feedback from coworkers on a Word document	"Have Your Team Review a Word Document," page 333
Share a workbook with coworkers	"Share a Workbook with a Coworker," page 338

Have Your Team Review a Word Document

Have Others Comment on a Document Using Annotations and Revision Marks

Let's say you just completed a new product proposal, and you want to send it out electronically to have the rest of the team or managers review it.

During the team review, you want to give some reviewers authority to make changes directly to the document, but limit others to inserting only comments. Using revision marks and annotations, you can determine how reviewers mark changes in an electronic version of your document.

And if you need to highlight certain sections for special attention, the Word Highlight button makes it a snap to shade sections that you want people to notice.

Key Features

Revision Marks

Annotations

Highlight Button

Document Protection

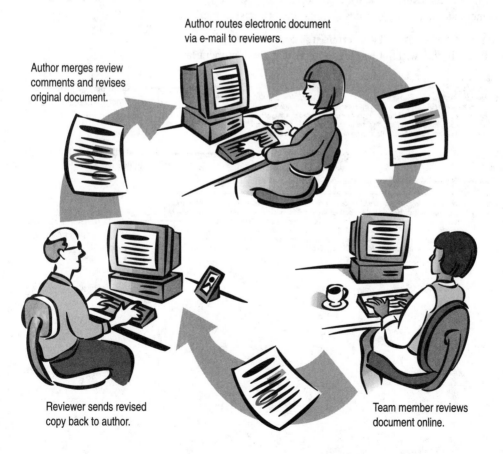

Author routes electronic document via e-mail to reviewers.

Author merges review comments and revises original document.

Reviewer sends revised copy back to author.

Team member reviews document online.

Get a Document Ready for Review

Before routing the document, decide how you want reviewers to comment, and then lock or protect the document to prevent unauthorized changes.

To have reviewers comment without making changes in the original document   Use annotations. Have reviewers click Annotation (Insert menu), and then type their comments, or annotations, in the Annotations pane. Word inserts the reviewer's initials and numbers each remark in sequence.

To have reviewers make changes directly to the document   Use revision marks. Revision marks show text or art that is added, deleted, or moved. When you review revisions, Word displays who made a change and the date and time of the revision.

To add protection to the document   Click Protect Document (Tools menu), and then click Annotations or Revisions. Protecting the document automatically enables annotations or revision marks.

If you add a password   Make certain it is one you'll remember. If you forget it, you will not be able to unprotect the document later.

For Help, double-click.
In the Word online index look up:
annotations
revision marks

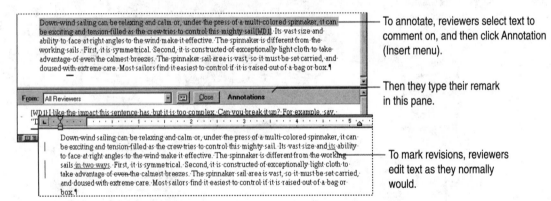

To annotate, reviewers select text to comment on, and then click Annotation (Insert menu).

Then they type their remark in this pane.

To mark revisions, reviewers edit text as they normally would.

Include instructions for reviewers If you lock a document for annotations only, tell reviewers how to insert annotations. If you lock a document for revision marks, tell reviewers that revision marks will automatically appear when they make changes to the document.

Bothered by revision marks? Tell reviewers they can turn off revision marks while editing by clearing the Show Revisions On Screen check box in the Revisions dialog box (Tools menu).

Want reviewers to focus on key sections only? If you used the Highlight button to mark text, tell reviewers they can find these sections by clicking Find (Edit menu), and then clicking Highlight in the Format box.

Highlight button

Inserting Voice Annotations

Reviewers with sound cards and microphones installed in their computers may prefer to insert voice annotations, or a combination of voice and text.

Instruct reviewers to insert voice annotations by clicking the Insert Sound Object button in the Annotations pane. To insert both text and voice, they should type the text first. Then, in the document pane, move the insertion point to the right of the annotation mark and record the voice annotation.

To listen to a voice annotation, click Annotations (View menu), click the annotation, and then double-click the sound symbol.

Incorporate Review Comments

Before you begin incorporating review comments, click Unprotect Document (Tools menu).

To merge revisions   Evaluating and incorporating review comments is more manageable if you merge everyone's revision marks and annotations into the original document.

Open the revised document, and then click Revisions (Tools menu). Click the Merge Revisions button and click the name of the original document in the File Name box.

To review annotations   Click Annotations (View menu).

To review revision marks   Click Revisions (Tools menu). Then click the Review button.

For Help, double-click.
In the Word online index look up:
merging documents with revision marks
reviewing documents, viewing annotations

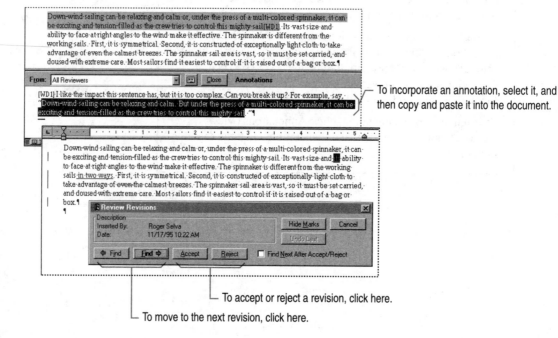

To incorporate an annotation, select it, and then copy and paste it into the document.

To accept or reject a revision, click here.

To move to the next revision, click here.

 Want to delete annotation marks?   Select the mark and press DELETE to delete the mark and the associated annotation.

Want to print annotations?   Click Print (File menu), and then click Annotations in the Print What box.

Next Steps

To	See
Make formatting changes to your document	"Make Your Word Document Look Great," page 161
Make the final version of the document available to a wider audience	"Share Documents Electronically," page 326

Share a Workbook with a Coworker

You've created a workbook, and now you want help from your coworkers in completing, verifying, and updating the information. You'd like everyone to see the most recent data. You'd like to tell your coworkers what parts they're responsible for as you work together to update the information.

Microsoft Excel can merge everyone's changes; you view the group's progress every time you save.

Key Features

 Cell Notes

Shared Lists

Get your workbook ready for sharing.

Note assignments and instructions right in the cells.

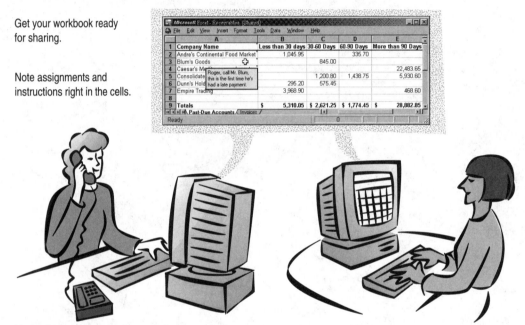

Your colleagues then view the worksheet.

Microsoft Excel lets everyone work on the same worksheet file at once ... and keeps the information up to date.

Before you start, make sure all users have current software and access to a shared resource

- Everyone who shares a workbook needs Microsoft Windows 95 and Microsoft Excel for Windows 95.

- Users must edit the workbook on a mutually shared resource, such as a network drive.

 Did you know that you can also route workbooks to other users? Routing sends a workbook to each user in succession and returns it to you with their cumulative edits. For details, see "Share Documents Electronically," page 326.

Prepare Your Workbook To Be Shared

Anyone in your workgroup can share a workbook over your network with little preparation, but you can do some things in advance to make the collaboration go more smoothly. For example, your group can use your aged-receivables worksheet to collect past-due customer accounts. You want to let your coworkers know which customers to call, so you add *cell notes* so that everyone can view your instructions as tips. You want everyone to update the amounts owed and add more cell notes as they work, but you don't want them to change any of the formulas.

For Help, double-click. In the Microsoft Excel online index look up:
cell notes, adding
unlocking cells
worksheets, protecting

On your worksheet, select the cell you want to add a note to. Click Note (Insert menu).

Type your instructions for each cell.

Unlock the cells that everyone will edit. Uncheck the Locked check box (Format menu, Cells command, Protection tab).

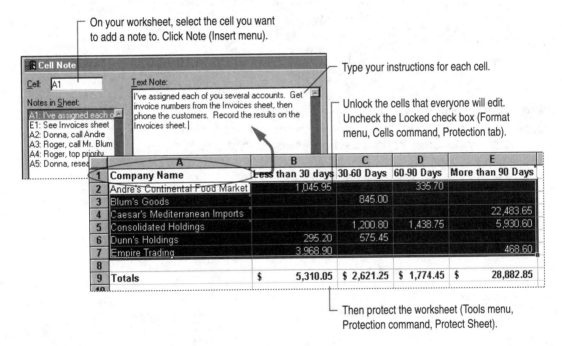

Then protect the worksheet (Tools menu, Protection command, Protect Sheet).

Want to keep your formulas out of sight? Before you protect the worksheet, you can hide them. Select a formula, click Cells (Format menu), and check Hidden on the Protection tab.

Should I consider using a Microsoft Access database? For information that will help you choose the right Office application for your needs, see "Where Should You Store Your Contact Information?," page 294.

Collaborate, and Watch Everyone's Progress

Share the workbook: Put it out on your network. Click Shared Lists (File menu), click the Editing tab, and then check Allow Multi-User Editing. Now your team can get started on the work.

Have your team members click Save (File menu) after adding or changing information. Save the file yourself, and you are updated with everyone's saved changes.

For Help, double-click. In the Microsoft Excel online index look up:
using shared lists
cell notes, displaying and hiding

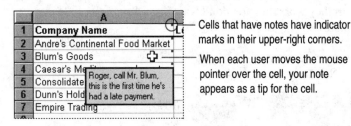

Cells that have notes have indicator marks in their upper-right corners.

When each user moves the mouse pointer over the cell, your note appears as a tip for the cell.

Tired of seeing the notes?   Once you've read them, turn them off: Use the Note Indicator check box (Tools menu, Options command, View tab). Or print them out: Check the Notes check box (File menu, Page Setup command, Sheet tab).

What Kinds of Shared Editing Can We Do?

Shared lists are great for data entry, list management, and data consolidation. You can change values, add and delete rows and columns, move rows and columns, and even sort and filter the worksheet. As each user saves the workbook, changes are merged and reconciled.

What if two of us change the same cell? When the second user to make a change tries to save the workbook, a dialog box presents information about both changes. The last person to save can decide which change to keep. For details, look up **conflicts in shared lists** in the Microsoft Excel online index.

How do we keep track of who changed what? You can save your changes and get updates from other users automatically, at an interval that you set. For details, look up **updating shared lists** in the Microsoft Excel online index.

You can see information about which changes users have decided to keep. When you share the workbook, check Show Conflict History (File menu, Shared Lists command, Editing tab).

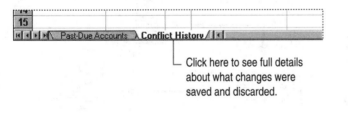

└ Click here to see full details about what changes were saved and discarded.

Create an Online Manual

For Example—an Employee Handbook, Policy Manual, or Systems Guide

You're in charge of creating a procedures manual for your company, let's say an employee handbook. You need to make sure the manual is universally accessible and always up to date. Also, you want to let users quickly browse and retrieve information. Finally, you'd like to include color and graphics—but you don't want to pay higher printing costs. (In fact, you wouldn't mind eliminating printing costs altogether!)

The solution: Create an online manual. This topic describes how to set up the manual's structure and design and then collaborate on it with your workgroup. You can use these techniques for any multiuser authoring task, such as an annual report or periodical.

Key Features

Styles

Fields

Master Documents

Manual Template

The project lead sets up the structure and design of the manual, and then makes it available over the network.

Multiple authors collaborate on the manual simultaneously.

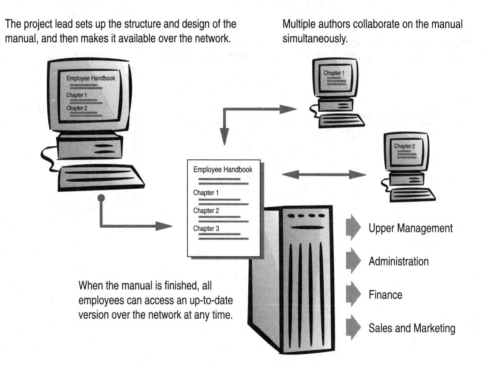

When the manual is finished, all employees can access an up-to-date version over the network at any time.

Upper Management

Administration

Finance

Sales and Marketing

So you want to create a printed manual?   This topic includes details on creating a professionally designed printed manual that includes the usual components, such as a cover page, table of contents, and index.

Create an Easy-to-Read Design

You want to design an online manual that's easy to read and easy to scan. Start by creating a template that sets up the fonts, colors, white space, and other elements you'll need.

First, click the New button. Then, type some sample headings and body text, and format them as shown in the following illustration.

 For Help, double-click.
In the Word online index look up:
styles

New button

Apply built-in heading styles: Select a heading and click a heading style in the Style box. Repeat for the other headings.

Change the text design: Select a heading or body text paragraph, format it the way you want, click in the Style box, press ENTER, and then click OK.

 Save the design as a template Click Save As (File menu), and then click Document Template in the Save As Type box. Name the new template, and then save it.

What Makes a Design Easy to Read?

To improve the legibility of on-screen text: Use large and plain fonts, heighten the contrast between text and the background color, and use white space generously. To highlight important information: Increase the font size, indent the text, or emphasize it with underlining or color.

Optimize the Screen for Online Viewing

You want users to read the manual on a "clean screen"—without distracting elements such as toolbars and nonprinting characters. To optimize users' screens, add a button to the template.

First, record a macro that "cleans the screen"   The macro should switch to normal view, turn on full screen view, and set view options (Tools menu, Options command, View tab) the way you want. Make sure to store the macro in the template you just created. For details, see "Automate Repetitive Tasks in Word," page 536.

Then, create the "clean screen" button   Click Field (Insert menu), click the MacroButton field name, and then click Options. Click the macro you created, click Add To Field, and then click OK twice. If you don't see the MACROBUTTON field, press ALT+F9.

For Help, double-click.
In the Word online index look up:
Full screen view
MACROBUTTON field
recording macros

To add a button graphic, click at the end of the macro name, press the SPACEBAR, and then click Picture (Insert menu). Resize the graphic, if necessary. — — Then, type some explanatory text.

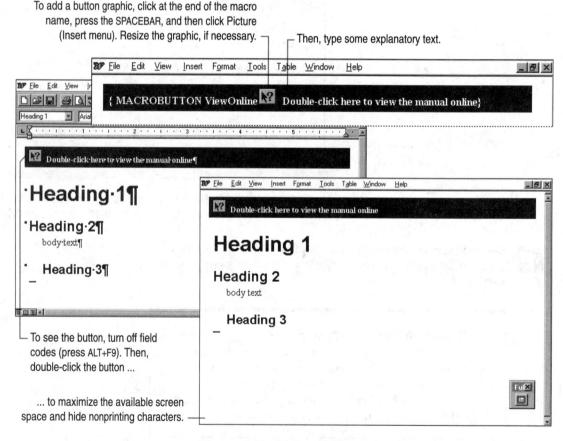

To see the button, turn off field codes (press ALT+F9). Then, double-click the button ...

... to maximize the available screen space and hide nonprinting characters. —

When you finish, click Save All (File menu), and then close the template.

Plan to Write the Manual by Yourself?

To start the new manual, click New (File menu), and then select the template you just created.

To outline, or not to outline Then, just start typing as usual. For a quick way to organize your manual, you can switch to outline view (View menu). If you decide not to outline the manual, make sure to use the built-in heading styles (Heading 1, Heading 2, and so on) for your headings. That way, you can easily create a table of contents and "jumps"—shortcuts for jumping from one part of the manual to another.

 For Help, double-click.
In the Word online index look up:
styles
views, outline view

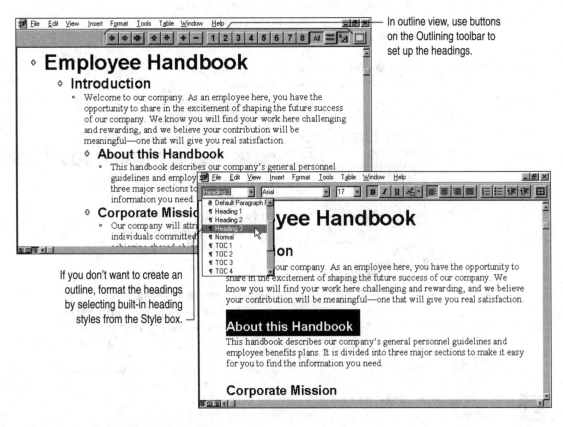

In outline view, use buttons on the Outlining toolbar to set up the headings.

If you don't want to create an outline, format the headings by selecting built-in heading styles from the Style box.

💡 **Where do you go from here?** For details on creating jumps, skip ahead to "For Easy Navigation, Create Simple 'Jumps.'"

What's all this about "master documents"? Since your manual has just one author, you can safely ignore any instructions related to master documents. (In case you're curious, a master document makes it easier for multiple authors to work on a document simultaneously.)

Plan to Write the Manual with a Group of Authors?

You'll create a *master document* that contains individual files (or *subdocuments*) for each topic in the manual. With a master document, there's no need to track topic names and locations, or to "build" the manual. And, you can store the master document on a network location so authors can view and edit it simultaneously.

For Help, double-click. In the Word online index look up: **master documents**

Create the master document   Click New (File menu), and then select the template you just created. Then, click Master Document (View menu). Type the outline for the entire manual—probably just the manual title, main topics, and subtopics. Select a heading and click either the Promote or Demote button to assign a heading level to it (Heading 1 for the title, Heading 2 for a main topic, and so on). Repeat for the other headings.

Promote and Demote buttons

Select the main topics and subtopics that you want to divide into separate subdocuments, and then click the Create Subdocument button.

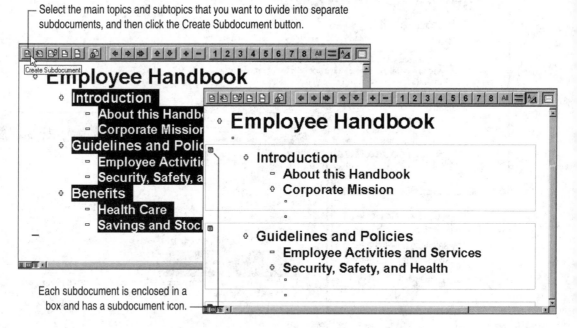

Each subdocument is enclosed in a box and has a subdocument icon.

Save the master document on a network location   Click the Save button, and type a name for the new document. Word automatically names the individual subdocuments. If you want to rename one, double-click its subdocument icon and click Save As (File menu).

Save button

Have Authors Protect Files Against Changes

Before any writing begins, make sure that authors know which subdocuments they've been assigned. Have authors take ownership of their subdocuments and set privileges for other authors to read-only recommended. This way, each author always has write access to his or her subdocuments, even if another author is viewing them.

For Help, double-click.
In the Word online index look up:
read-only files
locking, documents

The assigned author opens the master document and then unlocks a subdocument by clicking its icon and then clicking the Lock Document button.

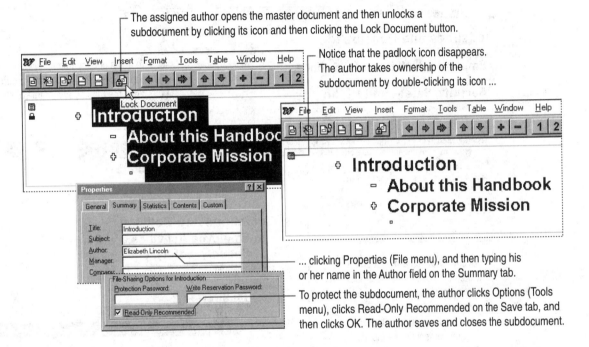

Notice that the padlock icon disappears. The author takes ownership of the subdocument by double-clicking its icon ...

... clicking Properties (File menu), and then typing his or her name in the Author field on the Summary tab.

To protect the subdocument, the author clicks Options (Tools menu), clicks Read-Only Recommended on the Save tab, and then clicks OK. The author saves and closes the subdocument.

Who can edit what? The author of the master document can edit the master document and all subdocuments. A subdocument should be edited only by the author whose name is listed on the Summary tab (Properties command, File menu).

Can you edit a subdocument even if you're not the author? You can, but it's not recommended. To temporarily unlock another's subdocument, click the Lock Document button.

Is there any way to prevent others from editing your subdocuments? To prevent changes, click Options (Tools menu), click the Save tab, and assign a write reservation password. For details, look up **passwords** in the Word online index.

Write, Edit, and Rearrange Topics

To start working on your topics, first open the master document. Then, unlock any subdocuments you plan to edit or rearrange. (If you're rearranging subdocuments, you also need to unlock the master document itself.) Then, modify the documents as shown in the following illustration and tips.

For Help, double-click. In the Word online index look up: **subdocuments**

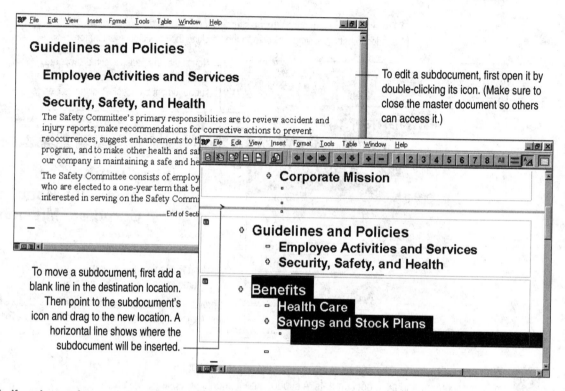

To edit a subdocument, first open it by double-clicking its icon. (Make sure to close the master document so others can access it.)

To move a subdocument, first add a blank line in the destination location. Then point to the subdocument's icon and drag to the new location. A horizontal line shows where the subdocument will be inserted.

 If you're moving a subdocument, "collapse" (or hide) the body text So that the subdocument is more compact, and it's easier to see what you're moving where. For details, look up **collapsing outlines** in the Word online index.

To delete a subdocument   Click its icon and press DELETE. Then, delete the subdocument from disk as usual.

To add an existing Word document   First, insert a blank line where you plan to add the Word document. Click in the blank line, and then click the Insert Subdocument button.

Insert Subdocument button

Protect your work!   Use the Automatic Save or Always Create Backup Copy option to help you recover work if there is a power failure or other problem. For details, look up **automatically saving documents** or **backing up documents** in the Word online index.

Keep Track of Changes

You can use the Word "version control" features to track changes made to the manual (who did what—and when). If you don't like the changes—or if a draft has been damaged—you can revert to a previous version.

Use annotations or revision marks To record the changes or comments made by each writer or editor. For details, see "Have Your Team Review a Word Document," page 333.

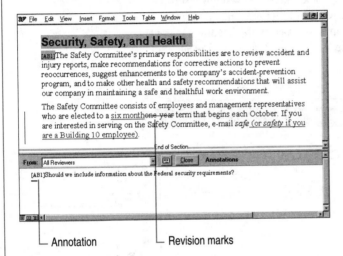

— Annotation   — Revision marks

Archive drafts Store each draft of the manual in a separate folder. That way, you can revert to a previous draft if a later one is lost or damaged.

Compare versions If you've archived drafts, you can mark the changes between different versions of the manual. For details, look up **comparing documents** in the Word online index.

For Easy Navigation, Create Simple "Jumps"

To help users navigate through the online manual, it's a good idea to include shortcuts for jumping from one location to another. For example, create a table of contents for the manual, and then jump to any topic in it. Or, create Hypertext buttons to jump to any location in the manual. This section and the following one show you how.

For Help, double-click. In the Word online index look up: **tables of contents**

Use a table of contents to jump to any topic   Open the master document and type an instruction like this: "Double-click a page number to go to a topic." Then, click where you want to insert the table of contents. Click Index And Tables (Insert menu). On the Table Of Contents tab, click Options. Specify the headings you want to include—probably Heading 2, Heading 3, and so on—and then click OK twice.

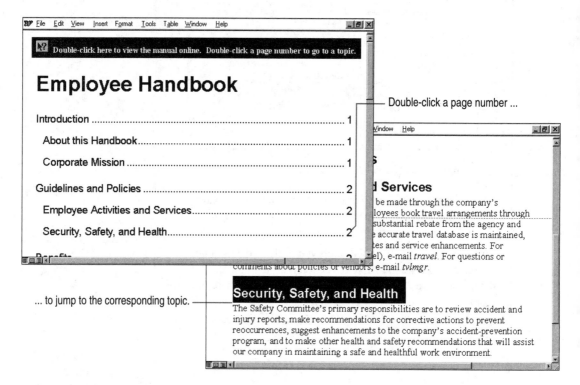

Update the table of contents   If you modify the headings or change the page breaks, update the table of contents by clicking in it and pressing F9.

Make it easier to view and work on the whole document   Switch from master document view to normal view. In this view, the master document looks like a single document; individual subdocuments are separated by section breaks.

Add Hypertext Buttons

First, mark the locations to jump *to* Open the master document and unlock any subdocuments you want to jump between. Then, mark each location to jump to: Select a heading, click Bookmark (Edit menu), and then give the location a name.

Then, create buttons to jump *from* Click where you want to put a button, click Field (Insert menu), and then click the GoToButton field name. Click Options, click the location to go to, click Add To Field, and then click OK twice. You'll see a GOTOBUTTON field. If you don't see the field, press ALT+F9.

For Help, double-click.
In the Word online index look up:
GOTOBUTTON field
bookmarks

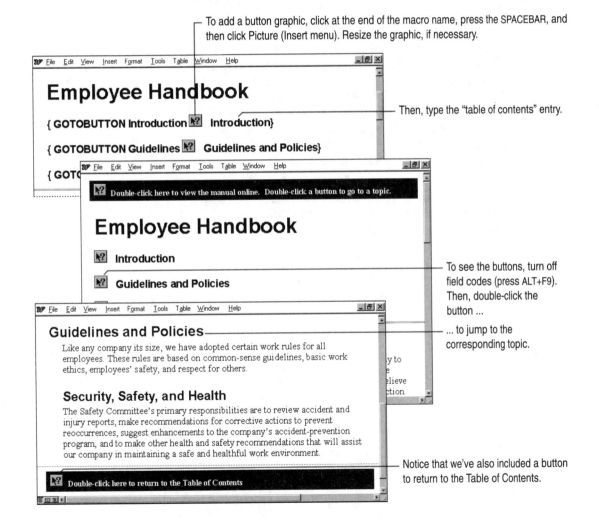

To add a button graphic, click at the end of the macro name, press the SPACEBAR, and then click Picture (Insert menu). Resize the graphic, if necessary.

Employee Handbook

{ GOTOBUTTON Introduction 🔲 Introduction}

{ GOTOBUTTON Guidelines 🔲 Guidelines and Policies}

{ GOTC

Then, type the "table of contents" entry.

🔲 Double-click here to view the manual online. Double-click a button to go to a topic.

Employee Handbook

🔲 Introduction

🔲 Guidelines and Policies

To see the buttons, turn off field codes (press ALT+F9). Then, double-click the button ...

... to jump to the corresponding topic.

Guidelines and Policies

Like any company its size, we have adopted certain work rules for all employees. These rules are based on common-sense guidelines, basic work ethics, employees' safety, and respect for others.

Security, Safety, and Health

The Safety Committee's primary responsibilities are to review accident and injury reports, make recommendations for corrective actions to prevent reoccurrences, suggest enhancements to the company's accident-prevention program, and to make other health and safety recommendations that will assist our company in maintaining a safe and healthful work environment.

🔲 Double-click here to return to the Table of Contents

Notice that we've also included a button to return to the Table of Contents.

Want to Distribute the Manual to a Wider Audience?

If you're looking for a way to share documents electronically with just about anyone—including users of the "information superhighway"—Word Viewer and Internet Assistant for Word are the solution.

What if your audience doesn't use Word?   Word Viewer is an easy-to-use standalone utility that lets your users view and print any Word document; there's no need to install the regular version of Word or any other document processing software on their computers. Keep in mind that your audience won't be able to edit the Word documents, and that some features, such as MACROBUTTON fields, are disabled.

Want to publish the manual on the Internet?   Use Internet Assistant to convert Word documents into HTML (Hypertext Markup Language), the standard format for the World Wide Web. Or, use Internet Assistant to create native-format Word documents with hypertext links, rich formatting, and OLE 2.0 embedded objects for use on the Web. As an added bonus, Internet Assistant includes a built-in Web browser, so you won't ever need to switch between editing and browsing applications.

You don't have Word Viewer or Internet Assistant—how do you get them?   Word Viewer comes with the CD versions of Windows 95 and Office for Windows 95. You can also obtain Word Viewer or Internet Assistant (free!) from Microsoft customer service, or you can download them from many electronic bulletin boards. (Note that you need to use the 32-bit version of Internet Assistant; the 16-bit version won't work with Word for Windows 95.)

Create a Printed Manual

Word includes a template that sets up the basic structure of a manual, includes ready-to-use elements such as margin notes and sidebars, and provides a professionally designed layout.

How to use the manual template Click New (File menu), click the Publications tab, and then double-click the manual template. The new document contains instructions on how to create the manual, so it's a good idea to print out a copy to consult as you fill in your own information.

Like the result—and want to use it to start your next manual? Delete any information you don't plan to include in future manuals. Click Save As (File menu), and then click Document Template in the Save As Type box. Name the new template, and then save it. Then select this template the next time you start a new manual.

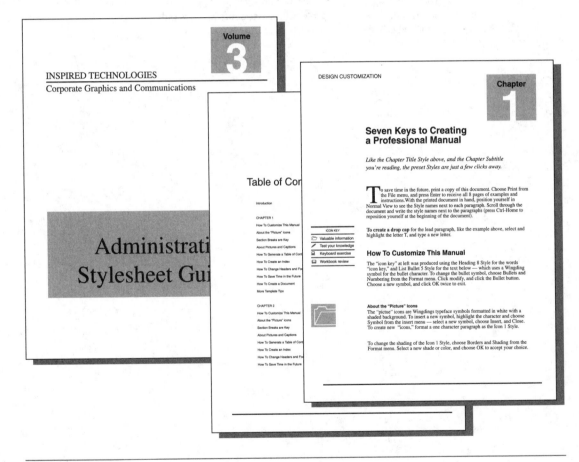

Next Steps

To	See
Create a simple schedule that includes topic names, authors, current status, and future milestones	"Create a Business Contact List in Microsoft Excel," page 300
Schedule team meetings, and track other tasks and appointments	"Schedule an Appointment," page 314; "Keep a To Do List," page 317
Modify the manual's formats— such as fonts, line spacing, margins	"Make Your Word Document Look Great," page 161
Solicit feedback on individual topics or the entire manual	"Have Your Team Review a Word Document," page 333
Protect the manual so end-users can't make unauthorized changes	**protecting documents** in the Word online index

Track Orders in a Shared Database

Use Microsoft Access in a Multiuser Environment

An Order Entry database is likely to be used by people throughout your company. For example, one person may enter an order taken over the phone, another may fill the order from inventory, someone else may pack and ship the order, and another person may check on order status for the customer. With the Microsoft Access Database Wizard, you can easily create a multiuser database that serves all of these needs.

Key Features

 Database Wizard

Multiuser Options

To complete the steps in this topic You need to have either Microsoft Office Professional for Windows 95 or an individual copy of Microsoft Access for Windows 95 installed.

 Want to set up other types of business databases? Use the Database Wizard to create many business and personal databases, including databases for asset tracking, event management, and resource scheduling. Refer to this topic for details on running the Database Wizard and on sharing information stored in your databases.

Create an Order Entry Database

First, set up a database to track your orders with the Microsoft Access Database Wizard. Start Microsoft Access, click Database Wizard, click OK, and then double-click Order Entry. Or, if you've already started Microsoft Access, click the New Database button, and then double-click Order Entry.

When the wizard asks you to choose fields, select the fields that you need. If you want to provide your coworkers with help in getting started on tracking orders, click the sample data option.

For Help, double-click.
In the Microsoft Access online index look up:
databases, creating

The wizard creates everything you need to enter orders and search your database, including a Switchboard for opening forms, tables, and reports.

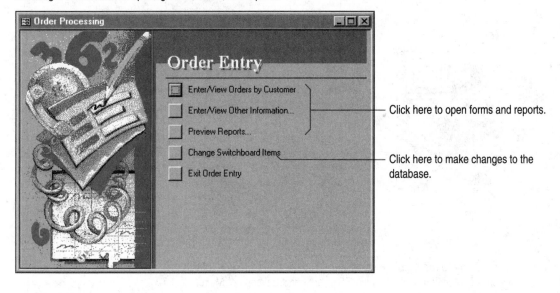

Click here to open forms and reports.

Click here to make changes to the database.

Protect your database with a password Click Security (Tools menu), and then point to Set Database Password. Type a password as directed. When you or your coworkers attempt to open the database, Microsoft Access will ask for the password.

Do you need more sophisticated security? Microsoft Access provides a Security Wizard that steps you through the process of setting up the protections you need. For details, look up **security, using Security Wizard** in the Microsoft Access online index.

Want a shortcut for opening your tables, queries, forms, and reports? Add them to the Microsoft Office Shortcut Bar. For details, see "Take a Shortcut to Work," page 36. Or, drag them to the Windows 95 desktop. For details, look up **shortcuts** in the Microsoft Access online index.

Want to see all the forms, reports, tables, and queries that make up your database? Click the Database Window button.

Database Window button

Share Your Order Entry Database

The Database Wizard creates a complete Order Entry database ready for data entry. Now, use the Windows Explorer to put the file in a location on your network where everyone can open it.

Once you've placed the database on a network, your coworkers can use its forms and reports by clicking one of the buttons on the Switchboard. To open the Orders By Customer form (the primary order entry form), a user clicks Enter/View Orders By Customer. Multiple users can enter data at the same time using this and other forms. Microsoft Access saves changes every time a user presses SHIFT+ENTER or moves to the next record.

For Help, double-click. In the Microsoft Access online index look up: **multiuser environment, workgroups described**

The pencil symbol shows that you are editing this record.

Several users can create new orders simultaneously, while other users view the latest status.

Prevent others from making changes to a form while you do Click Options (Tools menu), click the Advanced tab, and then click the Default Record Locking option that you want. For details, look up **locking records** in the Microsoft Access online index.

What happens if someone is editing while you are and has saved the changes? Microsoft Access will notify you and give you choices about how to proceed.

To view the most up-to-date changes to records Click Refresh (Records menu).

Do some users just look at orders and never make changes? These users can open the file in the read-only state. To open a database in read-only state, click the Open Database button, click the database, click the Commands And Settings button, and then click Open Read Only.

Open Database button

Commands And Settings button

When You Need to Modify the Database, Open It in Exclusive Mode

Making design enhancements while others are sharing the database can be confusing to your users. For example, if other users are sharing the database and you start making changes to table designs, the other users cannot use the data stored in the tables you're modifying. If other users have opened tables, you can't modify them.

You can exclude others from the database while you make changes and additions. That way, you prevent them from losing access to data while they're working. Choose a time when no one else is likely to be using the database, open it, and then click the Exclusive check box. For details, look up **exclusive mode** in the Microsoft Access online index.

Use Data from Other Applications or Databases

Microsoft Access makes it easy to work with data from elsewhere on your network. You can make data stored in other applications or databases a permanent part of your Microsoft Access database by pasting a copy or *importing* it. You can even work with data that will continue to be stored or maintained in other databases by *linking* the data to your Microsoft Access database.

Move data permanently into your database by pasting or importing   You can move data stored as text, as a Microsoft Excel list, or in a supported database format into Microsoft Access. Microsoft Access wizards can help you import your text files and Microsoft Excel lists.

For details, look up **importing data, basics** in the Microsoft Access online index, and **converting**

documents, **Microsoft Access** in the Microsoft Excel online index.

View and update data that's stored in another application by linking   What if you want to work with data that's stored and maintained in another database or in a different application, such as dBASE? Link a table in a supported database format to your Microsoft Access database. Users can then view and update the linked data just as they view and update data stored in Microsoft Access. The changes are saved and stored in the original application's file, so that users who work with the data using the original application can continue to do so.

For details, look up **linking data from other programs** in the Microsoft Access online index.

List in dBASE

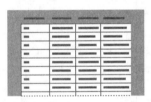

List in another database application

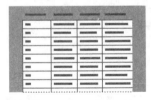

Customer table

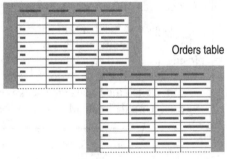

Orders table

Microsoft Access database

Next Steps

To	See
Learn more about using forms for data entry	**data, entering in Datasheet or Form view** in the Microsoft Access online index
Move Microsoft Excel data into Microsoft Access	"Move a Product List into Microsoft Access," page 379

PART 9

Budgeting with Microsoft Excel

Contents

Consolidate Budget Input

Working up an overall budget means combining the budgets of several groups or departments within your company. Determining how to allocate the available funds involves several rounds of proposals and reconsolidation. To project expenses and make adjustments, your department managers need worksheets from you that contain the right information. Design the worksheets so that you can easily roll up the figures you get from each department, as many times as they change.

Key Features

Copying Worksheets to Other Workbooks

3-D References

In the worksheets you prepare, each department enters its figures ...

Budget Worksheet – H. R.

Employee Costs	
110	Payroll
120	IRS/FICA

Subcontractors & Ser...	
201	Services
254	Advertising

Supplies and Materia...

| Total | |

Budget Worksheet – Sales

Employee Costs	
110	Payroll
120	IRS/FICA

Subcontractors & Services	
201	Services
254	Advertising

Supplies and Materials

| Total | |

Budget Worksheet – Marketing

Employee Costs	
110	Payroll
120	IRS/FICA

Subcontractors & Services	
201	Services
254	Advertising

Supplies and Materials

| Total | |

Consolidated Budget Input	FY1995	FY1996
Employee Costs	164,146	?
Subcontractors & Services	58,035	?
Supplies and Materials	902	?
Total	**223,083**	**?**

... and you combine them in a summary, the consolidation.

Prepare Your Budget Worksheet

Prepare a worksheet to use as a template. List every account to be budgeted across all departments. You'll use the template both to gather input and to consolidate it.

For Help, double-click. In the Microsoft Excel online index look up: **templates**

— Plan to include current figures for comparison.

	A	B	C	D	E
1	Budget Input				
2					
3	Account		FY 1995 Actual	FY 1996 Projected	
4					
5	Employee Costs				
6	110	Payroll			
7	120	IRS/FICA/Wk comp/State/SDI			
8	140	Retirement Plan			
9		Subtotal			
10					
11	Subcontractors & Services				
12	201	Telecommunication Services			
13	254	Advertising			
14		Subtotal			
15					
16	Total				

＼ Budget Worksheet ／

— Here's where you'll consolidate the new budget information.

Do you keep the current budget or actual figures in a database somewhere? Get the external data into a Microsoft Excel worksheet so that you can copy it into each department's worksheet. You don't have to retype the figures. For details, see "Get Sales Information from a Database," page 434.

Get Budget Projections from Each Department

Each department fills in its estimates using a copy of the template worksheet that you provide. For each department, you include only the accounts needed, and provide the figures from the current year by copying them into each department's worksheet.

Keep all accounts in the same rows and columns. Maintaining the same information in the same position across all worksheets allows you to consolidate their contents.

 For Help, double-click. In the Microsoft Excel online index look up: **copying sheets** **hiding cells**

Each department puts its figures into its own worksheet.

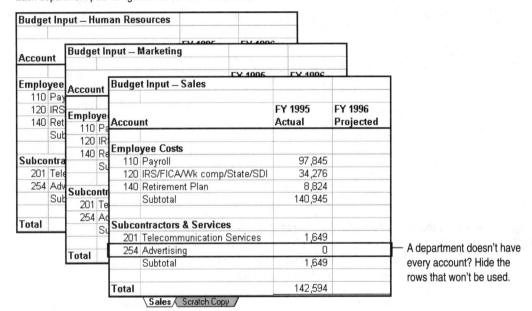

Budget Input — Sales		FY 1995 Actual	FY 1996 Projected
Account			
Employee Costs			
110	Payroll	97,845	
120	IRS/FICA/Wk comp/State/SDI	34,276	
140	Retirement Plan	8,824	
	Subtotal	140,945	
Subcontractors & Services			
201	Telecommunication Services	1,649	
254	Advertising	0	
	Subtotal	1,649	
Total		142,594	

— A department doesn't have every account? Hide the rows that won't be used.

Prevent changes to the worksheet layout   Unlock only the cells to receive input, then protect the worksheet from other editing. For details, look up **unlocking cells** and **worksheets, protecting** in the Microsoft Excel online index.

Give each department an official copy and a scratch copy   They'll appreciate an extra unprotected copy of the worksheet for their preliminary calculations.

Save the time and effort of copying the worksheets onto floppy disks   Route the workbooks to the departments. For details, see "Share Documents Electronically," page 326.

Combine the Input

As each department returns its filled-in worksheet, you need to combine the worksheets in one workbook where you can calculate the combined results. Copy each worksheet of budget projections into your consolidation workbook.

For Help, double-click. In the Microsoft Excel online index look up: **copying sheets**

For easy access to the worksheet tabs, arrange the workbook windows horizontally.

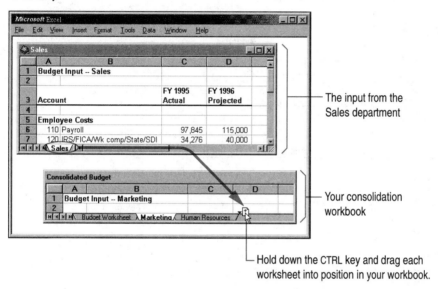

The input from the Sales department

Your consolidation workbook

Hold down the CTRL key and drag each worksheet into position in your workbook.

Consolidate the Combined Input

Use a copy of your template worksheet to set up the consolidation. You create a formula that adds up projections for each account across all the departmental worksheets. You indicate the range of worksheets the formula uses by including the first and last worksheet names in the formula, and you also include a reference to the cell on each worksheet to include in the consolidated total. The result appears on your consolidation worksheet.

For Help, double-click. In the Microsoft Excel online index look up:
formulas, entering 3-D references

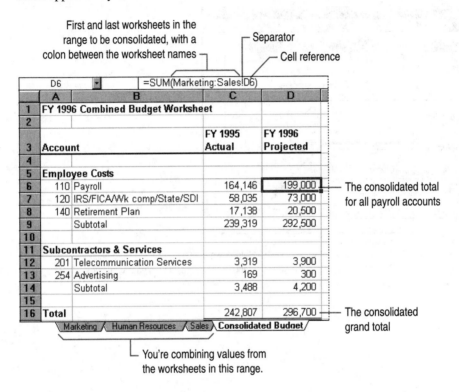

First and last worksheets in the range to be consolidated, with a colon between the worksheet names

Separator

Cell reference

D6 =SUM(Marketing:Sales!D6)

	A	B	C	D
1	FY 1996 Combined Budget Worksheet			
2				
3		Account	FY 1995 Actual	FY 1996 Projected
4				
5	Employee Costs			
6	110	Payroll	164,146	199,000
7	120	IRS/FICA/Wk comp/State/SDI	58,035	73,000
8	140	Retirement Plan	17,138	20,500
9		Subtotal	239,319	292,500
10				
11	Subcontractors & Services			
12	201	Telecommunication Services	3,319	3,900
13	254	Advertising	169	300
14		Subtotal	3,488	4,200
15				
16	Total		242,807	296,700

Marketing / Human Resources / Sales / **Consolidated Budget**

The consolidated total for all payroll accounts

The consolidated grand total

You're combining values from the worksheets in this range.

To enter the worksheet names in the formula Place the insertion point at the target location within the formula, and then click the appropriate worksheet tabs.

Copy formulas automatically Once you've entered the formula to consolidate one account, you don't have to type similar formulas for the rest of the accounts. If you used a relative cell reference, dragging the AutoFill handle or using the Copy and Paste commands will adjust the cell references accordingly for your other formulas. For details, look up **formulas, copying** and **relative cell references** in the Microsoft Excel online index.

Cope with revisions and late returns When you get another departmental worksheet after you've set up the consolidation, just drag a copy of the new worksheet between the tabs of the worksheets you refer to in the formula. The new worksheet consolidates automatically.

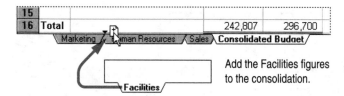

Add the Facilities figures to the consolidation.

Other Ways to Consolidate Your Figures

3-D references let you design your template worksheet any way you want. But they do require that the same information be in the same place on every worksheet.

Can I consolidate worksheets with different layouts? If the worksheets have similar data but in different areas or positions, you can name the corresponding range of cells on each worksheet. You can then combine data from same-name ranges on different worksheets. For details, look up **name-based consolidation** in the Microsoft Excel online index.

What if I need to compare my figures as well as combine them? You can use a PivotTable to consolidate and compare up to four worksheets. For details, look up **PivotTables, multiple consolidation ranges** in the Microsoft Excel online index.

A Multiuser Workbook Makes Getting the Input Easier

If your departments are on a network, you can use a multiuser workbook to speed the input-gathering process.

You create the worksheets for each department in one workbook and share it on the network. Each department updates its worksheet in this workbook. All departments can work simultaneously, and you can watch the input arrive and be consolidated.

For further information, see "Share a Workbook with a Coworker," page 338. For details, look up **shared lists** in the Microsoft Excel online index.

Important In a multiuser workbook, every authorized user in the workgroup can view all of the worksheets. So, use this distribution method only if it's acceptable for all departments to see each other's figures.

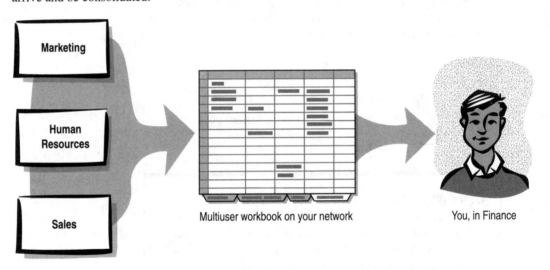

Marketing

Human Resources

Sales

Multiuser workbook on your network

You, in Finance

Next Steps

To	See
Analyze the results of the consolidation	"Develop Budgeting Alternatives," page 371
Consolidate data from worksheets with different layouts	**consolidating data** in the Microsoft Excel online index

Develop Budgeting Alternatives

Work with What-If Assumptions in Microsoft Excel

To balance a budget, you must find the best way to allocate the resources you have among departments. When initial projections exceed the available funds, you need to compare redistribution strategies. You can model different strategies in Microsoft Excel to analyze the pros and cons of different approaches. As you work through several rounds of negotiation and reallocation, you can adjust your models.

Key Features

Goal Seeking

Charts

By creating summaries and charts of the strategies you tried, you can demonstrate to your departments that you reached a fair allocation.

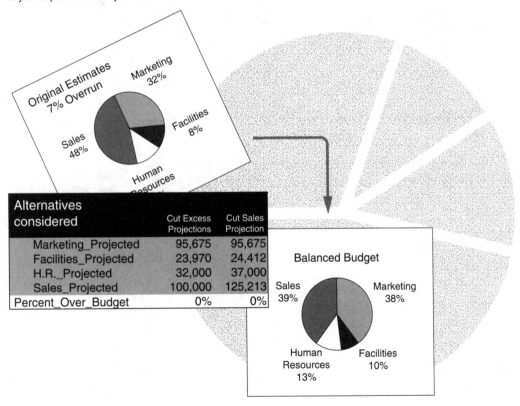

Original Estimates
7% Overrun

Marketing 32%

Facilities 8%

Sales 48%

Human Resources

Alternatives considered	Cut Excess Projections	Cut Sales Projection
Marketing_Projected	95,675	95,675
Facilities_Projected	23,970	24,412
H.R._Projected	32,000	37,000
Sales_Projected	100,000	125,213
Percent_Over_Budget	0%	0%

Balanced Budget

Sales 39%

Marketing 38%

Human Resources 13%

Facilities 10%

Find the Over- and Under-Budget Areas

You've rolled up account-by-account projections from several departments. Compare the projections to your target amounts: can you correct some shortfalls by redistributing funds among accounts? Simply subtracting the allocations from the projections can show you the problem areas and the surplus funds.

 For Help, double-click. In the Microsoft Excel online index look up: **cell references, formulas**

Subtract the value in cell E6 from the value in cell D6 ...

| F6 | =D6-E6 | | | | |

	A	B	C	D	E	F
1	FY 1996 Budget Worksheet					
2						
3			FY 1995		FY 1996	
4	Account		Actual	Projected	Allocated	Difference
5						
6	110	Payroll	164,146	199,000	180,000	19,000
7	120	IRS/FICA/Wk comp/State/SDI	58,035	73,000	66,000	7,000
8	140	Retirement Plan	17,138	20,500	18,500	2,000
9	201	Telecommunication Services	3,319	3,900	4,300	(400)
10	254	Advertising	169	300	250	50
11	301	Office Supplies	4,048	4,500	4,250	250
12	304	Miscellaneous Supplies	902	1,075	1,000	75
13						
14	Total		247,757	302,275	274,300	27,975
15						

... to see the discrepancies.

 More Power   Do you have a large number of accounts? Sort them to view the largest shortages. Click a cell that contains a shortfall amount, and then click the Sort Ascending button.

Sort Ascending button

Set Up a Model

You'll want to analyze where spending cuts will be most effective. For example, you might model the percentage of overrun by department and for the overall budget.

Name the cells you'll use for varying estimates, then use the cell names in formulas that calculate the results. Names are an alternative to cell references. Using names makes your formulas easy to read, plus names help you try out what-if scenarios. Also, you need to name cells in order to create a summary of your alternatives.

For Help, double-click. In the Microsoft Excel online index look up: **cell references, names creating formulas**

To name a cell, first select the cell, then click here and type the name.

F9   =Sales_Difference/Sales_Budgeted

	A	B	C	D	E	F
1	FY 1996 Department Totals					
2						
3		FY 1995	FY 1996			
4	Account	Actual	Projected	Allocated	Difference	Percent
5						
6	Marketing	69,958	95,675	97,000	(1,325)	-1%
7	Facilities	20,994	24,412	23,500	912	4%
8	Human Resources	32,890	37,000	36,800	200	1%
9	Sales	123,915	145,188	125,000	20,188	16%
10						
11	Totals	247,757	302,275	282,300	19,975	7%

The calculated percentage over budget

Name this cell Sales_Projected.

Name this cell Sales_Budgeted.

Name this cell Sales_Difference.

 A quick way to show numbers as percentages Use the Percent Style button on the Formatting toolbar.

 Percent Style button

Test Alternative Strategies

You'll want to see the effect of different reductions on each department and the bottom line. Using *goal seeking*, you can adjust a projection to achieve a specific percentage over or under budget. Goal seeking lets you set a target value for a formula, then adjusts one of the cells used in the formula to calculate your target value. For example, determine how much you'd have to lower the sales projection to reduce the total budget overrun to zero. Try changing different projections to see what it takes to balance the budget.

For Help, double-click. In the Microsoft Excel online index look up: **goal seeking**

Important The cell where you change the value (cell C9 in the example below) must contain a value, not a formula.

The value you want to change ⎯

⎯ Calculates the total percentage over budget for all departments

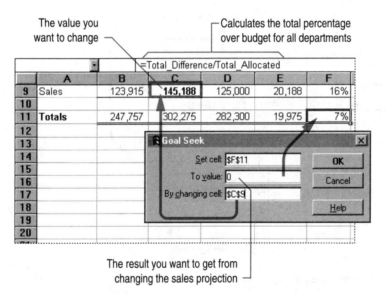

The result you want to get from changing the sales projection ⎯

 More Power Use Microsoft Excel Solver to change more than one value simultaneously to achieve this zero percent goal. For details, look up **Solver** in the Microsoft Excel online index.

Compare Alternatives

As you try different strategies to reduce the over-budget projections, you'll want to compare and refine approaches. You might be used to doing this by saving various copies of your worksheet and looking at them simultaneously.

Another way to compare, however, is to save different sets of projections on a single worksheet, as scenarios. Enter your values, either by goal seeking or by typing the values. Save these original values as a scenario, then enter and save other sets of values to try out other reallocation strategies. You can view each scenario on the same worksheet.

For Help, double-click. In the Microsoft Excel online index look up: **creating scenarios**

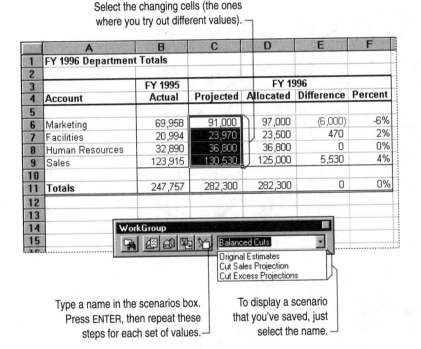

Select the changing cells (the ones where you try out different values).

Type a name in the scenarios box. Press ENTER, then repeat these steps for each set of values.

To display a scenario that you've saved, just select the name.

Reallocate Fairly

Once you decide how to balance the budget, use your model and scenarios to support the results. To show the departments how you reached a decision, create a summary report showing the scenarios you considered. Demonstrate the final distribution by creating a chart showing the division of resources. A pie chart is a good way to show the relationship of parts to a whole, so choose this chart type to show how the allocation is divided among departments. For other chart types, see "Create a Chart from Worksheet Data," page 216.

 For Help, double-click. In the Microsoft Excel online index look up: **scenarios, reports ChartWizard**

ChartWizard button

The summary uses the names you gave to the cells in your model.

Create a summary: Tools menu, Scenario; Summary button.

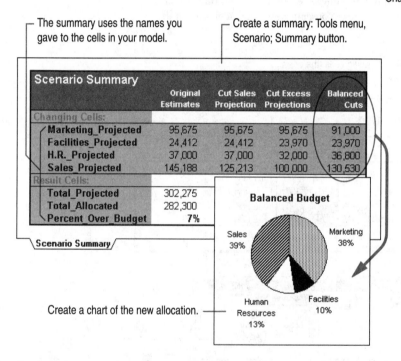

Create a chart of the new allocation.

 For comparison, chart the original figures too   To clarify why the final distribution is reasonable, present the two charts together with the summary of the alternatives you tried.

PART 10

Track Inventory Your Way

Set Up a Custom Inventory System

Contents

Design a Custom Inventory Database

Create a Database Application

You can create many common types of *database applications*—databases with their own custom interfaces—using the Microsoft Access Database Wizard. However, if the wizard doesn't create the database you need, or if you have data that doesn't fit into the tables the wizard creates, you can create a database from scratch and design your own interface.

The topics in this part show you how to create a custom Inventory database, but you can use the examples to create any type of database, or to customize an existing database. Use the following table to decide which topic to read for more information.

To	See
Create a database by moving data, such as a large product list stored in Microsoft Excel, into Microsoft Access tables	"Move a Product List into Microsoft Access," page 379
Add a table to your database to store additional information, such as a list of your company's suppliers	"Add Suppliers to Your Inventory Database," page 385
Customize tables to make data entry easier and to help ensure that data is entered accurately	"Make Data Entry Easy and Accurate," page 392
Create an attractive form that presents data on the screen just the way you like it	"Create a Great Looking Product Form," page 400
Summarize information that's stored in your database and print it in customized reports	"Create and Enhance an Inventory Report," page 407
Tie the tables, forms, and reports in your database together with a custom interface	"Turn Your Inventory Database into an Application," page 412

 Want the Database Wizard to create a database for you? See "Track Your Business Contacts in Microsoft Access," page 306.

Move a Product List into Microsoft Access

Convert Data from Microsoft Excel to Microsoft Access

Microsoft Excel does a great job of helping you create and maintain simple lists. But a list that has repeating data can become too large for Microsoft Excel (which has a limit of 16,384 rows in a worksheet) or may become difficult to maintain. Converting the list to Microsoft Access lets you create a new database, so you can add more entries. And Microsoft Access makes it much easier to manage your information. With a database, you store each fact in one place so that you only have to make a change once to update it everywhere it's used. Microsoft Access also can help make sure your data stays up to date and accurate.

If you're maintaining your information using a Microsoft Excel shared list, consider that Microsoft Access provides true multiuser capability, including locking out changes to entries that are being updated and making updates available to all users immediately.

Key Features

 Convert To Access Command

 Table Analyzer Wizard

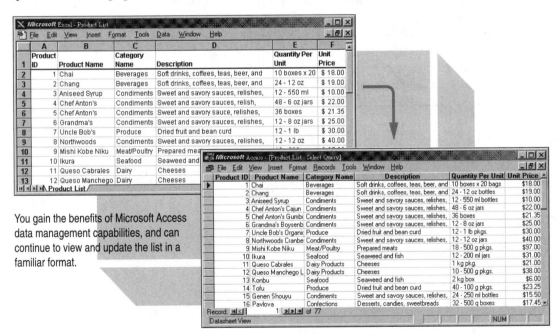

You gain the benefits of Microsoft Access data management capabilities, and can continue to view and update the list in a familiar format.

To complete the steps in this topic   You need either Microsoft Office Professional for Windows 95 or individual copies of Microsoft Access for Windows 95 and Microsoft Excel for Windows 95 installed. You also need the Microsoft Excel AccessLinks add-in installed and enabled. For details, look up **add-in programs, loading and unloading** in the Microsoft Excel online index. Your Microsoft Excel worksheet must be set up as a list. For list format guidelines, look up **lists, creating** in the Microsoft Excel online index.

Get the Help You Need While You Work

Expanded and improved online assistance is just a click away. It's the fastest way to get information so you can keep working.

Ask the Answer Wizard   Type a question in your own words. The Answer Wizard lists online Help topics related to your question. Double-click the Help button and then click the Answer Wizard tab.

Look it up in the online index   Instead of typing a question, use index entries provided in this book to find online topics related to your task. Double-click the Help button and then click the Index tab.

For details, see "Get Assistance While You Work," page 30. Or look up **Help** in the online index.

Convert Your List to Microsoft Access

Suppose you have a growing Product List worksheet that you would like to convert to a Microsoft Access database. This worksheet includes the same product categories and descriptions in multiple locations.

To begin converting your list to a Microsoft Access database, first open the Microsoft Excel workbook that contains your list worksheet. Click anywhere in the list, and then click Convert To Access (Data menu). A Microsoft Access wizard steps you through the process of converting your Microsoft Excel data into Microsoft Access.

For Help, double-click. In the Microsoft Excel online index look up: **converting documents, Microsoft Access**

One reason to move your list to Microsoft Access is to make data maintenance easier.

In a worksheet, you don't always catch different ways that you enter the same data.

	A	B	C	D	E	F
1	Product ID	Product Name	Category Name	Description	Quantity Per Unit	Unit Price
2	1	Chai	Beverages	Soft drinks, coffees, teas, beer, and	10 boxes x 20	$ 18.00
3	2	Chang	Beverages	Soft drinks, coffees, teas, beer, and	24 - 12 oz	$ 19.00
4	3	Aniseed Syrup	Condiments	Sweet and savory sauces, relishes,	12 - 550 ml	$ 10.00
5	4	Chef Anton's	Condiments	Sweet and savory sauces, relish,	48 - 6 oz jars	$ 22.00
6	5	Chef Anton's	Condiments	Sweet and savory sauce, relishes,	36 boxes	$ 21.35
7	6	Grandma's	Condiments	Sweet and savory sauces, relishes,	12 - 8 oz jars	$ 25.00
8	7	Uncle Bob's	Produce	Dried fruit and bean curd	12 - 1 lb	$ 30.00
9	8	Northwoods	Condiments	Sweet and savory sauces, relishes,	12 - 12 oz	$ 40.00

Product List

If repeating data changes, you have to update it by hand in each place that it occurs.

Important After you convert your list to Microsoft Access, you make all further changes directly in your database. You no longer work in the Microsoft Excel worksheet, and your changes aren't reflected in the original worksheet, so you can free up the disk space it occupies by archiving it.

You don't have to correct errors in repeating data before you convert Microsoft Access first stores your data exactly as it found it in your worksheet, and then helps you find and fix this kind of mistake.

Organize Your Data in Tables

When you finish converting, be sure to check I Would Like A Wizard To Analyze My Table After Importing The Data. The wizard analyzes your list and suggests the best way to organize your data into *tables*. Each table will receive the facts about a single subject. In tables as in worksheets, each column is called a *field*, and each row is called a *record*.

Using separate tables allows you to save each fact in one place. Then, you update each fact in a single place, but you can use it in many places. As a result, it's easier to maintain accurate information throughout your database.

The wizard also suggests *relationships* between the tables to make them work together. Relationships describe how the information in tables is shared.

For Help, double-click. In the Microsoft Access online index look up:
tables, overview
relationships, between tables

Your worksheet column headings become fields in the tables.

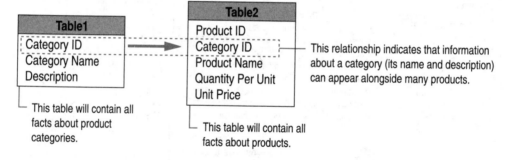

Table1
Category ID
Category Name
Description

This table will contain all facts about product categories.

Table2
Product ID
Category ID
Product Name
Quantity Per Unit
Unit Price

This table will contain all facts about products.

This relationship indicates that information about a category (its name and description) can appear alongside many products.

 Rename tables to reflect their contents   For example, change the name of Table1 to Categories and Table2 to Products. For details, look up **renaming tables** in the Microsoft Access online index.

Check that each table contains facts about only one subject   If fields belong in different tables, move them to where they belong.

When you convert your Product List worksheet   Microsoft Access creates a table named Data From Product List that backs up your list. You'll see the backup table when you click the Tables tab in the Database window of your new database. The backup table is provided in case there's a problem after you finish creating your new tables. You'll want to delete the Data From Product List table once you're sure your data is intact.

View and Update Your Data in Microsoft Access

When you accept the proposed tables and relationships, the Table Analyzer Wizard splits your data into tables and prompts you to correct errors in repeating data. Then tell the wizard to create a *query* for viewing and updating your list data. The query combines data from the tables in an arrangement similar to the original worksheet to ease your transition from a worksheet to a database.

 For Help, double-click. In the Microsoft Access online index look up: **viewing Table Analyzer Wizard query**

Although the query looks like your worksheet, it behaves in an enhanced way. Change a repeating entry in one place, and it's updated in every affected record. When you enter a new product name in a new record, Microsoft Access assigns it a new, unique product ID automatically. Enter a category name, and the associated description is displayed automatically.

You can use this query to create forms and reports to make your new database even more useful.

The query has the same name as your original list.

The field names are the column headings from your worksheet.

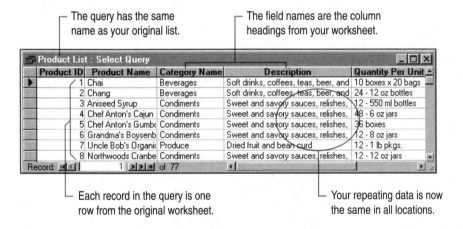

Each record in the query is one row from the original worksheet.

Your repeating data is now the same in all locations.

Important Changes you make in Microsoft Access don't affect your original list in the Microsoft Excel worksheet.

 Scroll through the records to make sure your data is set up correctly You might want to compare the records with your Microsoft Excel list to make sure that you made the right corrections to your data. Note, however, that records may not appear in the same order as in your original list.

Adding a new list entry is easy Click the New Record button, and begin typing.

New Record button

Other Ways to Get Data into Microsoft Access

What if my data isn't in a Microsoft Excel worksheet?   You can import data into Microsoft Access from many popular formats, including dBASE, Paradox, and other database applications, and even plain text from a word processor.

If your data is in a text file, the Microsoft Access Text Import Wizard makes it easy to convert the data to Microsoft Access tables. Just click Import (File menu, Get External Data submenu), in the File Of Type list click Text Files, click the file you want, and follow the instructions that appear on your screen. For details, look up **importing with Text Import Wizard** in the Microsoft Access online index.

What if I need to keep my data in a Microsoft Excel worksheet? You can link a worksheet to a Microsoft Access database.

The linked worksheet is included in your database as another table. You view and update the linked data as you would data stored directly in Microsoft Access, but the attached data continues to be stored in the Microsoft Excel worksheet. For details, look up **linking spreadsheets** in the Microsoft Access online index.

Next Steps

To	See
Fine-tune how your tables are set up and interrelated	**tables, overview** and **relationships, between tables** in the Microsoft Access online index
Add another table to your database	"Add Suppliers to Your Inventory Database," page 385
Make it easier to add data to your database	"Make Data Entry Easy and Accurate," page 392
Use the query you created to create forms that make it easy to view information and enter new data	"Create a Great Looking Product Form," page 400
Use the query you created to create reports that summarize your data	"Create and Enhance an Inventory Report," page 407

Add Suppliers to Your Inventory Database

Add a Table to Your Database

If you've followed the steps in the preceding topic, your Inventory database contains all the tables you need to store product information. But suppose that you need to add information about the suppliers who make your products. Just create a new table with the Table Wizard. Then tie your new table into the database so you can combine information from your tables any way you want.

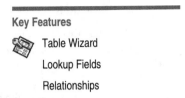

Key Features

Table Wizard

Lookup Fields

Relationships

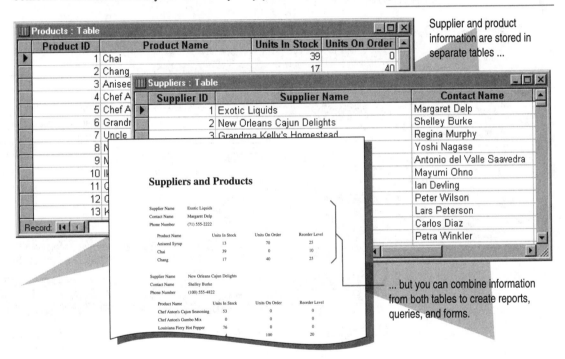

Supplier and product information are stored in separate tables ...

... but you can combine information from both tables to create reports, queries, and forms.

To complete the steps in this topic You need to have either Microsoft Office Professional or an individual copy of Microsoft Access installed. You must also have created Products and Categories tables; for details, see "Move a Product List into Microsoft Access," page 379. However, you can follow the steps in this topic to add any table to a database.

Create the Suppliers Table

When you need to add a new type of information to your database, add a table. The Table Wizard makes it easy to create tables. It provides a list of common fields for many different kinds of tables, so all you do is choose the fields you need.

Click the arrow next to the New Object button, click New Table, and then double-click Table Wizard. Click the Suppliers table, and then add the fields you want from the list.

New Object button

Click the Suppliers table to see the fields you can use.

Click the fields on the left in the order you want them to appear in the table ...

... and then click here to add each one to your table.

The wizard displays the table's datasheet, where you can enter information about suppliers.

 Can't find the type of table you want in the Table Wizard?   If the Table Wizard doesn't list the table you want to create, type field names and data into a blank datasheet. Click the arrow next to the New Object button, click New Table, and then double-click Datasheet View. For details, look up **creating tables by entering data in a datasheet** in the Microsoft Access online index.

New Object button

Add existing data to your table   If you have data in another application or format, such as a text file, import it by clicking Import (File menu, Get External Data submenu). For details, look up **importing data from other programs** in the Microsoft Access online index.

Add Supplier Information

When you finish with the wizard, it opens the table in Datasheet view, in which you type your information.

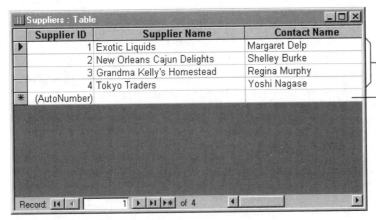

 For Help, double-click.
In the Microsoft Access online index look up:
datasheets, overview
adding records

Datasheet view displays more than one record at a time.

Type information about a supplier in the blank record at the end of the datasheet.

To change a field name Double-click the column header in the datasheet and type a new name. Be sure to do this before you create queries, forms, and reports, or you will have to change the field names in those, too.

Need to add another field? If you forgot to include a field or if the Table Wizard doesn't have a field you need, add it by clicking the header of the column that will follow the new field, and then clicking Column (Insert menu).

To further customize your table Open it in Design view and set *field properties.* For details, look up **tables, properties** in the Microsoft Access online index.

To open the Suppliers table after you've closed it Click the Database Window button, click the Tables tab, and then double-click the Suppliers table.

Database Window button

Want to create a form for entering supplier information? Click the arrow next to the New Object button, click AutoForm, and then type information into the form.

New Object button

Tie Supplier and Product Information Together

To tie the Suppliers table to the database, add a *lookup* field to the Products table. The lookup field displays a list of suppliers from which you can select the supplier for each product.

The Lookup Wizard makes it easy to add the field. Open the Products table by clicking the Database Window button, clicking the Tables tab, and then double-clicking the Products table. In the column header where you want to add the lookup field, click the right mouse button, and then click Insert Lookup Column. Follow the instructions on the screen, and be sure to tell the wizard that you want to choose names from the Suppliers table and display data from the Supplier Name Field.

 For Help, double-click. In the Microsoft Access online index look up: **lookup**

Database Window button

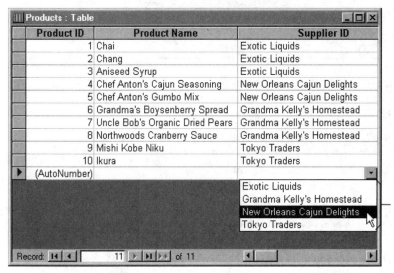

When you have finished with the Lookup Wizard, you can select a supplier from a list.

 Don't see anything in the list? If you haven't entered information in the Suppliers table, your list will be empty. Add information about your suppliers to the Suppliers table before using the list.

Add Fields to Track Inventory Levels

If you want your Products table to include the same fields that are used in the following topics, add four fields: UnitsInStock, ReorderLevel, UnitsOnOrder, and Discontinued. The easiest way to add several fields to a table is to use the Field Builder in Design view. Click the Database Window button, click the Tables tab, click the Products table, and then click Design.

Click the right mouse button where you want to add the field ...

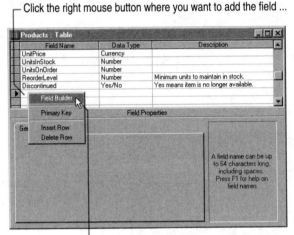

... click Field Builder, select the table that contains the field that you want to add, and then select the field.

If the Field Builder doesn't have the fields you want, type field names and select data types in blank rows in the upper portion of the window. For details, look up **tables, adding fields** in the Microsoft Access online index.

Viewing Relationships Between Tables

When you add a lookup field, Microsoft Access creates a *relationship* between the two tables, making them part of a unified database. When tables are related, you can combine data from each in queries, forms, and reports.

You can see the tables in your database and the relationships between them in the Relationships window. To open this window, in the Database window, click the Relationships button.

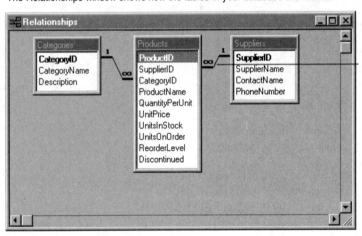

Relationships button

Each table is represented by a field list. The lines that connect field lists show the relationships between tables.

You can also set options for the relationships between tables to ensure that information entered in the tables is always appropriate. For example, you can make sure a product always has a valid supplier.

For details, look up **relationships, between tables** in the Microsoft Access online index.

The Relationships window shows how the tables in your database are related.

To set options for a relationship, double-click the relationship line.

Next Steps

To	See
Customize tables to make data entry easier and to help ensure that your data is entered accurately	"Make Data Entry Easy and Accurate," page 392
Create attractive forms to present data on the screen	"Create a Great Looking Product Form," page 400
Create custom reports to summarize and print information contained in your database	"Create and Enhance an Inventory Report," page 407

Make Data Entry Easy and Accurate

Now that your Inventory database includes all the tables you need, you can make data entry consistent, accurate, and easy. By setting *field properties* for your tables, you can have Microsoft Access fill in information for you and tell you when you've made a mistake.

Key Features

Table Design

Field Properties

Default Values

Validation Rules

Input Masks

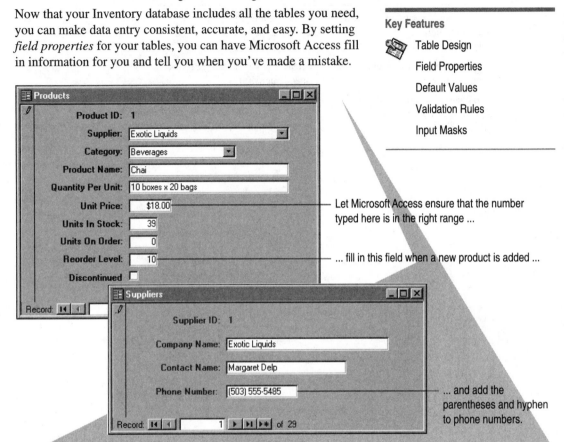

Let Microsoft Access ensure that the number typed here is in the right range ...

... fill in this field when a new product is added ...

... and add the parentheses and hyphen to phone numbers.

To complete the steps in this topic   You need to have either Microsoft Office Professional or an individual copy of Microsoft Access installed. You must also have created the Products, Categories, and Suppliers tables in "Move a Product List into Microsoft Access," page 379, and "Add Suppliers to Your Inventory Database," page 385. However, you can follow the steps in this topic to make data entry easier for any table you create.

Set Up Your Tables to Speed Data Entry

To control data entry and make it easier, you set *field properties* for the tables in your database. Properties control how a field behaves or looks. Once you set properties for a table, all forms and datasheets that use information from that table will use the settings.

You set field properties in a table's Design view. To open a table in Design view, click the Database Window button, click the Tables tab, click the table, and then click Design. Then, click the field whose properties you want to set.

 For Help, double-click. In the Microsoft Access online index look up: **tables, properties field properties**

Database Window button

Click a field ...

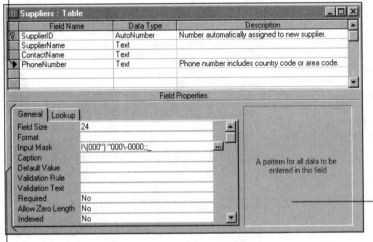

Look here for a brief explanation of what the selected property does.

... and then click a property here and type the new setting.

Important Set properties for a table before you create forms based on that table. If you set table properties after creating forms, some of the settings won't apply to the forms. After setting properties, click the Save button to save the table.

 Save button

 To create a form that uses your new property settings Save the table, click the arrow next to the New Object button, and then click AutoForm.

 New Object button

Let Microsoft Access Enter Information for You

Does your table have a field that almost always contains the same information? For example, do you usually reorder any item when you have only 10 in stock? Whenever you or your coworkers enter a new product into the database, you can have Microsoft Access automatically enter 10 in the Reorder Level box.

For Help, double-click. In the Microsoft Access online index look up:
DefaultValue property
writing expressions

Open the Products table in Design view, and then click the ReorderLevel field to display its properties.

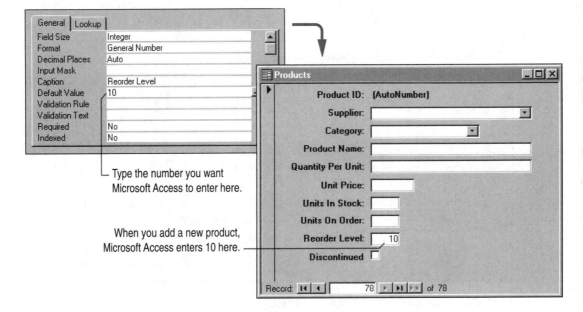

Type the number you want Microsoft Access to enter here.

When you add a new product, Microsoft Access enters 10 here.

Enter today's date automatically   In a Date field, you'll often want to enter the current date. Click the DefaultValue property box, and then type **=Date()**.

If you changed the information in a field that's automatically filled in, but want to change it back   Press ALT+CTRL+SPACEBAR. For other keyboard shortcuts, look up **keyboard shortcuts** in the Microsoft Access online index.

Limit the Information That Can Be Entered in a Field

Sometimes, you may want to limit what can be entered in a field. For example, suppose you want to make sure that numbers entered in the UnitPrice field are always greater than 0 and less than 1000. Limit the data that's allowed in a field by setting the ValidationRule property.

If your Products table isn't opened in Design view, open it. Then click the UnitPrice field to display its properties.

For Help, double-click.
In the Microsoft Access online index look up:
validation, rules
ValidationRule property
writing expressions

— Type the limits for the field here.

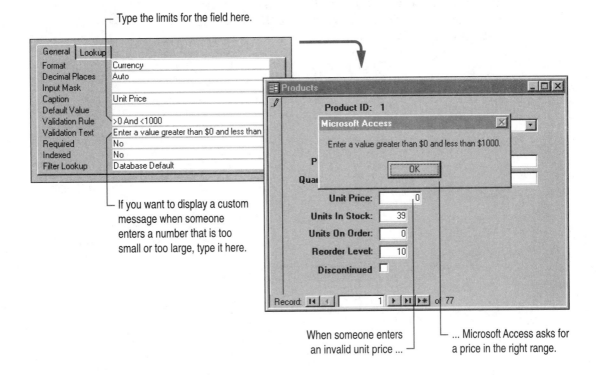

— If you want to display a custom message when someone enters a number that is too small or too large, type it here.

When someone enters an invalid unit price ...

— ... Microsoft Access asks for a price in the right range.

Did you know that Microsoft Access always checks to see that you've entered the right kind of data?   For example, if you try to enter text in a numeric field, Microsoft Access will tell you that you've entered the wrong type of data.

Want to compare a value in one field with the value in another field? Set the ValidationRule property for the table. For example, you can require that a product's unit price is always greater than its unit cost by comparing the fields in the table's validation rule. For details, look up **record-level validation** in the Microsoft Access online index.

Want to ensure that a field always contains a value?   In the field's Required property box, click Yes. For details, look up **Required property** in the Microsoft Access online index.

Simplify Typing Phone Numbers

You always enter supplier phone numbers with parentheses and hyphens, like this: (503) 555-5485. Save yourself some typing by letting Microsoft Access automatically add the parentheses and hyphen for you. Create an *input mask*.

Open the Suppliers table in Design view, and then click the PhoneNumber field to display its properties.

 For Help, double-click. In the Microsoft Access online index look up: **InputMask property**

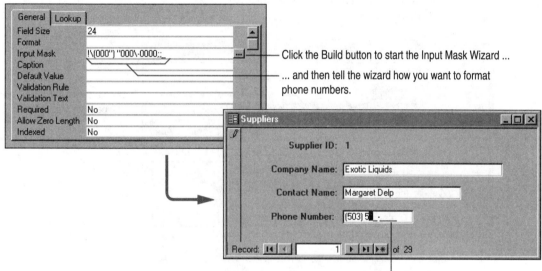

Click the Build button to start the Input Mask Wizard ...

... and then tell the wizard how you want to format phone numbers.

Microsoft Access adds the parentheses and dashes and ensures that you or your coworkers enter the right number of digits.

Do you have other data with format characters? You can have Microsoft Access automatically add format characters for other types of data, such as social security numbers or ZIP Codes. For details, look up **input masks, examples of** in the Microsoft Access online index.

Check Spelling and Correct Mistakes

No matter how careful you are when you enter information into your database, you'll occasionally misspell a word. Even minor spelling mistakes can compromise the integrity of your database. Another way to ensure that your data is accurate is to let Microsoft Access check your spelling. Microsoft Access can even automatically correct words that you frequently mistype.

To check spelling in a form or datasheet, select one or more fields or columns and click the Spelling button. You can check spelling for fields that store text, but not numbers or other types of data.

 Spelling button

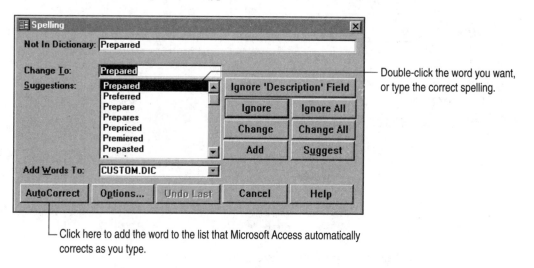

Double-click the word you want, or type the correct spelling.

Click here to add the word to the list that Microsoft Access automatically corrects as you type.

Next Steps

To	See
Create attractive forms to present data on the screen in your own way	"Create a Great Looking Product Form," page 400
Create custom reports to summarize and print information	"Create and Enhance an Inventory Report," page 407
Control how data is displayed in your tables, forms, and reports	**formatting** in the Microsoft Access online index
Get more information about properties that control how data in your tables looks and behaves	**tables, properties** in the Microsoft Access online index
Save typing by choosing information from a list	"Add Suppliers to Your Inventory Database," page 385

Create a Great Looking Product Form

Use a Product Form to Add Data to Your Inventory Database

Want a fast, efficient way for you and your coworkers to enter data about your growing product line into the Inventory database? Create a Product form. With a form, you see just one record at a time, so it's easy to see what to type and where to type it. Creating a form is a snap with the Microsoft Access Form Wizard. Then, in a few simple steps, you can customize your form to make it even easier to use.

Key Features

Form Wizard

Subforms

Form Design View

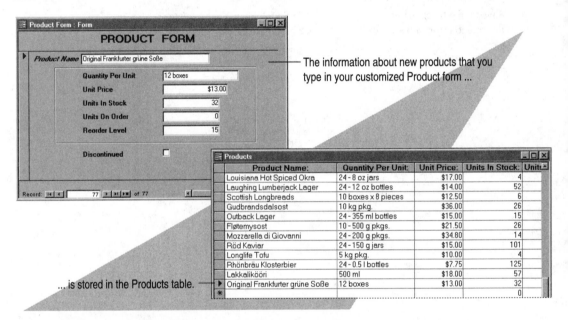

The information about new products that you type in your customized Product form ...

... is stored in the Products table.

To complete the steps in this topic You need to have either Microsoft Office Professional or an individual copy of Microsoft Access installed. You also need to create a Products table using the procedure in "Move a Product List into Microsoft Access," page 379, or with the Table Wizard. For details, look up **tables, creating** in the Microsoft Access online index. However, you can use the techniques in this topic to create customized forms for any Microsoft Access table.

Create the Form

With the Microsoft Access Form Wizard, creating a form is as easy as choosing from a list of fields in your database. Your form contains only the information you need, arranged and formatted to simplify data entry.

Click the arrow next to the New Object button, click New Form, and then double-click Form Wizard. Tell the wizard which table contains the fields you want to include in the form, and then choose only the fields you need. On the following screens, tell the wizard what you want the form to look like and what you want to call it.

 For Help, double-click.
In the Microsoft Access online index look up:
forms, creating

New Object button

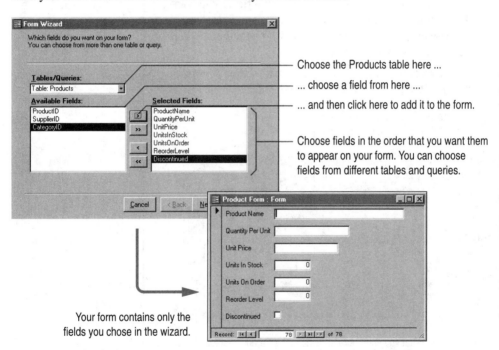

— Choose the Products table here ...

... choose a field from here ...

... and then click here to add it to the form.

— Choose fields in the order that you want them to appear on your form. You can choose fields from different tables and queries.

Your form contains only the fields you chose in the wizard.

 To see more than one record at a time Click the arrow next to the View button, and then click Datasheet View.

View button

Want a quick way to open your form for data entry? After opening the database, drag the form from the Database window to the Windows 95 desktop. To open the form from the Windows 95 desktop, double-click the form's icon. For details, look up **shortcuts** in the Microsoft Access online index.

Create a Form to Add Data to More Than One Table at a Time

You can increase the efficiency of data entry by creating forms that contain subforms (forms within other forms). For example, you could create a single form that lets you store information about each of your product categories, such as Beverages (the main form) and about the products in each category, such as coffee and tea (the subform). Use your form to enter or view data about both at once.

Start the Form Wizard. Choose the table and fields you want in the main form, and then choose the table and fields you want to include in the subform. Then, follow the instructions on the screen to lay out your form.

For more information on designing forms, look up **forms, creating** in the Microsoft Access online index.

What you enter here is saved in the Categories table. ┐

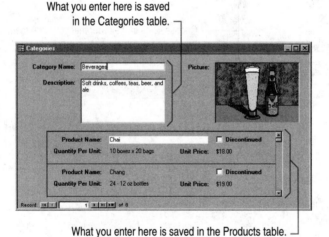

What you enter here is saved in the Products table. ┘

Adjust the Form's Layout

The Form Wizard created a simple form ready for data entry. But, suppose you want to rearrange the field names and the labels that identify them (called *controls*) to group related information together. Just switch to Design view to adjust the form's layout.

Click the arrow next to the View button, and then click Design View. Select a control that you want to move, and then reposition it on the grid. If you need to enlarge or reduce a control, select it and adjust it.

 For Help, double-click.
In the Microsoft Access online index look up:
controls, creating
forms, views (illustrated)

View button

Modify your form's layout in Design view.

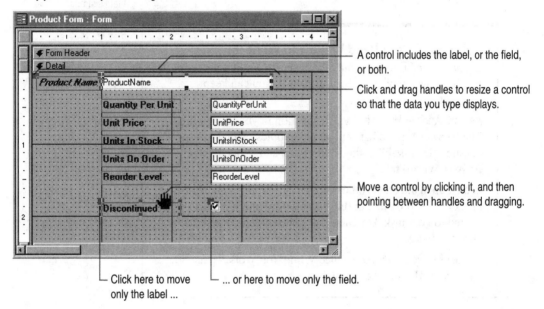

A control includes the label, or the field, or both.

Click and drag handles to resize a control so that the data you type displays.

Move a control by clicking it, and then pointing between handles and dragging.

Click here to move only the label ...   ... or here to move only the field.

Fine-tune the placement of a control Click the control, hold down the CTRL key, and then use the arrow keys to move the control in fine increments.

To move or realign more than one control at a time Click next to one of the controls, and then drag the pointer around the controls to select them (a box appears around the controls as you drag the pointer). Point between any two handles on the selected controls. When the pointer changes to an open hand, hold the mouse button down and drag the controls to a new location. For details, look up **controls, moving** in the Microsoft Access online index.

Need to add a field? Click the Field List button, and then drag the field you want from the list to the form.

Field List button

Get the Help You Need While You Work

Expanded and improved online assistance is just a click away. It's the fastest way to get information so you can keep working.

Ask the Answer Wizard Type a question in your own words. The Answer Wizard lists online Help topics related to your question. Double-click the Help button and then click the Answer Wizard tab.

Look it up in the online index Instead of typing a question, use index entries provided in this book to find online topics related to your task. Double-click the Help button and then click the Index tab.

For details, see "Get Assistance While You Work," page 30. Or look up **Help** in the online index.

Emphasize Important Information

You can also make your form easier to read by changing the font, size, and style of controls. For example, you can make your most important labels or field names bold and larger. Select one label or group of labels, and then use the Formatting toolbar to apply the format you want.

 For Help, double-click.
In the Microsoft Access online index look up:
Format Painter
forms, views (illustrated)

Select the control you want to format ...

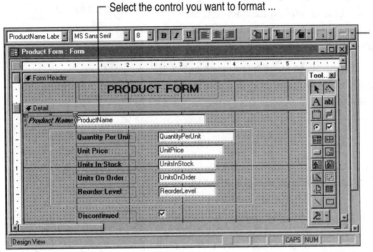

... and then choose the formats you want from the Formatting toolbar.

Guidelines

Add a title to your form Point to the top of the Detail section bar. When a two-headed arrow appears, click and drag the bar downward to create space for the title. Click the Label tool in the toolbox, click in the Form Header section to create a box for the title, and then type the title in the box. To format the title, click the label box to select it, and then use the Formatting toolbar to apply formatting.

Label tool

Add lines to your form Click the Line tool in the toolbox, click where you want the line to start, and then drag to draw it. For details, look up **lines, drawing on forms or reports** in the Microsoft Access online index.

Line tool

Copy a format quickly with the Format Painter   Click the control
whose format you want to copy, and then click the Format Painter
button once to copy to a single control, or double-click the button to
copy to multiple controls. Then, click each control you want to
format. If you're formatting multiple controls, you'll need to click
the Format Painter button again to turn off formatting.

Format Painter button

**Change the appearance and alignment of all controls on the form with
automatic formats**   Automatic formats include formatting
combinations such as bold lettering, etched field names, and
borders. Click the AutoFormat button on the Formatting toolbar, and
then choose the format you want.

AutoFormat button

Add a border around related controls to make them stand out   Click
the Rectangle tool in the toolbox, and then drag the pointer around
the controls you want to include.

Rectangle tool

Next Steps

To	See
Find specific information in your forms	**filters, creating** in the Microsoft Access online index
Find information contained in two or more tables	"Evaluate Sales Performance in a Microsoft Access Database," page 458, or **queries, creating** in the Microsoft Access online index

Create and Enhance an Inventory Report

Summarize Inventory Data in a Microsoft Access Report

Business is booming, and as a result you've greatly increased your inventory. To keep track of inventory flow, you want to create a monthly inventory report.

With the Microsoft Access Report Wizard, you can quickly create a polished report that calculates total units in stock and the percentage of overall total for each product category. Next month, simply run the report again. You'll get the latest facts and figures with no effort at all.

Key Features

Report Wizard

Report Design View

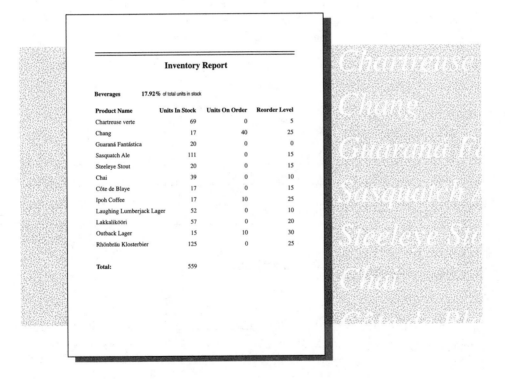

Inventory Report

Beverages	17.92% of total units in stock		
Product Name	**Units In Stock**	**Units On Order**	**Reorder Level**
Chartreuse verte	69	0	5
Chang	17	40	25
Guaraná Fantástica	20	0	0
Sasquatch Ale	111	0	15
Steeleye Stout	20	0	15
Chai	39	0	10
Côte de Blaye	17	0	15
Ipoh Coffee	17	10	25
Laughing Lumberjack Lager	52	0	10
Lakkalikööri	57	0	20
Outback Lager	15	10	30
Rhönbräu Klosterbier	125	0	25
Total:	559		

To complete the steps in this topic You need Microsoft Office Professional or an individual copy of Microsoft Access installed. You also need to have created Categories and Products tables by using the steps in "Move a Product List into Microsoft Access," page 379, or by using the Microsoft Access Table Wizard. However, you can use the techniques in this topic to produce reports for any type of data that you have in a Microsoft Access database.

Begin the Report

You'll want to organize your inventory report the same way you organize your inventory: by product category. That way, you'll be able to see the figures for all products of one type at a glance. And you'll want to include these facts about each product: product name, units in stock, units on order, and reorder level. Complete the picture by totaling the units in stock for each category and calculating the percentage of the grand total of units in stock that each category accounts for. Gathering this information from your database and laying it out in an attractive format is easy with the Report Wizard.

To create the report   Run the Report Wizard and follow its instructions. To run the Report Wizard, click the arrow next to the New Object button, and then click New Report. Double-click Report Wizard, choose the Category and Products tables, and add the fields that contain the information you need.

For Help, double-click.
In the Microsoft Access online index look up:
reports, creating

New Object button

The Report Wizard enables you to choose the fields you want in the report.

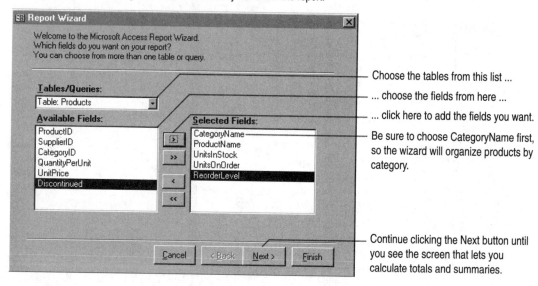

Choose the tables from this list ...

... choose the fields from here ...

... click here to add the fields you want.

Be sure to choose CategoryName first, so the wizard will organize products by category.

Continue clicking the Next button until you see the screen that lets you calculate totals and summaries.

Important   When the wizard asks you which fields you want to group on, accept the proposed field, CategoryName. For details, look up **records, grouping in reports** in the Microsoft Access online index.

Calculate Totals

Next, when you see the screen that asks about sort order, click Summary Options, and then tell the wizard to total the units in stock by clicking the Sum box in the Units In Stock field and to calculate a percentage of the total by clicking the Calculate Percent Of Total For Sums box. In the following screens, choose the style you want for your report, give the report a name, and you're done. The wizard does it all!

When you finish with the wizard, you'll see your report in Print Preview, which shows how the report will look when it's printed. Sometimes, you may want to check the report's overall layout first. In this case, click the Close Window button, click the arrow next to the View button, and then click Layout Preview.

 For Help, double-click.
In the Microsoft Access online index look up:
reports, calculating

Close Window
button

View
button

In Layout Preview, you see just enough of your report to evaluate the layout.

┌ The percentage of total products and...

┌ The top-level
  CategoryID Header

┌ ... total units for each category are
  calculated in the CategoryID Footer.

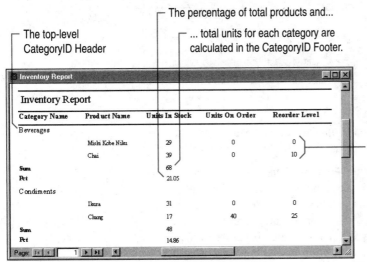

Product information makes up the
Detail section of the report.

 To see category totals without details about individual products In the Report Wizard, on the screen that calculates totals and summaries, click Summary Only.

Improve the Appearance of Your Report

The Report Wizard did a great job of laying out your data. But to make the report easier to read you'd like to realign some of the items, called *controls*. Adjusting the layout of a report is as easy as dragging its controls into new positions.

From Layout Preview, open the report in Design view by clicking the Close button.

 For Help, double-click. In the Microsoft Access online index look up: **controls, moving reports, customizing**

In Design view, you see each element of your report on a grid that shows its relative position on the page.

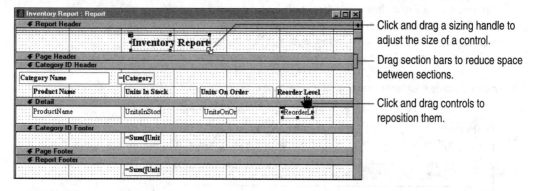

— Click and drag a sizing handle to adjust the size of a control.

— Drag section bars to reduce space between sections.

— Click and drag controls to reposition them.

Guidelines

Format headings so they stand out   Select the heading, and then choose the font or style you want from the Formatting toolbar.

Copy a format quickly with the Format Painter   Select the control that has the format you want to copy, and then click the Format Painter button once to copy the format to a single control, or double-click the Format Painter button to copy the format to multiple controls. Then click the control(s) you want to format. If you're formatting multiple controls, you'll need to click the Format Painter button to turn formatting off.

Format Painter button

Add labels for the fields in your report   Click the Label tool in the toolbox. Position the pointer where you want the upper left corner of the label to appear, and then click to insert the label box. Type text for the label in the box.

A

Label tool

Change the way page numbers look   Click Page Number (Insert menu), and then choose the format and placement for the numbers.

As you make layout changes, see how they look Click the arrow next to the View button, and then click Layout Preview. If you need to make more adjustments, click the Close Window button to return to Design view.

View button

Close Window button

Want to see how the report will look when it's printed? Click the arrow next to the View button, and then click Print Preview.

Eliminate blank pages Check to see that the combined width of the report and the margins doesn't exceed the paper size selected in the Page Setup dialog box. For details, look up **page setup** in the Microsoft Access online index.

Next Steps

To	In the Microsoft Access online index look up
Print an updated inventory report at the end of the month	**printing, reports**
Get specific facts about your inventory, such as which products are on order	**queries, overview**

Turn Your Inventory Database into an Application

Prepare a Database for Others to Use

Now that you have a complete Inventory database, you're almost ready to share it with your coworkers. Before you do, make it easy to use by creating a simple startup form that appears each time someone opens the database. Add buttons to the form that open the forms and print the reports your coworkers use most frequently. Then, secure your database from unauthorized use by creating a password.

These special touches not only make the database easier to use, they transform your database into a custom *application*.

Key Features

Startup Form

Command Button Wizard

Database Passwords

By creating a startup form that appears when someone opens the database application, you can make it easier for your coworkers to get their work done.

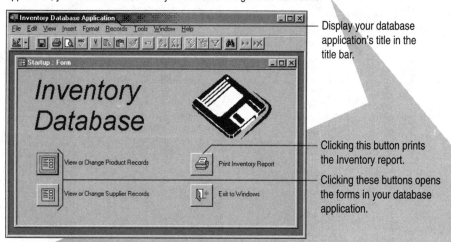

Display your database application's title in the title bar.

Clicking this button prints the Inventory report.

Clicking these buttons opens the forms in your database application.

To complete the steps in this topic   You need to have either Microsoft Office Professional or an individual copy of Microsoft Access installed. You also must have created a Product form and an Inventory report as described in "Create a Great Looking Product Form," page 400, and "Create and Enhance an Inventory Report," page 407. However, you can follow the steps in this topic to turn any database you create into an application.

Create a Startup Form

The first step in turning your database into a custom application is to create a *startup* form that appears whenever someone opens your database. A startup form looks like any database form, but it can include special text to identify the database and welcome users.

Click the arrow next to the New Object button, click New Form, and then double-click Design View. Add the text that you want to appear on the form.

 For Help, double-click.
In the Microsoft Access online index look up:
forms, creating
forms, properties

New Object button

— Click the Label tool ...

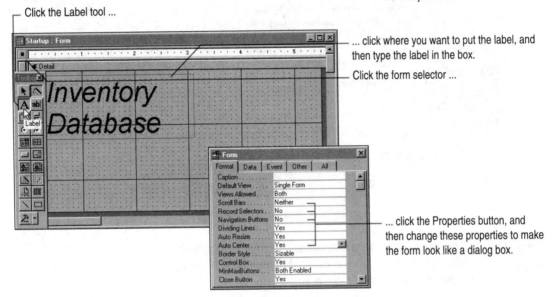

... click where you want to put the label, and then type the label in the box.

— Click the form selector ...

... click the Properties button, and then change these properties to make the form look like a dialog box.

 To change the font and size of the label Use the buttons on the Formatting toolbar.

Add a logo or clip art to the startup form For details, look up **OLE objects, adding to forms or reports** in the Microsoft Access online index.

Add Buttons That Open Forms and Reports

Next, add buttons that open the forms and print the reports in your database.

Adding buttons to a form is easy with the Command Button Wizard. In the toolbox, click the Command Button tool, and if the Control Wizards tool isn't selected, click it. Then, click where you want to put the button, and follow the instructions on the screen.

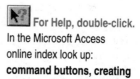 For Help, double-click.
In the Microsoft Access online index look up:
command buttons, creating

Command Button   Control Wizards
tool   tool

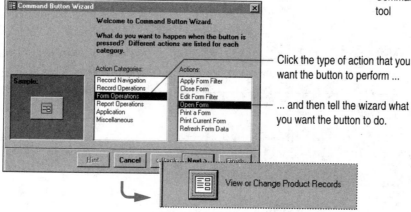

Click the type of action that you want the button to perform ...

... and then tell the wizard what you want the button to do.

The wizard creates the button for you.

 Use the Command Button Wizard to create buttons for many tasks
For example, use it to add a button that starts Microsoft Excel or Word, moves to another record, or closes the database.

Want to put text instead of a picture on a button? Tell the wizard what you want the button to say.

Want to add a description of what a button does? Use the Label tool in the toolbox.

Make Your Startup Form Open Automatically

Now, make your startup form appear automatically whenever someone opens the Inventory application. Further customize your new application by adding a title to the startup form's title bar and by choosing which standard Microsoft Access items you want to appear in your application. Click Startup (Tools menu).

 For Help, double-click. In the Microsoft Access online index look up: **startup dialog box**

Choose your startup form from the list.

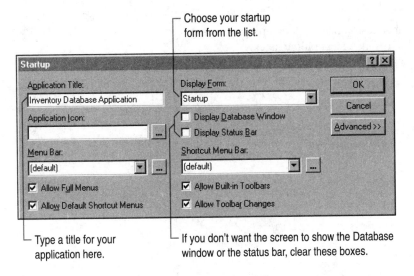

Type a title for your application here.

If you don't want the screen to show the Database window or the status bar, clear these boxes.

Create an icon so users can open your application from Windows without starting Microsoft Access first For details, look up **shortcuts** in your Windows 95 documentation.

Want to bypass the startup form and go directly to the Microsoft Access Database window? Hold down the SHIFT key when you open your database.

Display Custom Toolbars and Menus

For most applications, you'll want to display the standard Microsoft Access toolbars and menus. However, if you want to control which commands are available in your database application, or if you want to provide an easy way to run macros or Visual Basic program code, you can create custom toolbars or menus.

For details on toolbar customization, look up **customizing toolbars** in the Microsoft Access online index.

For details on customizing menus, look up **menu bar** in the Microsoft Access online index.

Protect Your Database with a Password

Your Inventory database application contains confidential information that you'll want to protect from unauthorized users. Prevent them from opening the application by creating a password.

Important To create a password, you must open the database for exclusive access. Close the database, click Open Database (File menu), select your database, click Exclusive, and then click Open.

For Help, double-click. In the Microsoft Access online index look up:
security, basics
passwords, adding database

Click Security (Tools menu), click Set Database Password, and then type the password.

⌐ Type a password ...

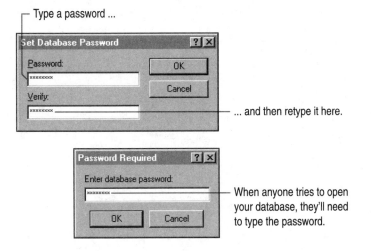

... and then retype it here.

When anyone tries to open your database, they'll need to type the password.

Record your password and keep it in a safe place If you forget the password, you won't be able to open your database.

For added security, change the password occasionally Click Security (Tools menu), and then click Remove Password. Then create a new password.

Need more sophisticated security? You can give each user in your workgroup permission to view or change a different set of objects and data. For details, see **security, users/groups** in the Microsoft Access online index.

Next Steps

To	See
See examples of Startup and Main Switchboard forms	Startup and Main Switchboard forms in the Northwind sample database
Create a simple database application using the Database Wizard	"Track Orders in a Shared Database," page 355
Learn Visual Basic programming and read about how to create your own database applications using Microsoft Access	*Building Applications with Microsoft Access for Windows 95,* available directly from Microsoft with the order form provided in your Microsoft Office package

PART 11

Prepare Customer Bids

Contents

Create a Price List

Create a Microsoft Access Report That Helps Sell Your Products

Need a price list that promotes both your company and your products? If you store product and price information in a Microsoft Access database, you can produce a professional-looking price list by creating a report. As prices change, update your price list simply by reprinting the report. Use the techniques in this topic to create attractive reports from data stored in any Microsoft Access database.

Key Features

Report Wizard

Report Design View

Product Price List

Beverages

Soft drinks, coffees, teas, beer, and ale

Product Name	Product ID	Quantity Per Unit	Unit Price
Chartreuse verte	39	750 cc per bottle	$18.00
Chang	2	24 - 12 oz bottles	$19.00
Guaraná Fantástica	24	12 - 355 ml cans	$4.50
Sasquatch Ale	34	24 - 12 oz bottles	$14.00
Steeleye Stout	35	24 - 12 oz bottles	$18.00
Chai	1	10 boxes x 20 bags	$18.00
Côte de Blaye	38	12 - 75 cl bottles	$263.50
Ipoh Coffee	43	16 - 500 g tins	$46.00
Laughing Lumberjack Lager	67	24 - 12 oz bottles	$14.00
Lakkalikööri	76	500 ml	$18.00
Outback Lager	70	24 - 355 ml bottles	$15.00
Rhönbräu Klosterbier	75	24 - 0.5 l bottles	$7.75
Sir Rodney's Marmalade	20	30 gift boxes	$81.00

To complete the steps in this topic   You need Microsoft Office Professional or an individual copy of Microsoft Access, and you need to have Microsoft Access installed.

Try It Out   The example in this topic uses the Northwind database included with Microsoft Access. If you like, you can open this database to experiment. If you want to perform the techniques described in this topic on your own database, create one by using the Database Wizard. For details, look up **databases, creating** in the Microsoft Access online index.

Begin the Report

As you set up your price list, you'll want to include all the details your customers need to place an order: product name and number, the quantity per unit, and unit price. If you carry many items, you'll also want to organize products by category; for example, you'll want to group information about all beverages together. Gathering this information from your database and laying it out in an attractive format is easy with the Report Wizard.

To create the report Run the Report Wizard and follow its instructions. Click the arrow next to the New Object button, click New Report, and then double-click Report Wizard. Next, select the tables and fields that contain the information you need. Continue to click the Next button until you come to the screen that asks what you want to call your report. Name the report, click the Finish button, and let the wizard do the rest of the work.

 For Help, double-click. In the Microsoft Access online index look up: **reports, creating**

New Object button

Choose the Categories and Products tables from this list ...

... choose each field you want from here ...

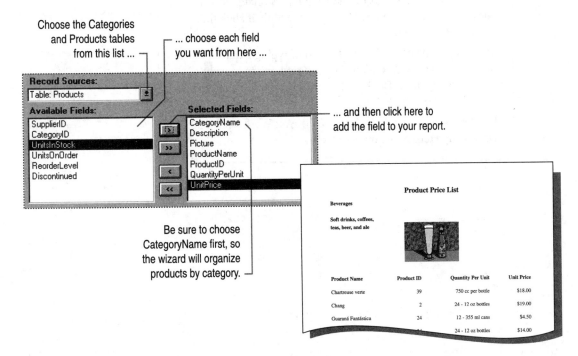

... and then click here to add the field to your report.

Be sure to choose CategoryName first, so the wizard will organize products by category.

The Report Wizard organizes your products by category.

To create a report from data stored in a Microsoft Excel for Windows 95 worksheet   In Microsoft Excel, click in the worksheet, and then click Access Report (Data menu).

Do you have pictures?   If you've stored pictures on your computer, you can add them to your database tables as OLE object data types, and then use them in reports and on forms. For more information on including a picture, image control, or OLE objects, look up **OLE objects, adding to forms or reports** in the Microsoft Access online index.

Get the Help You Need While You Work

Expanded and improved online assistance is just a click away. It's the fastest way to get information so you can keep working.

Ask the Answer Wizard   Type a question in your own words. The Answer Wizard lists online Help topics related to your question. Double-click the Help button and then click the Answer Wizard tab.

Look it up in the online index   Instead of typing a question, use index entries provided in this book to find online topics related to your task. Double-click the Help button and then click the Index tab.

For details, see "Get Assistance While You Work," page 30. Or look up **Help** in the online index.

Adjust the Report Layout

The Report Wizard produces an attractive price list, but you may want to move and realign information to reduce the space between items in your list. Adjusting the layout of a report is as easy as dragging an item, or *control*, into position. A control represents each of the fields you selected in the wizard.

To make changes to the layout of your price list, from Print Preview switch to Design view by clicking the Close Window button.

In Design view, you see each element of your report on a grid that shows its relative position on the page.

 For Help, double-click.
In the Microsoft Access online index look up:
reports, customizing
controls, creating
controls, moving

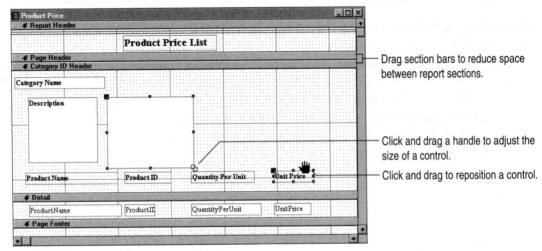

Close Window button

Drag section bars to reduce space between report sections.

Click and drag a handle to adjust the size of a control.

Click and drag to reposition a control.

Guidelines

Format several controls at once   Click near one of the controls, drag around the controls you want to format, and then choose a format from the Formatting toolbar.

Copy a format from one control to another   Select the control that has the format you want to copy, click the Format Painter button once to copy the format to one control or double-click the button to copy the format to multiple controls. Then, click the control(s) you want to format. If you're formatting multiple controls, you'll need to click the Format Painter button again to turn off formatting.

Format Painter button

Align data within a control   Select the control, and then click an alignment button on the toolbar.

Alignment buttons

 Did the Report Wizard include some controls you don't need?   Click the control, and then press DELETE.

As you make layout changes, see how they look   Click the arrow next to the View button, and then click Layout Preview. If you need to make more adjustments, click the Close Window button to return to Design view.

View
button

Close Window
button

Want to see how the report will look when it's printed?   Click the View button to switch to Print Preview.

Print One Category Per Page

Now, refine your design even further and make it even easier for your customers to find the products they are looking for by starting each product category on a new page.

In report Design view, click the CategoryID Header section bar, and then click the Properties button. In the Force New Page property box, click the arrow to display properties, and then click Before Section. To see the change, click the arrow next to the View button, and then click Layout Preview.

 For Help, double-click.
In the Microsoft Access online index look up:
reports, properties
reports, sections described

Properties button

Your customized price list

Product Price List

Beverages

Soft drinks, coffees, teas, beer, and ale

Product Name	Product ID	Quantity Per Unit	Unit Price
Chartreuse verte	39	750 cc per bottle	$18.00
Chang	2	24 - 12 oz bottles	$19.00
Guaraná Fantástica	24	12 - 355 ml cans	$4.50
Sasquatch Ale	34	24 - 12 oz bottles	$14.00
Steeleye Stout	35	24 - 12 oz bottles	$18.00
Chai	1	10 boxes x 20 bags	$18.00
Côte de Blaye	38	12 - 75 cl bottles	$263.50
Ipoh Coffee	43	16 - 500 g tins	$46.00
Laughing Lumberjack Lager	67	24 - 12 oz bottles	$14.00
Lakkalikööri	76	500 ml	$18.00
Outback Lager	70	24 - 355 ml bottles	$15.00
Rhönbräu Klosterbier	75	24 - 0.5 l bottles	$7.75
Sir Rodney's Marmalade	20	30 gift boxes	$81.00

 Eliminate blank pages Check to see that the combined width of the report and the margins doesn't exceed the paper size selected in the Page Setup dialog box. For details, look up **page setup** in the Microsoft Access online index.

To print the report Click the Print button.

Print button

Add a Cover to Your Report

If you have a cover sheet saved as a Microsoft Word file, or a logo saved as art, use it to create a cover for your report. To use a Word file, from the Database window, click the Reports tab, click the name of the report, and then click Design. Click on the Report Header section, click Object (Insert menu), and then click Word. Click Create From File, click the Browse button, click the file that contains your cover sheet, and then click OK. To make the cover print on a separate page, click the

Report Header section bar, click the Properties button, and then change the Force New Page property to After Section.

For more information on creating covers or importing objects from Word, see "Create Letterhead and Matching Envelopes," on page 133, and look up **OLE objects, adding to forms or reports** in the Microsoft Access online index.

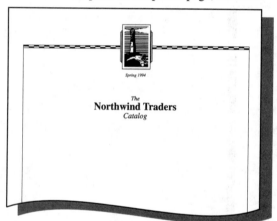

Spring 1994

The
Northwind Traders
Catalog

Next Steps

To	See
Ask specific questions about data stored in more than one table	"Evaluate Sales Performance in a Microsoft Access Database," page 458
Create a report from a query	**reports, creating** in the Microsoft Access online index

Prepare a Customer Quote

Get Information from a Price List and Calculate Discounts

To get the customer's order, you need to put together a quote that showcases your company's products. You tailor the product offerings and discounts to the customer's needs. But you also consider how much profit your company makes on the order. Microsoft Excel makes it easy for you to put together the information for your quotes and present it to your client.

To simplify organizing the information in your quote, use your own online quote form, or create one based on the Microsoft Excel sales quote template.

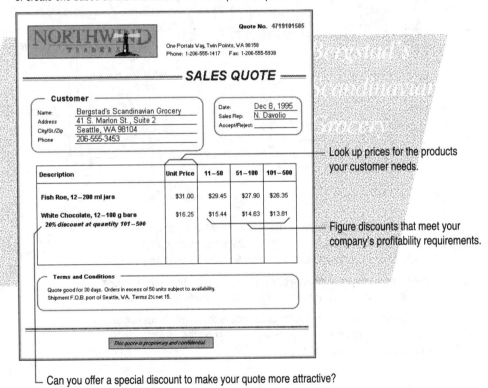

Look up prices for the products your customer needs.

Figure discounts that meet your company's profitability requirements.

Can you offer a special discount to make your quote more attractive?

Look Up Prices

The first step is to get the product and pricing information for your quote. You know your product lines, and you know that prices fluctuate. Your company frequently updates its standard price list.

Here's a fast and easy way to check on prices.

 For Help, double-click.
In the Microsoft Excel online index look up:
formulas, entering
VLOOKUP worksheet function

When you select a product name in cell B2, the VLOOKUP function in cell B4 searches for the product in the price list below.

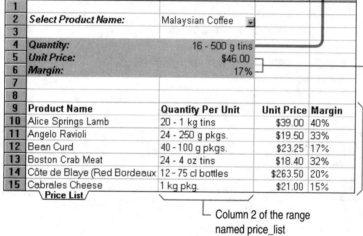

The function returns the information for this product from column 2, Quantity Per Unit.

Similar formulas find the price and profit margin information for you.

Cell range named price_list

Column 2 of the range named price_list

 Use the Function Wizard to enter the VLOOKUP function Click the Function Wizard button, and then follow the wizard's instructions. For details, look up **Function Wizard** in the Microsoft Excel online index.

Use named ranges to make your formulas easier to read For details, look up **creating range names** in the Microsoft Excel online index.

Use Visual Basic for applications to create the drop-down list of products For details, look up **drop-down list boxes, creating** in the Microsoft Excel online index.

f×

Function Wizard button

> ### Is Your Price List Stored Outside of Microsoft Excel?
> Use Microsoft Query to get the data from your company's database into a worksheet. Query can read most database formats and update the data for you as it changes. For more information, see "Get Sales Information from a Database," page 434.

Select Products that Meet Profit Requirements

Do you want to quote only products in a certain price or profitability range? You can filter your price list to show only products that meet your requirements. Just enter the column heading and criteria in two unused cells. Then click Advanced Filter (Data menu, Filter submenu).

For Help, double-click. In the Microsoft Excel online index look up:
filtering data
complex criteria

Filter the Margin column to see only the rows for products that return a 25% or greater profit.

	A	B	C	D
1				
2	*Select Product Name:*	Fish Roe		
3				
4	*Quantity:*	12 - 200 ml jars		*Margin*
5	*Unit Price:*	$31.00		>=25%
6	*Margin:*	32%		
7				
8				
9	Product Name	Quantity Per Unit	Unit Price	Margin
10	Alice Springs Lamb	20 - 1 kg tins	$39.00	40%
11	Angelo Ravioli	24 - 250 g pkgs.	$19.50	33%
13	Boston Crab Meat	24 - 4 oz tins	$18.40	32%
18	Chef Anton's Gumbo Mix	36 boxes	$21.35	28%
19	Cloudberry Liqueur	500 ml	$18.00	32%
20	Courdavault Raclette Cheese	5 kg pkg.	$55.00	35%

\ Price List /

Do you have simple filtering criteria? If you're using uncomplicated criteria and don't need to see the column heading and criteria on your worksheet, you can use AutoFilter to filter your list. For details, look up **AutoFilter** in the Microsoft Excel online index.

Extract and Quote the Prices

What discounts can you offer and still turn a profit? Given a base price and profit rate, construct a simple model that will answer this question. Using information copied from your price list, calculate the effects of different discounts. Then copy the product information and discount prices to your quote form.

For Help, double-click. In the Microsoft Excel online index look up:
formulas, entering
copying cell contents

Copy the product name, unit price, and margin from your price list to cells B2, B3, and C3.

In cell B4, multiply the unit price by the discounted percentage in cell A4.

	B4	=Unit*(100%-A4)			
	A	B	C	D	E
1		**Price**	**Margin**		
2	Product	Fish Roe			
3	Unit Price	$31.00	32%		
4	5%	$29.45	27%		
5	10%	$27.90	22%		
6	15%	$26.35	17%		
7					
8	Product	White Chocolate			
9	Unit Price	$16.25	35%		
10	5%	$15.44	30%		
11	10%	$14.63	25%		
12	15%	$13.81	20%		

The formulas in these cells subtract the discount percentage from the margin.

Name cell B3 Unit.

Next Steps

To	See
Use an online form to write up the quote	"Create a Form for Online Customer Quotes," page 198
Fax the quote to your customer	"Create a Fax Cover Sheet," page 129

PART 12

Find the Magic Numbers

Analyze and Report Sales Data

Contents

What Method Should You Use to Analyze Your Sales Data?

Microsoft Excel and Microsoft Access provide you with complete flexibility to analyze and summarize data. Regardless of where your data originates, you can use all of the powerful features of both applications to create the summaries, reports, and charts you need.

The topics in this part show you how to proceed, depending on where your data is stored initially. Topics elsewhere in this book and in online Help show you other analysis methods that you can apply to data, sales or otherwise.

For Data Stored in Microsoft Access

Use the following table to decide which topics to read for more information.

If you want to ...	Do this ...
Create a detailed report that organizes, subtotals, and summarizes your data	Run the Microsoft Access Report Wizard. For information about the types of reports you can create and the steps to follow, look up **reports, creating** in the Microsoft Access online index.
Create a chart to summarize your data graphically	Run the Microsoft Access Chart Wizard. See "Create a Chart from a Database," page 230.
Create a summary that cross-tabulates your data	Create a Microsoft Access crosstab query. For details, look up **crosstab queries, creating to summarize data** in the Microsoft Access online index.
Create a Microsoft Excel summary table that lets you change your view of the data dynamically	Create a Microsoft Excel PivotTable. For details, see "Create a Sales Summary from a Microsoft Access Database," page 465.
Organize, subtotal, and summarize the data using Microsoft Excel	Use the Analyze It With MS Excel button to output a snapshot of the data to a Microsoft Excel worksheet. Then see "Create a Detailed Sales Report," page 439. When your data changes, you must repeat these steps for updated results.

For Data Stored in Microsoft Excel

Use the following table to decide which topics to read for more information.

If you want to ...	Do this ...
Create a detailed report that organizes, subtotals, and summarizes your data	Add automatic subtotals to your data. For details, see "Create a Detailed Sales Report," page 439.
Create a chart to summarize your data graphically	Run the Microsoft Excel ChartWizard. For details, see "Create a Chart from Worksheet Data," page 216.
Create a summary table that lets you change your view of the data dynamically	Create a Microsoft Excel PivotTable. For details, see "Create a Sales Summary," page 446.
Create a detailed Microsoft Access report without making changes to your original worksheet	Run the Microsoft Access Report Wizard directly from your Microsoft Excel worksheet. For details, see **Report Wizard (Microsoft Access)** in the Microsoft Excel online index.

If Your Data Is Stored Somewhere Other Than in Microsoft Access or Microsoft Excel

Both Microsoft Access and Microsoft Excel let you work with data from external sources.

Import files into or link files to your Microsoft Access database

Importing a file copies a snapshot of its contents into your database. Linking allows you to work with a file that continues to be maintained in its originating application. For information about the file types and formats that you can import and link and details of the procedures, look up **importing data from other programs** and **linking data from other programs** in the Microsoft Access online index.

Bring data into your Microsoft Excel worksheet using Microsoft Query

You can analyze external data in Microsoft Excel and refresh the data in your worksheet when it changes. See "Get Sales Information from a Database," page 434.

Get Sales Information from a Database

Bring Data from Almost Anywhere to Your Microsoft Excel Worksheet

Chances are you work with data stored away from your PC. For instance, your company may compile sales statistics on a networked mainframe.

Use familiar spreadsheet analysis tools on that data, without retyping it. Out of mountains of detailed data, extract just the portions relevant to your work (How well did my product sell?).

Key Features

Microsoft Query

Select just the data you need, and return it to Microsoft Excel for further analysis.

Before you start, install and enable the following:

- The correct Open Database Connectivity (ODBC) driver for your data source. To find out which driver you need, see the person who manages the database you plan to use. For details, look up **ODBC drivers** in the Microsoft Excel online index.

- The Microsoft Query add-in. If you chose the Typical installation option for Microsoft Excel rather than the Custom/Complete option, you'll need to run the Setup program to get this add-in. Click the Converters, Filters, and Data Access option, click Change Option, click Data Access, click Change Option, and then check Microsoft Query. For details, look up **installing add-in programs** and **data sources** in the Microsoft Excel online index.

Set Up a Link to Your Database

The first time you get the external data, you need to open a new workbook and do some setup. Starting from a blank worksheet, click Get External Data (Data menu) to define your database as another data source. When you name a new data source, you associate your database with one of the ODBC drivers installed on your machine.

In the Select Data Source dialog box, click Other, and then click New to add your data source. In the ODBC Setup dialog box, you'll want to assign a name that brings your particular database to mind.

Important If you don't see the Get External Data command, you may not have enabled the Query add-in after installing it. Make sure you check the MS Query Add-In check box (Add-Ins command, Tools menu).

For Help, double-click. In the Microsoft Excel online index look up: **Query (Microsoft), starting**

For Help on dialog box options, click this button.

You use Microsoft Query both to contact your external database and to return the data to your worksheet.

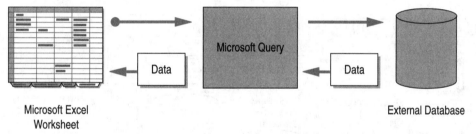

Microsoft Excel Worksheet

Microsoft Query

External Database

What Databases Can I Read?

You can work with just about any popular database format, mainframe or microcomputer. You can open dBASE .DBF files that aren't too large directly into Microsoft Excel worksheets. Or, using the approach described here, you can use ODBC drivers to tap databases like Microsoft Access, SQL Server, FoxPro, and Paradox.

Missing the driver you need? Check with Microsoft, because new ones frequently become available. Also check with your database vendor, who might know about additional drivers.

When all else fails See whether you can get a text-file version of the data. Import the text file into Microsoft Excel, and go from there. For details, look up **importing data** in the Microsoft Excel online index.

View What's in Your Database

Now select your data source and click Use to browse through the available data. Query shows you the information in database *tables*. Each table is a grid much like a worksheet. Columns are fields (categories); rows are data records.

In the Microsoft Query online index look up:
**Table pane, adding tables
fields, adding**

You want to know how many orders each salesperson is getting for each product category. Add the tables you want to take a closer look at: employees, orders, products, and categories. Then drag each field that has data you want to the lower part of the query window.

Important   Each data source has different requirements. Your data source might require you to enter a password and might include one table or several. For information about your particular requirements, contact the person who manages your external database.

The Query window lets you view and select external data.

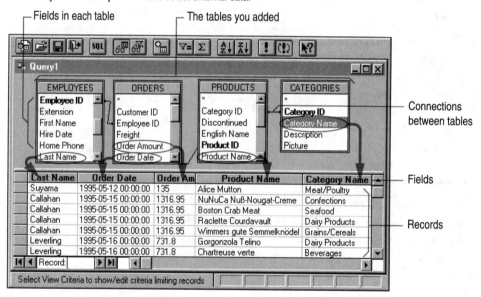

To view the Microsoft Query online index   From the Query window click Contents (Help menu) and then click the Search button.

Try It Out If you have Microsoft Access, you can query the Northwind sample database. The example illustrated here uses the Northwind database as the data source. Or you can use the .DBF files included with Microsoft Excel that simulate the Northwind database.

Is the data slow to appear? Turn off Auto Query With Auto Query off, you can quickly arrange the fields you want, without waiting for the data to appear. When you're ready to see the data, use the Query Now button.

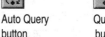

Auto Query button

Query Now button

Sift Out the Data You Want, and Return It to the Worksheet

Your database may well have far more records than the 16,384-row limit of your worksheet. You'll want to exclude data you don't need, such as products tracked by other sales managers.

In the Microsoft Query online index look up:
criteria, adding
exiting Microsoft Query

First, click a product that you want to view information for.

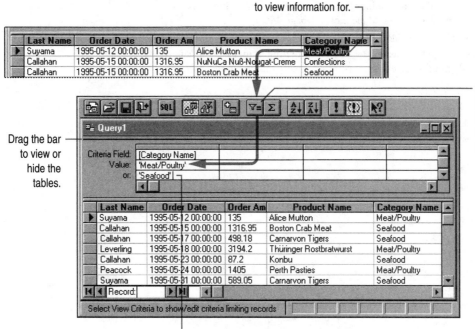

Drag the bar to view or hide the tables.

Next, click the Funnel button to display just that product's data.

To choose another category from a list, double-click here, and then click Values in the Edit Criteria dialog box.

When you're finished, bring the data back to your Microsoft Excel worksheet   Click the Return Data button when you're ready to return the data to your Microsoft Excel worksheet for further analysis.

Return Data button

To rearrange the columns   Click a column to select it, and then drag it.

Format your data in the query, not the worksheet   If you save the query by clicking Save (Query File menu), you can repeat it next month, with new data. You'll get the same column order and other selections. But any formatting and arranging you did to the data in the worksheet is lost when you bring in the new data.

Next Steps

To	See
Format the data (make the column headings bold, display amounts in dollars, and so forth)	"Make Your Microsoft Excel Worksheet Look Great," page 206
Analyze the data (determine total sales by product, who sold the most of each product, and so forth)	"Create a Sales Summary," page 446
Repeat the query when next month's figures come in	**opening a query** in the Microsoft Query online index

Create a Detailed Sales Report

Insert Subtotals on Your Detail Worksheet

Do you have detailed data and want to see totals? For instance, you might receive information about orders as each is filled over the course of several months. You might need to calculate the total sales for each region and total product sales across the regions. Microsoft Excel can rapidly organize and sum up this kind of data for you.

Your order information is compiled day by day ...

... but you need totals by region.

	A	B	C	D
1	Date	Product	Region	Amount
2	12-May-95	Produce	UK	135.00
3	15-May-95	Produce	Spain	1,
4	16-May-95	Dairy	Sweden	7
5	18-May-95	Produce	Italy	3,1
6	22-May-95	Dairy	Norway	1
7	23-May-95	Grain	Sweden	1
8	24-May-95	Grain	Germany	1,4
9	25-May-95	Dairy	France	1,
10	26-May-95	Produce	Denmark	1,8
11	31-May-95	Produce	Netherlands	8
12	12-Jun-95	Grain	Spain	1,0
13	13-Jun-95	Produce	Sweden	

Region	Amount
Denmark Total	4,101.50
Finland Total	1,103.50
France Total	1,171.00
Germany Total	5,606.38
Italy Total	7,265.26
Netherlands Total	595.05
Norway Total	6,766.59
Spain Total	11,773.00
Sweden Total	10,027.54
UK Total	10,911.71
Grand Total	$ 59,321.53
Number of Grain Orders	24
Total Grain Orders	$ 16,900.87

With Microsoft Excel you can get the totals easily, without tedious calculation or complex programming.

Arrange the Data by Product and Region

First group together the data you want to total. Click the Sort command (Data menu), and sort the data by region.

Sorting both alphabetizes the regions and groups the orders for each region together.

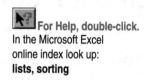

For Help, double-click. In the Microsoft Excel online index look up: **lists, sorting**

	A	B	C	D	E	F
1	Date	Product	Region	Amount		
2	9-Jun-95	Dairy	Denmark	1,148.00		
3	26-May-95	Produce	Denmark	1,530.00		
4	7-Jun-95	Produce	Denmark	1,423.50		
5	5-Jun-95	Dairy	Finland	192.10		
6	12-Jul-95	Dairy	Finland	351.00		
7	2-Jun-95	Grain	Finland	560.40		
8	17-May-95	Dairy	Germany	498.18		
9	30-May-95	Dairy	Germany	470.00		
10	7-Jul-95	Dairy	Germany	747.00		
11	24-May-95	Grain	Germany	1,405.00		
12	30-May-95	Grain	Germany	470.00		
13	30-May-95	Produce	Germany	470.00		
14	26-Jun-95	Produce	Germany	17.40		

You don't have to select the list before sorting   Just click any cell in the column you want to sort upon, and then sort. Microsoft Excel determines where your data starts and ends and applies your commands to the full extent. For more information about setting up lists that are easy to sort, see "Create a Business Contact List in Microsoft Excel," page 300.

Subtotal Each Region

With regional data grouped together, you can total each region's sales in a single operation. Click the Subtotals command (Data menu). In the Subtotal dialog box, at each change in region, use the Sum function, and add a subtotal to the Amount column.

For Help, double-click. In the Microsoft Excel online index look up: **automatic subtotals**

┌─ Outline symbols show how your data is grouped. ┌─ In one command, you added a total for each region.

	A	B	C	D	E
1	**Date**	**Product**	**Region**	**Amount**	
2	9-Jun-95	Dairy	Denmark	1,148.00	
3	26-May-95	Produce	Denmark	1,530.00	
4	7-Jun-95	Produce	Denmark	1,423.50	
5			**Denmark Total**	$ 4,101.50	
6	5-Jun-95	Dairy	Finland	192.10	
7	12-Jul-95	Dairy	Finland	351.00	
8	2-Jun-95	Grain	Finland	560.40	
9			**Finland Total**	$ 1,103.50	
10	25-May-95	Dairy	France	1,171.00	
89	3-Jul-95	Produce	UK	909.91	
90	6-Jul-95	Produce	UK	850.50	
91			**UK Total**	$ 10,911.71	
92			**Grand Total**	$ 59,321.53	

You also calculated the grand total at the end of the list. ─┘

 Want to subtotal selected parts of your data? Filter first For example, you might want to see totals for only some of the regions. By clicking AutoFilter (Data menu), you can filter on the region and then add subtotals. For more information, look up **filtering data** in the Microsoft Excel online index.

More Power

Want to total product sales within each region?   You can add product totals in addition to the regional totals and grand total. First click Sort (Data menu) to sort the data by two columns: Sort by region, and then by product. Then create subtotals for the regions.

Repeat the Subtotals command at each change in product, but don't replace the current (regional) subtotals. For details, look up **nested subtotals** in the Microsoft Excel online index.

Add averages, counts, and other summaries   You can use any of several functions to summarize your data. For details, look up **subtotals, summary functions** in the Microsoft Excel online index.

Print each subtotaled group on a separate page, automatically Insert page breaks automatically when you create the totals.

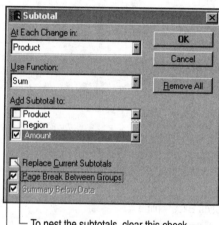

— To nest the subtotals, clear this check box the second time you subtotal.

— Check here to print each subtotaled group on a separate page.

View the Summary Without the Detail

In a long list of data, it's inconvenient to scroll to see the subtotals. When you add subtotals, your worksheet is outlined for you automatically. Outlining lets you choose the level of detail to view.

For Help, double-click. In the Microsoft Excel online index look up: **outlines, expanding and collapsing**

— When you click here, you see only the totals.

— Click here to view the detail again ...

		C	D
	1	Region	Amount
+	5	Denmark Total	$ 4,101.50
+	9	Finland Total	$ 1,103.50
+	11	France Total	$ 1,171.00
+	23	Germany Total	$ 5,606.38
+	28	Italy Total	$ 7,265.26
+	30	Netherlands Total	$ 595.05
+	40	Norway Total	
+	51	Spain Total	
+	75	Sweden Total	
+	89	UK Total	
–	90	Grand Total	

... or click to display the detail for a particular region.

		C	D
	1	Region	Amount
+	5	Denmark Total	$ 4,101.50
+	9	Finland Total	$ 1,103.50
+	11	France Total	$ 1,171.00
+	23	Germany Total	$ 5,606.38
·	24	Italy	3,194.20
·	25	Italy	438.43
·	26	Italy	3,194.20
·	27	Italy	438.43
–	28	Italy Total	$ 7,265.26
+	30	Netherlands Total	$ 595.05
+	40	Norway Total	$ 6,766.59
+	51	Spain Total	$ 11,773.00
+	75	Sweden Total	$ 10,027.54
+	89	UK Total	$ 10,911.71
–	90	Grand Total	$ 59,321.53

If you want just the totals without the detail, use a PivotTable instead of outlining For details, see "Create a Sales Summary," page 446.

Hide columns that you don't want to see For details, look up **hiding cells** in the Microsoft Excel online index.

Count Orders for a Product Across Regions

You also want to know how many orders were filled for a particular product, but the products sell across regions, so the data isn't grouped together. You can count these orders using the function, COUNTIF, that counts the rows containing a particular product name.

With the Function Wizard, it's easy to set this up.

In this example, the formula in cell D93 counts the number of rows that contain the word "Grain" in column B.

 For Help, double-click.
In the Microsoft Excel online index look up:
COUNTIF worksheet function
Function Wizard

f_x

Function Wizard button

Enter the range of cells that contains the product names.

For the criteria, type the name of the product that you want to count.

		A	B	C	D
	87	3-Jul-95	Produce	UK	909.91
	88	6-Jul-95	Produce	UK	850.50
	89			UK Total	$ 10,911.71
	90				
	91			Grand Total	$ 59,321.53
	92				
	93			Number of Grain Orders	24
	94				

D93   =COUNTIF(B2:B88,"Grain")

Your COUNTIF formula counts only the rows for Grain orders.

 Want to know which regions are over quota? COUNTIF can compare each row with the amount of your sales quota. For example, if the quota is $3000 per region, you could use the formula `=COUNTIF(D2:D87,">3000")`. For details, look up **expressions, operators** in the Microsoft Excel online index.

You can count empty cells, as well as those containing values For details, look up **COUNTBLANK worksheet function** in the Microsoft Excel online index.

If you're using a PivotTable, you can count instead of total there too For details, look up **PivotTables, summary functions** in the Microsoft Excel online index.

Total the orders for each product   The SUMIF function adds only the amounts for the product you specify in the formula. For details, look up **SUMIF worksheet function** in the Microsoft Excel online index.

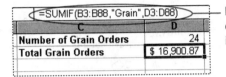

C	D
Number of Grain Orders	24
Total Grain Orders	$ 16,900.87

Looking through the data in column B, if SUMIF finds Grain, it adds the amount in column D.

Find errors in formulas quickly   If a cell where you've entered a formula displays an error message, such as DIV/0!, Microsoft Excel can show you where the error is. Use the Auditing toolbar to find the source of the error. For details, look up **tracing errors** in the Microsoft Excel online index.

Get the Help You Need While You Work

Expanded and improved online assistance is just a click away. It's the fastest way to get information so you can keep working.

Ask the Answer Wizard   Type a question in your own words. The Answer Wizard lists online Help topics related to your question. Double-click the Help button and then click the Answer Wizard tab.

Look it up in the online index   Instead of typing a question, use index entries provided in this book to find online topics related to your task. Double-click the Help button and then click the Index tab.

For details, see "Get Assistance While You Work," page 30. Or look up **Help** in the online index.

Create a Sales Summary

Use PivotTables to Summarize Sales Data

You may have more data than you can easily summarize manually, for example, details about every order placed for your products. What you want is the big picture. How are the products selling? Who is selling the most of each product?

From the same data, you can create two instant summaries, called *PivotTable* dynamic views, to answer your questions. If you work with sales figures or other similar business data, Microsoft Excel can rapidly produce the summaries you want from the detail you have.

Key Features

PivotTable Wizard

ChartWizard

Given date, amount, and product for each order ...

	A	B	C	D
1	**Name**	**Order Amount**	**Order Date**	**Product**
2	Annabella Dodsworth	$ 135.00	12-May-95	Meat
3	Michael Suyama	$ 1,316.95	15-May-95	Meat
4	Andrew Fuller	$ 731.80	16-May-95	Seafood
5	Michael Suyama	$ 498.18	17-May-95	Meat
6	Andrew Fuller	$ 3,194.20	18-May-95	Seafood
7	Linda Callahan	$ 173.40	22-May-95	Seafood
8	Michael Suyama			

... summarize how each product is selling by creating a PivotTable automatically—no formulas to enter.

	A	B	C	D	E
1	**Sales by Product**	Order Date			
2	Product	May Sales	June Sales	July Sales	Grand Total
3	**Meat**	33,905.34	52,824.09	21,246.03	**$ 107,975.46**
4	**Seafood**	67,810.68	105,648.18	42,492.06	**$ 215,950.92**
5	**Grand Total**	$ 101,716.02	$ 158,472.27	$ 63,738.09	**$ 323,926.38**

You can also compare the results visually, with a chart.

What Information Is Buried in Your Data?

Your company probably keeps a separate record describing each order processed. Scanning the list shows that you have to consider hundreds of orders just for the products you track. You want a fast way to see how much each representative has sold of each product.

	A	B	C	D	E
1	**Name**	**Order Amount**	**Order Date**	**Product**	
2	Annabella Dodsworth	$ 135.00	12-May-95	Meat	
3	Michael Suyama	$ 1,316.95	15-May-95	Meat	
4	Andrew Fuller	$ 731.80	16-May-95	Seafood	
5	Michael Suyama	$ 498.18	17-May-95	Meat	
6	Andrew Fuller	$ 3,194.20	18-May-95	Seafood	
7	Linda Callahan	$ 173.40	22-May-95	Seafood	
8	Michael Suyama	$ 87.20	23-May-95	Seafood	
9	Janice Leverling	$ 1,405.00	24-May-95	Meat	
10	Andrew Fuller	$ 1,171.00	25-May-95	Meat	
11	Michael Suyama	$ 1,530.00	26-May-95	Seafood	
12	Michael Suyama	$ 470.00	30-May-95	Meat	

You have a row of facts for every order.

There's too much detail to see what's going on; you want total orders per sales rep, not a list of every order.

You're interested in monthly totals rather than day-by-day sales.

Guidelines: Setting Up Data for a PivotTable

To create a PivotTable, you start with data arranged as follows.

Label your columns PivotTables use your column headings to cross-tabulate your data. For example, you can summarize orders by product or by salesperson (Name).

Use one worksheet row for each record A PivotTable summarizes data stored in rows.

Make sure any dates are in date format Select the dates (for example, column C in the above illustration), choose Cells (Format menu), and then click the Number tab. For details, look up **formatting dates** in the Microsoft Excel online index.

If a column contains repeating information, spell each entry the same way each time Entries that are the same, such as seafood or meat entries in a Product column, can be grouped together automatically in the PivotTable. Avoid extra spaces.

[?] For Help on dialog box options, click this button.

Who Is Selling the Most Product?

A PivotTable can answer this question in a flash. Select a cell in your source data. From the Data menu, click PivotTable, and then follow the wizard's directions. Create the PivotTable on a new worksheet in your workbook automatically: once you've arranged the fields, click Finish.

 For Help, double-click. In the Microsoft Excel online index look up: **PivotTable Wizard**

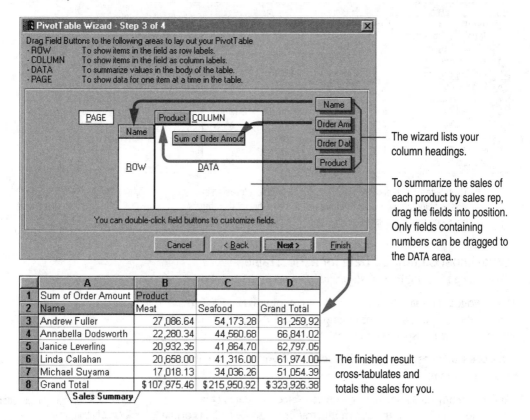

The wizard lists your column headings.

To summarize the sales of each product by sales rep, drag the fields into position. Only fields containing numbers can be dragged to the DATA area.

	A	B	C	D
1	Sum of Order Amount	Product		
2	Name	Meat	Seafood	Grand Total
3	Andrew Fuller	27,086.64	54,173.28	81,259.92
4	Annabella Dodsworth	22,280.34	44,560.68	66,841.02
5	Janice Leverling	20,932.35	41,864.70	62,797.05
6	Linda Callahan	20,658.00	41,316.00	61,974.00
7	Michael Suyama	17,018.13	34,036.26	51,054.39
8	Grand Total	$107,975.46	$215,950.92	$323,926.38

Sales Summary

The finished result cross-tabulates and totals the sales for you.

 Add commas or currency signs, or adjust the decimal places   Select a number in the data area of the PivotTable. Click PivotTable Field (Data menu), and then click the Number button to apply number formatting.

Rank the top sales representatives   Select a cell in the Grand Total column, and then click the Sort Descending button.

To pivot the table, just drag the gray field buttons   You don't need to start the PivotTable Wizard again to change the layout of your summary. For example, you could exchange the positions of the Name and Product buttons to view the products in the rows and the sales reps in the columns.

Sort Descending button

How Well Are Products Selling Over Time?

Run the wizard to create another PivotTable to show the sales performance of each product (ROW area) by order date (COLUMN area). This view still has too much detail and too many columns to see at once. You want to see monthly totals instead of daily details. A PivotTable can quickly group the dates by month. Place the new PivotTable on a separate worksheet in your workbook: When you make changes to the original data, your PivotTables are updated automatically and can grow and expand.

For Help, double-click. In the Microsoft Excel online index look up:
grouping PivotTable data
refreshing PivotTable data

The Group command lets you group dates automatically by weeks, months, quarters, or years.

Sum of Order Amount	Order Date					
Product	5/12/95	5/15/95	5/16/95	5/17/95	5/18/95	
Meat	405	3950.85	2195.4	1494.54	9582.6	
Seafood	810	7901.7	4390.8	2989.08	19165.2	
Grand Total	1215	11852.55	6586.2	4483.62	28747.8	

Product Summary

Click here, then right-click and choose Group and Outline, Group.

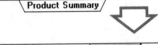

Dates are now grouped by months.

Sum of Order Amount	Order Date			
Product	May	Jun	Jul	Grand Total
Meat	33905.34	52824.09	21246.03	107975.46
Seafood	67810.68	105648.18	42492.06	215950.92
Grand Total	101716.02	158472.27	63738.09	323926.38

Product Summary

Reuse the same data when you make a new PivotTable   When you start the PivotTable Wizard to create a different summary, choose Another PivotTable. Because Microsoft Excel reuses its internal data from your first PivotTable, your workbook stays smaller and changes you make to your source data are reflected faster in your PivotTables.

Did you know that you can also make a PivotTable directly from external data?   As with all PivotTables, when you use data outside your worksheet, your table can be updated automatically when the data changes. You'll need to install Microsoft Query and the appropriate ODBC drivers to access external data sources. Then, choose the External Data Source option in the PivotTable wizard. For details about installing Microsoft Query, see "Get Sales Information from a Database," page 434.

Page Fields Provide Another Way to Group Information

You can create a series of PivotTables and view each in turn using a page field. A page field lets you display your data in three dimensions.

For example, you could edit the Sales by Product PivotTable to use the Name column as a page field. This field lets you view the sales by product for each sales representative, or for all representatives combined.

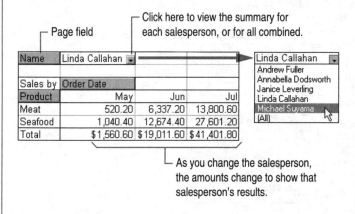

Page field

Click here to view the summary for each salesperson, or for all combined.

As you change the salesperson, the amounts change to show that salesperson's results.

For PivotTables with many fields, page fields are a great way to keep your tables compact and readable. For details, look up **PivotTables, page fields** in the Microsoft Excel online index.

Compare Sales Results Graphically

Your product summary lets you consider the totals, but there's a better way to compare the two product lines. You can create a chart from a PivotTable as you would from any data. As you make changes to the PivotTable or refresh the underlying data, the chart updates too.

To create a chart, first select the data in the PivotTable, and then use the ChartWizard to choose the chart and format you want. For details, see "Create a Chart from Worksheet Data," page 216.

Note To select data that includes a field button, drag from the lower right to the upper left corner.

 For Help, double-click.
In the Microsoft Excel online index look up:
charts in Excel, creating
ChartWizard

ChartWizard button

A column chart compares data over time, showing variations.

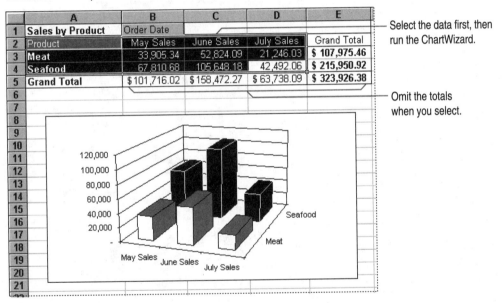

	A	B	C	D	E
1	**Sales by Product**	Order Date			
2	Product	May Sales	June Sales	July Sales	Grand Total
3	**Meat**	33,905.34	52,824.09	21,246.03	**$ 107,975.46**
4	**Seafood**	67,810.68	105,648.18	42,492.06	**$ 215,950.92**
5	**Grand Total**	$101,716.02	$158,472.27	$63,738.09	**$ 323,926.38**

Select the data first, then run the ChartWizard.

Omit the totals when you select.

 To place the chart on the same worksheet as the data, remember to click and drag When you start the ChartWizard, you draw a box to position the chart using the cross-hair pointer.

Is your sales data broken down geographically? Map it You can view where your sales are concentrated on a map of your region or country. For details, see "Display Data on a Map," page 246.

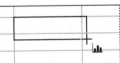

ChartWizard cross-hair pointer

Next Steps

To	See
Forecast future sales based on your recent results	"Create a Sales Forecast," page 453

Create a Sales Forecast

You collect and analyze sales figures not just to see how you're doing, but in the hope of predicting future results. What are the trends in your recent sales, and how can you expect them to affect future sales?

With Microsoft Excel forecasting functions you can apply sophisticated statistical analysis techniques to your data. And, you don't have to be a statistician or study involved mathematics to create realistic sales projections. You can also use these techniques to project expenses, inventory requirements, stock prices, and other business trends.

Forecast sales one month ahead, or several months.

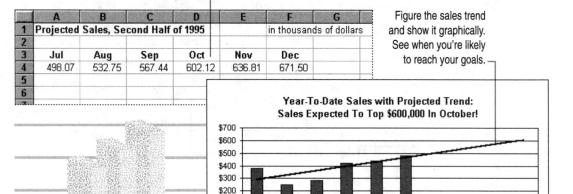

	A	B	C	D	E	F	G
1	Projected Sales, Second Half of 1995					in thousands of dollars	
2							
3	Jul	Aug	Sep	Oct	Nov	Dec	
4	498.07	532.75	567.44	602.12	636.81	671.50	
5							
6							

Figure the sales trend and show it graphically. See when you're likely to reach your goals.

Year-To-Date Sales with Projected Trend: Sales Expected To Top $600,000 In October!

Forecast Next Month's Sales

To predict next month's sales based on the results in recent months, use the FORECAST function. The Function Wizard helps you to enter the formula.

 For Help, double-click.
In the Microsoft Excel online index look up:
FORECAST worksheet function
Function Wizard

Double-click a cell ...

... and then click here to start the Function Wizard.

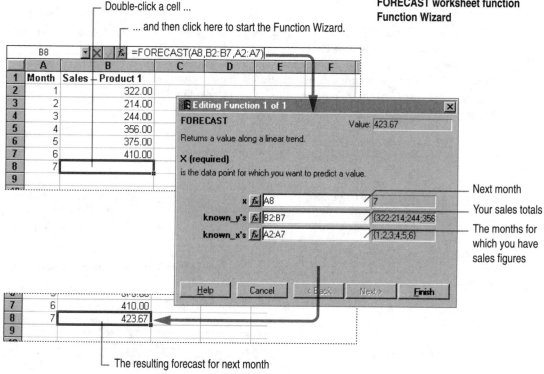

Next month

Your sales totals

The months for which you have sales figures

The resulting forecast for next month

 Use the Function Wizard to learn more about functions If you want more detail than the Step 2 screen provides, click the Help button in the Function Wizard for full reference information about the function.

f_x

Function Wizard button

Determine Sales Trends

Will sales continue to go up or down, and how fast? You can calculate the likely direction using the TREND function.

Use the TREND formula to predict the results for the next several months, even if you don't have actual results for recent months. A formula that calculates several values at once uses a range of cells, called an *array*, to display the set of results. Before entering the function, select enough cells for all of the results.

For Help, double-click.
In the Microsoft Excel online index look up:
TREND worksheet function
arrays

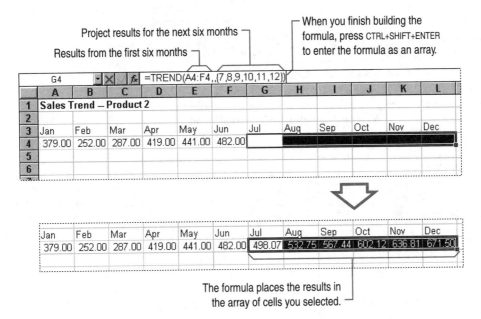

Project results for the next six months ⌐

Results from the first six months ⌐

When you finish building the formula, press CTRL+SHIFT+ENTER to enter the formula as an array.

The formula places the results in the array of cells you selected.

Calculate a trend quickly using AutoFill Select your data for past months, use the right mouse button to drag the fill handle, and then choose Linear Trend or Growth Trend from the shortcut menu. For details, look up **data entry, filling cells** and **trend series** in the Microsoft Excel online index.

Chart a Trendline

Another way to project a trend is to chart a trendline. A trendline shows the direction of your sales visually.

Use the ChartWizard to create a column chart. Click the chart, and then double-click the first column. Click Trendline (Insert menu), and then select the type of trendline you want. For more information about creating charts, see "Create a Chart from Worksheet Data," page 216.

For Help, double-click. In the Microsoft Excel online index look up: **trendlines in Excel charts** **ChartWizard**

Chart the dates in cells C2:L3.

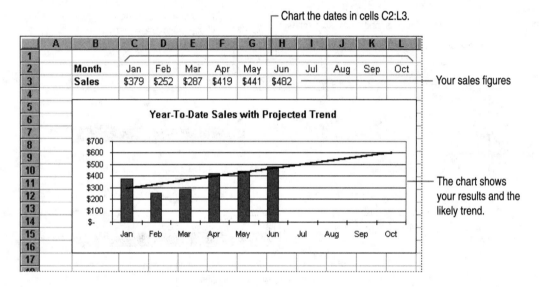

Your sales figures

The chart shows your results and the likely trend.

 Change the look of your chart   For details, see "Customize the Look of a Chart," page 236.

What If My Sales Don't Follow a Simple Trend?

Trendlines describe future sales well when you have a simple, linear increase or decrease.

First sales are up, then they're down To see the trend within all the spikes and dips, add a *moving average* trendline to your chart. By computing a series of averages from parts of your data, this trendline smoothes out the fluctuations to show the pattern more clearly. For details, look up **moving average trendlines** in the Microsoft Excel online index.

My sales are really taking off! If your sales are doubling or tripling, you're seeing exponential growth. Use the GROWTH function instead of TREND to forecast this kind of expansion. For details, look up **GROWTH worksheet function** in the Microsoft Excel online index.

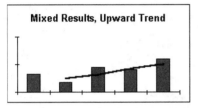

Moving average trendline

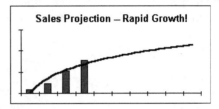

Logarithmic trendline

Next Steps

To	See
Include your forecasts in a report	"Create a Business Plan," page 154
Perform a complete statistical analysis of your sales figures	The Analysis ToolPak add-in package. Also, see "Analyze Data from an Experiment," page 480

Evaluate Sales Performance in a Microsoft Access Database

Use a Query to Find Out How Your Sales Force Is Doing

How are sales this month? Who's selling the most? If you've set up a Microsoft Access database for tracking customer orders, you can quickly check your employees' monthly totals to see how your sales force is doing. Then, rank your sales staff to see who your top performers are. Use the techniques in this topic to find similar information stored in any Microsoft Access database.

Key Features

Simple Query

Expressions

Sorting Records

September Orders

Employees

Last Name	First Name	Total
Leverling	Janet	$611.90
Peacock	Margaret	$558.70
Davolio	Nancy	$377.40
Dodsworth	Anne	$301.20
Callahan	Laura	$240.4
King	Robert	$193.7
Fuller	Andrew	$169.3
Suyama	Michael	$168.9

Top Employees

Last Name	First Name	Total
Leverling	Janet	$611.90
Peacock	Margaret	$558.70
Davolio	Nancy	$377.40

To complete the steps in this topic You need to have either Microsoft Office Professional or an individual copy of Microsoft Access installed. You also need to use the Table Wizard to create Employees, Orders, and Order Details tables, as illustrated in this topic. In the Order Details table, be sure to include an Amount field that shows the amount of each item ordered. For help designing tables and deciding which fields to include, look up **tables, creating** in the Microsoft Access online index.

Begin the Query

To see how your sales force is doing, you need to see the details about each item ordered: who placed the order, the date it was placed, and the amount charged for each item. These facts are stored in three tables: Employees, Orders, and Order Details. When you need to find information that's stored in two or more tables and that meets certain criteria, such as orders filled in September, create a *query* in the Query Design window.

Click the arrow next to the New Object button, click New Query, and then double-click New Query. Choose the tables and fields that contain the details you need.

 For Help, double-click. In the Microsoft Access online index look up:
queries, overview
queries, creating
queries, design

New Object button

Choose the tables that contain the information you need ...

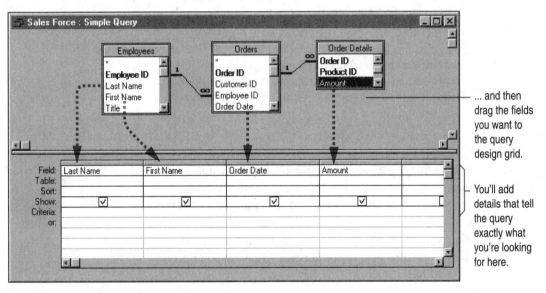

... and then drag the fields you want to the query design grid.

You'll add details that tell the query exactly what you're looking for here.

 Want to add all the fields from a table? Double-click the title bar on the field list, and then drag all fields to the grid.

What Is a Query and When Do I Use One?

A query is just a question you ask of your database to find the information you need. You use a query when you want to do one or more of the following:

- Ask a question about data that's stored in more than one table; for example, when you need to see sales figures for your sales force, as illustrated in this topic.

- Ask a question that includes certain criteria; for example, when you want to see a list of all employees who were hired between January and June.

- Save the question you are asking so you can reuse it; for example, when you want to use the same query to review sales figures for another period of time.

- Use the answer to your question to create forms and reports; for example, when you want to create a form for entering data into a table or a formatted report showing employee names and their total sales. (For details, look up **forms, creating** or **reports, creating** in the Microsoft Access online index.)

If you have a simple question, such as what are the names and phone numbers of all employees, then use the Simple Query Wizard. Click the arrow next to the New Object button, click New Query, and then double-click Simple Query Wizard. Otherwise, use the Query Design window, as illustrated in this topic.

When you're viewing a form or datasheet, you can quickly select information of a particular type by filtering. For details, look up **filters, creating** in the Microsoft Access online index.

For more information about queries, look up **queries, creating** in the Microsoft Access online index.

Show Only Last Month's Orders

Unless you tell it otherwise, your query finds all orders filled since you set up your database. To see only the orders filled last month, you ask the query to find only orders that meet that criteria. Specify criteria whenever you need to refine or limit the information that the query looks for. To limit the dates of orders the query finds, type beginning and ending dates (an *expression*) in the Criteria row under the Order Date field.

To see the results of your query, click the arrow next to the View button, and then click Datasheet View.

 For Help, double-click.
In the Microsoft Access online index look up:
queries, using criteria
queries, expressions in

View button

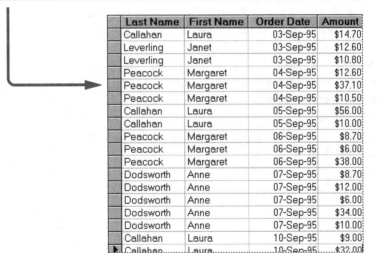

Type the beginning and ending dates here ...

... to see all orders filled in September.

Don't bother typing the number symbols   When you leave the field, Microsoft Access automatically adds them.

Did you make a mistake when you set up the query?   Click the View button to display the query design grid, and then change the query by adding or deleting fields or by changing the contents of the cells.

View button

See orders for another range of dates   Change the dates in the Between expression.

Have Microsoft Access prompt you for start and end dates each time you run the query   For details, look up **parameter queries** in the Microsoft Access online index.

Get the Help You Need While You Work

Expanded and improved online assistance is just a click away. It's the fastest way to get information so you can keep working.

Ask the Answer Wizard   Type a question in your own words. The Answer Wizard lists online Help topics related to your question. Double-click the Help button, and then click the Answer Wizard tab.

Look it up in the online index   Instead of typing a question, use index entries provided in this book to find online topics related to your task. Double-click the Help button, and then click the Index tab.

For details, see "Get Assistance While You Work," page 30. Or look up **Help** in the online index.

Calculate Each Employee's Grand Total

Your query finds every order filled by each employee during the month. See the total orders filled by each employee by asking the query to calculate the total. To perform a calculation in any numeric field, add a Total row to the query design grid, and then choose the type of calculation you want in the Total cell under that field.

For Help, double-click.
In the Microsoft Access online index look up:
totals in queries
Total row

Click the Totals button to add a
Total row to the query design grid.

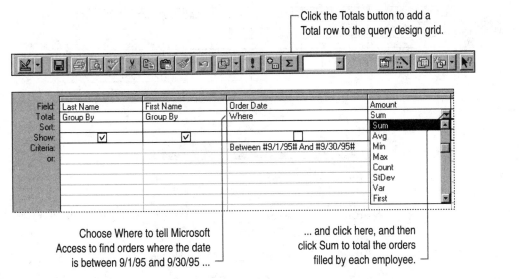

Choose Where to tell Microsoft
Access to find orders where the date
is between 9/1/95 and 9/30/95 ...

... and click here, and then
click Sum to total the orders
filled by each employee.

Want to find an average or a minimum or maximum value for a field?
In the Total cell under the field you want to calculate, click the drop-down list, and then click the type of calculation you want. For details, look up **aggregate functions** in the Microsoft Access online index.

Want to find the minimum and maximum values of the same field?
Add the field to the grid twice, and then click the type of calculation you want in the Total cells. For example, add the Amount field and click Min in the Total cell, and then add the Amount field again and click Max.

Rank Your Sales Staff

Now that you have the information you need, sort it so it's easier to see who's selling the most. To sort the contents of a field, in the Sort cell under the field, select the order in which you want the information sorted. Rank employees by sorting grand totals in descending order.

For Help, double-click.
In the Microsoft Access online index look up:
sorting data
sort order, queries

Field:	Last Name	First Name	Order Date	Amount
Total:	Group By	Group By	Where	Sum
Sort:				Descending
Show:	☑	☑	☐	Ascending
Criteria:			Between #9/1/95# And #9/30/95#	Descending
or:				(not sorted)

— Click here and select Descending ...

Last Name	First Name	SumOfAmount
Callahan	Laura	$451.00
Peacock	Margaret	$231.60
King	Robert	$205.00
Leverling	Janet	$140.20
Davolio	Nancy	$110.70
Dodsworth	Anne	$70.70
Buchanan	Steven	$31.90
Fuller	Andrew	$18.50

... to rank employees by sales totals.

Want to sort by more than one field?   Microsoft Access sorts fields from left to right. In the query design grid, arrange the fields in the order you want the sorts performed, and then click the sort order for each field you want to sort. For details, look up **sorting records in queries** in the Microsoft Access online index.

Find your top achievers   Click the Top Values button, and then click the value you want, such as 25% to see the top 25 percent of orders filled, or type in the value you want to see, such as 5 to see the top five order totals.

Top Values button

Next Steps

To	In the Microsoft Access online index look up
Print the results of your query in a report	**reports, creating**
Find other information about an employee	**Filter By Form**

Create a Sales Summary from a Microsoft Access Database

Use Microsoft Excel PivotTable Dynamic Views in Microsoft Access

A Microsoft Access sales database keeps details about each order readily available. But you want to see the big picture of your sales results, not the detail. You want answers to specific questions about how sales representatives and products are doing.

With Microsoft Access, you can bring the power of Microsoft Excel to bear on your data, automatically, so you can make comparisons and focus on the information you seek. Wizards show you how to do quick, on-the-fly summaries.

Key Features

 Simple Query Wizard

PivotTable Wizard

 PivotTables

Combine your detailed sales figures into a summary ...

Sales Results : Simple Query

Last Name	Product Name	Order Date	Order Amount
Leverling	Chocolade	02-Jan-95	$86.70
Leverling	Sirop d'érable	02-Jan-95	$726.75
Davolio	Chang	02-Jan-95	$182.40
Leverling	Jack's New England Clam Chowder	02-Jan-95	$193.00
Davolio	Spegesild	02-Jan-95	$420.00
Leverling	Ipoh Coffee	02-Jan-95	$782.00
Fuller	Geitost	02-Jan-95	$40.00
Leverling	Boston Crab Meat		
Leverling	Tarte au sucre		
Leverling	Côte de Blaye		
Peacock	Côte de Blaye		

Record: 1 of 1020

... then compare who is selling the most of each product ...

First Quarter Sales	Sold By					Grand Total
Product Name	Buchanan	Callahan	Davolio	Dod	00	Grand Total
Alice Mutton	$585.00	$234.00	$2,702.70	$1	00	$9,146.70
Aniseed Syrup		$300.00	$40.00		00	$1,192.00
Boston Crab Meat		$512.00	$73.60		00	$5,751.20
Camembert Pierrot	$693.60	$1,847.20	$1,362.72	$1		$21,811.57
Carnarvon Tigers		$498.18	$2,723.50		30	$12,455.35
Grand Total	$28,896.55	$74,487.76	$80,273.63	$46	70	$579,292.95

... and see the total results.

To complete the steps in this topic You need to have either Microsoft Office Professional for Windows 95 or individual copies of Microsoft Access for Windows 95 and Microsoft Excel for Windows 95 installed. You also need to have sales data stored in a Microsoft Access database.

Choose the Data to Analyze

Formulate the question you want to answer: How much of each
product did each representative sell? Your first step is to create a
query. A query is just a question that you ask about your data. In the
Database window, click the New Object button, click New Query,
and then double-click Simple Query Wizard.

 For Help, double-click.
In the Microsoft Access
online index look up:
queries, overview

The answer to your question involves facts about products, sales
representatives, and the amounts and dates of orders. As you browse
through the fields in various tables and queries in your database,
select the fields that contain these facts.

Choose a table or query to
display the fields it contains. — ┌ Browse until you find the fields you want.

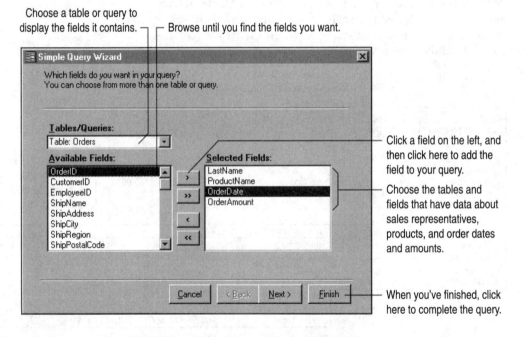

Click a field on the left, and
then click here to add the
field to your query.

Choose the tables and
fields that have data about
sales representatives,
products, and order dates
and amounts.

When you've finished, click
here to complete the query.

Take data from any related table or query in your sales database   For
example, the query in this topic uses fields from Employees, Products, and
Orders tables, plus an Order Amount field that is calculated in another
query. For details, look up **bringing together data in multiple tables,
queries** in the Microsoft Access online index.

View the results of your query   Click the arrow next to the View button,
and then click Datasheet View.

When you finish, save the query   You'll use the query later in this topic to
create summary tables using Microsoft Excel.

View button

Summarize by Product and Salesperson

Your query has pulled together the raw data, but it raises more questions. How can you total and compare the amount of each product sold by each sales representative? Starting from your query, you can create a PivotTable to calculate grand totals and compare results.

In the Microsoft Access Database window, click the New Object button, click New Form, and then click PivotTable Wizard. Then select your query and use its fields to lay out the PivotTable.

New Object button

Drag the fields to lay out the PivotTable.

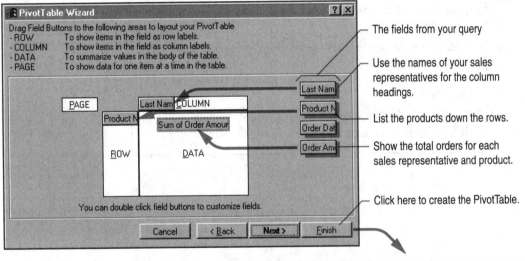

The fields from your query

Use the names of your sales representatives for the column headings.

List the products down the rows.

Show the total orders for each sales representative and product.

Click here to create the PivotTable.

The layout of your fields in the resulting PivotTable

Sum of Order Amount	Last Name			
Product Name	Buchanan	Callahan	Davolio	Dodsworth
Alice Mutton	$585.00	$234.00	$2,702.70	$1,402.80
Aniseed Syrup		$300.00	$40.00	$740.00
Boston Crab Meat		$512.00	$73.60	$644.00
Camembert Pierrot	$693.60	$1,847.20	$1,362.72	$1,583.55
Carnarvon Tigers		$498.18	$2,723.50	$625.00

Important Because the finished PivotTable is a Microsoft Excel object, you must have Microsoft Excel installed on your computer before you run the PivotTable Wizard.

Can't read some field names?   Double-click a long field name so you can view all of its characters.

Use Microsoft Access tables and queries to create PivotTables   For details, look up **PivotTables** in the Microsoft Access online index.

Get the Help You Need While You Work

Expanded and improved online assistance is just a click away. It's the fastest way to get information so you can keep working.

Ask the Answer Wizard   Type a question in your own words. The Answer Wizard lists online Help topics related to your question. Double-click the Help button and then click the Answer Wizard tab.

Look it up in the online index   Instead of typing a question, use index entries provided in this book to find online topics related to your task. Double-click the Help button and then click the Index tab.

For details, see "Get Assistance While You Work," page 30. Or look up **Help** in the online index.

View and Compare the Results

Your PivotTable appears in a new Microsoft Access form that is created to receive it. When the PivotTable Wizard finishes, Microsoft Excel is activated so that you can change the layout of the PivotTable.

Now it's easy to compare the sales of each product for each sales representative by viewing the PivotTable in different ways. Just drag the fields to change the view of the PivotTable. Or edit the PivotTable further in Microsoft Excel. Unlike Microsoft Access crosstabs, where the table layout is fixed, the PivotTable is dynamic: Microsoft Excel recalculates it for you automatically as you make changes. When you finish, save the Microsoft Access form.

For Help, double-click. In the Microsoft Access online index look up: **editing embedded objects**

Your PivotTable is a Microsoft Excel worksheet embedded in a Microsoft Access form.

The button in this position controls the row contents.

The button in this position controls the column contents.

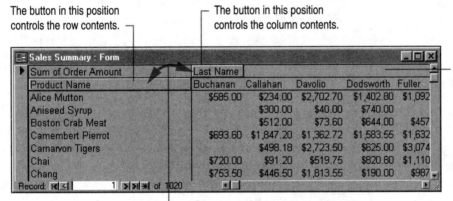

Change the layout of the PivotTable by double-clicking it, and then dragging the buttons.

To view the products across the columns and the sales representatives down the rows, just drag the buttons to swap their positions.

 To reactivate Microsoft Excel for further editing Open the form and double-click the PivotTable.

More Power: Use the Full Power of Microsoft Excel

While you're editing your PivotTable, you have all of the Microsoft Excel features at your disposal. For example, you can rank the products from most to least sold, display just the products you want to focus on, or filter out products with sales above or below your quota.

For details, look up **sorting**, **hiding cells**, and **filtering** in the Microsoft Excel online index. To get to the Microsoft Excel online index quickly, simply double-click your PivotTable, click Help Topics (Help menu), and then click Index.

View the Sales by Quarter

What if you also want to compare the sales of each product on a quarter-by-quarter basis? You can create another PivotTable from the same query, showing the sales performance of each product (ROW area) by order date (COLUMN area).

This PivotTable has too much detail and too many columns to see all at once. But by editing it in Microsoft Excel, you can quickly group the dates to see quarterly totals. When you finish with the Microsoft Access PivotTable Wizard, double-click the resulting PivotTable to activate Microsoft Excel and change the layout.

For Help, double-click. In the Microsoft Excel online index look up: **grouping PivotTable data**

Sum of Order Amount	Order Date							
Product Name	1/2/95	1/3/95	1/4/95	1/5/95	1/6/95	1/9/95	1/10/95	1/11
Alice Mutton								
Aniseed Syrup								
Boston Crab Meat		$938.40						
Camembert Pierrot							$1,734.00	
Carnarvon Tigers								
Chai								
Chang	$182.40						$190.00	

To summarize the sales by quarter, click here, and then right click and choose Group and Outline, Group. Choose Quarters from the list.

Sum of Order Amount	Quarters	Order Date				
	Qtr1			Qtr2		
Product Name	Jan	Feb	Mar	Apr	May	
Alice Mutton	$1,872.00	$2,620.80	$468.00	$3,170.70		
Aniseed Syrup	$790.00			$250.00	$40	
Boston Crab Meat	$1,398.40	$2,263.20	$184.00	$920.00		
Camembert Pierrot	$4,998.00	$4,377.50	$2,136.90	$5,718.80	$63	
Carnarvon Tigers	$3,046.88	$1,562.50	$1,012.50	$2,875.00		
Chai	$1,512.00	$2,052.00	$378.00	$1,741.50	$612	
Chang	$1,426.90	$760.00	$921.50	$2,189.75	$1,001	

Click each quarter, and then right click and choose Group and Outline, Hide Detail.

Sales by Quarter	Quarters	Order Date			
	Qtr1	Qtr2	Qtr3	Qtr4	Grand Total
Product Name					
Alice Mutton	$4,960.80	$3,278.70	$810.00	$97.20	$9,146.70
Aniseed Syrup	$790.00	$290.00		$112.00	$1,192.00
Boston Crab Meat	$3,845.60	$1,432.00	$384.00	$89.60	$5,751.20
Camembert Pierrot	$11,512.40	$5,782.72	$2,846.25	$1,670.20	$21,811.57
Carnarvon Tigers	$5,621.87	$3,373.18	$1,439.30	$2,021.00	$12,455.35
Chai	$3,942.00	$2,353.50	$1,574.55	$609.69	$8,479.74
Chang	$3,108.40	$3,191.05	$269.05	$2,157.80	$8,726.30

Orders for each product are totaled by quarter.

Next Steps

To	See
Export the data from your Microsoft Access query to a Microsoft Excel worksheet for further analysis	**exporting data to another file format** in the Microsoft Access online index

Create an Executive Sales Summary

Insert Information from Microsoft Excel in a Top-Level Report Written in Word

You may be responsible for writing a report combining regional sales reports in a top-level summary that your company may use to identify market and sales trends and to make corporate planning decisions.

Your challenge is to combine information from different regional reports and worksheets into a meaningful summary. Word makes the job easier by enabling you to organize, write, and automatically format the report.

Key Features

Link Microsoft Excel Data

AutoFormat

Style Gallery

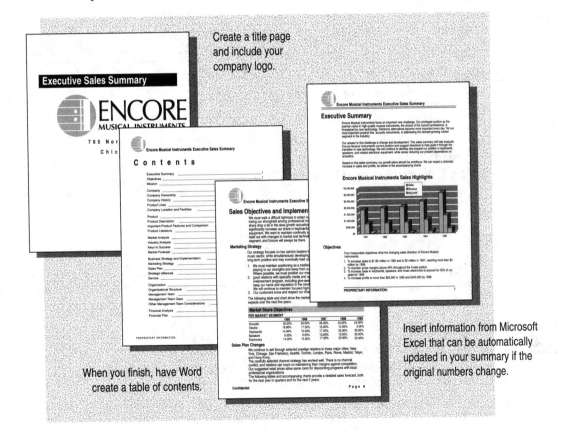

Create a title page and include your company logo.

When you finish, have Word create a table of contents.

Insert information from Microsoft Excel that can be automatically updated in your summary if the original numbers change.

Organize and Write the Summary

To begin, create a new document by clicking the New button.

If you want to create an outline   Switch to outline view (View menu), and then type all the headings and subheadings you want to include in the summary. When you finish the outline, you will probably find it easier to write the text of the report if you switch to normal view (View menu).

If you don't want to create an outline   Just start writing. If you want a table of contents, make sure that you use the Style box to format headings with the built-in heading styles, Heading 1, Heading 2, and so on. Word uses heading styles to create a table of contents.

For Help, double-click.
In the Word online index look up:
views, outline view
styles
outlines

Heading 1

Style box

Using Outline View

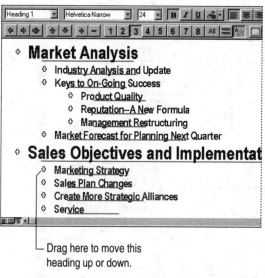

— Drag here to move this heading up or down.

Using Heading Styles

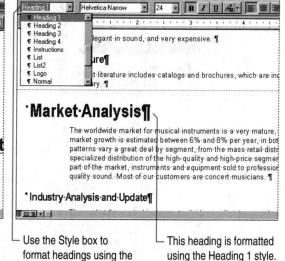

— Use the Style box to format headings using the built-in heading styles.

— This heading is formatted using the Heading 1 style.

Want to change the look of a built-in style?   Change the formatting in a paragraph that has the style you want to change. Select the paragraph, click in the Style box, and then press ENTER. Click OK to redefine the style. Word changes all paragraphs formatted with that style.

Insert frequently used text or graphics the easy way   All you do is select the item you want to reuse—a word, a phrase, your company name, or a graphic—click AutoCorrect (Tools menu), and type an abbreviation. To insert the item in your document, type the abbreviation and a space or punctuation.

For Help on dialog box options, click this button.

Insert and Summarize Sales Figures

The easiest way to insert information, such as regional spreadsheet summaries, text, or graphics, is to copy and paste it.

But if your sales information is likely to change, you can *link* the figures to your summary. Just copy the cells you want in Microsoft Excel. In your Word document, click Paste Special (Edit menu), and then select the Paste Link check box.

Charts make information easy to understand. With Microsoft Excel, it's easy to create and format a chart and then paste or link it to your executive summary. For details, see "Add a Chart to a Document or Presentation," page 223.

For Help, double-click. In the Word online index look up:
linked objects, overview
figures, copying and moving

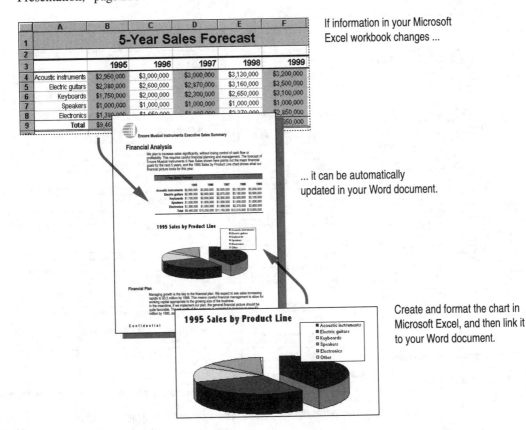

If information in your Microsoft Excel workbook changes ...

... it can be automatically updated in your Word document.

Create and format the chart in Microsoft Excel, and then link it to your Word document.

Need to see more of the document as you work? To remove rulers, toolbars, or other screen elements, click Full Screen (View menu). Choose commands using shortcut keys or display shortcut menus by clicking the right mouse button. To use the menu bar, click the top of your screen.

Give the Report a Professional Look

Appearance counts, especially in an executive-level report. To achieve a professional appearance with a minimum of effort, have Word do the formatting.

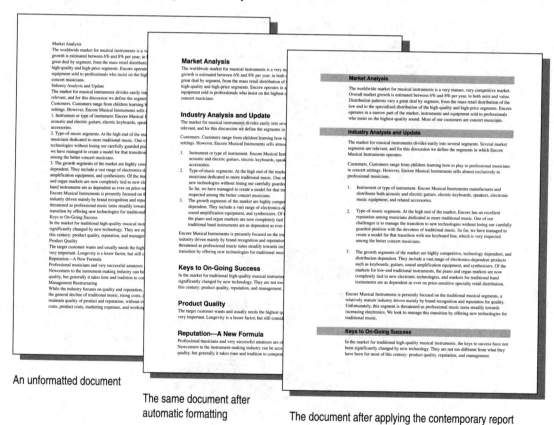

For Help, double-click.
In the Word online index look up:
AutoFormat

Have Word automatically format your document   To automatically format your executive summary, click AutoFormat (Format menu).

Use template styles to add professional polish   Once styles are applied (manually or using AutoFormat), you can choose a document "look" using your own styles or those from the Word built-in templates. Click Style Gallery (Format menu), and then choose the template that gives you the look you want.

An unformatted document

The same document after automatic formatting

The document after applying the contemporary report template in the Style Gallery

Want to add page numbers? Click Header And Footer (View menu), type the text you want, and then use the toolbar buttons to add the page numbers, date, or time.

Need to change the layout or page orientation for parts of your report? Divide your document into sections, and then format each section the way you want. For details, look up **sections** in the Word online index.

Add captions to text, worksheet summaries, and pictures To insert a caption number, select the item, and then click Caption (Insert menu). If you want, add a brief description.

Helpful hints as you work Watch the Word TipWizard for helpful hints and assistance as you work. To display the TipWizard, click the TipWizard button on the toolbar.

TipWizard button

What if you formatted the document manually? You can copy formatting to other parts of your document using the Format Painter button. Just select the formatted text, click the Format Painter button, and then select the text you want to format. To copy formatting multiple times, double-click the Format Painter button, and then select the paragraphs you want to format. When you finish, click the Format Painter button again.

Format Painter button

Create a Table of Contents

If you used the Word built-in heading styles, Heading 1, Heading 2, Heading 3, and so on, it's easy and quick to create a table of contents.

Place the insertion point in your report where you want the table of contents to appear. Click Index And Tables (Insert menu), and then click the Table of Contents tab. Select the format you want, and then click OK. For details, look up **tables of contents** in the Word online index.

Create a PowerPoint Presentation

Are you scheduled to present your executive sales summary to potential investors or associates? If you used the Word built-in heading styles, you can quickly create a PowerPoint slide presentation.

When you open your Word document in PowerPoint, PowerPoint uses the heading styles to create presentation slides. Each Heading 1 becomes the title of a slide, and Heading 2 through Heading 5 are successive levels of indented text. For details, see "Transfer Information Between PowerPoint and Other Applications," page 268.

Next Steps

To	See
Route the summary to your associates	"Share Documents Electronically," page 326
Chart regional or national figures in Microsoft Excel or Graph	"Add a Chart to a Document or Presentation," page 223
Format a chart	"Customize the Look of a Chart," page 236

PART 13

Analyze Scientific and Engineering Data

Contents

Analyze Data from an Experiment

Have you been performing calculations like exponential smoothing and Fourier analysis using a dedicated math package? Did you know that you can do the same number crunching in Microsoft Excel, and use all of the convenient and powerful analysis and formatting capabilities of Microsoft Excel on your results?

Key Features

 Analysis ToolPak

Important   Make sure you've installed the Analysis ToolPak add-in module. If you chose the Typical installation for Microsoft Excel rather than Custom/Complete, you'll need to run the Setup program to get this add-in. After installation, enable the Analysis ToolPak by clicking Add-Ins (Tools menu). You can work with data sets up to 16,384 rows by 256 columns and up to 255 characters per cell.

⌐ Analysis of variance calculates
  the comparison factors you need.

	A	B	C	D	E
1	Anova: Single Factor				
2					
3	SUMMARY				
4	Groups	Count	Sum	Average	Variance
5	Sample Taken	16	10.10069444	0.631293403	0.002652422
6	Temperature	16	364.9	22.80625	0.863291667
7					
8					

Sample Taken Residual Plot

Normal Probability Plot

Sample Taken Line Fit Plot

Residuals
2
1
0
-1
-2

Temperature
25
24
23
22
21

Temperature
25.0
24.0
23.0
22.0
21.0

13:00 14:12 15:24 16:36 17:48

Sample Taken

♦ Temperature
■ Predicted Temperature

⌐ The regression analysis
  tool automatically charts
  its results.

Set Up Your Data

Place each data series in a row or column. Each tool has specific input requirements.

The analysis tools store their output where you specify: elsewhere on the worksheet, on another worksheet, or in another workbook.

For Help, double-click.
In the Microsoft Excel online index look up:
Analysis ToolPak

	A	B
1	**Sample Taken**	**Temperature**
2	13:01	23.0
3	13:25	22.5
4	13:45	21.0
5	14:02	21.2
6	14:18	22.0
7	14:36	22.2
8	14:48	22.8
9	15:05	23.3
10	15:10	23.9
11	15:35	23.8
12	15:55	24.2
13	16:07	23.7
14	16:19	23.0
15	16:39	22.9
16	16:45	23.3
17	16:55	22.1

— Identify your variables for the resulting analysis, or let the tools create labels for you.

— Your input range

More power Bring external data directly into your worksheet. Microsoft Excel can read most database formats, or you can import text files. For examples, see "Get Sales Information from a Database," page 434.

If you aren't a statistician and all you want is a simple forecast See "Create a Sales Forecast," page 453. For some straightforward techniques to analyze uncomplicated data, see "Create a Sales Summary," page 446, and "Create a Detailed Sales Report," page 439.

Run the Analysis

Use the Data Analysis command (Tools menu) to select the type of analysis you want.

Important If you don't see this command, you may not have enabled the Analysis ToolPak after installing it. Use the Add-Ins command (Tools menu) to enable the Analysis ToolPak.

 For Help, double-click.
In the Microsoft Excel
online index look up:
Descriptive Statistics analysis tool

	A	B	C	D
1	Sample Taken		Temperature	
2				
3	Mean	0.631293403	Mean	22.80625
4	Standard Error	0.012875418	Standard Error	0.232283726
5	Median	0.630208333	Median	22.95
6	Mode	#N/A	Mode	23
7	Standard Deviation	0.051501671	Standard Deviation	0.929134902
8	Sample Variance	0.002652422	Sample Variance	0.863291667
9	Kurtosis	-1.137247717	Kurtosis	-0.359166577
10	Skewness	-0.158973114	Skewness	-0.493724094
11	Range	0.1625	Range	3.2
12	Minimum	0.542361111	Minimum	21
13	Maximum	0.704861111	Maximum	24.2
14	Sum	10.10069444	Sum	364.9
15	Count	16	Count	16
16	Confidence Level(95.0%)	0.02744332	Confidence Level(95.0%)	0.495101346

The Descriptive Statistics tool calculates the parameters you want for further analysis.

Want details about tools? For algorithms used by the tools and other details, look up the tool you want to know about in the Microsoft Excel online index. For a list of the available analysis tools, click Data Analysis (Tools menu.)

Next Steps

To	See
Create scatter plots and other charts from your data or analysis results	"Display Scientific Data in a Chart," page 483
Include the analysis in your thesis, journal article, or other paper	"Create a Thesis or Dissertation," page 523

Display Scientific Data in a Chart

When your data has pairs or grouped sets of values, you can display it effectively in an xy (scatter) chart. This chart type is commonly used for displaying scientific and engineering data.

- An xy (scatter) chart has two value axes, instead of one value axis and one category axis like most chart types.

- Another difference is that data can be shown in uneven intervals, or clusters.

- Optional chart items that can be helpful in analyzing data are trendlines for prediction and error bars to show the margin of error.

Key Features

XY (Scatter) Chart Type

Trendlines

Error Bars

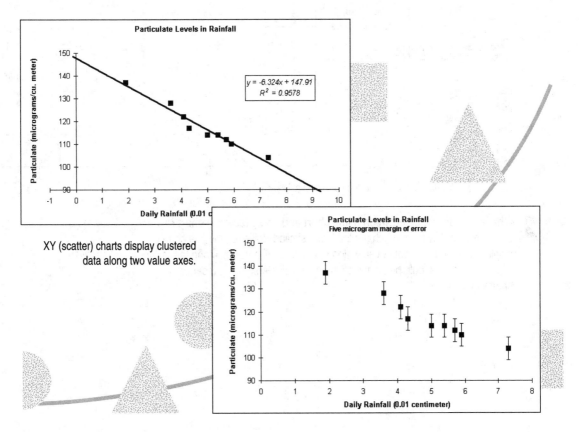

XY (scatter) charts display clustered data along two value axes.

Create an XY (Scatter) Chart

Select the data you want to display in the chart. The selection should not include text labels, because they will be interpreted as values. If there is more than one *y* value for each *x* value, see "If Your Data Has Multiple *Y* Values," later in this topic, more information.

For Help, double-click. In the Microsoft Excel online index look up: **charts in Excel, creating**

Let the ChartWizard help you create the chart   After selecting the data, click the ChartWizard button and select the xy (scatter) type in step 2 of the wizard. For more information about creating charts, see "Create a Chart from Worksheet Data," page 216.

ChartWizard button

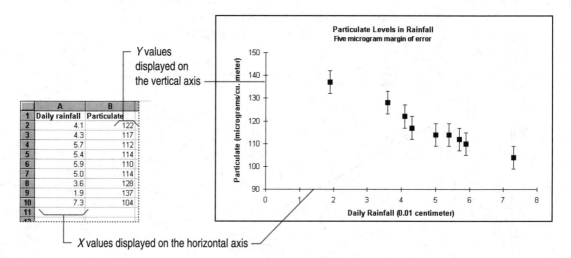

Y values displayed on the vertical axis

	A	B
1	Daily rainfall	Particulate
2	4.1	122
3	4.3	117
4	5.7	112
5	5.4	114
6	5.9	110
7	5.0	114
8	3.6	128
9	1.9	137
10	7.3	104
11		

X values displayed on the horizontal axis

What's the difference between a line chart and an xy (scatter) chart? Line charts and xy (scatter) charts look very similar. However, the line chart displays categories of data evenly along the *x* axis, with values along the *y* axis. When data should be displayed in uneven clusters, the xy (scatter) chart works better.

If Your Data Has Multiple *Y* Values

When your data has two or more *y* values corresponding to each *x* value, arrange the data as shown to get the chart you want. If your data series are in rows instead of columns, the *x* values should be in the top row with the *y* values in rows below.

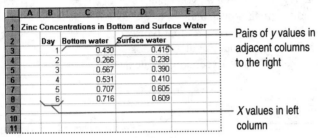

Pairs of *y* values in adjacent columns to the right

X values in left column

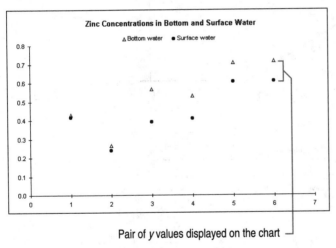

Pair of *y* values displayed on the chart

Predict Forward or Backward with a Trendline

To predict beyond actual data (also known as regression analysis), add a trendline to a data series. Select the data series and click Trendline (Insert menu). Specify the trendline type you want; optionally, you can display a trendline label with the line equation, the R-squared value (a measure of reliability), or both.

For Help, double-click. In the Microsoft Excel online index look up: **trendlines in Excel charts**

What types of trendlines are available?   Depending on your data, choose from linear, logarithmic, polynomial, power, and exponential. Each type is calculated differently. Try different types to find the most useful one. For information about calculation, look up **equations, chart trendlines** in the Microsoft Excel online index.

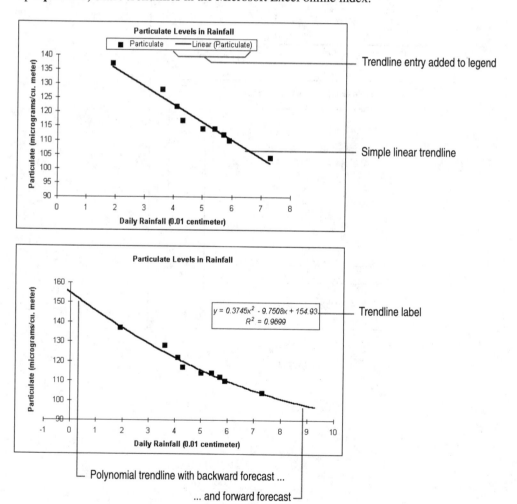

Trendline entry added to legend

Simple linear trendline

Trendline label

$$y = 0.3745x^2 - 9.7508x + 154.93$$
$$R^2 = 0.9699$$

Polynomial trendline with backward forecast ...

... and forward forecast

The trendline belongs to the data series A trendline is calculated from the values in the associated data series. If you delete or move the data series, the trendline is also deleted or moved. If you want to change the type of trendline you use, double-click the line and make your change in the Format Trendline dialog box.

Modify the trendline Change the trendline's type (for example, from linear to polynomial), change its color or line style, give it a name or add a label. Make the changes you want in the Format Trendline dialog box.

Format the trendline label Work with a trendline label like any other data label: double-click it. Then change the font, change the way numbers are displayed, or add a border or background color. To move the label, select it and drag to the new location. For information on formatting data labels, look up **data labels in Excel charts** in the Microsoft Excel online index.

Other chart types can have trendlines, too You can add trendlines to 2-D bar, column, and line charts, but not to 3-D charts. For information on working with different chart types, look up **choosing chart type** in the Microsoft Excel online index.

Use moving averages and regression trendlines for business data Another trendline that is available is the moving average. All types of trendlines are useful for business data. For more information, see "Create a Sales Forecast," page 453. For information about using the TREND function on worksheet data, look up **TREND worksheet function** in the Microsoft Excel online index.

? For Help on dialog box options, click this button.

Show "Plus or Minus" with Error Bars

When it's useful to indicate the degree of uncertainty for a data series—the "plus or minus" range—add error bars. Select the data series and click Error Bars (Insert menu). Then specify the display you want and how the error amount should be obtained.

How is the error amount obtained?   Specify as the error amount a fixed value or a percentage of each value in the data series, automatically calculate the standard deviation or standard error, or refer to custom error values in a worksheet range. For more information on how error amounts are calculated, look up **equations, calculating error amounts** in the Microsoft Excel online index.

For Help, double-click.
In the Microsoft Excel online index look up:
error bars in Excel charts

For Help on dialog box options, click this button.

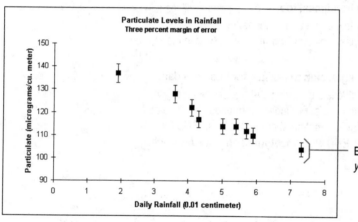

Error bar calculated as percentage of *y* value, with end marker displayed

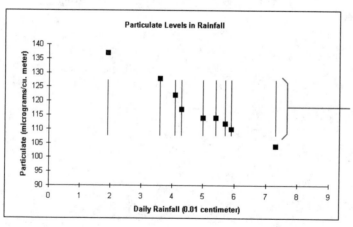

Error bar showing one standard deviation, with no end marker

The error bars belong to the data series Error bars are obtained from the values in the associated data series. If you delete or move the data series, the error bars are also deleted or moved.

Modify the error bars To change the color, style, and line weight for all error bars associated with a data series, double-click one error bar. Change the look on the Patterns tab, and change other characteristics on the X Error Bars tab and the Y Error Bars tab.

Other chart types can have error bars, too You can add error bars to 2-D area, bar, column, and line charts, but not to 3-D charts. For information about working with different chart types, look up **choosing chart type** in the Microsoft Excel online index.

Next Steps

To	See
Custom-format a chart and save the formatting to use for other charts	"Customize the Look of a Chart," page 236
Link or embed a chart in a Word document or a PowerPoint presentation	"Add a Chart to a Document or Presentation," page 223

PART 14

Order for the Court

Creating Legal Documents

Contents

Create a Pleading

Use Word to Create and Track Legal Documents

If you need to create a pleading to initiate or to continue a legal proceeding, it's fast and easy to use the Word Pleading Wizard to set up the pleading.

The Pleading Wizard sets up a basic document that you can modify to comply with the court's rules of procedure. Additionally, you can add a table of authorities, table of contents, and a title page.

Key Features

Pleading Wizard

Footnotes

Table of Authorities

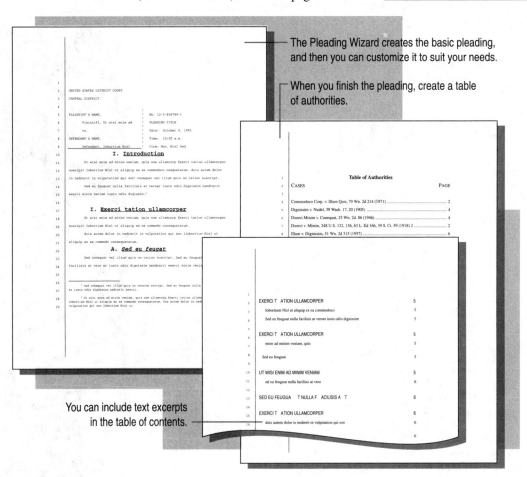

The Pleading Wizard creates the basic pleading, and then you can customize it to suit your needs.

When you finish the pleading, create a table of authorities.

You can include text excerpts in the table of contents.

Create a Basic Pleading

To start the Pleading Wizard, click New (File menu), click the Other Documents tab, and then double-click the Pleading Wizard icon. The wizard asks you a series of easy-to-answer questions. Your answers determine how Word sets up the basic page elements of the pleading.

For example, you will tell the wizard what line numbering and spacing, margin settings, and page number style you want, and you'll choose from three styles for the caption box. You'll also fill in the attorney, defendant, plaintiff, case number, and pleading title information.

For Help, double-click.
In the Word online index look up:
page setup

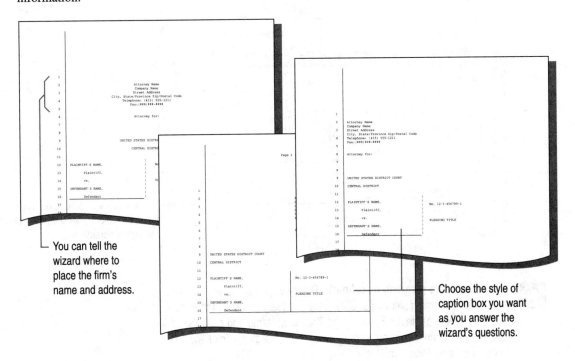

You can tell the wizard where to place the firm's name and address.

Choose the style of caption box you want as you answer the wizard's questions.

Customize and Write the Pleading

When you finish the wizard, you can modify the layout and formatting to suit your needs just as you would in any other Word document.

For example, you may want to change column spacing in the caption box, or add lines. Because the caption box is a three-column table, you can drag the column gridline to adjust it.

Then write the text of the pleading. If you want to cite text from another source and make it single-spaced, just select the text, click the Style box, and then choose the Single Spacing style.

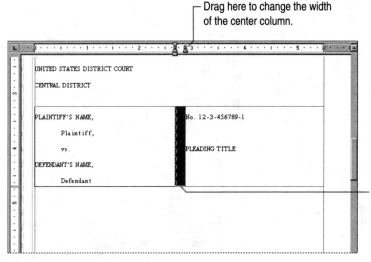 **For Help, double-click.** In the Word online index look up: **tables**

Drag here to change the width of the center column.

To add a line, place the insertion point in the column, press ENTER, and then type a parenthesis.

 Want to use this pleading next time?   Delete anything you don't plan to use in your upcoming pleadings. Click Save As (File menu), and then click Document Template in the Save File As Type box. Name and save the new template, and then when you want to start a new pleading, click New (File menu), and select this template.

Add Footnotes

When you need to expand upon or include other citations or text, you can insert a footnote. To insert a footnote, click Footnote (Insert menu). Click AutoNumber or type a custom mark.

To separate footnotes from the pleading text, Word automatically inserts a short horizontal line. Or, if the footnote continues onto the next page, Word inserts a longer separator line.

You can underline citations and format the footnote text just as you would any other text.

 For Help, double-click.
In the Word online index look up:
footnotes and endnotes

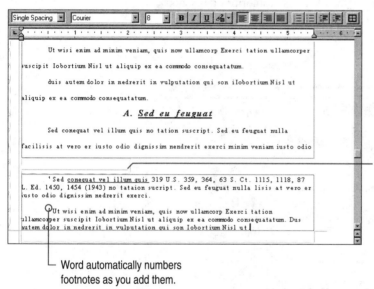

Word adds a short separator line for footnotes that do not go beyond one page.

Word automatically numbers footnotes as you add them.

Want to add a footnote continuation notice? For footnotes that continue on the next page, add a continuation notice. In normal view, click Footnotes (View menu). In the drop-down list box at the top of the footnote pane, click All Footnotes, click Footnote Continuation Notice, and then type the text of the notice.

Add a Table of Authorities

Mark citations   Before you create a table of authorities, scroll through the text to find the first long citation, or have Word search for common abbreviations such as *v.*, *ID.*, *Ibid*, *Cong.*, *Sess.*, or *in re*. Select the text for the first citation and then press ALT+SHIFT+I.

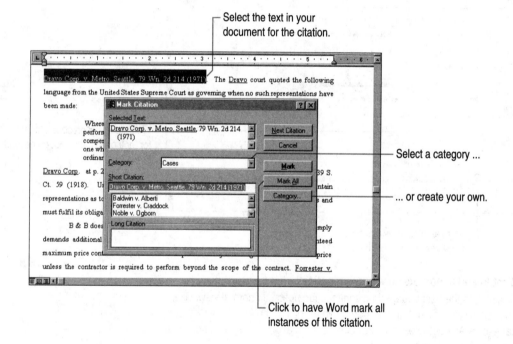

For Help, double-click.
In the Word online index look up:
tables of authorities

Edit or type the short citation, and choose a category. Then click the Mark or Mark All button.

Create the table of authorities   Place the insertion point where you want the table to appear in your pleading. Click Index And Tables (Insert menu), and then click the Table Of Authorities tab. Choose the format and any other options you want.

Select the text in your document for the citation.

Select a category ...

... or create your own.

Click to have Word mark all instances of this citation.

Making Changes to a Table of Authorities

Edit the entries Before you make any changes, display paragraph marks, if they aren't displayed already, by clicking the Show/Hide ¶ button on the toolbar.

To edit a table of authorities, move to the entry within the pleading and change only the text between the quotation marks. To delete an entry, select the entire entry including the brackets, and then press DELETE or BACKSPACE.

Update the table To have the table of authorities reflect editing changes, click Index And Tables (Insert menu). Click the Table Of Authorities tab, click OK, and then click Yes.

Create a Table of Contents

If you want a table of contents with headings only If you used the built-in heading styles, Heading 1, Heading 2, and so on, skip to "To create the table of contents," later in this section. If you did not use the Word built-in heading styles, just use the Style box to format the headings.

If you want to include text excerpts in a table of contents You need to mark excerpts by selecting the text and then pressing ALT+SHIFT+O. In the Entry box, make any changes you want, and then click the Mark button.

To create the table of contents Place the insertion point where you want the table of contents to appear. Click Index And Tables (Insert menu), and then click the Table Of Contents tab. If you want headings only, choose the options you want, and you're done. If you want to include text excerpts, click the Options button, and then select the Table Entry Fields check box.

For Help, double-click.
In the Word online index look up:
tables of contents
styles

You can omit or include line numbers on the title page.

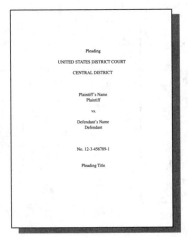

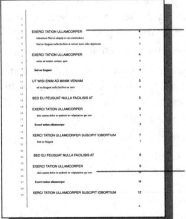

Word automatically includes the first three heading levels in a table of contents. For example, this text is formatted using the Heading 2 style.

Include excerpts from text in the table of contents, and choose the heading level you want for each excerpt.

Want to add a title page?   To include a title page, place the insertion point at the very beginning of your document. Type the title page text, and add graphics if you want. Then place the insertion point at the end of the title page text, click Break (Insert menu), and under Section Breaks, click Next Page. If you already included page numbers and want to omit the page number from the title page, click Header And Footer (View menu). Click the Page Setup button, and then click Different First Page. Then, delete the page number by selecting it and pressing DELETE.

Need to update the table of contents?   If you make changes to the pleading, you'll want to update the table of contents. To do this, place the insertion point in the table of contents, click the right mouse button, and then click Update Field. You can choose to update only page numbers or the entire table of contents.

Next Steps

To	See
Fax the document to a client	"Create a Fax Cover Sheet," page 129
Get comments on the pleading	"Have Your Team Review a Word Document," page 333
Change the formatting	"Make Your Word Document Look Great," page 161

Create a Legal Contract

Use Microsoft Word to Create and Track Legal Documents

Whether you are writing a contract or corporate bylaws, Word provides tools to help you create the document efficiently.

For example, use AutoText to quickly insert standard text, and have Word add page numbers to cross-references as you write. Later, use revision marking to track revisions and to produce black-lined and clean copies.

Key Features

AutoText

Cross-references

Revision Marks

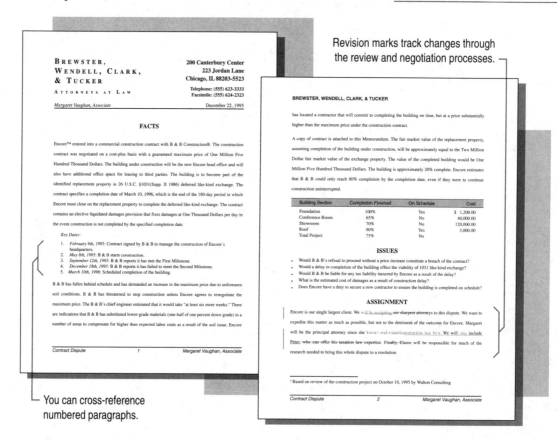

Revision marks track changes through the review and negotiation processes.

You can cross-reference numbered paragraphs.

Create and Format the Contract

Chances are you'll want to begin the contract by revising an existing one or by using your firm's template. Open the contract or template by clicking Open (File menu). If you want to start from scratch or create a new template, click the New button.

If you start from scratch, type or insert basic elements, such as the firm's name and logo. Then revise or create standard headers and footers for the document. Click Header And Footer (View menu), and type the text. Use the buttons on the Header And Footer toolbar to insert the elements you want.

 For Help, double-click.
In the Word online index look up:
headers and footers
tables

Switch Between Header
And Footer button

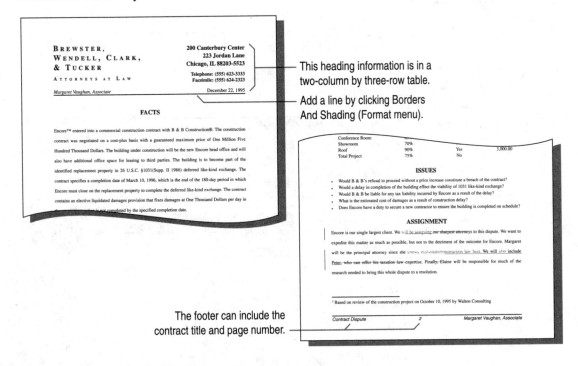

This heading information is in a two-column by three-row table.

Add a line by clicking Borders And Shading (Format menu).

The footer can include the contract title and page number.

 Create a template you can use next time Delete information you won't need in future contracts. Then click Save As (File menu), and click Document Template in the Save As Type box. Name the new template, and then when you want to start a new contract, click New (File menu), and select this template.

Align text elements precisely Insert a table by clicking the Insert Table button and then dragging to select the number of rows and columns you want. Then, type the text you want in the table.

Insert Table button

Write the Contract

Now, write or revise the text of the contract. As you write, be sure to use the Style box to apply built-in heading styles.

Add cross-references   You can cross-reference headings that use built-in heading styles, footnotes and endnotes, and items with captions. Just type the text for the cross-reference in your document, and click Cross-reference (Insert menu).

Insert boilerplate text   When you want to insert text you use frequently, copy it into your current document, and make it an AutoText (Edit menu) entry.

For Help, double-click.
In the Word online index look up:
cross-references
AutoText
numbering paragraphs

Heading 1

Style box

Type the first part of the cross-reference sentence in your document, and then click Cross-reference (Insert menu).

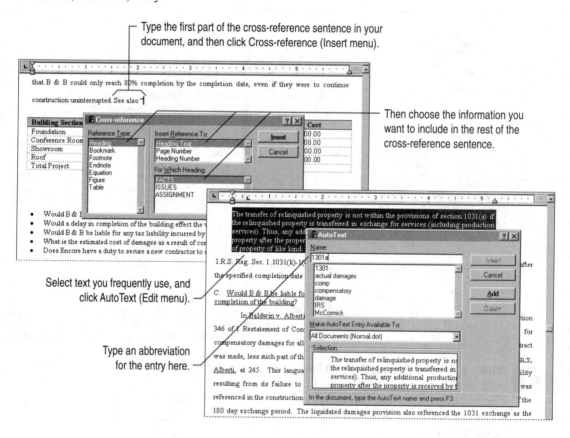

Then choose the information you want to include in the rest of the cross-reference sentence.

Select text you frequently use, and click AutoText (Edit menu).

Type an abbreviation for the entry here.

AutoText button

Add your favorite tools to a Word toolbar If you want quick access to your favorite tools, such as AutoText, click Customize (Tools menu), and then click the Toolbars tab. Under Categories, click Insert, and then drag the AutoText button to any toolbar. For details, look up **customizing toolbars** in the Word online index.

? For Help on dialog box options, click this button.

Want to number paragraphs or headings? To number paragraphs, select the paragraphs, and then click Bullets And Numbering (Format menu). To number headings, click Heading Numbering (Format menu).

Add cross-references to numbered paragraphs Select the paragraphs you want to cross-reference, and then click Bookmark (Edit menu). Type a name for the bookmark, and choose the Add button. Then click Cross-reference (Insert menu) and select Bookmark. In the Insert Reference To box, click Paragraph Number, and then click the name of the bookmark you want in the For Which Bookmark box.

Add a footnote Move the insertion point where you want the footnote reference mark to appear. Click Footnote (Insert menu).

Have Word automatically update the document date Click Date And Time (Insert menu), and then click the Update Automatically (Insert As Field) check box.

Get the Help You Need While You Work

Expanded and improved online assistance is just a click away. It's the fastest way to get information so you can keep working.

Ask the Answer Wizard Type a question in your own words. The Answer Wizard lists online Help topics related to your question. Double-click the Help button and then click the Answer Wizard tab.

Look it up in the online index Instead of typing a question, use index entries provided in this book to find online topics related to your task. Double-click the Help button and then click the Index tab.

For details, see "Get Assistance While You Work," page 30. Or look up **Help** in the online index.

Track Changes Through the Negotiation Process

Use either of these methods to track changes to legal documents.

Protect the document for revisions before sending it to reviewers
Click Protect Document (Tools menu), and then click Revisions.
Any changes reviewers make will be marked.

To incorporate changes in a revised document, remove protection by
clicking Unprotect Document (Tools menu). Click Revisions (Tools
menu), and then click the Review button. Each revision is marked
with the reviewer's name, date, and time.

**If the document has already been revised without using revision
marks**   Then have Word compare the revised version to the original
and mark the differences. Before you do this, make sure the original
and edited documents have different filenames, or are in different
folders if they have the same filename. Then open the edited version
of the document and click Revisions (Tools menu). Click the
Compare Versions button, and then open the original document.

As Word compares the two documents, it marks differences. You
can review and incorporate the changes as described previously.

For Help, double-click.
In the Word online index look up:
protecting documents
revision marks

For Help on dialog box options,
click this button.

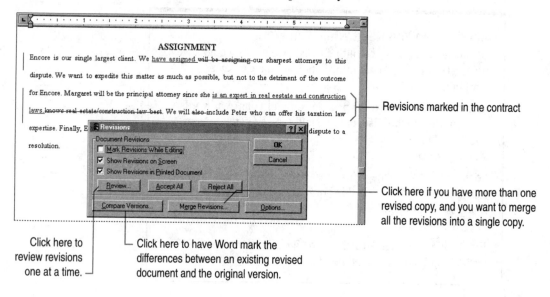

Revisions marked in the contract

Click here if you have more than one
revised copy, and you want to merge
all the revisions into a single copy.

Click here to
review revisions
one at a time.

Click here to have Word mark the
differences between an existing revised
document and the original version.

Want to send a document to several reviewers simultaneously? First, protect the document for revisions as described earlier. When you get the revision-marked copies back, merge those revisions into the original document by clicking Revisions (Tools menu), and then clicking the Merge Revisions button.

Insert Annotations Instead of Revision Marks

Instead of making changes in the document, reviewers can insert annotations by clicking Annotation (Insert menu) and then typing their comments in a separate annotation pane. Word marks the comment in the document with the reviewer's initials and a reference number.

To review annotations, double-click the annotation mark in your document, or click Annotations (View menu.)

Next Steps

To	See
Fax the document to a client	"Create a Fax Cover Sheet," page 129
Get comments on the document	"Have Your Team Review a Word Document," page 333
Change the formatting	"Make Your Word Document Look Great," page 161

PART 15

The Home Office

Contents

Create a Resume and Cover Letter

a.k.a. Curriculum Vitae or CV

Creating a resume from scratch may be the first step in your job search. Or, you might want to create an online version of your resume so you can easily update or customize it. Whatever your reasons, you need a resume that stands out from the rest.

The Resume Wizard or the resume templates help you create a resume that highlights your skills and experiences. You can also use the Letter Wizard to produce a cover letter and matching envelope.

Key Features

Resume Wizard

Letter Wizard

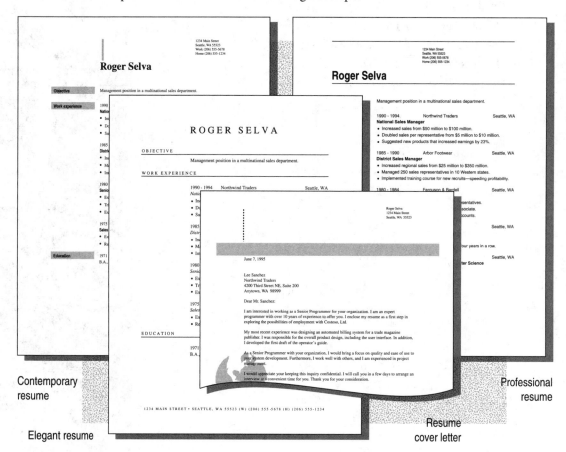

Contemporary resume

Elegant resume

Professional resume

Resume cover letter

Use the Resume Wizard to Get Started

To start the Resume Wizard, click New (File menu), click the Other Documents tab, and then double-click Resume Wizard. In English versions of Word distributed outside the U.S. and Canada, the Resume Wizard is called the Curriculum Vitae Wizard.

The Resume Wizard "interviews" you and uses your answers to set up the resume's basic content and layout. When the wizard finishes, the new resume appears—all you need to do is fill in the details.

For Help, double-click.
In the Word online index look up:
templates
wizards

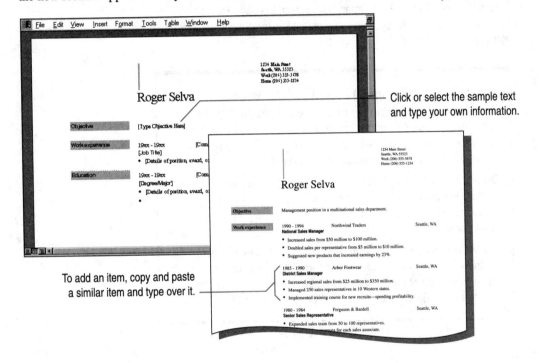

Click or select the sample text and type your own information.

To add an item, copy and paste a similar item and type over it.

Need a cover letter and envelope?   On the final step of the Resume Wizard, you can jump to the Letter Wizard to create these items. (For more details, see "Write a Cover Letter" and "Print an Envelope," later in this topic.) Use the Window menu to switch between the cover letter and resume.

Try on a different resume design   Click Style Gallery (Format menu), and then click a resume template (Contemporary, Elegant, or Professional).

Like the result—and want to use it to start your next resume?   Delete any information you don't plan to include in future resumes. Click Save As (File menu), and then click Document Template in the Save As Type box. Name and save the new template. Then select this template the next time you start a new resume.

Use a Resume Template Instead of the Wizard?

The Resume Wizard and the resume templates produce the same result—an attractive, ready-to-complete resume. Here's the difference: The wizard lets you choose layout options step by step, while the templates have a preset layout.

To use a resume template, click New (File menu), click the Other Documents tab, and then double-click a resume template. Then, select the sample text and type your information.

Create your own personalized template   Add your name, address, and any other standard information you want to include in each resume. Then, save the modified resume as a template (for details, see the tip earlier in this topic).

Add a Second Page — or More

If you decide to include multiple pages, add your name, phone number, and the page number to the top of each page. That way, the recruiter can easily tell if pages are missing or out of order.

Click Header And Footer (View menu). Click the Page Setup button, and then click Different First Page on the Layout tab. If necessary, click the Show Next button on the Header And Footer toolbar to switch to the header for the second and subsequent pages.

 For Help, double-click.
In the Word online index look up:
first page header or footer

Page Setup button

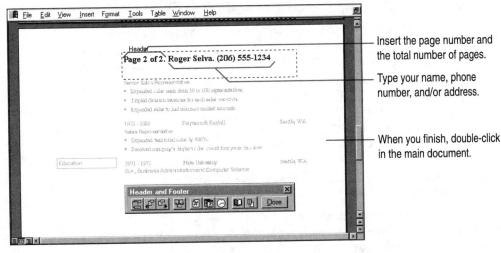

Insert the page number and the total number of pages.

Type your name, phone number, and/or address.

When you finish, double-click in the main document.

 Use automatic page numbers In the header, type **Page**, and then click the Page Numbers button. Type **of**, click Field (Insert menu), and then click the NUMPAGES field. The page numbers are automatically updated when you print, or you can update the page numbers at any time by selecting them and pressing F9.

Page Numbers button

Stuck with a couple of lines on a second page? To fit the resume on one page, click the Print Preview button and then the Shrink To Fit button.

Shrink To Fit button

Proofread and "Wordsmith" as You Work

First impressions count in a resume, so the last thing you want to do is overlook a few typos or misspellings. The spelling checker and thesaurus can work like your own personal editor—fixing mistakes and suggesting more precise and varied words.

 For Help, double-click.
In the Word online index look up:
thesaurus
spell checking
AutoCorrect

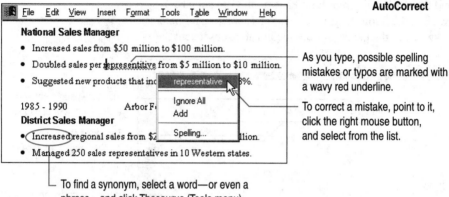

As you type, possible spelling mistakes or typos are marked with a wavy red underline.

To correct a mistake, point to it, click the right mouse button, and select from the list.

To find a synonym, select a word—or even a phrase—and click Thesaurus (Tools menu).

Don't see wavy lines under spelling mistakes?   Click Options (Tools menu), click the Spelling tab, and then click Automatic Spell Checking.

Don't want to make the same mistake twice?   When the spelling checker questions a mistake you frequently make, point to it, click the right mouse button, click Spelling, type or select a correction, and then click AutoCorrect. The next time you make the same mistake, Word will fix it for you.

Tired of the spelling checker questioning your name?   When the spelling checker questions a word that's spelled correctly, point to it, click the right mouse button, and then click Add. The word is then stored in a custom dictionary, and the spelling checker won't bother you about it again.

Write a Cover Letter

Grab a recruiter's attention by including a polished, professional cover letter that tailors your skills and achievements to the job description. Word's ready-to-use cover letter gives you a head start.

If you created a cover letter at the same time that you created a resume, use the Window menu to switch to it and fill in the details. Otherwise, use the Letter Wizard to create a cover letter (make sure to click the Prewritten Business Letters option); for details, see "Write a Business Letter," page 120.

For Help, double-click.
In the Word online index look up:
prewritten business letters
wizards

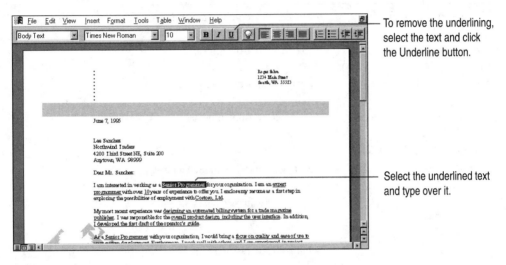

To remove the underlining, select the text and click the Underline button.

Select the underlined text and type over it.

Make sure the cover letter design matches the resume If it doesn't, click Style Gallery (Format menu), and then click the appropriate letter template.

Record the recruiter's address for follow-up correspondence Use your Microsoft Exchange personal address book or Schedule+ Contact List. For details, look up **address book** or **contact list (Schedule+)** in the Word online index.

Print an Envelope

If you selected Create An Envelope Or Mailing Label on the final step of the Letter Wizard, you're ready to start. If you didn't, it's not too late—with the cover letter on screen, click Envelopes And Labels (Tools menu). Change any options you want, insert the envelope into the printer as shown in the Feed box, and click Print.

For Help, double-click. In the Word online index look up: **envelopes**

Next Steps

To	See
Add even more visual impact	"Make Your Word Document Look Great," page 161
Fax a copy of the resume	"Create a Fax Cover Sheet," page 129
E-mail a copy of the resume	"Share Documents Electronically," page 326
Schedule an interview	"Schedule an Appointment," page 314
Create follow-up correspondence	"Write a Business Letter," page 120
Keep track of contacts	"Manage Contacts with Schedule+," page 296
	"Create a Business Contact List in Microsoft Excel," page 300
	"Track Your Business Contacts in Microsoft Access," page 306

Figure the Monthly Payment on a Loan

Know All About Your Loan Before You Get to the Bank

Microsoft Excel includes a template that you can use to figure out everything you need to know about *amortizing* a loan, whether you're borrowing or lending money.

To begin, click New (File menu), click the Spreadsheet Solutions tab, and double-click Loan Manager. Then follow the directions on the template.

Key Features

Spreadsheet Solutions

Templates

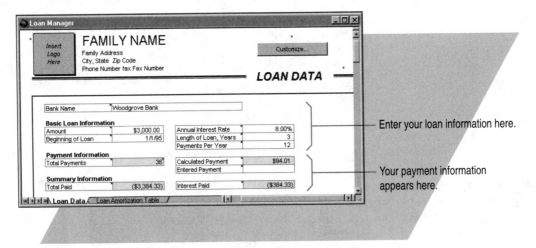

Enter your loan information here.

Your payment information appears here.

How does amortization work? Each time you make a loan payment, you pay off some of the original amount that you borrowed (called the *principal*). Each payment also includes *interest* that the lender charges for allowing you to use the money. Each month, the interest portion of the payment decreases and the principal portion increases, while the actual payment stays the same. This is the amortization effect; a convenience that allows you to pay a fixed amount of money each month.

What is an "entered" payment? The "Entered Payment" box allows you to specify the payment you want instead of having the template calculate it for you. You should always enter a number larger than the calculated payment. The additional amount is applied to the principal.

The Amortization Table

While the Loan Data tab shows you what your monthly payment will be, you might want more information. Click the Loan Amortization Table tab to view detailed data for individual payments.

 For Help, double-click.
In the Microsoft Excel online index look up: **amortization**

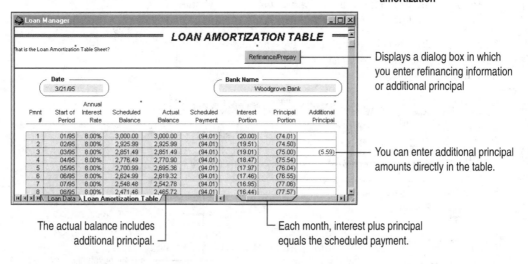

Displays a dialog box in which you enter refinancing information or additional principal

You can enter additional principal amounts directly in the table.

The actual balance includes additional principal.

Each month, interest plus principal equals the scheduled payment.

Why pay additional principal?   If, instead of the $94.01 monthly payment in our example, we pay a round $100, the additional $5.59 is applied directly to the principal. As a result, the loan is paid off three months earlier, saving $187 in interest. Try adding different amounts in the Additional Principal column to see how it affects your loan. If you set the amortization table to display years instead of months, multiply the monthly additional principal amount by 12.

On-screen tips   Cells with small red dots in the upper right corner contain CellTips that appear when you move the mouse pointer over the cell. These tips give you more information about using the template.

Changing the number of periods in the table   You can set the amortization table to display any number of rows of detail. If your loan is to be amortized over 30 years, for example, you'll want to display all 360 months of the loan. To adjust the number of rows in the table, click the Customize button on the Loan Data tab.

Move the mouse pointer over a cell with this indicator for a CellTip

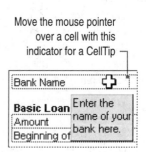

The Spreadsheet Solutions Templates

The Spreadsheet Solutions tab in the New Workbook dialog box contains a number of templates you might find useful, including the following that are focused on your personal needs.

- **The Car Lease template** Helps you find the "hidden" interest rate when leasing a car, and provides assistance with various negotiation options.
- **The Personal Budget template** Helps you set up and manage your personal finances.

More Spreadsheet Solutions templates The following Spreadsheet Solutions templates are available in addition to those listed above: Business Planner, Change Request, Expense Statement, Invoice, Personal Budget, Purchase Order, Sales Quote, and Timecard. If the template you want does not appear on the Spreadsheet Solutions tab, you need to run Setup again to install it. For more information about Setup, see "Install and Start Microsoft Office," page 25.

Customizing Each template includes a Customize button that activates a sheet where you can enter your name, address, and other personal information that is used throughout the template.

You can also add a logo of your choice, or change the font used to display personal information. After you finish customizing, click Save As (File menu), and select Template in the Save As Type box to save the workbook with your personal information, eliminating the need to re-enter it each time you use the template.

Special toolbars Each Spreadsheet Solutions template includes a special toolbar, each of which has similar tools designed to help you use the template more efficiently.

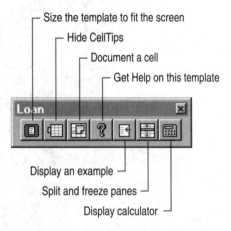

Size the template to fit the screen
Hide CellTips
Document a cell
Get Help on this template
Display an example
Split and freeze panes
Display calculator

Organize Your Music Collection

Set Up a Microsoft Access Database to Catalog Your Music Collection

Has your collection of CDs, tapes, and albums grown so large that you can't find the selections you want to hear or all recordings by your favorite artists? Use the Microsoft Access Database Wizard to create a database for cataloging your collection. Then, when you need to find just the right selections or print a list of your entire CD collection, just tell your database what you need.

To complete the steps in this topic   You need Microsoft Office Professional or an individual copy of Microsoft Access for Windows 95, and you need to have Microsoft Access installed.

 Want to set up other types of personal databases?   Use the Database Wizard to create many personal and business databases, including databases for tracking people or expenses, cataloging book collections, and organizing recipes. Refer to this topic for details on running the Database Wizard and on finding information stored in your databases.

Create a Music Database

With the Database Wizard, you can create everything you need to catalog your music collection and find the information you want.

To run the wizard Start Microsoft Access, click Database Wizard, click OK, and then click the Music Collection folder. Or, if you've already started Microsoft Access, click the New Database button, and then double-click Music Collection. When the wizard asks you to choose fields, select all fields. If you want help in getting started on cataloging your collection, check the sample data option. Click the Next button until you come to the final screen, and then click the Finish button.

New Database button

The wizard creates everything you need to catalog and search your database, including a Switchboard for opening forms, tables, and reports.

 If you need to return to the Switchboard while in the Music Collection database Click the Database Window button, click the Forms tab, and then double-click Switchboard.

Database Window button

To create a new database while working in Microsoft Access Click the New Database button, and then click Blank Database or select the type of database you want.

New Database button

What Your Database Contains

The Music Collection database contains four tables in which
different facts about your music collection are stored (Albums,
Artists, Music Categories, and Tracks); three forms for
entering data about different aspects of your collection
(Albums, Artists, and Music Categories); and reports that list
albums by artist, albums by category, tracks by album, and
albums by format (CD, audio tape, or album). (In the Music
Collection database, album refers to all three formats.) To see
the forms, tables, and reports, click the Database Window
button.

Catalog Your Music Collection

Now that you have a database, add data about your music collection.
You'll enter most of the information you need on the Albums form.

On the Music Collection Switchboard, click the Enter/View Albums
button. If the form shows sample data, use it as an example of what
to enter in each field. When you've finished entering details about
your music collection, close the form to return to the Switchboard.

 For Help, double-click.
In the Microsoft Access
online index look up:
forms, overview
adding records

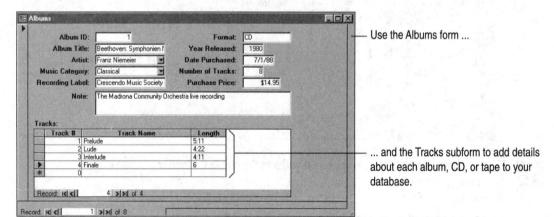

Use the Albums form ...

... and the Tracks subform to add details
about each album, CD, or tape to your
database.

Want to track additional details about artists and music categories?
Use the Artists and Music Categories forms.

Find the Selections by Your Favorite Artist

In the mood to hear something by your favorite artist? Quickly search your database for a list of that artist's selections by filtering with the Albums form.

From the Music Collection Switchboard, click Enter/View Albums. Click the Filter By Form button, and then choose the details you want to search for.

 For Help, double-click.
In the Microsoft Access online index look up:
Filter By Form

Filter By Form button

Choose your favorite artist ... ┐ ┌ ... and the music category ...

... and then click the Apply Filter button to see details about the first album by that artist that Microsoft Access finds.

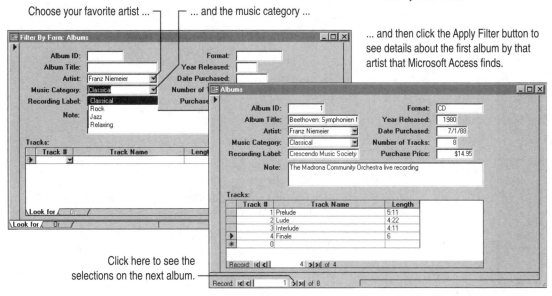

Click here to see the selections on the next album.

 To find all works by a particular artist or all albums in a particular category As you work in the Albums form, select the data in the field that contains the information you want to see, for example, Chopin in the Artist field, and then click the Filter By Selection button.

 Filter By Selection button

To find data that meets either of two criteria For example, to find recordings by either Beethoven or Chopin, click the Filter By Form button, click the field that contains the first criterion, click the arrow that appears to the right of the field, and then click the criterion, such as the artist's name. Then, click the Or tab, click the arrow next to the field that contains the second criterion, click the second criterion, and then click the Apply Filter button.

 Filter By Form button

 Apply Filter button

To see all records after filtering Click the Remove Filter button.

 Remove Filter button

Next Steps

To	Click
Print a list of CDs or of titles on other formats	Preview Reports on the Music Collection Switchboard

Create a Thesis or Dissertation

Tools and Tips for Academics—or Anyone Who's Writing a Long, Complex Document

Word provides built-in tools to help you design, set up, and complete a master's thesis, doctoral dissertation, or other academic paper or report. Word sets up a "skeleton" thesis for you to fill in, and includes time-saving tools for adding illustrations and captions, inserting footnotes and endnotes, and compiling a list of illustrations, an index, and a table of contents. All you need to do is focus on what you know best—researching and writing.

Key Features

Thesis Template

Footnotes and Endnotes

Index

Table of Contents

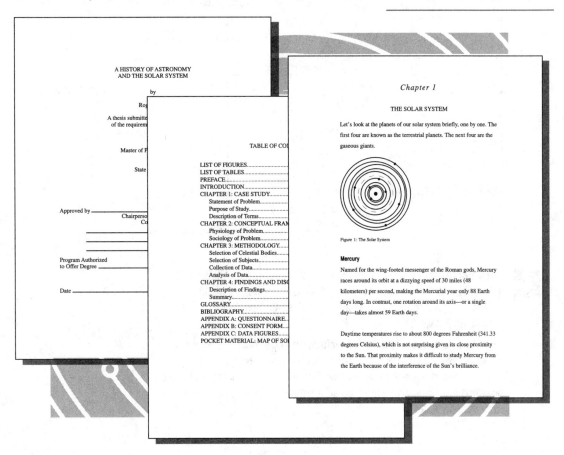

A HISTORY OF ASTRONOMY
AND THE SOLAR SYSTEM

by

Rog

A thesis submitte
of the requirem

Master of P

State

Approved by

Chairperso
Co

Program Authorized
to Offer Degree

Date

Chapter 1

THE SOLAR SYSTEM

Let's look at the planets of our solar system briefly, one by one. The first four are known as the terrestrial planets. The next four are the gaseous giants.

Figure 1: The Solar System

Mercury

Named for the wing-footed messenger of the Roman gods, Mercury races around its orbit at a dizzying speed of 30 miles (48 kilometers) per second, making the Mercurial year only 88 Earth days long. In contrast, one rotation around its axis—or a single day—takes almost 59 Earth days.

Daytime temperatures rise to about 800 degrees Fahrenheit (341.33 degrees Celsius), which is not surprising given its close proximity to the Sun. That proximity makes it difficult to study Mercury from the Earth because of the interference of the Sun's brilliance.

In this topic, the term "thesis" Refers to any academic paper.

Use the Thesis Template to Get Started

To start a new thesis, click New (File menu), click the Publications tab, and then double-click the Thesis template.

The template sets up a "skeleton" thesis, with placeholders for the title page, abstract, acknowledgments, glossary, chapters, bibliography, and so on. The template also takes care of the thesis layout and design. All you need to do is fill in the content.

For Help, double-click.
In the Word online index look up:
templates
copying text and graphics

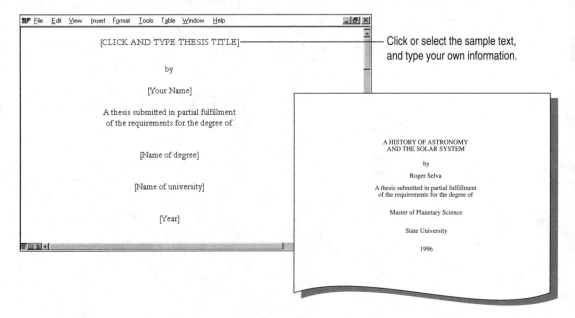

Click or select the sample text, and type your own information.

What *not* to fill in?   Don't fill in the table of contents, list of figures, or index, since Word can automatically generate these items for you. For details, see "Create a Table of Contents," "Illustrate Your Points," and "Create an Index," later in this topic.

Want to add another chapter or include an appendix?   In normal view, select an existing chapter placeholder plus the page break that follows it. Then, copy and paste the chapter placeholder. The placeholder's title and body text are already formatted, so all you need to do is select and type over the sample text.

Use Styles for One-Stop Formatting

To speed up formatting, use the thesis template's built-in *styles*—which let you apply several formats at once. To apply any style, select a paragraph, and then click a style in the Style box.

 For Help, double-click.
In the Word online index look up:
styles

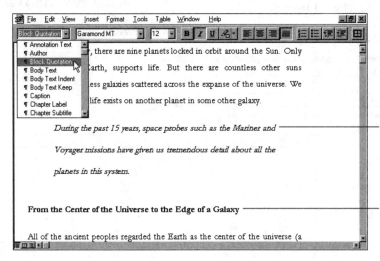

For example, apply the Block Quotation style to in-text quotations ...

... or apply the Heading 1 style to main headings.

Need to find out which built-in styles are available? Click Style Gallery (Format menu), click the thesis template, and then click Style Samples.

Want to modify a built-in style? Select a paragraph and make the formatting changes you want. (For example, to single space block quotations, click Paragraph (Format menu), click the Single Spacing option, and then click OK.) Then, click in the Style box, press ENTER, and then click OK. Word automatically updates all paragraphs that have the style you modified.

? For Help on dialog box options, click this button.

Want to Automatically Format Text?

The AutoFormat feature in Word can work behind the scenes to format text—such as lists or headings—as you type. For example, to create a bulleted or numbered list, type an asterisk (*) or the number **1.**, press SPACEBAR, type the first item, and then press ENTER. To finish the list, press ENTER twice. For details, look up **AutoFormat** in the Word online index.

Illustrate Your Points

Word makes it a snap to add illustrations to your thesis—including maps, photos, charts, diagrams, graphics, drawings, and so on. Once you've inserted the illustrations, you can easily add numbered captions and create a list, or table, of figures.

For Help, double-click.
In the Word online index look up:
pictures, importing and inserting
captions
tables of figures

To insert a picture, click Picture (Insert menu).

To insert a caption, click Caption (Insert menu). You can type an optional description.

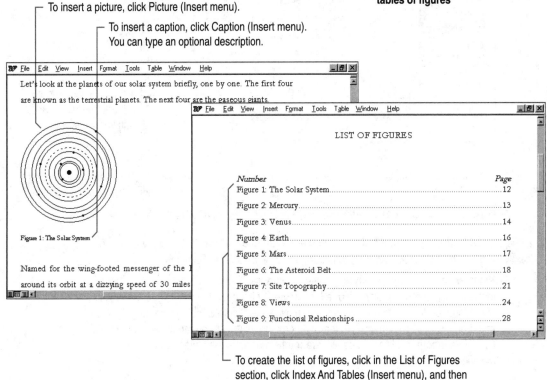

To create the list of figures, click in the List of Figures section, click Index And Tables (Insert menu), and then select the options you want on the Table Of Figures tab.

 Want to automatically add a caption each time you insert an illustration? First, turn on automatic captions: Click Caption (Insert menu), click AutoCaption, select the item you want to caption, select a label and position, and then click OK. Next, insert your illustrations, and watch the captions automatically appear.

Need to update caption numbers? If you've moved or deleted captioned items, update the caption numbers by pressing CTRL+A to select the entire document and then pressing F9.

Need to update the list of illustrations? If you've added or deleted illustrations—or changed the page breaks in the thesis—update the list of illustrations by clicking in the List Of Figures section and pressing F9.

Insert Tables for Facts and Figures

To insert a table, click the Insert Table button, and then drag over the grid to select the number of rows and columns. Then, enter text and format the table as shown in the following illustration.

 For Help, double-click.
In the Word online index look up:
tables

Insert Table button

Type your text in the cells.
Press TAB to jump between cells.

	Distance from Sun (millions of kilometers)	
Planet	Maximum	Minimum
Mercury	69.187	45.052
Venus	107.803	106.194
Earth	151.246	146.419
Mars	249.395	

To make the text single-spaced and aligned on the left, select the table, click Paragraph (Format menu), and select Single Spacing, Left Alignment, and 0 (zero) Spacing After.

Distance from Sun (millions of kilometers)		
Planet	Maximum	Minimum
Mercury	69.187	45.052
Venus	107.803	106.194
Earth	151.246	146.419
Mars	249.395	205.952

To automatically format and resize the table, click in the table, click Table AutoFormat (Table menu), and then select a design.

 Need to create a really wide table? Just position the table sideways on the page. Select the table, click Page Setup (File menu), and then click Landscape Orientation on the Paper Size tab.

Want to add table captions or create a list of tables? See the previous section, "Illustrate Your Points."

Add Equations Such as $y = \sqrt[3]{b - m}\left(c^a + k - u\right)$

Click Object (Insert menu), and then click Microsoft Equation on the Create New tab. For details, look up **Equation Editor** in the Word online index.

Want to add equation captions or create a list of equations? See the previous section, "Illustrate Your Points."

Insert Footnotes or Endnotes

When you insert footnotes or endnotes, Word automatically positions them—don't worry about measuring how much space to leave at the bottom of the page. And Word automatically numbers the notes, so the numbers are always correct even if you add, delete, or move notes around in the document.

For Help, double-click. In the Word online index look up: **footnotes and endnotes**

Click where you want to put the number or symbol.

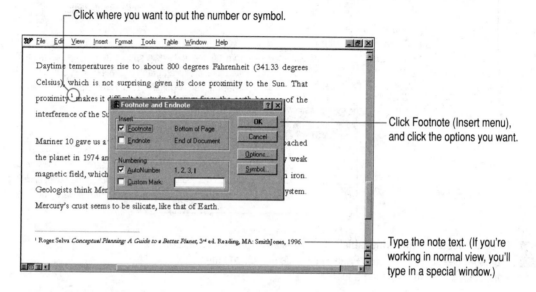

Click Footnote (Insert menu), and click the options you want.

Type the note text. (If you're working in normal view, you'll type in a special window.)

 Want to edit or delete a note?   To edit a note, double-click its number or symbol in the main document; the insertion point jumps to the corresponding note so you can edit it. To delete a note, select and delete its number or symbol in the main document; Word automatically deletes the corresponding note.

Include Short Citations

First, save each short citation—such as "(Selva, 1983)"—as an AutoCorrect entry. Here's how: Type the short citation, select it, click AutoCorrect (Tools menu), type a unique abbreviation—such as **se83**—and then click OK. When you're ready to insert the short citation, type the appropriate AutoCorrect abbreviation, and then type a space or other punctuation.

Create an Index

To create an index, you'll mark the words or phrases you want to include in the index, and then create the finished index. Word gives you plenty of options for customizing the index—for example, create multiple levels of index entries, including "See" cross-references, and choose from several index designs.

 For Help, double-click.
In the Word online index look up:
indexes
XE (Index Entry) fields

Select the text you want to index and press ALT+SHIFT+X.

Edit the entry (if necessary), select any options, and then click the Mark button.

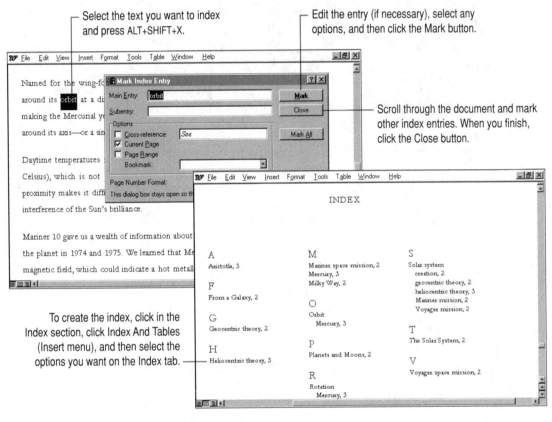

Scroll through the document and mark other index entries. When you finish, click the Close button.

To create the index, click in the Index section, click Index And Tables (Insert menu), and then select the options you want on the Index tab.

 Want to edit the index? When you mark an index entry, it's followed by a *field* that looks something like this: { XE "Callisto" \t "*See* Moons" }. If you don't see any fields, click the Show/Hide ¶ button. To edit an entry, change only the text between the quotation marks. To delete an entry, delete the entire field—including the brackets. Make sure to hide the fields before you create the index; otherwise, page numbers may not be correct.

¶
Show/Hide ¶ button

Need to update the index? If you've added or deleted index entries—or changed the page breaks in the document—update the index by clicking in the Index section and pressing F9.

Create a Table of Contents

To create a table of contents, just tell Word which styles you used for the titles and headings in your thesis. Then, Word can list the corresponding titles and headings (and their page numbers) in the table of contents.

For Help, double-click. In the Word online index look up: **tables of contents**

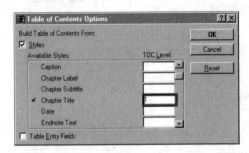

To create the table of contents, click in the Table of Contents section, and then click Index And Tables (Insert menu). On the Table Of Contents tab, click the Options button. Type **1** beside the Chapter Title and Section Label styles. Clear the numbers beside any other styles.

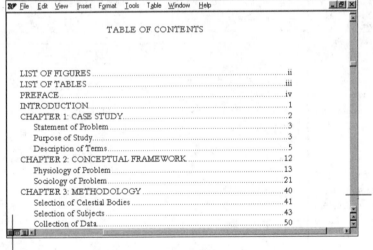

To include chapter numbers and headings in the table of contents, see the following tips.

Click OK twice to see the compiled table of contents.

Why does the table of contents include an entry for the "Table of Contents" title? The "Table of Contents" title has the Section Label style, so Word picks it up along with the other section labels. Here's how to solve this problem: Click in the table of contents, press CTRL+SHIFT+F9 to convert it to normal text, and then delete the "Table of Contents" entry. Or, to permanently omit this entry from the table of contents, change the title's style *before* you create the table of contents: Select the title, select "Section Label" in the Style box, type a new name, and then press ENTER.

Want to include chapter numbers in the table of contents? Just type the appropriate chapter number (for example, "Chapter 1:") in front of each chapter in the table of contents.

Want to include other headings in the table of contents? First, make sure you've applied the built-in heading styles (Heading 1, Heading 2, and so on) to the headings in your thesis. Then, create the table of contents as previously described—however, in the Table Of Contents Options dialog box, type **2** beside Heading 1, type **3** beside Heading 2, and so on.

Need to update the table of contents? If you've added, deleted, or edited titles—or changed the page breaks in the thesis—update the table of contents. If you've deleted the "Table of Contents" entry or added chapter numbers, select all the table of contents entries, and then recreate the table of contents as previously described. If you haven't modified the table of contents, you can quickly update it by clicking in the Table Of Contents section and pressing F9. Make sure that creating the table of contents is the last step in completing your thesis so that it will reflect the correct page numbers for all parts of the thesis.

Track Research Notes in an Access Database

Instead of using index cards, legal pads, or piles of books with dog-eared pages, get organized and store your research notes in a simple database. Then, use your electronic "index cards" to quickly reorganize and retrieve the information. For example, you can view the information in a separate report, or insert it directly into your thesis. For details, look up **creating a database** in the Microsoft Access online index.

Create a Printed or Online Questionnaire

If you plan to interview your research subjects, solicit feedback, or create a consent form, you can create a printed or online questionnaire (or other form) to capture the information.

What are the advantages of using an online questionnaire? You don't need to retype the information! For example, store an online questionnaire on your laptop computer when you conduct field research, or email the questionnaire to subjects in distant locations. Online

questionnaires can contain advanced features such as text entry fields, check boxes, and drop-down lists. And, you can save the information to a delimited text file—a file in which a special character separates different kinds of information—so you can export it to a spreadsheet or database for easy retrieval or further analysis.

For details, see "Create a Printed or Online Form in Word," page 191.

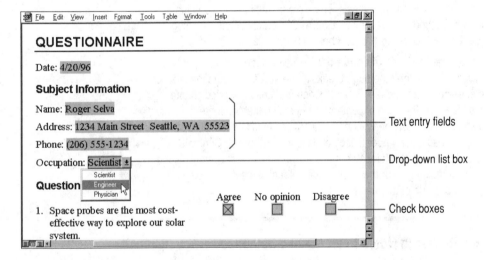

Next Steps

To	See
Modify the thesis formatting—such as fonts, line spacing, margins, etc.	"Make Your Word Document Look Great," page 161
Include a chart or graph in your thesis	"Add a Chart to a Document or Presentation," page 223
Store and track research notes	**databases, creating** in the Microsoft Access online index
Create a printed or online questionnaire	"Create a Printed or Online Form in Word," page 191
Organize your daily tasks and activities	"Keep a To Do List," page 317
Schedule appointments with advisors, research subjects, etc.	"Schedule an Appointment," page 314
Have a colleague review your work in progress	"Share Documents Electronically," page 326, or "Have Your Team Review a Word Document," page 333

PART 16

Automate and Program Office

Delegate Your Most Tedious Work

Contents

Automate Repetitive Tasks in Word

Let's say you want to reformat the tables in several hundred documents, and you want all tables to have the same layout, although they will differ in data. You think to yourself, "There must be a way to automate this task with Word." In fact, there is. You can create a *macro* that can make this mundane task easy to accomplish.

To create a macro, you use the Macro Recorder and record actions so that you can have Word perform the task again with the click of a button. For example, in each successive document, you can run a formatting macro and Word will repeat all the formatting actions you recorded.

Key Features

AutoFormat

Macros

Let Word perform your repetitive tasks for you.

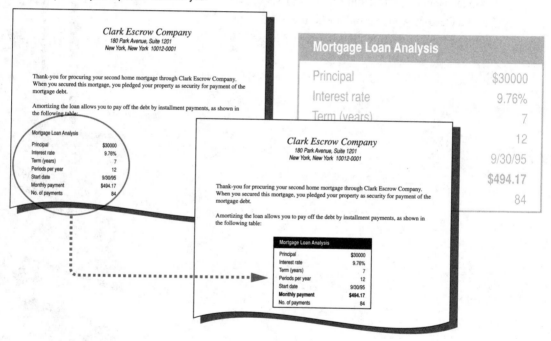

Record the Macro

Make sure the insertion point is where you want it to be, such as within a table. Then, to start the Macro Recorder, click Macro (Tools menu), and click the Record button. Once you click OK in the Record Macro dialog box, Word is in "record mode" and any actions you take are recorded in a macro. For example, if you want to record formatting a table, you would next choose the sequence of commands necessary to format the table. For details, look up **tables, formatting** in the Word online index.

For Help, double-click.
In the Word online index look up:
macros, recording
tables, formatting

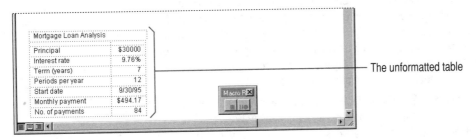

The unformatted table

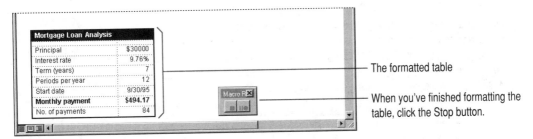

The formatted table

When you've finished formatting the table, click the Stop button.

 A note about the macro recorder When the macro recorder is on, you can use the mouse to choose commands or click the scroll bar, but you can't use the mouse to move the insertion point or select text in your document. Use your keyboard instead.

Try Out Your Macro

Open a new document with a table you need to format. Place your insertion point on the first cell that will be formatted by the macro. Click Macro (Tools menu), choose the macro you recorded, and click the Run button. In a flash, all the steps you recorded are executed and the table is formatted.

Now save the document, close it, and open up a new document. You're ready to run the macro again.

For Help, double-click.
In the Word online index look up:
macros, running

WordBasic, the language of macros   Macros are recorded in WordBasic language. Although you can always create new macros by simply recording your actions, with a little study, you can also learn how to write macros and customize them to increase their usefulness. For example, by writing a few lines of WordBasic, you could modify the macro recorded earlier to open each file with a table and close it after formatting.

For information on WordBasic, look up **WordBasic** in the Word online index. For more in-depth information, see the *Microsoft Word Developer's Kit*, available anywhere computer books are sold or directly through Microsoft Press.

Insert the same text quickly   Use AutoText to store text and graphics, along with any formatting they have, so that you don't need to type or create them again. Click AutoText (Edit menu) to insert an AutoText entry as many times and in as many documents as you want. For details, look up **AutoText** in the Microsoft Word online index.

To access reference Help for WordBasic   You need to install the WordBasic Help file. For details about installing additional Word components, see "Install and Start Microsoft Office," page 25. Once you've installed WordBasic Help, click Help Topics (Help menu), click the Contents tab, and then double-click WordBasic Reference.

More Power: Assigning a Macro to a Button

To make the new macro easily accessible, you can assign the macro to a new button on a toolbar. Click Customize (Tools menu). Select the Macros category and the macro you recorded. Drag the macro to the toolbar you want to add it to.

Drag the macro onto any active toolbar.

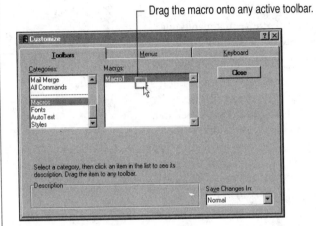

Select a custom button image, and click the Assign button. Your macro will be accessible instantly from the toolbar where you placed the button.

For details, look up **macros, assigning** in the Word online index.

Automate Repetitive Tasks in Microsoft Excel

Let's say you have a task in Microsoft Excel that you need to perform often, for example, a list of data in which you want to call out certain numbers. The list is very long, and it would be tedious to search each cell and manually format only those that meet your criteria. A macro—a program you write or record that stores instructions for Microsoft Excel—can do that work for you.

You could write a macro from scratch to change cell color but it's often easier to use the Macro Recorder. With the Macro Recorder turned on, any actions you take in Microsoft Excel are stored in a macro. After recording, you can go back and edit or add to the macro.

Key Features

  Macros

Visual Basic for Applications

You're repeatedly asked to format a list of data so that certain numbers stand out.

	A	B	C	D	E
1	City	Date	Fee	Attendance	Books Sold
2	Philadelphia	1/31/95	$ 1,965	145	31
3	Providence	2/2/95	$ 1,964	111	73
4	Detroit	2/14/95	$ 1,881	376	
5	Atlanta	2/8/95	$ 1,880	149	
6	Charleston	1/29/95	$ 1,822	328	
7	Topeka	2/20/95	$ 1,775	66	
8	Vancouver, B.C.	3/13/95	$ 1,740	69	
9	Washington, D.C.	1/27/95	$ 1,724	499	
10	Boise	3/17/95	$ 1,706	118	
11	Denver	3/19/95	$ 1,558	436	
12	Albuquerque	3/29/95	$ 1,552	206	
13	Chicago	2/12/95	$ 1,544	222	
14	Dallas	2/24/95	$ 1,497	444	
15	Santa Fe	3/27/95	$ 1,429	440	
16	Houston	2/25/95	$ 1,267	238	
17	New Orleans	3/31/95	$ 1,233	415	

Book tour statistics

	A	B	C	D	E
1	City	Date	Fee	Attendance	Books Sold
2	Philadelphia	1/31/95	$ 1,965	145	31
3	Providence	2/2/95	$ 1,964	111	73
4	Detroit	2/14/95	$ 1,881	376	58
5	Atlanta	2/8/95	$ 1,880	149	95
6	Charleston	1/29/95	$ 1,822	328	124
7	Topeka	2/20/95	$ 1,775	66	12
8	Vancouver, B.C.	3/13/95	$ 1,740	69	59
9	Washington, D.C.	1/27/95	$ 1,724	499	151
10	Boise	3/17/95	$ 1,706	118	84
11	Denver	3/19/95	$ 1,558	436	38
12	Albuquerque	3/29/95	$ 1,552	206	62
13	Chicago	2/12/95	$ 1,544	222	60
14	Dallas	2/24/95	$ 1,497	444	72
15	Santa Fe	3/27/95	$ 1,429	440	154
16	Houston	2/25/95	$ 1,267	238	35
17	New Orleans	3/31/95	$ 1,233	415	59

Book tour statistics   Module1

Record a Macro

To turn on the Macro Recorder, click Record Macro (Tools menu), and then click Record New Macro. A module sheet is created in your workbook, and any actions you take in Microsoft Excel are now stored in the macro named "Macro1" on the Module1 sheet. You can switch to this sheet any time by clicking on the Module1 tab at the end of the workbook.

 For Help, double-click. In the Microsoft Excel online index look up: **macros, recording**

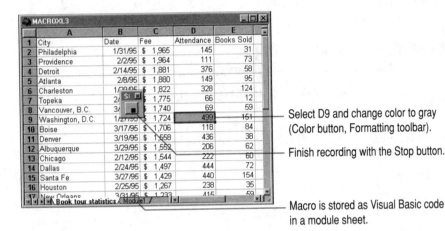

Select D9 and change color to gray (Color button, Formatting toolbar).

Finish recording with the Stop button.

Macro is stored as Visual Basic code in a module sheet.

Where is my macro? When you run the Macro Recorder, Microsoft Excel automatically inserts a module sheet in your workbook and stores your macro on it in Visual Basic for applications. To see the macro, click the module tab.

To see online Help for Visual Basic You must install the Visual Basic Help file. For details about installing additional components, see "Install and Start Microsoft Office," page 25. To see Visual Basic Help after installation, click Help Topics (Help menu), click the Contents tab, then double-click Getting Started with Visual Basic.

If you want to choose manually which cell is formatted Make sure you select the cell you want formatted before you start the Macro Recorder. Then, later you can run the macro on any cell you choose.

Modify Your Macro to Handle the Entire Task

The macro is recorded in Visual Basic code, but it only reformats cell D9. If you want to format more cells automatically, such as all cells with a value greater than 400, you will need to modify the Visual Basic code. Do this by clicking the Module1 tab and adding Do...Loop and If...Then statements.

For Help, double-click. In the Microsoft Excel online index look up: **macros, editing**

Macro 1 as originally recorded

This is the name of the macro, Macro1.

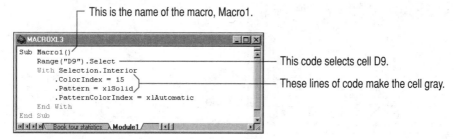

This code selects cell D9.

These lines of code make the cell gray.

Macro 1 after modifications

These lines select the sheet and cell to start the data search.

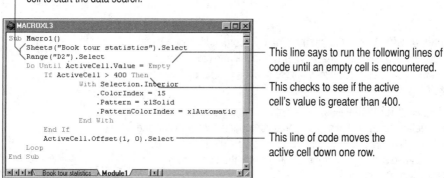

This line says to run the following lines of code until an empty cell is encountered.

This checks to see if the active cell's value is greater than 400.

This line of code moves the active cell down one row.

 You can get help at any point To get Help on a Visual Basic keyword, such as Select or ActiveCell, place the cursor in the keyword and press F1.

To learn how to write code See the *Microsoft Excel/Visual Basic for Windows 95 Programmer's Guide*, available wherever computer books are sold or directly from Microsoft Press. For introductory information, click Help Topics (Help menu), click the Contents tab, then double-click Getting Started with Visual Basic.

Running Your Macro

With the modifications made, Macro1 will now search through all the cells of a column of numbers and change to gray the color of those cells containing a value greater than 400. To run this macro, switch to the worksheet, click Macro (Tools menu), select the Macro1 macro, and click Run.

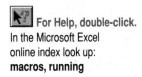

For Help, double-click. In the Microsoft Excel online index look up: **macros, running**

	A	B	C	D	E
19	Salt Lake City	3/21/95	$ 1,190	275	37
20	New York	1/23/95	$ 1,180	205	147
21	Cleveland	2/10/95	$ 1,073	128	32
22	Anchorage	3/15/95	$ 1,038	179	98
23	Phoenix	3/23/95	$ 955	87	38
24	Los Angeles	3/5/95	$ 941	265	47
25	Seattle	3/11/95	$ 936	279	109
26	St. Louis	2/18/95	$ 920	354	19
27	Memphis	2/6/95	$ 910	493	45
28	San Francisco	3/7/95	$ 904	171	145
29	Boston	1/25/95	$ 821	385	146
30	Portland	3/9/95	$ 781	485	33
31	Indianapolis	2/22/95	$ 776	186	64
32	Minneapolis	2/16/95	$ 771	445	18
33	Miami	2/4/95	$ 757	221	41
34					

Book tour statistics / Module1

The macro will stop when it reaches the first empy cell in column D.

Making Your Macro Accessible

You can make your macro more accessible to your coworkers by assigning it to a new button on a toolbar. Then, once you've opened the worksheet with data to be formatted, all you have to do is click the button to run the macro.

For details, look up **macros, assigning** in the Microsoft Excel online index.

Extending the Usefulness of This Macro

It would be easy to modify Macro1 to make it even more useful. For example, if you want to identify the cells in column E with fewer than

50 books sold, you would make the following changes so that all cells with a value of less than 50 will be formatted as yellow.

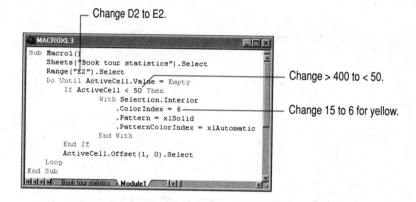

Change D2 to E2.

```
MACROXL3                                    _ □ ×
Sub Macro1()
    Sheets("Book tour statistics").Select
    Range("E2").Select
    Do Until ActiveCell.Value = Empty          Change > 400 to < 50.
        If ActiveCell < 50 Then
            With Selection.Interior
                .ColorIndex = 6                 Change 15 to 6 for yellow.
                .Pattern = xlSolid
                .PatternColorIndex = xlAutomatic
            End With
        End If
        ActiveCell.Offset(1, 0).Select
    Loop
End Sub
  Book tour statistics \ Module1
```

Next Steps

To	See
Learn more about Microsoft Excel Visual Basic for applications	**Getting Started with Visual Basic** in the Microsoft Excel online Help Contents
	Sample.xls in the Examples Folder of the Microsoft Excel Program directory

Create a Custom Application in Microsoft Excel

Microsoft Excel is a powerful platform for developing custom applications. With Visual Basic for applications and the Microsoft Excel extensive object library, you can make your workbook easy to use, even for someone new to Microsoft Excel. Specify a starting point with a *startup sheet*. Add buttons, drop-down boxes, and other *controls* to automate complex tasks such as data analysis.

Key Features

Objects

Microsoft Visual Basic for applications

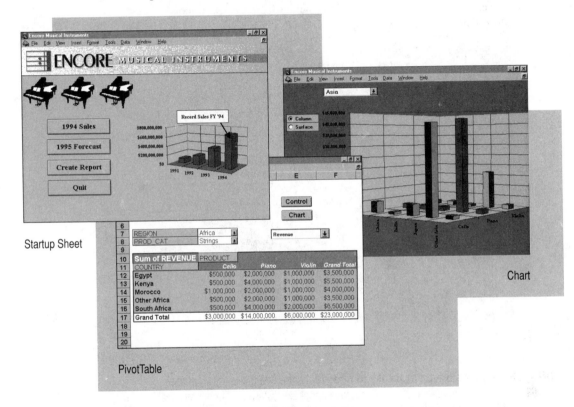

Startup Sheet

PivotTable

Chart

Important This topic provides some examples of what you can do to create an application. For details on writing code in Visual Basic or on using the Microsoft Excel object library, see Visual Basic Help. For details on installing Visual Basic Help if you have not already done so, see "Install and Start Microsoft Office," page 25. To access Visual Basic Help, click Help Topics (Help menu), click the Contents tab, and then double-click Getting Started with Visual Basic.

Create a Startup Sheet

Create a *startup sheet* to provide a clear starting point for those using your application. Add buttons that, when clicked, display specific sheets, generate reports automatically, or close the application. Spruce up the opening sheet with pictures imported from drawing programs such as Microsoft Paintbrush, or embed other objects such as charts.

Use the Create Button button on the Forms toolbar or Drawing toolbar to add buttons to the Startup sheet. You make the buttons "active" by attaching macros you have written or recorded in Visual Basic. For more information, see "Assign a Macro to a Button or Other Control," later in this topic.

For Help, double-click. In the Microsoft Excel online index look up:
creating, controls
graphic objects in Excel

Create Button button

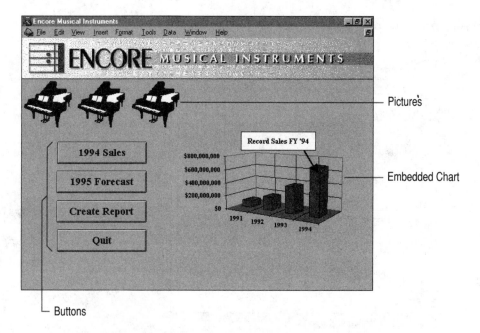

Pictures

Embedded Chart

Buttons

 Make your startup sheet easy to find Make the first tab in the workbook the startup sheet, and give it an obvious name like "Startup." Then, save the workbook with this first sheet displayed so that it will be the first thing users see when they open the workbook. For information on moving and naming worksheet tabs, look up **tabs (sheet)** in the Microsoft Excel online index.

Protecting your startup sheet You can protect your startup sheet and other forms in your custom application from accidental data changes, button realignment, and so on. For details, look up **protecting** in the Microsoft Excel online index.

Make Using a PivotTable Easy

A PivotTable provides a powerful means to analyze and summarize large amounts of data. Creating and using a PivotTable isn't always easy, however. With the addition of a drop-down box and a few buttons, you can automate changing the view on data or quickly display another sheet, such as a chart sheet created from the PivotTable.

To insert a drop-down box, or any other control, use the Forms toolbar. Click Toolbars (View menu). Once you've added the drop-down box, you can attach a Visual Basic macro. For general information on attaching a macro to a control, see "Assign a Macro to a Button or Other Control," later in this topic.

 For Help, double-click.
In the Microsoft Excel online index look up:
**PivotTables
creating, controls**

Drop-Down button

Page fields can be added automatically when you create the PivotTable. ⌐

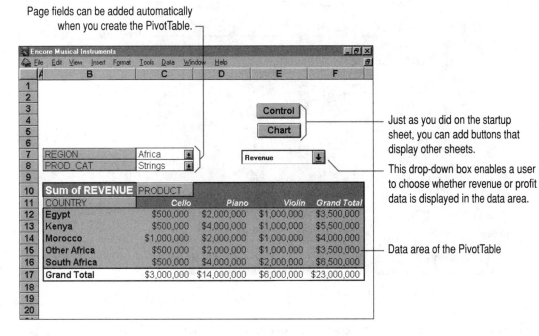

Just as you did on the startup sheet, you can add buttons that display other sheets.

This drop-down box enables a user to choose whether revenue or profit data is displayed in the data area.

Data area of the PivotTable

 Never created a PivotTable before? Create a PivotTable by using the PivotTable Wizard. For an example of how to create a PivotTable, see "Create a Sales Summary," page 446. For details about creating PivotTables and using page fields, look up **PivotTables** and **page fields** in the Microsoft Excel online index.

Format a PivotTable When you select the AutoFormat Table option in the PivotTable Wizard, Microsoft Excel formats your PivotTable for you. You can select a different format after the PivotTable is created. For details, look up **PivotTables, formatting** in the Microsoft Excel online index.

Automate Content and Format Changes in a Chart

You can customize your chart so that users have easy control over the display of data. Because a chart is already linked to its source data, all you have to do to quickly change how data is displayed in a chart is to automate changing the source data.

For example, on a chart created from a PivotTable, you can add a drop-down box that allows users to change which page is displayed on the PivotTable. This changes what section of data is displayed in the chart. You can also add option buttons that quickly change the chart format.

For Help, double-click. In the Microsoft Excel online index look up: **charts in Excel, creating**

Option buttons change the chart type to one of two views.

Drop-down box changes the Region page field on the PivotTable. Chart displays the selected region.

Jumps back to PivotTable sheet.

 Formatting a chart   Format your chart to make it easier to read. The quickest and easiest method is to apply a built-in or custom autoformat to the chart. You can also select the chart area or plot area and then globally apply colors, patterns, borders, and text fonts. For more information, see "Create a Chart from Worksheet Data," page 216 and "Customize the Look of a Chart," page 236.

Assign a Macro to a Button or Other Control

You specify what happens when a user clicks a control you've added by assigning a *macro* to it. A macro is a sequence of code created in Visual Basic that tells Microsoft Excel what to do. You can write a macro from scratch, or you can record it by clicking Record Macro (Tools menu). For an introduction to using the Macro Recorder and to editing Visual Basic code, see "Automate Repetitive Tasks in Microsoft Excel," page 540.

Once it's written or recorded, assign the macro to the control. Hold down the CTRL key as you select the control, and then click Assign Macro (Tools menu). If you are creating a button, you have the option of recording or assigning a macro as you add the button to your worksheet by using the Assign Macro dialog box, which appears when you add the button.

For Help, double-click.

In the Microsoft Excel online index look up:
macros, assigning
creating controls

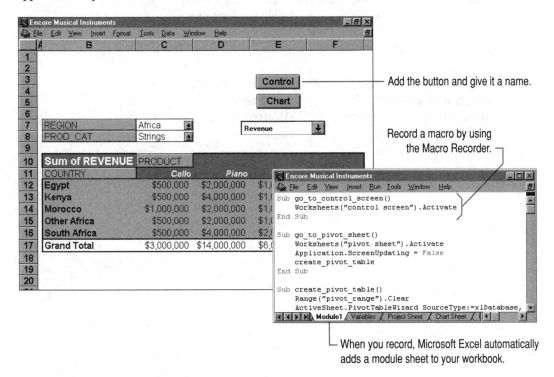

Add the button and give it a name.

Record a macro by using the Macro Recorder.

When you record, Microsoft Excel automatically adds a module sheet to your workbook.

Getting help on Visual Basic   Writing a macro can be as easy as turning on the Macro Recorder and making a few mouse clicks, or it may require significant research and writing time. For details on getting more information about Visual Basic, see "Getting to Know Visual Basic," later in this topic.

Protect your macro from being changed   Hide the module sheet by clicking Hide (Edit menu). If you want to protect the sheet with a password as well, do it first by clicking Protection (Tools menu) For details, look up **hiding sheets** and **protecting** in the Microsoft Excel online index.

Communicate with Other Applications at the Click of a Button

You can program buttons to do some fairly sophisticated tasks. Consider the "Create Report" button on the startup sheet. A click of this button opens Word and creates a report using data from the PivotTable sheet. For more information on controlling and communicating with other applications, look up **communicating with other applications** in the Microsoft Excel online index.

Note   You must have Visual Basic Help installed to see Visual Basic subjects in the online index. For information about installing additional components, see "Install and Start Microsoft Office," page 25.

Other Ways to Automate Microsoft Excel

Microsoft Excel has other controls you can add to create a custom application. For example, you can create a menu, a button on a toolbar, a control on a worksheet, or a custom dialog box.

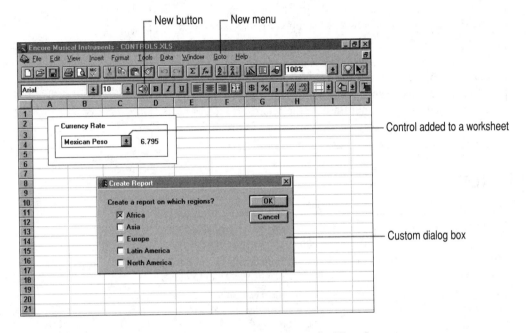

New button — New menu

Control added to a worksheet

Custom dialog box

- For details on creating menus, look up **custom menus in Visual Basic, creating** in the Microsoft Excel online index.

- For details on adding a new button to a toolbar, look up **new buttons (toolbar)** in the Microsoft Excel online index.

- For details on creating controls on a worksheet, look up **creating controls** in the Microsoft Excel online index.

- For details on creating custom dialog boxes, look up **creating dialog boxes** in the Microsoft Excel online index.

 To see Visual Basic subjects in the online index You must install Visual Basic Help. For information about installing additional components, see "Install and Start Microsoft Office," page 25

> **Getting to Know Visual Basic**   Visual Basic and the Microsoft
> Excel object library provide a seemingly infinite array of ways
> to automate tasks in Microsoft Excel. If you're new to Visual
> Basic, you will probably find helpful an introductory book
> such as *Microsoft Excel Visual Basic for Applications
> Step-by-Step*, available wherever computer books are sold or
> directly from Microsoft Press.
>
> Microsoft Excel itself provides a comprehensive online
> reference for the objects Microsoft Excel supports. For
> information on accessing and using this information, look up
> Getting Started with Visual Basic in the Microsoft Excel
> online Help Contents.

Next Steps

For information on	See
Creating custom applications	*Developing Microsoft Excel 5 Solutions*, Microsoft Press
Microsoft Excel Visual Basic for applications	Getting Started with Visual Basic in the Microsoft Excel Help Contents
	Microsoft Excel/Visual Basic for Windows 95 Step-by-Step, Microsoft Press
	Microsoft Excel/Visual Basic for Windows 95 Programmer's Guide, Microsoft Press
	Sample.xls in the Examples Folder of the Microsoft Excel Program directory

Automate Repetitive Tasks in Microsoft Access

Put Macros and Visual Basic for Applications to Work in Your Forms

When you set up a database, you'll want it to be as easy to use as possible, especially when it comes to repetitive tasks like data entry. With Microsoft Access, it's easy to automate tasks like changing values in one field when the value in another changes or printing reports by creating macros or writing Visual Basic procedures.

Key Features

Macros

Command Button Wizard

Visual Basic

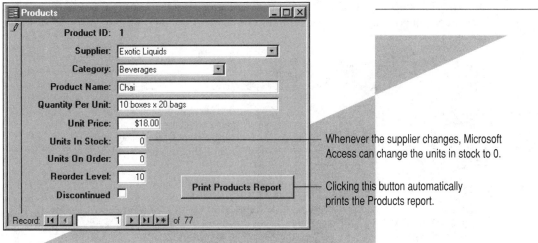

Whenever the supplier changes, Microsoft Access can change the units in stock to 0.

Clicking this button automatically prints the Products report.

To complete the steps in this topic   You need to have Microsoft Office Professional or an individual copy of Microsoft Access installed. You also need a Products form and a report. For details, see "Create a Great Looking Product Form," page 400, and "Create and Enhance an Inventory Report," page 407. However, you can use the steps in this topic to add command buttons to any form and to create any macro.

Create a Macro to Change a Field's Value

When you find yourself repeating the same tasks, such as changing the number in the Units In Stock box to 0 every time you change suppliers for a product, create a macro to change the number for you.

Your action, changing the supplier, causes an *event* to occur (in macro language, an AfterUpdate event). By creating a macro, you can tell Microsoft Access which *action* you want it to take when this event occurs.

Creating a macro is easy with the Macro Builder. Open the form in Design view by clicking the Database Window button, clicking the Forms tab, clicking the Products form, and then clicking Design. Click the SupplierID text box, click the Properties button, and then click the Event tab.

 For Help, double-click.
In the Microsoft Access online index look up:
macros, defined
macros, creating
events, described

Database Window
button

Properties
button

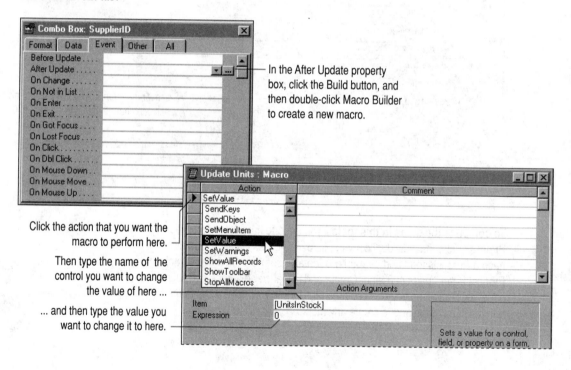

In the After Update property box, click the Build button, and then double-click Macro Builder to create a new macro.

Click the action that you want the macro to perform here.

Then type the name of the control you want to change the value of here ...

... and then type the value you want to change it to here.

Click the Save button to save the macro Microsoft Access runs the macro whenever the supplier changes.

Save button

Respond to other common events You can create macros that tell Microsoft Access what to do when a user opens a form (the Open event), moves from one record to another (the Current event), or clicks a specific button (the Click event), among other things. For details, look up **events, described** in the Microsoft Access online index.

What other actions can a macro perform? A macro can display a message to the user (the MsgBox action), perform a Microsoft Access menu command (the DoMenuItem action), or simulate typing on the keyboard (the SendKeys action), among other actions. For details on any macro action you see in the Macro window, click the action and press F1.

Want a macro to perform a series of actions in response to a single event? Select each action you want to perform in a separate row of the Macro window. Microsoft Access performs the actions row by row.

Add a Command Button That Prints a Report

Do you frequently print a report after updating your database? Add a button to your form that automatically prints the report.

Creating buttons that perform actions is easy with the Command Button Wizard. If you haven't opened the Products form in Design view, do so. In the toolbox, click the Command Button tool, and if the Control Wizards tool isn't selected, click it, too. Click where you want to put the button, and then follow the wizard's instructions.

Command
Button tool

Control
Wizards tool

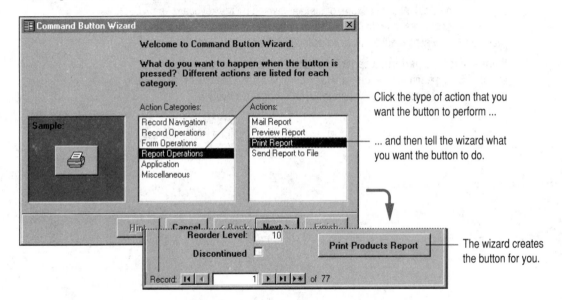

Click the type of action that you want the button to perform ...

... and then tell the wizard what you want the button to do.

The wizard creates the button for you.

 Use the Command Button Wizard to create buttons that perform many other actions   Buttons can automatically open other forms, move between records, and add or delete records, among other things. For details, look up **command buttons, creating** in the Microsoft Access online index.

Programming in Visual Basic

When the Command Button Wizard creates a button, it actually writes a Visual Basic *event procedure* to perform the action you want. You can see the event procedure for the Print Products Report button by opening the button's property sheet, selecting the OnClick property, and then clicking the Build button.

Using the Visual Basic programming language, you can edit or add to the instructions the Command Button Wizard creates. Or, you can write your own event procedures to customize Microsoft Access even further. For details, look up **event procedures** in the Microsoft Access online index.

The Module window shows the Visual Basic code for the active form.

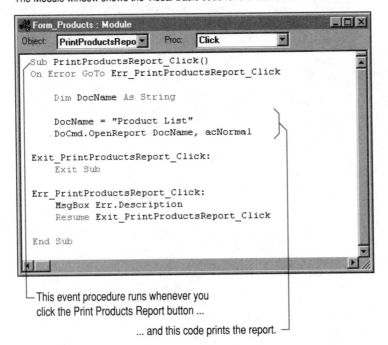

```
Sub PrintProductsReport_Click()
On Error GoTo Err_PrintProductsReport_Click

    Dim DocName As String

    DocName = "Product List"
    DoCmd.OpenReport DocName, acNormal

Exit_PrintProductsReport_Click:
    Exit Sub

Err_PrintProductsReport_Click:
    MsgBox Err.Description
    Resume Exit_PrintProductsReport_Click

End Sub
```

This event procedure runs whenever you click the Print Products Report button ...

... and this code prints the report.

Next Steps

To	See
See examples of how to use macros to automate work in forms and reports	The Northwind sample database, which Setup installs with Microsoft Access
Learn Visual Basic programming and read about creating custom database applications using Microsoft Access	*Building Applications with Microsoft Access for Windows 95*, available directly from Microsoft using the order form provided with Microsoft Office

Accessibility for People with Disabilities

Microsoft is committed to making its products and services easier for everyone to use. This appendix provides information about the following features, products, and services that make Microsoft Windows, Microsoft Windows NT, and Microsoft Office applications more accessible for people with disabilities:

- Microsoft Office applications' accessibility

- Microsoft services for people who are deaf or hard-of-hearing

- Access Pack for Microsoft Windows NT, a software utility that makes using Windows NT easier for people with motion or hearing disabilities

- Keyboard layouts designed for people who type with one hand or a wand

- Microsoft software documentation on audiocassette, floppy disk, or compact disc (CD)

- Third-party utilities to enhance accessibility

- Hints for customizing Microsoft Windows or Microsoft Windows NT

- Other products and services for people with disabilities

Note The information in this section applies only to users who purchased Microsoft products in the United States. If you purchased Windows or Windows NT outside the United States, your package contains a subsidiary information card listing Microsoft support services telephone numbers and addresses. You can contact your subsidiary to find out whether the types of products and services described in this appendix are available in your area.

Microsoft Office Applications' Accessibility

In addition to Microsoft Windows and Microsoft Windows NT accessibility products and services, several features of Microsoft Office applications make them more accessible for people with disabilities. For more information, look up **accessibility** in the Microsoft Excel, Word, PowerPoint, or Microsoft Access online index.

Microsoft Services for People Who Are Deaf or Hard-of-Hearing

Through a text telephone (TT/TDD) service, Microsoft provides people who are deaf or hard-of-hearing with complete access to Microsoft product and customer services.

You can contact Microsoft Sales Information Center on a text telephone by dialing (800) 892-5234 between 6:30 A.M. and 5:30 P.M. Pacific time. For technical assistance in the United States, you can contact Microsoft Support Network on a text telephone at (206) 635-4948 between 6:00 A.M. and 6:00 P.M. Pacific time, Monday through Friday, excluding holidays. In Canada, dial (905) 568-9641 between 8:00 A.M. and 8:00 P.M. Eastern time, Monday through Friday, excluding holidays. Microsoft support services are subject to Microsoft prices, terms, and conditions in place at the time the service is used.

Access Pack for Microsoft Windows NT

Microsoft distributes an Access Pack for Microsoft Windows NT, which provides people who have motion or hearing disabilities with better access to computers running Windows NT. (If you are running Microsoft Windows 95, these same Access Pack features are already built in. For more information, look up **accessibility** in the Microsoft Windows 95 online index.) The Microsoft Windows NT Access Pack contains several features that:

- Allow single-finger typing of SHIFT, CTRL, and ALT key combinations.

- Ignore accidental keystrokes.

- Adjust the rate at which a character is repeated when you hold down a key, or turn off character repeating entirely.

- Prevent typing extra characters if you unintentionally press a key more than once.

- Enable you to control the mouse cursor by using the keyboard.

- Enable you to control the computer keyboard and mouse by using an alternative input device.

- Provide a visual cue when the computer beeps or makes other sounds.

Access Pack for Microsoft Windows NT is included in the Microsoft Application Note WNO789. If you have a modem, you can download Wno789.exe, which is a self-extracting archive file, from the following network services:

- CompuServe®

- GEnie™

- Microsoft OnLine

- Microsoft Download Service (MSDL), which you can reach by calling (206) 936-6735 any time except between 1:00 A.M. and 2:30 A.M. Pacific time. To reach MSDL, use the following communications settings:

For this setting	Specify
Baud rate	1200, 2400, 9600, or 14400
Parity	None
Data bits	8
Stop bits	1

- Various user-group bulletin boards (such as the bulletin-board services on the Association of PC User Groups network)

- In /SOFTLIB/MSLFILES on the Internet servers FTP.MICROSOFT.COM and WWW.MICROSOFT.COM

People within the United States who do not have a modem can order the Access Packs on disk by calling Microsoft Sales Information Center at (800) 426-9400 (voice) or (800) 892-5234 (text telephone). In Canada, they can call (905) 568-3503 or (905) 568-9641 (text telephone).

Keyboard Layouts for Single-Handed Users

Microsoft distributes Dvorak keyboard layouts that make the most frequently typed characters on a keyboard more accessible to people who have difficulty using the standard "QWERTY" layout. There are three Dvorak layouts: one for two-handed users, one for people who type with their left hand only, and one for people who type with their right hand only. The left-handed or right-handed keyboard layouts also can be used by people who type with a single finger or a wand. Users do not need to purchase any special equipment to use these features.

Microsoft Windows and Microsoft Windows NT already support the two-handed Dvorak layout, which can be useful for coping with or avoiding types of repetitive-motion injuries associated with typing. To get this layout, choose the Regional Settings or International option from the Windows Control Panel. The two layouts for people who type with one hand are distributed as Microsoft Application Note GA0650. This application note is also contained in file Ga0650.exe on most network services and on the Microsoft Download Service. For instructions on obtaining this application note, see the preceding section, "Access Pack for Microsoft Windows NT."

Microsoft Documentation in Alternative Formats

People who have difficulty reading or handling printed documentation may obtain many Microsoft publications from Recording for the Blind, Inc. Recording for the Blind distributes these documents to registered, eligible members of their distribution service, either on audiocassettes or on floppy disks. The Recording for the Blind collection contains more than 80,000 titles, including Microsoft product documentation and books from Microsoft Press. Contact Recording for the Blind at the following address or phone numbers for information on eligibility and availability of Microsoft product documentation and books from Microsoft Press:

Recording for the Blind, Inc.   Phone: (609) 452-0606
20 Roszel Road   Fax: (609) 987-8116
Princeton, NJ 08540

Third-Party Utilities to Enhance Accessibility

A wide variety of third-party hardware and software products are available to make personal computers easier to use for people with disabilities. Among the different types of products available for the MS-DOS, Microsoft Windows, and Microsoft Windows NT operating systems are:

- Programs that enlarge or alter the color of information on the screen for people with visual impairments.

- Programs that describe information on the screen in braille or synthesized speech for people who are blind or have difficulty reading.

- Hardware and software utilities that modify the behavior of the mouse and keyboard.

- Programs that enable users to "type" using a mouse or their voice.

- Word or phrase prediction software that allows the user to type more quickly and with fewer keystrokes.

- Alternative input devices, such as single switch or puff-and-sip devices, for those who cannot use a mouse or a keyboard.

For more information on obtaining third-party utilities, see "Getting More Information for People with Disabilities," later in this section.

Customizing Microsoft Windows
or Microsoft Windows NT

There are many ways you can adjust the appearance and behavior of Microsoft Windows or Microsoft Windows NT to suit varying vision and motor abilities without requiring any additional software or hardware. These include ways to adjust the appearance as well as the behavior of the mouse and keyboard. The specific methods available depend on which operating system you are using. Application notes are available describing the specific methods available for each operating system.

See the appropriate application note for information related to customizing your operating system for people with disabilities. For information on obtaining application notes, see "Access Pack for Microsoft Windows NT," earlier in this section.

Operating system	Application note
Microsoft Windows 3.0	Ww0786.txt
Microsoft Windows 3.1	Ww0787.txt
Microsoft Windows for Workgroups 3.1	Wg0787.txt
Microsoft Windows NT 3.1 and 3.5	Wn0789.exe
Microsoft Windows 95	WN1062

Getting More Information for People with Disabilities

For more information on Microsoft products and services for people with disabilities, contact:

Microsoft Sales	Voice telephone:	(800) 426-9400
Information Center	Text telephone:	(800) 892-5234
One Microsoft Way	Fax:	(206) 635-6100
Redmond, WA 98052-6393		

The Trace R&D Center at the University of Wisconsin–Madison produces a book and a compact disc that describe products to help people with disabilities use computers. The book, titled *Trace ResourceBook*, provides descriptions and photographs of about 2,000 products. The compact disc, titled *CO-NET CD*, provides a database of more than 18,000 products and other information for people with disabilities. It is issued twice a year. To obtain these directories, contact:

Trace R&D Center	Voice telephone:	(608) 263-2309
S-151 Waisman Center	Text telephone:	(608) 263-5408
1500 Highland Avenue	Fax:	(608) 262-8848
Madison, WI 53705-2280		

For general information and recommendations on how computers can help specific people, consult a trained evaluator who can best match your needs with the available solutions. An assistive technology program in your area will provide referrals to programs and services that are available to you. To locate the assistive technology program nearest you, contact:

National Information System	Voice/text telephone:	(803) 777-4435
Center for Developmental	Fax:	(803) 777-6058
Disabilities		
Benson Building		
University of South Carolina		
Columbia, SC 29208		

Index

(number symbol)
    in database queries 462
    in Microsoft Excel worksheet cells 74, 77, 207
= (equal sign) in worksheet formulas 76
=(Formula) field 194
1-2-3, Lotus *See* Lotus 1-2-3
35mm slides 90
3-D charts
    formatting 236–245
    rotating 245
    when to use 219
3-D references 368, 369

A

academic papers *See* theses
Access *See* Microsoft Access
accessibility 559–565
AccessLinks add-in 380
accounts for shared database use 357
action items
    See also tasks, individual
    making new slides from 290
    noting during electronic presentations 290
actions, macro 554
add-ins
    AccessLinks 380
    Analysis ToolPak 480–482
    data access objects (DAO) 198
    getting help with 34
    installing 29
    loading 29
    Microsoft Data Map 246
    Microsoft Organization Chart 278
    Microsoft Query 434–438
    starting 29
    Template Wizard With Data Tracking 198–205

address books, electronic
    See also contact lists
    and Microsoft Exchange 121, 124
    as mailing lists for form letters 178, 182
    using in Word 60, 121, 124, 126, 130
addresses
    See also address books, electronic; mailing labels
    adding to form letters 178
    creating contact lists in Microsoft Excel 300–305
    for envelopes 124
    importing into worksheets 300
    inserting from personal address book 60, 121, 124, 126, 130
    printing on mailing labels 182, 185–186
    where to store 294, 295
agendas, meeting 322
aligning
    data in worksheet cells 209
    text using Word Formatting toolbar 65, 163
alphabetizing *See* sorting
amortizing loans 515–516
Analysis ToolPak
    enabling 480, 482
    installing 480
    listing tools 482
    running analyses 482
    setting up data 481
analysis, statistical 480–482
Analyze It With MS Excel button 432
analyzing data
    sales 431–471
    scientific 480–482
    which method to use 432–433
anchors, frame 147
animation 286
annotation pane (Word) 334
annotations (Word)
    defined 334
    deleting marks 336

Not finding what you want? Your subject may be in online Help.
Click Help Topics (Help menu), then follow the directions in the dialog box.

Not finding what you want? Your subject may be in online Help.
Click Help Topics (Help menu), then follow the directions in the dialog box.

Not finding what you want? Your subject may be in online Help.
Click Help Topics (Help menu), then follow the directions in the dialog box.

Not finding what you want? Your subject may be in online Help.
Click Help Topics (Help menu), then follow the directions in the dialog box.

Not finding what you want? Your subject may be in online Help.
Click Help Topics (Help menu), then follow the directions in the dialog box.

Not finding what you want? Your subject may be in online Help.
Click Help Topics (Help menu), then follow the directions in the dialog box.

Not finding what you want? Your subject may be in online Help.
Click Help Topics (Help menu), then follow the directions in the dialog box.

Not finding what you want? Your subject may be in online Help.
Click Help Topics (Help menu), then follow the directions in the dialog box.

Not finding what you want? Your subject may be in online Help.
Click Help Topics (Help menu), then follow the directions in the dialog box.

Not finding what you want? Your subject may be in online Help.
Click Help Topics (Help menu), then follow the directions in the dialog box.

Not finding what you want? Your subject may be in online Help.
Click Help Topics (Help menu), then follow the directions in the dialog box.

Not finding what you want? Your subject may be in online Help.
Click Help Topics (Help menu), then follow the directions in the dialog box.

Not finding what you want? Your subject may be in online Help.
Click Help Topics (Help menu), then follow the directions in the dialog box.

Not finding what you want? Your subject may be in online Help.
Click Help Topics (Help menu), then follow the directions in the dialog box.

Not finding what you want? Your subject may be in online Help.
Click Help Topics (Help menu), then follow the directions in the dialog box.

Not finding what you want? Your subject may be in online Help.
Click Help Topics (Help menu), then follow the directions in the dialog box.

G

Not finding what you want? Your subject may be in online Help.
Click Help Topics (Help menu), then follow the directions in the dialog box.

Not finding what you want? Your subject may be in online Help.
Click Help Topics (Help menu), then follow the directions in the dialog box.

Not finding what you want? Your subject may be in online Help.
Click Help Topics (Help menu), then follow the directions in the dialog box.

Not finding what you want? Your subject may be in online Help.
Click Help Topics (Help menu), then follow the directions in the dialog box.

Not finding what you want? Your subject may be in online Help.
Click Help Topics (Help menu), then follow the directions in the dialog box.

Not finding what you want? Your subject may be in online Help.
Click Help Topics (Help menu), then follow the directions in the dialog box.

Not finding what you want? Your subject may be in online Help.
Click Help Topics (Help menu), then follow the directions in the dialog box.

Not finding what you want? Your subject may be in online Help.
Click Help Topics (Help menu), then follow the directions in the dialog box.

Not finding what you want? Your subject may be in online Help.
Click Help Topics (Help menu), then follow the directions in the dialog box.

Not finding what you want? Your subject may be in online Help.
Click Help Topics (Help menu), then follow the directions in the dialog box.

Not finding what you want? Your subject may be in online Help. Click Help Topics (Help menu), then follow the directions in the dialog box.

Not finding what you want? Your subject may be in online Help.
Click Help Topics (Help menu), then follow the directions in the dialog box.

Not finding what you want? Your subject may be in online Help.
Click Help Topics (Help menu), then follow the directions in the dialog box.

Not finding what you want? Your subject may be in online Help.
Click Help Topics (Help menu), then follow the directions in the dialog box.

Not finding what you want? Your subject may be in online Help.
Click Help Topics (Help menu), then follow the directions in the dialog box.

Not finding what you want? Your subject may be in online Help.
Click Help Topics (Help menu), then follow the directions in the dialog box.

Not finding what you want? Your subject may be in online Help.
Click Help Topics (Help menu), then follow the directions in the dialog box.

Not finding what you want? Your subject may be in online Help.
Click Help Topics (Help menu), then follow the directions in the dialog box.

Not finding what you want? Your subject may be in online Help. Click Help Topics (Help menu), then follow the directions in the dialog box.

Not finding what you want? Your subject may be in online Help.
Click Help Topics (Help menu), then follow the directions in the dialog box.

Not finding what you want? Your subject may be in online Help.
Click Help Topics (Help menu), then follow the directions in the dialog box.

Not finding what you want? Your subject may be in online Help.
Click Help Topics (Help menu), then follow the directions in the dialog box.

Not finding what you want? Your subject may be in online Help.
Click Help Topics (Help menu), then follow the directions in the dialog box.

Not finding what you want? Your subject may be in online Help.
Click Help Topics (Help menu), then follow the directions in the dialog box.

Not finding what you want? Your subject may be in online Help.
Click Help Topics (Help menu), then follow the directions in the dialog box.

Not finding what you want?   Your subject may be in online Help.
Click Help Topics (Help menu), then follow the directions in the dialog box.

Not finding what you want? Your subject may be in online Help.
Click Help Topics (Help menu), then follow the directions in the dialog box.

Not finding what you want? Your subject may be in online Help.
Click Help Topics (Help menu), then follow the directions in the dialog box.

Not finding what you want?   Your subject may be in online Help.
Click Help Topics (Help menu), then follow the directions in the dialog box.